Housing Development

CW00554135

For the first time in one place *Housing Development* brings together information on housing production, housing provision and the housing environment, highlighting the theoretical and policy contexts in which housing development takes place as an integrated process. Previously, knowledge about housing has been available only from widely disparate sources focused on the traditional disciplines of construction, design, building control, planning, economics, sociology and psychology, leaving scope for a fresh holistic overview of how the separate inputs into the housing development process actually interact in practice.

Housing Development reviews the full range of factors that have influenced the location, siting, quality and viability of housing in the United Kingdom, and explores the reasons for different housing outcomes in different situations, past and present. Chapters include discussion of housing demand and need, the private house-building industry, social housing and the role of government, planning and land supply, site appraisal and estate layout, dwelling construction and design, finance, procurement and marketing, technical innovation, sustainable development, urban capacity, refurbishment and comparisons with housing in other European countries.

Students will be familiarised with important topical issues, such as flooding, contamination, urban regeneration and mixed-use development, and helped in their career choices through reference to the wide range of enterprises, agencies and institutions that employ staff in pursuit of housing development. Architects, building contractors, surveyors and other professionals will also gain useful insights into the background to perennial housing development problems and the significance of trends currently affecting the successful realisation of housing projects.

This user-friendly volume also includes learning objectives, indicative educational assignments, suggested topics for dissertations and theses, priorities for commissioned research, annotated guides to further reading, a glossary of terms, an extensive index and details of relevant websites. A selection of maps, diagrams, tables and photographs are included in support of the ideas discussed.

Andrew Golland is Senior Research Fellow and **Ron Blake** is Visiting Research Fellow at the Centre for Residential Development, Nottingham Trent University.

Housing, Planning and Design Series

Editors: Nick Gallent and Mark Tewdwr-Jones,
The Bartlett School of Planning, University College London

This series addresses critical issues affecting the delivery of the right type of housing, of sufficient quantity and quality, in the most sustainable locations, and the linkages that bind together issues relating to planning, housing and design. Titles examine a variety of institutional perspectives, examining the roles of different agencies and sectors in delivering better quality housing together with the process of delivery – from policy development, through general strategy to implementation. Other titles will focus on housing management and development, housing strategy and planning policy, housing needs and community participation.

Housing in the European Countryside
Edited by Nick Gallent, Mark Shucksmith and Mark Tewdwr-Jones

Housing Development: theory, process and practice
Edited by Andrew Golland and Ron Blake

Forthcoming:
Planning and Housing
Nick Gallent and Mark Tewdwr-Jones

Housing Development

Theory, process and practice

Edited by Andrew Golland
and Ron Blake

Routledge
Taylor & Francis Group

LONDON AND NEW YORK

First published 2004
by Routledge
11 New Fetter Lane, London EC4P 4EE

Simultaneously published in the USA and Canada
by Routledge
29 West 35th Street, New York, NY 10001

Routledge is an imprint of the Taylor & Francis Group

Typeset in Galliard by
Florence Production Ltd, Stoodleigh, Devon
Printed and bound in Great Britain by
TJ International Ltd, Padstow, Cornwall

British Library Cataloguing in Publication Data
A catalogue record for this book is available from the British Library

Library of Congress Cataloging in Publication Data
A catalog record for this book has been requested

ISBN 0–415–23432–8 (hbk)
ISBN 0–415–23433–6 (pbk)

To our families . . .

Contents

Contributors

Andrew Golland is a Senior Research Fellow at the Centre for Residential Development, Nottingham Trent University. A chartered surveyor, he includes in his research interests housing needs studies, housing market monitoring, land assembly and urban capacity assessment.

Ron Blake is a Visiting Research Fellow at the Centre for Residential Development, Nottingham Trent University. A chartered town planner and Fellow of the Royal Geographical Society, he includes in his research interests social trends, land use change, urban regeneration and the reuse of disused airfields and railways.

Paul Collins is Head of Postgraduate Studies in the Faculty of Construction, Computing and Technology at Nottingham Trent University. A chartered surveyor, he includes in his research interests property development, facilities management, marketing strategy and green roof design.

Kathleen Dunmore is a Senior Research Fellow at the Centre of Residential Development, Nottingham Trent University, and a member of the Three Dragons housing consultancy. An advisor to English Partnerships, local authorities and house-builders, she focuses her research on the links between affordable housing, land supply and the planning process.

Mike Gillen is a Senior Lecturer in the Faculty of Design, Architecture and Building at the University of Technology, Sydney, Australia. A former researcher in the Centre for Residential Development at Nottingham Trent University, he continues to focus his academic interests on the structure and performance of the private house-building industry.

Chris Nicol is Monitoring and Evaluation Co-ordinator for the Capital City Partnership, Edinburgh. A chartered town planner and former researcher in the Centre for Residential Development at Nottingham Trent University, he includes in his academic interests house-price indicators, urban capacity assessment and innovation in housing production.

Michael Oxley is Professor of Housing and Head of the Centre for Residential Development at Nottingham Trent University. An Associate of the Chartered Institute of Housing, he includes in his research interests the economics of housing supply, residential development viability and comparative housing markets in Europe.

Gavin Tunstall is a Senior Lecturer in Building, Real Estate and Construction Management at Nottingham Trent University. A chartered architect, he includes in his research interests sustainable dwelling construction, residential estate layout and housing design theory.

Acknowledgements

Many colleagues have kindly provided information, comments and advice during our research for the book. We are particularly grateful to the following: John Adams, Viv Aldred, Ron Biggin, Kirsten Bunch, Paul Bywater, Christine Carr, Marilyn Charlesworth, the late Rafe Clowes, Lin Cousins, Simon Cox, Peter Crane, Martin Culshaw, Alan Fewkes, Mike Fox, Nick Gallent, Graham Gardner, Juanita Gonzales-Metcalf, Matt Gregory, Allison Heller, John Herington, Andy Hey, Alan Hooper, Roger Humber, Owen Jones, Dave King, Marianna Knight, Bob Line, Stef Lubynskyj, Rod McEchrane, Janice Mee, Laurence Monkhouse, John Moohan, Vincent Nadin, Judith Nathanail, Paul Nathanail, Bridget Neville, Sean Nicholson, Ken Orchard, Adam O'Rourke, Sandra Price, Dave Priest, Barry Redfearn, Richard A. (Dick) Rogers, Mike Rosenbaum, Ben Roskrow, Paul Russell, Ian Smalley, Nigel Stuart-Baker, David Towell, Christopher Walker, Martin Ward, John Weir, Desmond Wiltshaw and Ian Woodland.

Special thanks are due to Linda Dawes of Belvoir Cartographics & Design for producing the figures, to Denise Holland and Emma Spillings for typing and helping to edit the manuscript at Nottingham Trent University, and to Donna Gregory of Florence Production for perfecting the text. Finally, we are indebted to our publishing editors, Andrew Mould and Melanie Attridge at Routledge, for their patient support throughout the project.

Abbreviations

ADAS	Agricultural Development and Advice Service
AIM	Alternative Investment Market
ALG	Association of London Government
AMA	Association of Metropolitan Authorities
AONB	Area of outstanding natural beauty
BME	Black and Minority Ethnic (association)
BPEO	Best Practicable Environmental Option
BRE	Building Research Establishment
BRECSU	Building Research Energy Conservation Support Unit
BSI	British Standards Institution
BSRIA	Building Services Research and Information Association
CABE	Commission for Architecture and the Built Environment
CACI	California Analysis Centre Incorporation
CAP	Common Agricultural Policy
CBD	Central business district
CC	Countryside Commission
CCT	Compulsory Competitive Tendering
CCTV	Closed Circuit Television
CDA	Comprehensive Development Area
CDM	Construction, Design and Management
CEN	Comité Européen de Normalisation (European standardisation organisation)
CHAC	Central Housing Advisory Committee
CIBSE	Chartered Institution of Building Services Engineers
CIEH	Chartered Institute of Environmental Health
CIH	Chartered Institute of Housing
CIOB	Chartered Institute of Building
CIPFA	Chartered Institute of Public Finance and Accountancy
CIRIA	Construction Industry Research and Information Association
CITB	Construction Industry Training Board
CPO	Compulsory Purchase Order
CPRE	Council for the Protection of Rural England
CRD	Centre for Residential Development, Nottingham Trent University
CSO	Central Statistical Office
DEFRA	Department for Environment, Food and Rural Affairs

DETR	Department of the Environment, Transport and the Regions
DIY	Do it yourself
DLG	Derelict Land Grant
DLO	Direct Labour Organisation
DLT	Development Land Tax
DNH	Department of National Heritage
DoE	Department of the Environment
DoT	Department of Transport
d.p.a.	dwellings per acre
DPC	Damp proof course
d.p.h.	dwellings per hectare
DTI	Department of Trade and Industry
DTLR	Department for Transport, Local Government and the Regions
EIA	Environmental Impact Analysis
EIP	Examination in Public
EMDA	East Midlands Development Agency
EP	English Partnerships
ESA	Environmentally Sensitive Area
ETSU	Energy Technology Support Unit
EU	European Union
FoE	Friends of the Earth
FTSE	Financial Times Stock Exchange (index)
GDO	General Development Order
GIA	General Improvement Area
GIS	Geographical Information Systems
GLA	Greater London Authority
GOEM	Government Office for the East Midlands
GOR	Government Offices for the Regions
GRO	General Register Office
HAA	Housing Action Area
HAG	Housing Association Grant
HBF	House Builders Federation
HGCR	Housing Grants, Construction and Regeneration (Act)
HIP	Housing Investment Programme
HMO	House in multiple occupation
HMLR	Her Majesty's Land Registry
HRA	Housing Renewal Area
ICRCL	Inter-Department Committee on the Redevelopment of Contaminated Land
ICE	Institution of Civil Engineers
IT	Information Technology
JRF	Joseph Rowntree Foundation
LA	Local authority
LAW	Land Authority for Wales

LGMB	Local Government Management Board
LOTS	Living over the Shop
LP	Local Plan
LPA	Local planning authority
LSVT	Large scale voluntary transfers
LUS	Land Utilisation Survey (also known as Land Use Survey)
MHLG	Ministry of Housing and Local Government
MIRAS	Mortgage Interest Relief of Source
NGO	Non-governmental organisation
NHBC	National House-Building Council
NHER	National Home Energy Rating
NHF	National Housing Federation
NHMB	New Homes Marketing Board
NIMBY	Not in my Back Yard
NLUD	National Land Use Database
NPFA	National Playing Fields Association
ODPM	Office of the Deputy Prime Minister
OS	Ordnance Survey
ONS	Office for National Statistics
PAG	Planning Advisory Group
PAZ	Plan d'Aménagement de Zone
PDA	Potential Development Area
PDL	Previously Developed Land
p/e	price/earnings (ratio)
PFI	Private Finance Initiative
plc	public limited companies
POS	Plan d'Occupation du Sol
POS	Public Open Space
PPG	Planning Policy Guidance
p.p.h	persons per hectare
Quango	Quasi-autonomous non-governmental organisation
RDA	Regional Development Agency
RIBA	Royal Institute of British Architects
RICS	Royal Institute of Chartered Surveyors
RPG	Regional Planning Guidance
RPI	Retail Price Index
RSL	Registered social landlord
RSPB	Royal Society for the Protection of Birds
RTB	Right to buy
RTPI	Royal Town Planning Institute
SAP	Standard Assessment Procedure (for energy performance in buildings)
SBS	Sick Building Syndrome
SBP	Secured by Design

SEPA	Scottish Environment Protection Agency
SHG	Social Housing Grant
SI	Statutory Instrument
SLOAP	Space Left Over After Planning
SNAL	Syndicat National des Aménageurs Lotisseurs
SP	Structure Plan
SPG	Supplementary Planning Guidance
SRB	Single Regeneration Budget
SSSI	Site of Special Scientific Interest
SUDS	Sustainable urban drainage systems
TCI	Total Cost Indicators
TCPA	Town and Country Planning Association
T&G	Tongued and grooved
TRADA	Timber Research and Development Association
UCO	Use Classes Order
UDC	Urban Development Corporation
UDP	Unitary Development Plan
UK	United Kingdom
UPVC	Unplasticised polyvinyl chloride
URBED	Urban and Economic Development Group
VAT	Value added tax
WIP	Work in progress
ZAC	Zone d'Aménagement Concert

Part One

Introduction

Plate 1.1 Home: an icon of our times: R. N. E. Blake.

Chapter 1

Aims, scope and structure of the book

Ron Blake and Andrew Golland

Preamble

The right to 'a decent home' has been at the centre of political debate in Britain for a century and a half, and the phrase is now firmly embedded in government policy (DETR, 2000a). Laws to improve sanitary conditions in the poorest housing areas were enacted from the mid-nineteenth century onwards and by the dawn of the twentieth century Ebenezer Howard's pioneering vision of 'garden cities' had set frameworks for town planning and residential layout that are still relevant today. In an advanced industrial society, founded on European and North American principles of regulated wealth creation, the notion of decency is necessarily a fluid one, tempered by rising incomes, changing life-styles, consumer preferences, widening expectations and periodically adjusted thresholds defining what should ideally be provided and what can be afforded. Housing, as a major component of the nation's infrastructure, is thus evolutionary and dynamic and repays close observation at frequent intervals.

Housing development, which will be defined more fully below, is the business of supplying houses of the right type, in the right numbers, in the right locations and at the right time. In essence the business of housing development focuses on issues of quantity, quality and accessibility – three aspects of provision that could each sustain a separate wide-ranging investigation. This book purposely embraces all the critical dimensions of housing development. It probes the web of relationships between them in search of a deeper understanding of how today's residential environment has been shaped by past events, is currently being shaped and could be better shaped with the benefit of more complete knowledge. It is appropriate therefore to continue this opening discussion with a cursory glance at some of the underlying factors that influence the complex milieu in which housing development is taking place at the present time. The reasons for embarking upon a project with an integrative thrust will quickly become clear.

Characteristics of housing

One of the most important advances in the British construction industry over the past two decades is the recognition that housing development is a multi-faceted process in which virtually all aspects of everyday life have some input. While housing production and house-buying have always been cyclic and susceptible to oscillations in the economy, house-builders have only recently begun to address the specific requirements of their customers and to take seriously on board the challenges of environmental conservation and design. It is important therefore to grasp where the house-building sector has come from, how it is responding to current pressures for change and where it is heading.

Previous books on aspects of housing have stressed the multiple significance of the dwelling in psychological, sociological, cultural and economic terms. A dwelling universally provides humans with shelter from adverse weather, facilities for cooking and food preparation, security against intruders, a controlled environment for raising children, caring for the elderly and nursing the sick, private space for dispensing hospitality, and storage room for personal and family possessions. A recent American work (Garber, 2001) has interpreted the house as a mother, a body, a trophy, a lover and a dream. In developed economies a dwelling also represents a 'positional good' that defines social status, and acts as a hedge against inflation, collateral for other borrowing, a source of rental income and a generator of capital when the need arises.

Homes are the core ingredient of neighbourhoods, villages and towns, and have influenced the siting of schools, shops, health centres and children's play areas. Together with community facilities and local roads, houses make up the 'residential landscape' that most people fondly associate with their childhood and adolescence. As patterns of employment have become looser since the Second World War, home-making has emerged as a key driver of the economy by virtue of increased property transactions, tax revenues and purchase of household goods and services. Housing availability exerts an increasing influence over where modern employers locate their premises and the volume of new house completions is a robust indicator of economic health at regional level. Whereas housing was traditionally clustered around factories, harbours and access points to public transport, the entrepreneur of today is more sensitive to where key personnel aspire to live for reasons other than economic survival. Accordingly, he is inclined to seek premises close in travel time to pools of qualified job seekers who have already made residential decisions based on environmental, educational and social-class criteria.

Modern dwellings are generally more durable than in the past because of the higher quality of materials, craftsmanship and infrastructure they are legally required to embody. Durability is also an important reason why a significant number of households are able to move confidently to another geographical area in order to secure a home that is better suited to their space requirements or budget at a particular stage in the membership's life-cycle. The matching of housing demand with housing supply, whether through the free market or subsidy arrangements, is responsible for the wide range of professional services that currently sustain the housing development process, for example mortgage lenders, local authority building inspectors, property insurers and marketing consultants. Their respective contributions will become clear as the different stages of the development process are examined.

Trends affecting housing development

Housing development in Britain over the past couple of decades has been affected by undercurrents that are partly global, partly European and partly domestic in origin. Globalisation of manufacturing, paradoxically, has emphasised regional inequalities particularly where large factory and institutional closures have taken place. On the other hand, the advent of information technology as the basis of new forms of employment has made it less necessary in principle for whole working communities to migrate from one region to another as occurred, for example, in coal-mining and steel-making as late as the 1950s. Extensions to the motorway network, combined with more fuel-efficient and reliable automobiles, have reduced the absolute necessity for families to change their area of residence purely to stay in work. Yet house-builders have continued to exploit sites close to highway and rail junctions in response to demand from house-buyers to be flexibly located relative to changing career opportunities.

Agricultural surpluses across the European Union have helped governments relax the post-war imperative to protect the countryside primarily for food production, thus giving housing development a role as an instrument for diversifying the rural economy. Redundant farmyards redeveloped for housing are a familiar sight in many rural districts. They symbolise the growing dominance of urban needs over the rural environment. Running counter to this trend are the efforts of planning authorities to re-populate inner-urban areas following a century of spontaneous and planned outward migration. An embarrassing rise in urban dereliction due to the decommissioning of obsolete factories, gas works and hospitals has fortuitously created niches for 'city living' on a scale unimagined a generation ago. Remediation of contaminated land is now a prerequisite of redevelopment for housing and many consultancies with relevant expertise have sprung up. Housing development thus has a geo-environmental as well as socio-economic and aesthetic dimensions.

Residential new-build on small, previously developed, sites, and the conversion of redundant industrial and public buildings to residential apartments, have

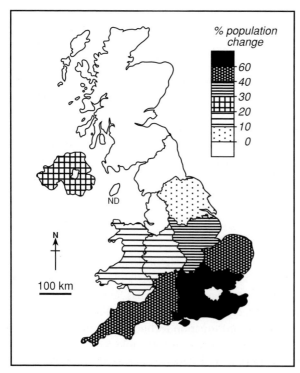

Figure 1.1
Percentage population change in
the UK by region, 1951–2001.
Source: Census of Population

% population
change

60
40
30
20
10
0

ND

N

100 km

presented special challenges to the house-building industry, calling for an inter-disciplinary approach closer to the traditions of urban conservation than to mass-production. Thus the attitude of the house-builder has had to change. This has demanded a greater awareness of the potential value of regeneration and a retreat from the adversarial relationships that divided builders, architects, surveyors and planners and impeded the raising of standards in residential developments during much of the twentieth century. The maturing of the housing development process is a further theme that will surface periodically in the book.

These are just a few of the trends influencing the current demand for homes, the capability of the industry to supply them, and the capacity of the environment to accommodate them. Population growth is obviously a key driver of demand, although pressures on housing vary greatly between regions (see Figure 1.1). There are countless ramifications of demand, for example the rising numbers of young adults and elderly people wanting single-person accommodation is manifest in the falling average size of dwellings and gardens. The appetite for interesting home improvements is undoubtedly responsible in part for the huge popularity of TV programmes featuring DIY disasters, 'makeovers' and house-hunting adventures. Media companies have certainly raised public awareness of the standard of house-hold amenities, but they have also exploited for entertainment the rising incidence of crime against domestic property and residential neighbourhoods.

The impact of recent events

Material for the book was mainly gathered during 2001 – a momentous year for Britain, the West and the world. The year's events introduced new and dormant issues that reinforce the timeliness of a new look at housing. Celebration of the millennium drew many Britons to reassess progress in the domestic environment since Romano-British and Domesday times. Similarly, the passing of the twentieth century provoked thoughts about the impact of two world wars on the planning of cities, transportation systems and the countryside. Racial tension in England's northern cities, coupled with influxes of asylum seekers in the south, raised questions about the effectiveness of policies for social inclusion. Dramatically, the terrorist attack of 11 September 2001 on the World Trade Center highlighted the fragility of modern urban life in a world dogged by bigotry, disaffection and political instability.

Widespread and repeated flooding in southern and central England raised questions about the wisdom of siting new housing developments in low-lying areas, while a recurrence of foot-and-mouth disease in northern and western counties cast doubt on the long-term viability of stock-rearing communities. On winning the general election of June 2001 New Labour announced, as part of its second-term programme, a commitment to reform the planning system, including proposals to speed up the development control process while simultaneously raising standards of design and community involvement in decision-making. Much was made in the press about the lack of affordable housing in London for key workers such as bus drivers, teachers and police constables. By the end of the year the average price of a house in Britain had edged towards the symbolic figure of £100,000 (and approaching double that figure in the Metropolis), but the idea of a 'seller's pack' to inform house-buyers of what to look out for was not embraced with great enthusiasm by the property professions.

In the aftermath of the election, the three main political parties each debated housing and planning issues through fringe meetings at their respective annual conferences. Significantly, Labour's focus was 'where will we house the key workers?'. The Liberal Democrats addressed the choice 'four million new homes for town or country?' while the Conservatives asked 'should we plan for the homes we need?'. From the titles of these debates, the party-political dimension of housing development boils down to three key issues: special housing need, location of development and responsibility for delivery. Coincidentally, 2001 was a census year in which new socio-economic data about the nation was gathered to inform politicians and their advisers on appropriate courses of action.

Continuing job losses in electronics, telecommunications and finance, arising indirectly from turbulence in the US stock market, were expected to depress the UK economy, yet the housing market throughout 2001 remained stubbornly buoyant in most regions. Oddly, Britain recorded its lowest annual house-building rate since the 1920s, a dip blamed by frustrated developers on land shortages and inflated house prices caused by planning controls. Intriguingly, housing concerns figured only obliquely in a government 'Quality of Life' survey conducted during the year.

All this suggests that current debates about housing revolve more around user-requirements, environmental impacts and geographically specific shortfalls than around the traditional issues of widespread homelessness and grossly sub-standard household conditions. Opinions still differ as to whether there is a real national shortage of appropriate housing, or merely the wrong distribution due to an unbalanced and unpredictable economy.

Aims of the book

This is not primarily a 'how to do it' book or even a polemic on what should be done with respect to housing. Formulae and specifications are therefore kept to a minimum and recommendations for alternative action take up a relatively small part of the discussion. The essential content relates to *what is done, why it is done* and *how it fits in* with the general scope of housing development. Emphasis is placed on the relationship between the different sectors of house-building and the different stages in the housing development process.

The overarching aim of the book is to provide a basic reference on the housing development process that is accessible, factual, theoretical, entertaining and practical. That such a reference is not already available will become increasingly evident as the successive debates unfold together with references to their supporting literature. As well as being multi-disciplinary in scope, the book adheres to the philosophy of 'joined-up thinking' favoured by the present government and implicitly takes a 'holistic' approach to all of housing's key dimensions: environment, design, property management, economic development and urban regeneration.

A special attempt is made to bridge the gap between 'big picture' issues such as sustainability and social inclusion and the 'small picture' issues of project delivery, profitability and local accountability. To emphasise the link between these broad levels of enquiry, generic and topical issues are purposely juxtaposed within each of the focal areas of discussion. In the same spirit, the book seeks to co-ordinate a range of methodologies taken from different sectors of housing development, and to create new typologies of issues and challenges that illuminate the subject in a broader way. Defining the parameters and overall scope of housing development is considered a worthy goal in itself and the book seeks to present clear and concise definitions throughout.

Bridge-building between the many actors in the housing development process is a further aim, not merely for the intellectual enrichment of synergistic research but as a contribution to the construction industry's operations, customer satisfaction and enhancement of the public realm. The book aims in particular to span the divide between practitioners and academics: two camps that can learn a great deal from one another through an inclusive and integrative treatise. Much is made of why some situations affecting housing development are predictably recurrent while others appear to occur with little or no warning. An important subsidiary aim therefore is to find historical explanations for all current situations and to identify the probable triggers that brought them recently to the fore. In everything examined we try to codify professional responses and assess a range of options for avoiding or minimising problems in the future.

Returning to the basic aim, our mission has been to produce a comprehensive overview that does for housing development what J. Barry Cullingworth and Vincent Nadin (2002) have done for the study of town and country planning. In emulation of the above-cited work, *Housing Development* addresses its specialised subject at all the key spatial scales – local, urban, rural, sub-regional, regional, national and international – with the crucial addition of a 'micro-environmental' scale representing the individual dwelling house. Cutting across the spatial scales, in the form of a matrix of housing concerns, are other important scales that can be expressed here as simple dichotomies, for example, public/private, high-rise/low-rise and retrospective/futuristic. The book attempts thereby to elucidate each of the main housing development problems not only in terms of spatial occurrence but also in relation to the agencies involved, the techniques applied and the scientific know-how required for decision-support.

As for target readership, we have no stereotypical audience in mind. We believe the subject to have a wide potential appeal, ranging from house-building companies to university departments and the discerning home-buyer. Realistically, we envisage the chief beneficiaries to be larger commercial house-builders, public-sector housing providers, town and country planners, and postgraduate and senior undergraduate students on construction, surveying and environment related courses. These particular groups would alone be sufficient to justify a general book on housing development, but other professionals and academics could also gain useful insights into their daily work from a wider understanding of the housing field. Environmental health officers, education and parks departments, local building contractors, builders' suppliers, interior designers and civic conservation groups are among those who could enhance their activities through a greater awareness of what professionals in related sectors are doing and aspire to do.

Within the academic sphere we see a number of applications beyond straightforward preparation for essays and examinations. The text is arranged to provide a rounded contextual background for theses and dissertations across a wide disciplinary spectrum. Chapter headings and appendices should help highlight topic areas that are currently under-researched or are under-represented in particular institutions' syllabuses. Themes for seminars, conferences and invited speakers can be gleaned from the section headings, illustrations and examples described. Contact details of relevant national organisations provide a further source for staging academic activities and events. Sixth-form tutors may find the contents of assistance when advising students on applications to university, while careers officers may find the book handy for placing graduates in appropriate jobs.

An extensive references section is designed to take readers beyond general discussion and into specialised areas of enquiry that the book cannot, and does not aspire to, address in ultimate depth. A final aim therefore is to introduce the academic reader to a range of professional material not normally available in institutional libraries, and reciprocally to reveal to the practitioner the fundamental and thought-provoking texts that would not normally find a place on office shelves yet would nevertheless be worthwhile reading for stimulation and mid-career development.

Scope and structure of the book

Drawing together a wide diversity of inputs between two covers has necessitated a careful structuring of the material to produce a coherent whole. Rather than simply collate existing socio-economic, land-use, constructional, design, management and marketing knowledge in a combined volume of 'best practice', we have attempted to re-examine each of these conventional approaches to housing development within an appropriate theoretical framework, to emphasise the importance of a co-ordinated delivery process.

The book is divided into five parts, comprising: (One) a contextual introduction (this chapter); (Two, Three and Four) three main groupings of chapters representing broad approaches to the subject area; and finally (Five) a synthesis of the study's key findings. Part One sets the tone of the book through its summary of long-term and recent trends and by spelling out the basic agenda which can be summarised as the unification and synthesis of disparate knowledge within the extensive field of housing development.

Part Two can be characterised as a grouping of chapters covering nationwide concerns that need to be properly understood before the full significance of more detailed aspects can be absorbed. Opening the part, Chapter 2 explores the historical and geographical dimensions of housing development and thereby establishes a rationale for the British public's sentimental attachment to home, garden and neighbourhood. Chapter 3 considers the supply and demand equation with regard to housing in basic economic and political terms, while Chapter 4 examines the current performance of the UK private house-building industry from the structural and organisational angles. Chapter 5 completes the part with an explanation of the vital contribution made by affordable housing to social inclusion and the national economy.

Part Three addresses the key professional activities involved in producing good housing development. Much of the factual content reiterates rather than expands upon what experts already know. However, the act of summarising the responsibilities of several distinct professions and trades in rapid sequence reveals important links that have remained obscured by the traditionally segmented approach. Academic readers with no practical experience in construction and property should gain useful insights into the shaping of the built environment from this part of the study. Chapter 6 examines the statutory land-use planning system in the UK and the parallel, largely commercial activity of acquiring the requisite amount of land to realise successful housing developments. Chapter 7 moves a step further down the spatial ladder to the appraisal of individual development sites and describes how these are engineered and laid out with infrastructure to accommodate a requisite number of dwelling units at an acceptable density. Chapter 8 outlines the main considerations in constructing a dwelling that meets the performance criteria of structural integrity, energy efficiency, sustainable materials, safety and aesthetic impact on its surroundings. To conclude the part, Chapter 9 focuses on the financial considerations of individual house-building companies and housing associations with particular reference to sources of capital, construction procurement methods and marketing of the finished product.

Part Four draws together four superficially rather different topics that share one characteristic in common: they deal with innovations and issues that have more to do with the future than received practice. Chapter 10 reviews the implications of the global sustainability agenda for land-use planning with specific reference to the role of urban-capacity assessments as an instrument of containment and regeneration. Chapter 11 considers in depth the roles of refurbishment, conversion, conservation and estate modification in the achievement of Britain's 'urban renaissance'. Chapter 12 looks comparatively at the mechanisms by which housing is supplied in certain other European countries as possible exemplars of good practice for adoption in this country. To conclude, Chapter 13 addresses innovation and emerging trends in dwelling construction and design, including 'green architecture', 'mass production', 'lean building' and 'self-build' together with radical settlements such as 'eco-villages'.

Part Five contains a single discussion: Chapter 14 reflects on the rapidly changing character of an historically conservative industry and area of social provision against the backcloth of an increasingly regulated urban, rural and global environment. The chapter also draws up a number of recommendations concerning how the housing development process could be made more effective for the twenty-first century in the opinion of the many experts consulted during the book's compilation.

Definitions

Unless otherwise stated (as in Chapter 12) the study relates to the United Kingdom (UK) of Great Britain (GB) and Northern Ireland. In certain areas of activity, for example land-use planning, England and Wales share a legal system while Scotland and Northern Ireland each have their own slightly different system. Space does not permit full regard to be paid to differences between parts of the UK, and therefore the housing development situations described tend to be those currently operating in England and Wales. Wherever possible statistics have been compiled for the UK, but in some instances data sets are available for England and Wales only or are difficult to reconcile across all the constituent countries. To avoid confusion, the geographical unit is clarified in all statistical citations. For simplicity and stylistic variation, the terms 'Britain' and 'British' are used as shorthand for the UK.

Various terms derived from the master word 'house' have already been introduced and some are explained in the glossary. Their respective meanings are mainly self-explanatory from the context, but in certain cases there are nuances that require special clarification. The thematic title 'housing development' refers primarily to *the dynamic process whereby housing is developed*, but there is also a secondary meaning of *physical development that consists of houses*. The former meaning can include activities that are non-physical (such as finance) while the latter is quite often preceded by the indefinite article (for example, 'Beaumont Leys is *a problematical development*'). In planning and property law 'development' (unqualified) has a wider connotation that embraces changes of land use that may not involve building operations at all, for example parking caravans. For the purposes of this study all manner of preparatory and remedial works, such as landscaping, surveillance and fire control, are embraced by the definition since they materially assist in 'developing' residential properties and areas. Housing provision, stemming from concepts of economic and social development, likewise falls within the remit of the study.

For the most part the terms used in the book are those in everyday professional use, but some usages may be confusing to the non-professional reader and therefore must be clarified. 'Dwelling' is preferred where the intended meaning is a unit of domestic accommodation (which may include apartments and maisonettes). 'Home' has largely replaced the noun *house* in the house-building industry because of its emotional appeal to customers (despite 'a home' traditionally denoting a care institution). 'Home-owner' is now almost universally used in marketing literature, probably because 'householder' includes rent-paying tenants. The vaguer term 'residential development' appears to be on the wane, but is used in planning, estate agency and academe to distinguish new housing from industrial, commercial and institutional developments.

Finally, there are difficulties peculiar to the English language with rendering composite nouns and adjectives consistently. 'Blend-words' (e.g. the noun *house-builder*) are not yet widely accepted on this side of the Atlantic, while the use of separate words adjectivally (e.g. free standing garages) can detract from understanding. Preference is therefore given to the hyphen, a device that usefully highlights word function (e.g. the *house-building* industry) and, interestingly, is employed by one of the leading professional bodies (NHBC) in its title.

In summary

From these introductory remarks it is already clear that housing development is a very wide canvas that is perpetually being re-touched by events. At the same time it has a colourful past that needs interrogating in search of answers to contemporary problems. Because the number of chapters in the book has necessarily been limited, some major issues such as density, land availability and design guidance are not reflected in chapter titles as such, but every effort has been made to cover them at appropriate points in the study. Countless articles, reports, bulletins and guidance notes have been consulted, and their essence distilled into a single work which, we believe, paints in the wider picture obscured by the detail of much existing literature.

To conclude, the book represents the combined effort of eight writers who are all currently working, or have recently worked, at the Nottingham Trent University's Centre for Residential Development (CRD). The Centre resides within the School of Property and Construction (formerly the Faculty of Construction and the Environment) and is one of two busy research foci within the School. CRD benefits from being located in a diverse school containing building technologists, construction managers, designers, land and property practitioners, environmental health and safety professionals, housing economists and other experts with team-based consultancy experience. Two courses in Residential Development, at BSc (Honours) and Master of Science levels, are sustained by CRD's research and the students' integrated projects and dissertations have provided many ideas and examples for the book.

Discussion point

1   With reference to this chapter and the chronology provided in Appendix A, identify what appear to have been the three most critical influences on the shaping of Britain's housing development industry over the past two centuries.

Part Two

The Political Economy of Housing
Development

Chapter 2

Historical, demographic and land-use perspectives

Ron Blake and Chris Nicol

Introduction

Housing development, both as a dynamic process and a feature of the landscape, is ultimately the product of history and geography. The historical perspective focuses on chains of events, decisions made by individuals, families, groups and governments, and how those decisions have shaped the built environment. The geographical perspective focuses on the influence of terrain, natural resources and location on social and economic activity, and the evolution of patterns of land use and settlement to which housing belongs. Cognate disciplines such as sociology and architecture straddle the divide between history and geography while others such as archaeology, demography and land administration also have strong temporal and spatial dimensions. In this chapter the salient historical and geographical dimensions of housing development are considered, drawing experience from a wide disciplinary spectrum. A concise evolution of the British dwelling house is presented first, highlighting the significance of period and place in the evolution of different construction methods and building styles. Long-term and recent population and socio-economic trends are then outlined as drivers of housing need, coupled with a brief review of census enumeration and analysis techniques including examples of problems encountered in the interpretation of results. Finally, the position of housing development within urban structure is assessed, with particular reference to sources of land-use data and models of land-use disposition and change.

House-building through history

No house-building project should be embarked upon without some reference to history. There are two main respects in which historical knowledge can exert a positive influence on housing outcomes. First, an appreciation of substructure and local surroundings can help maximise the value of 'environmental capital' inherent in a site. Second, lessons can be learnt from the documentation of past achievements and mistakes. Grand projects, for example high-rise flats, are one obvious area where hindsight can be constructive. The legacy of poor workmanship is another area where the shortcomings of past practices can be profitably investigated. A widespread abuse of history is seen in the slavish copying of past styles in ignorance of local building traditions, for example, the stone cladding of perfectly adequate brick-built terrace houses. On the other hand, certain expressions of dubious taste have proved marketable with the passage of time, for example, the excessively ornate masonry in large Victorian houses is now prized by home-owners and protected by conservation policies. Names given to new dwellings, streets and estates can assist in the preservation of local history provided they are carefully researched, but if gratuitous or inaccurate, their effect can be counter-productive.

Value judgements aside, the character of dwellings is strongly influenced by a combination of geology, geomorphology and landscape ecology. Where these assets have been acknowledged and creatively exploited the residential environment can be immeasurably enhanced, for example, by the incorporation of long-established hedgerows and ponds into housing estate layouts. Within existing built-up areas dwelling construction and design are more likely to be governed by the footprint of previous and surrounding buildings, and in town and village alike the availability of local materials and craft skills is often reflected in the fabric and façade of new residential property. At every stage in Britain's history the parallel traditions of 'vernacular' (local) and 'classical' (international) style have influenced the form of dwellings, sometimes skilfully blended within a single structure and at other times juxtaposed in adjacent properties. A chronological account of the British dwelling, set against the background of evolving rural and urban settlement patterns, is therefore indispensable to a complete understanding of how housing development operates today.

Geology and building tradition

Britain is based upon an exceedingly diverse geology that has contributed not only to local landscape contrasts but also to a rich domestic architecture (Barley, 1961). It is difficult to travel more than about 10km without passing over contrasting rock-types that are reflected in the building materials and construction methods used. Broadly, the country divides into an 'upland' zone and a 'lowland' zone, demarcated by a line extending from the Tees to the Exe. North and west of that line the rocks are predominantly hard, older than 300 million years, associated with rugged terrain, and the basis of a largely pastoral economy (Stamp, 1962). South and east of the line the rocks are overwhelmingly soft, young in geological terms, associated with low and smooth landforms, and supportive of predominantly arable farming. In consequence, stone and slate characterise the buildings of the uplands whereas brick, tiles and plasters are more prevalent in the lowlands (Figure 2.1). There are, of course, many exceptions to this simple duality, most notably the middle Jurassic limestones of the Cotswolds and south Lincolnshire where attractive honey-coloured stone cottages grace the countryside (Clifton-Taylor, 1972). Within lowland England there is a noticeable contrast between the 'pink' bricks manufactured from upper Jurassic clays around Peterborough and Bedford, and the 'yellow' bricks made from post-glacial material of wind-blown origin in the London basin. Red bricks, which characterise the industrial Midlands and North West, are derived from the Triassic clays that overlap the Carboniferous rocks of the nation's traditional coal-mining areas.

Figure 2.1 Geological outcrops influencing the availability of materials for house-building.
Source: British Geological Survey maps

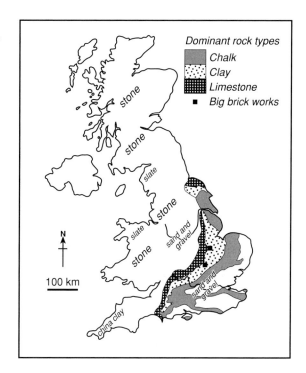

Settlement patterns from prehistory

The pattern of Britain's peopling is a story of successive colonisation and forest clearance, initially to create farmland and villages and later to make way for urban settlements, industries and long-distance communications. 'Clearing of the waste' (a term denoting human displacement of primeval forests, heath, moor and fen) made its first impact on Britain's landscape in the New Stone Age some 5,000 years ago. During the ensuing Bronze and Iron Ages, the most effective clearances took place on the light soils of the chalk and limestone escarpments of southern Britain, centred on great ceremonial sites such as Stonehenge, the Avebury Rings and Maiden Castle. At that time much of southern, eastern and central Britain was still densely forested and beyond the capability of the tools then available. Lightly forested areas in more extreme regions, for example Cornwall and the Orkneys, have surviving evidence of circular stone-built dwellings, facilitating roof construction by means of converging poles (Cunliffe, 1995). A lakeside village site at Glastonbury, Somerset, was kept above flood level by stout wooden piling. In the drier areas settled in prehistoric times, postholes offer the principal clues to dwelling construction.

Housing development in Roman times and the Dark Ages

Roman dwellings built in Britain were relatively substantial, although few examples survive above ground level because their materials were plundered by later settlers.

More than 600 country villas were constructed by Romans in what is now termed central-southern England, several with mosaic ceramic interiors, under-floor heating and robust outbuildings, as exemplified at Chedworth, Gloucestershire. Flint and tiles, rather than brick, were the principal building materials, many of which were later recycled for church building. As a military power, Rome made only a limited contribution to village development in Britain and within the towns only a few domestic basements have survived because the majority were obliterated in medieval times. Canterbury is a notable exception. Rome's presence in Britain ended around AD 400 as a result of sustained barbarian attacks from the mainland of northern Europe. Mass colonisation had a number of consequences germane to the study of housing, most importantly a proliferation of rural settlements and radical land-use changes on an unprecedented scale. Lowland England became a primarily Anglo-Scandinavian domain of closely spaced agricultural villages and market towns, while upland Britain remained a predominantly Celtic domain characterised by more dispersed patterns of settlement. Britain's medieval countryside was neither homo-geneous nor static, however, and domestic buildings evolved differently in each locality in response to natural resources, technology, and political events such as baronial and borderland wars (Roberts, 1987).

Medieval and Tudor housing

The clustering of cottages around village greens, or hugging lanes in unbroken rows, was a reflection of the feudal economy that discouraged personal mobility and investment in roads. For nostalgic reasons these variants on the nucleated village are keenly sought after by modern home-buyers. Some thriving villages were aban-doned during the Middle Ages due to plague, planned re-forestation, landscape enhancement, coastal erosion, and the enclosure of open fields to create lucrative sheep runs (Hoskins, 1955). Reclamation of marginal land occurred through squat-ting, changes in tenure created 'daughter' settlements, and many obsolete houses were replaced either *in situ* or on new sites (Ward, 2002).

Britain's status as a defensible island allowed the countryside to evolve in comparative peace, reflected in a proliferation of large unfortified houses dating from late medieval times. The patchwork of small fields created by enclosures has been adapted to great advantage in the modern village expansions where mature hedgerows and hedgerow trees help 'contain' new housing. Village planning is a discipline where an appreciation of local history is indispensable. As for construc-tion and design, few dwellings have survived unaltered from the medieval period because of fragile materials. While the Norman Conquest in the eleventh century introduced great castles and cathedrals to the landscape, the feudal system retarded innovation in domestic architecture. The better quality houses were usually sited within the outer walls of a castle as defence from outlaws.

The predominant dwelling type in medieval villages was the single-storey, single-room 'cruck', constructed like an upturned boat (Barley, 1961). Earth infill for walls and thatch for roofs meant discomfort and rapid deterioration. Manor houses were also timber-framed, normally consisting of one large room with the floors covered by rushes and skins and a 'smoke hole' in the roof. Stone vaulting of the kind found in churches was too expensive for ordinary domestic buildings, so cross-beams were inserted to create structural stability and to support galleries and upper floors in the larger properties. To prevent rotting, the bases of vertical timbers were sometimes charred and fixed in a stone plinth (Gibberd, 1945).

Despite the abundance in England of clay, bricks did not become widespread until after 1500 when Flemish refugees introduced brick-making along with weaving (Woodforde, 1976). The brick enabled load-bearing walls to become integral to dwelling construction and design from the Tudor period onwards, although timber-frame technology continued to be important into the seventeenth century, when reserves became seriously depleted due to the demands of shipbuilding, windmills and iron forges (Hoskins, 1955). A significant related innovation was the brick chimney, which increased thermal efficiency, reduced fire risk and provided opportunities for decorative 'twisting'. Glass also became cheaper and saw expression in small, closely spaced windows with heavy stone frames and mullions. Further characteristics of the Tudor house were the decorative 'battlement' and the ornamental 'moat', both redundant hangovers from medieval times and a reminder that nostalgia for a more chivalrous age was already fashionable five centuries ago.

Town houses remained a minority possession until the mid-nineteenth century when the proportion of Britons living in urban areas outnumbered the rural population for the first time (Briggs, 1963). Relatively big towns such as Norwich had become centres of industry by Tudor times, but were not polluted by industrial effluent in the modern sense. Defence, shipbuilding, sea-borne trade and agricultural prosperity provided most of the wealth for town improvement up to the industrial revolution. Late-medieval towns, Nottingham being another example, had been constricted either by defensive walls or the right to fill open fields, which had the effect of pushing building densities up in a piecemeal manner (Beckett, 1997). As a consequence, dwellings typically had jettied upper floors, cellars and outbuildings at the rear. Unco-ordinated encroachment onto streets accounts, in part, for the interesting alignment and charming resultant townscape admired by later generations (Burke, 1976). While narrow streets and over-hangs provided shelter, they also assisted the spread of fire and infection and impeded the passage of horses and carts as business expanded. Most dwellings contained workshops and stores at the back or upstairs and could therefore be described, in today's terminology, as 'mixed-use development'.

Impact of the Renaissance

Early hints of architectural innovation in English residential building are evident at Eton College, Hampton Court and Wollaton Hall, near Nottingham. These famous houses, more palatial than domestic in scale, display a blend of medieval and neo-classical styles characteristic of Tudor England. A gradual transition from timber-frame to brick-and-block construction was accelerated at the beginning of the seventeenth century by King James I, whose experience of robust stone build-ings in Scotland led him to recommend 'bricks not sticks' for the improvement of London. Classical architecture was introduced to London by Inigo Jones who is best remembered for designing the residential square of Covent Garden at the request of King Charles I in the 1620s. This 'greenfield' site on part of the Duke of Bedford's estate was modelled on cathedral cloisters, and provided a dignified alternative to the cramped streets of the medieval capital nearby. The Great Fire of 1666, confined to the old city, resulted in by-laws specifying that permanent mater-ials should be used for the rebuilding.

Later, London squares were designed around communal gardens overlooked by the houses and 'key-holder' access helped foster a sense of identity among the professional classes, who were the clients for this new type of residential area. Other prosperous cities, such as Bristol and Bath and spa towns such as Cheltenham, saw the development of crescents and circuses to accommodate the growing number of merchants, aristocrats and landed gentry wanting to live in state-of-the-art urban surroundings in the latter half of the eighteenth century. Edinburgh took the bold step of establishing a New Town alongside the squalid multi-storey tenements of the old hill-top city, and created a landscaped park from marshy ground between the two built-up areas. Georgian Britain saw the emergence of a speculative house-building industry, dominated by Thomas Cubitt who organised gangs of craftsmen and labourers to handle the volume of work. Pattern books of house types and interiors were another developer's innovation of the period. London's rapid west-ward expansion was financed in large measure on gambling, slavery and prostitution – a reminder of the economics behind housing output at that time.

Effects of industrialisation

The industrial revolution, beginning in the mid-eighteenth century, originated in rural areas where coal mining, iron-making and canal building transformed regional landscapes, particularly the Midlands and the southern Pennines. While new wealth helped finance the improvement of houses in both country and town, rapid increases in house-building to accommodate rural labourers migrating into urban areas led to a marked deterioration in the environment. Terraces of shoddily built dwellings were squeezed into poorly drained sites left over between factories and canal wharves. When the railways system expanded after 1830, demolition of slum areas for stations and goods yards exacerbated town cramming, while viaducts sweeping over existing built-up areas had the effect of isolating groups of dwellings in dingy backland pockets. Thus the substitution of brick and slate for timber and thatch was not automatically positive; poor standards of workmanship often went hand in hand with mass dwelling production even where theoretically more robust building materials were being used (Briggs, 1963).

Development in late Victorian and Edwardian times

Standards of dwelling construction nevertheless improved gradually during the Victorian era, due to rises in prosperity, scientific knowledge, technical proficiency and reform. A marked reduction in density due to legislation governing room size and the provision of back gardens is indicated by maps (a) and (b) of Figure 2.2 where an area of Nottingham's notorious back-to-back dwellings is contrasted with later by-law terraces of the type immortalised in the film *Saturday Night and Sunday Morning* (1960).

Dwelling design for the educated classes reflected a return of puritan values that favoured villas with a large number of rather gloomy rooms concealed by over-vegetated gardens. The late-Victorian house thus contrasted with the Georgian town house, although the terrace format survived for land economy reasons in some prosperous urban neighbourhoods. Paradoxically, there was a fashion in the latter half of the nineteenth century for Gothic elaboration and exotic features imported from the Empire, all of which made for a fussy urban environment oddly at variance with the ethos of manufacturing and trade. Resistance to the cosmopolitan values of mainland Europe may perhaps explain the sombre ornamentation of the large Victorian dwelling.

During the nineteenth century it occurred to a minority of successful industrialists that output could be increased by improving the living conditions of their employees. Robert Owen, Titus Salt, George Cadbury, William Lever and others all moved their factories from congested inner-urban environments to urban-fringe sites and used the lower cost of land to provide dwellings with gardens for their workers. Cadbury's model village at Bournville, near Birmingham, inspired the urban visionary Ebenezer Howard to develop his concept of the 'garden city' in which the amenity value of the rural cottage would be combined with access to urban facilities. Suburban railways, horse-drawn buses and trams were already making it possible for the late-Victorian bourgeoisie to enjoy homes with gardens (Figure 2.2c), although it was another generation before the artisan and clerical worker would also be able to enjoy real greenness in the home plot.

Inter-war developments

The First World War (1914–18) proved a major threshold in dwelling design and provision. Prime minister Lloyd George famously promised 'homes for heroes' after the poor general health of recruits to military service and factory production became public knowledge. The Tudor Walters report (1918) advocated public subsidy to local authorities to build housing for rent at a recommended density of 12 dwellings per acre (30 per hectare), contrasting with 40 d.p.a. (100 d.p.h) in the average terrace housing. Council estates were typically laid out with a radial-concentric street pattern, influenced by neo-classical town planning but distinguished by semi-detached or short rows of three to six dwellings designed in the 'arcadian' (rustic) style (Figure 2.2d).

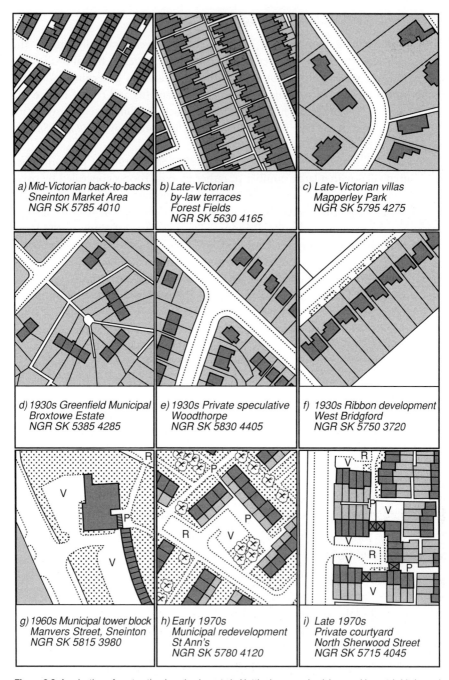

Figure 2.2 A selection of contrasting housing layouts in Nottingham emphasising road layout (white), garden size (grey) and communal open space (stipple).

Source: Authors' fieldwork and OS base maps

Notes: R = road space, V = vehicular outside parking, P = public footway. All developments are extant except area in map (a) which was demolished in the 1930s. The width of each map represents 100 m.

In the two decades 1919–39 approximately 4 million dwellings were built, about 1.5 million by the public sector and 2.5 million by the private sector. This addition to the housing stock was more than the net increase in population of 3 million. By 1940 roughly 40 per cent of Britons were living in dwellings of twentieth-century age, overwhelmingly with sizeable gardens. Low-density housing built in the private sector was characterised by a repetitive grid with semi-detached and detached dwellings as the predominant house-types (Figure 2.2e) although recent research (Whitehand and Carr, 1999, 2001) refutes the popular image of total suburban monotony. Provision of incidental public open space was certainly less than in municipal estates. Speculative housing development between the wars was encouraged by low agricultural land prices, lack of effective planning controls, a low bank rate, and the fact that many suburban market gardens could not get manure due to the replacement of draught horses by motor vehicles (Cherry, 1972). Local dairy farms suffered increasing competition from refrigerated transport and many were therefore sold for development. Other characteristic forms of new housing were 'ribbon' and 'pepper-pot' development, both responses to the falling cost of petrol. Ribbon development was unsatisfactory because it obscured the traveller's view of the countryside and gave the impression that land-take for housing was greater than it actually was (Figure 2.2f). It either precluded road widening or led to the erosion of front gardens when roads were widened; it retarded social interaction between neighbours on opposite sides of the highway; it produced unsightly 'wirescape' as residents acquired telephones; it increased the likelihood of

Plate 2.1 Inter-war ribbon development on the A52 trunk road at Spondon, east of Derby. The poor environment and splitting of the local community are very evident from this illustration: R. N. E. Blake.

Plate 2.2 An example of inter-war 'pepper-pot' development near the Thanet Way (A299) at Whitstable, Kent. Since the photograph was taken an unadopted access road for motor vehicles has been laid: R. N. E. Blake.

accidents as owners installed separate driveways; and it required milk floats and dust-carts to stop and start on the main carriageway. As we shall see, further development of this kind was restricted in the mid-1930s and its effects moderated by the provision of slip-roads to reduce conflict between local and through traffic (Plate 2.1). Pepper-pot development, consisting of isolated house plots in fields, was awkward for emergency vehicles especially where the owner failed to provide a metalled drive (Plate 2.2). In coastal areas such as Essex, Kent and Sussex 'plotlands' were created to encourage ex-servicemen to build bungalows for retirement. Peacehaven, on the South Downs, is the classic example of this characteristic legacy of the 1920s (Ward, 2002).

Wartime and post-war developments

The Second World War (1939–45) saw a virtual moratorium on house-building as construction resources were diverted to military works. Ironically, some wartime airfields and depots have latterly become the foci of controversial proposals for new settlements, e.g. Upper Heyford, Oxfordshire (Blake, 2001). After 1945 hutted camp sites were used to accommodate local homeless people and refugees from war-torn Europe. In design terms the Second World War proved less of a threshold than the preceding conflict and much new housing in both the public and private sectors continued to be constructed along inter-war lines. Record annual housing outputs of the order of 300,000–400,000 homes were achieved during the ministry of Harold Macmillan in the 1950s, the principal design legacy in the public sector being high-rise flats (Figure 2.2g). The decade also saw the advent of 'open-plan' layouts under American influence (Figure 2.2h) and the 'invasion' of commuter villages by suburban-style estates (Nairn, 1955; Brett, 1965). It can be seen from the examples illustrated in Figure 2.2 that some of the design innovations materialised a decade or more after the ideas were first promoted. Since 1970 housing developers have responded to the general tightening up of density with a proliferation of house-types attuned to company marketing strategies and branding. The return of the garden wall following advocacy of defensible space in 'design guides' is arguably the most visible public gain of the recent period.

Greater diversity in the residential landscape is particularly evident in the medium-rise, private-sector 'ensemble' development associated with the current urban renaissance and its forerunner developments of the type exemplified in Figure 2.2i. Looking back, the post-war period can be divided broadly into the first 25 years, when *quantity* of output was the priority, and the remainder of the twentieth century when *quality* of output driven by environmental and consumer imperatives dominated the house-building industry. The early post-war years were characterised by provision of greater space inside and around the dwelling and amenities not yet available in all homes (e.g. fixed baths, running hot water, lifts in tenements). The past three decades have seen much greater emphasis on energy efficiency, maximisation of ground use and design-led enclosure: all being traceable to concerns about the Earth's dwindling resources triggered by the Vietnam war, 'flower power' and the oil crisis. Manned exploration of outer space undoubtedly had a deep influence on thinking about domestic space.

Demographic and socio-economic perspectives

Britain is among the world's most densely populated countries (*c.*240 persons per km^2) and possesses one of the most agriculturally productive and enchanting landscapes. With their deep affection for the countryside and traditional architecture, the British public look to conservation bodies to protect their rural heritage, yet underlying these environmental concerns there is a buoyant demand for new homes. Since fewer than 10 per cent of Britain's population need to live in rural areas to exploit and manage natural resources, there is inevitably a philosophical debate over where development should properly be allowed to take place. Before considering the capacity of the environment to absorb housing development, it is first necessary to consider where the demand is coming from. The disciplines of demography, sociology and human geography can yield some of the answers, and by gathering, co-ordinating and interpreting factual evidence on patterns and trends of demand, a clearer picture of the drive for housing development emerges.

Demographic change

Though there is a broad spatial consonance between population and housing, this relationship is neither constant nor straightforward due to changes in household size. The Census, first conducted during the Napoleonic wars, provides a robust record of demographic change in Britain over two centuries of industrial transformation.

In 1801 the presently constituted UK contained fewer than 12 million people whereas today (2001) it contains almost 59 million (Table 2.1). The fastest proportional increase (90 per cent) took place in the half-century 1801–51, although the following half-century 1851–1901 saw a larger volumetric increase (of 16 million).

During the twentieth century the population increase has been almost 21 million, with higher volumetric and percentage growth rates during the first half-century than have occurred since 1951. This slowing is primarily the result of a declining birth rate related to changing social behaviour rather than the effect of fatalities in two world wars or net outward migration. It is already clear therefore that the post-war surges in house-building have not been directly fuelled by increases in population, but are attributable to other factors such as the desire for more individual space within the home, or moving to a different type of home or area by preference rather than necessity.

A progressive fall in average household size is also evident from the figures in Table 2.1. The average has fallen from well over 4 persons per household to 2.3 during the twentieth century. This is due to education, delayed child bearing, a fashion for few or no children, more elderly people surviving to live alone and more young and middle-aged people choosing a single life-style. Thus projections of the number of houses needed are related not simply to the number of extra people, but to the size of the family or household unit combined with its members' joint income. Inter-regional, intra-regional and international migration rates are also relevant in making predictions, as *natural* change (the balance between births and deaths) is only one component of overall change.

What we know about population and household conditions emanates primarily from the General Register Office (GRO). The key outputs of GRO are the decennial Census and the mid-year estimates derived from a combination of Census baselines and year-by-year assessment of births, deaths, immigration and emigration. The Census was instituted largely in response to the onset of the industrial revolution and a resultant acceleration in the rate of urbanisation. For the study of housing it is also pertinent to note the establishment of the Ordnance

Table 2.1 Total population, numbers of dwellings and average household size in the UK, 1801–2001

Year	Population (millions)	Occupied dwellings (millions)	Average number of persons per dwelling
1801	11.6	2.1	5.5
1851	22.3	4.1	5.4
1901	38.2	8.0	4.8
1951	50.2	14.2	3.6
2001	58.8	25.4	2.3

Source: Adapted from Census of Population

Survey (1791) which has provided an enduring spatial basis for population enumeration and analysis (Rhind, 1983). At each successive Census there have been innovations to expand the scope and make the statistics more useful. In 1851 birthplace was added to the questions, in 1911 aggregates at local authority level were first published and in 1951 household amenities (running hot water, inside toilet and fixed bath) were recorded. Tenure type was first recorded from 1961 and journey to work from 1981. Such changes make long-range comparison problematic, however, especially with regard to migration, ethnicity and household conditions. A particular deterioration in data availability occurred after 1971 as a consequence of local government reorganisation. The previous distinction between urban districts/boroughs and rural districts, which had enabled demographic contrasts to be made between town and country, was rendered more difficult by the new enlarged districts comprising an admixture of rural and urban land uses that conceals important socio-economic distinctions. While computing techniques have made it possible in principle to recreate old administrative areas from small-area statistics (parishes, wards and enumeration zones), longitudinal comparison is extremely difficult for the non-specialist researcher.

Problems with the 2001 Census

However, the outcome of the latest Census proved controversial for other reasons. The adjusted result of 58.8 million was 0.9 million lower than a previously published mid-year estimate upon which the government's published spending plans had been based. The discrepancy was most acute in inner London where the Borough of Westminster, for example, stands to lose a substantial slice of its housing grant if the Census figure prevails. A depressed 'official' figure could also affect the chances of housing developers getting planning permission since less demand is implied. Westminster council have accused the Office for National Statistics (ONS) of 'statistical treachery' in reducing the borough's population estimate by a staggering 64,000 (*The Independent*, 1 October 2002).

The national discrepancy of 0.9 million is attributed by ONS to an earlier over-estimate in the mid-year estimates of net migration (the excess of inward migrants over emigrants). It now appears that since 1991 more people have left Britain to live elsewhere than was previously thought and that the real contribution of net migration to total inter-censal growth (of 2.3 million) was only 0.7 million and not 1.6 million. Greater out-migration is almost certainly attributable to young males being attracted to exciting work opportunities in the Mediterranean and 'trendy global cities' such as Melbourne and Toronto. The probable implications for housing are delayed child-rearing in the short term, but an eventual return to Britain in the longer run expressed by a demand for city apartments rather than conventional family homes in the suburbs. Taking the wider view, this may be further evidence of the underlying trend towards single-living, delayed parenthood and participation in a global life-style focused on cities rather than small towns. There has been further comment on the increasing tendency of young women to choose a high-risk life-style involving frequent travel abroad to work and the implications this might have for fertility rates.

Population structure

In addition to the 'missing million' young men, Britain's population is getting older. Census 2001 indicates that for the first time there are more people over the age of 60 (21 per cent) than under 16 (20 per cent). Furthermore, there is now a significant proportion of the population aged over 85, a five-fold increase since 1951. This clearly reflects improvements in nutrition, medical care and housing conditions, but has important implications for the provision of appropriate housing as more people reach an advanced age. Much of the press comment and public reaction has focused on the question of how a diminishing working age group pays for the care of the older generation. Government estimates about migration were based on a certain size of working, and thereby tax-paying, population. With a dent in the size of the young workforce, the Chancellor may have to consider raising taxes from those in employment and suspending tax breaks for the affluent retired. The Treasury and the Bank of England are reconsidering growth prospects for the national economy, including a revised assessment of housing need in response to the unexpected findings of the latest Census. The scenario of working till the age of 70, straight after a decade in which retirement before 60 was becoming an attractive prospect for many, has embarrassing political implications and an obvious effect on the housing market. Should falls in the Stock Market lead to a wider recession, the relationship between the working age group, school-leavers and the older age groups is likely to change markedly. There are also likely to be knock-on effects regarding policy towards asylum seekers and economic migrants. The argument that these people are a drain on the economy has to be revised and inward migration could be encouraged as a means of reinvigorating the workforce, with implications for the provision of appropriate housing for foreign migrants.

As well as a change in the age structure of the population, there has been a shift in the balance between males and females. In an egalitarian society there should not, in theory, be any housing implication: but there is. Historically, despite risks in childbirth, there were more females in the older age groups due to the higher death rate of men through heart disease, industrial accident and wars. The 2001 Census revealed that Britain had 1.7 million more women than men, and symbolically more than 30 million women for the first time ever. In all age groups over 21 women are now more numerous than men. Feminisation of the workforce is one possible explanation for the emigration of young men who are said to no longer have a distinctive place in society and are reacting to negative images of maleness in popular culture (*The Independent*, 2 October 2002). With more females as well as more elderly people in the community there are serious questions concerning safety in public places. Design of estates and parks, with improved surveillance and warden services, is an emergent issue in residential design. Britain is said to have a poor 'work–life' balance, made worse by breakdown in the family structure through divorce and involuntary single living. The taxation issue is likely to cause further friction between the age groups in addition to antipathy between the sexes over who dominates in the home.

Another important finding of 2001 was the differential rate of population change between regions over the past couple of decades. There is nothing new about regional contrasts but the recent pattern of gains and losses is strongly indicative of the social changes affecting contemporary Britain. Against a national increase of 2.4 million (4 per cent) since 1981, all regions have risen in population except for the North East, North West and Scotland. The West Midlands, Yorkshire and Humberside and Wales (jointly representing the rest of heavy-industrial Britain) all grew by small numbers and below the national percentage rate. The East Midlands grew at twice the rate, but the most spectacular increases were registered in the east of England (11 per cent) and the South West (12 per cent). London grew at close to the national rate and Northern Ireland at slightly over twice the rate due to its high traditional birth rate. A net gain of over half a million in the South West, marginally out-performing the similarly rural Eastern region, has been sustained by affluent older people moving in for a comfortable retirement by the sea. One of the most popular destinations in this regard is Christchurch, Dorset, where opportunities for walking, swimming and sailing are fuelling the demand for homes from fit pensioners with the means to command prime locations. Apart from the ultimate strain on health and care services, this influx effectively debars young locals on low incomes and the unemployed from entering the housing market. The negative effect on society is not confined to the areas of inward migration. A Cabinet Office study released in July 2002 (*The Guardian*, 27 July) painted a dramatic picture of thousands of 'original' Londoners decamping to rural and coastal areas, leaving behind a metropolis depleted of social capital and populated increasingly by young migrants from overseas. Thus not only in size but also in its ethnic composition, London is becoming progressively less representative of the country as a whole. The current (2001) regional population densities are given in Figure 2.3.

Demographic forecasting

Forecasting is primarily a central government responsibility, although estimates are also made by local authorities for small areas using local knowledge such as employment trends. It is important therefore to draw a primary distinction between wider trends that have a degree of inevitability and local trends that can be more easily manipulated by policy decisions. National population forecasting is done initially by the Government Actuary's Department who interpret the Census and its annual updates to produce scenarios for decades ahead. Thirty years ago the official forecast population for the UK at the end of the twentieth century was 66 million (Thompson, 1970). Based on assumptions of 'white hot' economic growth (to paraphrase prime minister Harold Wilson) this figure proved to be an overestimate of about 10 per cent. Forecasting techniques were improved during the 1970s and by the mid-1980s the officially predicted figure for 2001 was uncannily

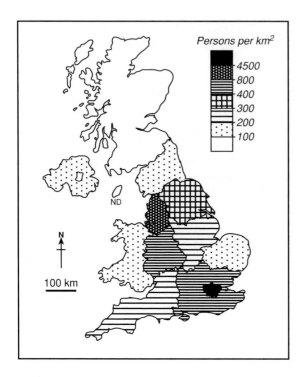

Figure 2.3 Population density in the UK in 2001 by standard region.
Source: Office for National Statistics

Persons per km²

4500
800
400
300
200
100

ND

N

100 km

close to the Census result discussed above. The projected population of the UK in 2021 is 63 million and is expected to stabilise around that figure until mid-century.

Population forecasts are based on four key components: births, deaths, in-migration and out-migration within given geographical areas. The first two components are responsible for 'natural change' and the last two for 'migratory change'. When births exceed deaths over a given period the natural change is positive, and it is negative when deaths exceed births. Similarly, when in-migration exceeds out-migration there is 'net migration', i.e. an increase attributable to movements across the area's boundary. The final balance between natural and migratory components determines whether the overall trend is upwards or downwards. Generally, natural change is the easier component to estimate as robust records of births and deaths have long been kept by local registrars and medical authorities. Migration is far more difficult to estimate due to the fact that movements abroad and between regions are not recorded in the same systematic way.

Forecasts have traditionally been made using simple arithmetic and geometric trends constructed from past data, ratios transferred from other areas with comparable socio-economic structure, and regression techniques involving dependent variables such as employment and infrastructure (Field and McGregor, 1987). In each of these the chief problem is the unreliability of external factors as indicators of population potential. Demographers therefore prefer the 'cohort survival' method which disaggregates the present population into age/sex bands and predicts the fertility rate for women and the lifespan of both genders using medical and other assumptions. One of those assumptions is the loss of current inhabitants though out-migration, a trend that could result in delayed family formation if those departing are mainly young adults. Migration in either direction is a complicating factor for cohort-survival analysis as it is far less predictable than either the birth rate or the death rate. Moreover, in-migrants have their own fertility rate based on the cultural norms of the country of origin and this will influence the future birth rate in proportion to the age and sex of the arrivals. 'Growth composition analysis' (another name for cohort survival) is therefore most reliable where the migratory element is small. In Britain it is customary to conduct population forecasts at regional level, as this provides the best balance of data for reconciling migratory movements with predictions of natural change.

Housing forecasting

For allocating public funds, and especially for marketing housing as a product, the forecasting of household formation is as important as population numbers and structure. As well as total numbers of houses needed per area it is useful to know the size and type of dwellings likely to be wanted to satisfy different types of households. Classification of households on a dynamic basis, using categories such as 'founding', 'expanding', 'stable' and 'contracting', is therefore a necessary refinement of demographic forecasting. In principle, forecasts of household formation should follow population and socio-economic forecasts driven by industrial location, employment growth and environmental preferences. In practice land use policy and house-building rates have a strong influence on where people can actually live. Housing forecasting is therefore more complicated than pure demographic forecasting.

Field and MacGregor (1987) identify five ingredients of housing forecasting, namely: future population, future households, existing housing stock, estimated deficit or surplus between household formation and housing stock, and land requirements. The third and the last are important components of forecasting housebuilding possibilities although not drivers of demand in the way that demographic trends clearly are.

Land-use data for residential development

Astonishingly, figures on the amount of land occupied by housing development in Britain are elusive. No baseline statistic for the size of the housing footprint has been found for any date or geographical area, and therefore no time-series estimates of the changing spatial significance of housing relative to other key land uses can be presented here. A statistic of the hectarage and percentage area of the UK occupied by houses and gardens is simply not available from any known source. Given the prominence of housing in the urban environment it is disappointing that information on this aspect is so vague. There are several branches of housing research where precise land-use data would be illuminating, not least the derivation of a meaningful expression of density for consistent comparison over time and geographical space. It is therefore worth probing this deficiency and presenting those fragments of information that provide some clues to the impact of housing on land use at the national level.

For a densely populated and urbanised society, Britain is conspicuously deficient in land-use data for built-up areas generally (Fuller *et al.*, 1994). Spectacular advances have been made over the past three decades in monitoring rural land-cover by remote sensing, but the images have not been resolved into the same land-use classes as those employed by urban planning authorities to control function and occupancy (Brown *et al.*, 2002). No comprehensive national land-use survey on Ordnance Survey (OS) sheet-lines has ever been conducted by a department of government, consequently neither planners, researchers nor members of the public have any reliable source of enlightenment on the evolving footprint of housing. It is noteworthy that the *Annual Abstract of Statistics* contains no table of land uses from which the areal extent of housing expansion can be monitored and evaluated. The reasons for this situation are complex but boil down to a longstanding belief among politicians and civil servants that the relevant facts are routinely gathered at local level and could be rapidly collated if needed for central policy making. It was implicit in early post-war planning legislation that local authorities would indeed gather such data as part of the plan review process, but the practice was abandoned before the first national data-bank was compiled (Blake, 1981). Other official bodies such as the District Valuer and the Land Registry have placed no spatially comprehensive outputs in the public domain, as it is not in their remit to produce land-use maps for sale. For decades it has been claimed that a foolproof methodology is on the horizon and that traditional methods of data acquisition are no longer cost-effective. The past decade has seen increasing reliance by government on the National Land Use Data Base (NLUD) for monitoring the reclamation of 'brown-field' (previously used) sites, but there is no section within this source recording land-use *stock*, i.e. the actual hectarages occupied by different land-use types in each administrative area at successive dates. In recognition of this deficiency, research into the feasibility of gathering land-use stock data was commissioned by DoE (Dunn and Harrison, 1994) but no action appears to have been taken yet. Results of tests carried out by Ordnance Survey in conjunction with the 2001 Census may shed light on this subject in due course.

Urgently needed are *local* hectarages for housing at successive dates based on identical survey methods, so that assumptions about land-take can be confirmed and debated. A realistic goal would be a comprehensive land-use survey conducted at the start of each decade, coinciding with the population Census. Geographical Information Systems (GIS) have the capacity to synthesise ground-truth and socio-economic data and issue results far more rapidly than in the past. Ordnance Survey, Office for National Statistics and the Centre for Ecology and Hydrology have conducted experiments along these lines but no district council consulted by the present authors in a recent sample survey could supply even the crudest estimate of the land-use breakdown in its area. What, then, is known about the housing footprint? Chronologically, the following facts have been gleaned from published and unpublished sources. The (first) Land Utilisation Survey of Britain (LUS1), organised in the 1930s by the celebrated geographer L. Dudley Stamp of the London School of Economics, divided residential land between 'houses with gardens' (mapped in purple) and houses with very small or no gardens (mapped in red). Because Stamp's main objective was to assess food-growing potential, his 'purple' category also included allotments, nurseries and orchards and thereby concealed the housing component in a conflated notation and statistic (Stamp, 1962). Similarly, Stamp's 'red' area included industrial, commercial and institutional development and was even less representative of its housing component. Given that the survey was conducted by volunteers from universities and secondary schools, it is understandable that generalisation was felt necessary. What Stamp's survey illustrates is the point that key data assumed to exist can in practice prove to be non-existent.

A repeat survey restricted to England and Wales was carried out in the early 1960s by Alice Coleman of King's College, London, using a revised classification of land uses designed to assist planners in controlling the rapidly evolving post-war landscape. However, despite a greatly expanded number of land-use categories, housing was mapped under a (grey) 'settlement' notation that also included commercial and institutional land uses such as shops and schools. The umbrella figure for settlement that emerged from subsequent area measurement was 7,758 km^2 (5.1 per cent of the national land mass). This was the first published indication from a spatially complete survey of housing's post-war extent, albeit inflated by ancillary land-use categories (Coleman, 1976). A revised survey handbook assigning housing to a free-standing (pink) category was later published in anticipation of a 'Third Land Use Survey' (Coleman and Shaw, 1980), but that project failed to attract funding for reasons intimated above. Special re-surveys to inform the structure planning process were commissioned independently by a number of county councils, e.g. Merseyside and Surrey, but the results were not circulated and are effectively unavailable for housing studies.

In 1996 a sample survey of Great Britain entitled *Land Use – UK* was organised by the Geographical Association to fill a knowledge vacuum that had defied officialdom for decades (Walford, 1997). For a larger national area (including Scotland, but not Northern Ireland) a figure of 11,240 km^2 was recorded as 'residential' land, extrapolated from the percentage land-cover in those 'urban' and 'rural' grid-squares sampled as part of the survey's design. This result was a generous estimate of housing because the surveyors (again volunteers) were instructed to include estate roads and minor landscaping under the definition. Thus in both this and Coleman's survey of three decades earlier the concept of 'housing land' was greater than the core area of the dwelling-plus-garden, though the reason for the exaggeration was different in each case. Quite apart from differences in the geographical areas surveyed and the use of spatial sampling in the latter project, the field instructions were different, illustrating the hazards of trying to determine an accurate footprint for any land-use category capable of comparison over time.

As with demographic data, the results of land-use surveys can be adjusted pro rata to give more accurate figures. If Coleman's early-1960s statistic for 'settlement' is raised in proportion to population to include all of the UK, and then reduced to eliminate the non-residential component (estimated at one hectare in four), the residential footprint for the UK 40 years ago emerges as 6,690 km^2 (2.7 per cent of the land mass). If Walford's figure for the mid-1990s is raised proportionally to include Northern Ireland, the national footprint for 'residential' land emerges as 11,565 km^2 (4.7 per cent). Unfortunately, it is difficult to adjust Walford's figure downwards because neither the average proportion of housing development under estate roads and landscaping, nor the extent to which generalisation was practised by surveyors, is known. Thus the apparent increase of 4,875 km^2 of housing land (74 per cent) over 35 years is manifestly exaggerated, even bearing in mind the scale of suburbanisation and village expansion that took place during that period. Nonetheless, it is salutary to have established that the UK's housing footprint has probably never exceeded 5 per cent of the national land surface.

In urban areas the coverage by housing is of course far greater, and in rural growth parishes new housing estates can increase the local housing footprint quite dramatically (Brett, 1965). Results from the Second Land Use Survey (Coleman, 1976) show housing, commercial uses and institutions (the 'grey' area) occupying almost exactly half (49 per cent) of the developed area. The other half consists of factories, utilities, roads, railway, tended open space and miscellaneous development. By screening out the non-residential component, the proportion of Britain's urban footprint devoted to housing falls below 40 per cent, consistent with a figure presented by Field and MacGregor (1987) which, incidentally, is one of the few estimates on this subject in print. In Walford's 'urban' squares, the housing percentage area was closer to half due to the inclusion of estate roads. The suspicion that houses, gardens and enclosed residential landscaping might be less extensive than the above figures suggest was tested in an exercise conducted jointly by Nottingham City Council planning department and the Faculty of Environmental Studies at Nottingham Polytechnic in 1991. Designed to coincide with the 1991 Census, the entire 75 km^2 of the city were surveyed by field inspection using a classification scheme that identified different ground covers within functional cartilages enabling dwellings and their gardens to be separately mapped for area-measurement purposes. Results showed that housing land, narrowly defined, occupied just 31 per cent of the municipal area (or 37 per cent when farmland, allotments and natural ground within the city boundary were excluded from the calculation). Based on its share of the national population (0.47 per cent in 1991), Nottingham's area under housing (23.25 km^2), when crudely extrapolated in proportion to that share, gave a national land-take estimate of 4,882 km^2 – less than half Walford's estimate. This result was predictable given that the Nottingham survey had deliberately excluded residential roads and landscaping in order to discern the true footprint of dwellings and gardens.

We have now reached the point where the figures for land use are so discrepant as to have limited practical application to housing policy until accounting methods can be refined. All that the data can do is to put housing's territorial demand into some perspective and provide a broad indicator of how much space is actually available to the average household within its defended living space. From a strategic point of view, more robust figures on the housing footprint at the local authority level would permit densities to be analysed and areas to be compared by government for policy and resource allocation purposes. At the present time there are no reliable figures and the above discussion merely serves as proof of this situation. If such a fundamental issue as land-take is so imprecisely monitored, it raises the possibility that other data-sets relevant to housing might also be defective.

The above discrepancy introduces another important principle that may help explain the complexities of land for housing. Best and Rogers (1973) derived a 'density/size rule' which states that the provision of developed land per thousand persons is inversely proportional to the size of settlement. Thus a big city like Nottingham (population 275,000) would be expected to have less land under housing per head than a medium-sized town or a village at the opposite end of the settlement continuum. This is explained, in broad terms, by the concentration of high-density accommodation in cities and the tendency for domestic gardens in smaller settlements to merge imperceptibly into quasi-agricultural land uses. It is probable that the local planning surveys from which Best made his calculations included paddocks, orchards and allotments as part of the 'built-up' areas especially in villages. Best (1981) later identified a 'pivotal density' above which large urban areas were tending to become less densely developed as a consequence of decentralisation policies, and below which rural areas were becoming more densely developed due to the shift of population towards smaller towns and key villages. Three decades on from that research, the balance appears to be shifting back to a greater contrast in densities along the urban-rural continuum as urban regeneration and 'city living' policies push urban densities up and keep greenfield development in check as part of 'sustainable development'. A comprehensive testing of changes in the density/size relationship is still awaited.

In his research Best was obliged to use statutory local development plans in the absence of pure land-use maps. The main deficiencies of forward plans are that they apply to the future and always generalise residential zones. Access roads, play areas, communal landscaping, health centres and small shops are not normally differentiated and therefore they exaggerate the residential footprint. It is also significant that the statistical distribution of land uses in local plans is no longer presented in tabular form in written planning documents. Only new allocations of development land are expressed in hectares, which precludes any longitudinal assessment of the territorial impact of housing within the plan area.

Spatial models of housing development

Since the 1920s scholars have recognised that urban settlements consist of zones of contrasting socio-economic and physical character. These zones have been conventionally represented in diagrammatic form (Figure 2.4). This mode of analysis

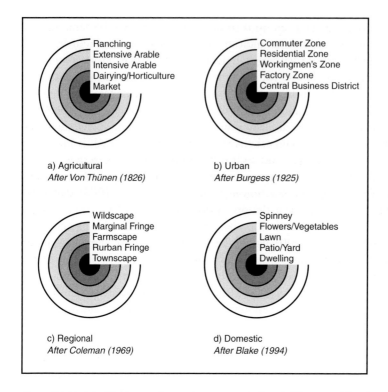

a) Agricultural
After Von Thünen (1826)

Ranching
Extensive Arable
Intensive Arable
Dairying/Horticulture
Market

b) Urban
After Burgess (1925)

Commuter Zone
Residential Zone
Workingmen's Zone
Factory Zone
Central Business District

c) Regional
After Coleman (1969)

Wildscape
Marginal Fringe
Farmscape
Rurban Fringe
Townscape

d) Domestic
After Blake (1994)

Spinney
Flowers/Vegetables
Lawn
Patio/Yard
Dwelling

Figure 2.4 Models of land use and ground-space organisation at different spatial scales.
Sources: various, as indicated

stems from the principle that the point of maximum local accessibility (typically a market place, bridge-head or waterfront) is competed for by all the potential land users within the tributary area. As a result, the most powerful economic and political interests end up commanding positions at the core, while the weaker interests are relegated to the periphery. A sequence of concentric bands emerges, based on the sum of responses to land values, amenity and travel-time. Figure 2.4 depicts this idea with a set of four concentric 'models' beginning with (a), a nineteenth century conception of rural space and concluding with (d), a domestic garden (Blake, 1994). Models (b) and (c) can be further explored in a number of texts on urban social geography (e.g. Knox and Pine, 2000).

In the 'pre-industrial' era, wealthy people lived close to their businesses, which were centrally located in order to take advantages of transport nodes. Artisans' homes were typically sited in streets immediately behind the prime locations while the poorest people occupied the town's edge, some employed on farms and in other rural industries as still occurs in agricultural societies. With industrialisation, the land directly surrounding the central business quarter became simultaneously less habitable for respectable families and increasingly valued by landlords who saw the opportunity to accommodate migrant workers at high density. Thus a belt of mixed-use development, comprising factories, warehouses, railways, tenements and cramped terrace houses, displaced what, in towns such as Nottingham, had constituted the entire built-up area a century earlier (Beckett, 1997). Environmental and social stresses led these 'zones of transition' to be branded 'twilight areas' on account of their dinginess and high incidence of malaise. The artisans and middle-class professionals tended to move into a ring of new development beyond the historic town boundary, while the well-to-do settled on the urban rim as roads and public transport were improved (Figure 2.4b). In effect, the industrial era reversed the social gradient and created a framework for 'filtering', whereby each social group moved centrifugally to a better area as the 'lower orders' pressed onto their domain from the inside. This process of 'invasion and succession' is part of the ecological approach to urban analysis and is particularly applicable to the absorption of ethnic minorities such as Jews from Eastern Europe during the twentieth century.

The neo-classical economic principles used to explain the zonal phenomenon lie in the 'access/space trade-off' model (Evans, 1985). This works from the premise that with every unit of distance away from the urban core, the amount of space available increases geometrically and therefore larger building plots in theory, become affordable. For the home-buyer (via the efforts of the house-builder or housing provider) there is a trade-off between the reduced cost of peripheral land and the added cost of travel back to the centre where it is assumed that the main income-generating opportunities lie. There have been many elaborations, and criticisms of this model, including its assumption that all economic activity is concentrated at the core and its failure to acknowledge contrasts in terrain, orbital communications, external centres of employment, planned intervention in the property market, and irrational behaviour. Early critics of the concentric-bands theory of urban structure pointed to distinctive wedge-shaped sectors caused by river-based transport corridors where industry and low-class housing extended to the urban rim because higher-class communities had not bothered to compete for the flood-prone environment. By the same token, ridges with commanding views, particularly up-wind of smoky industries, for example in Sheffield, permitted good-quality housing to thrive close to the centre at the expense of the normal commercial activities. The polycentric structure of modern cities is a further reason for rejecting the neat ring-based diagrams, although concentric zones in miniature are widely discernible, for example, around suburban railway stations.

All in all, this conceptualisation of residential space has proved robust and even the sternest critics acknowledge that it provides a benchmark for evaluating more advanced methods of urban analysis. The residential paradox, whereby poor people came to live closest to the economically most productive zone, can be explained by the fact that each family consumed very little space. Therefore the land-lords were able to draw a high combined rent from their properties, exceeding the amount affordable by a single family of greater means. Most inner-urban dwellings had no ancillary space other than a communal yard. The rent took a dispropor-tionate slice of the occupants' wages, which were kept low on the assumption that travel-to-work costs were negligible. The recent 'gentrification' of inner-urban

areas can be seen as a response to de-industrialisation, a shift of blue-collar employment to the 'outer city', and the rediscovery of the cultural advantages of urban life
in a 'post-industrial' society (Herington, 1984). Perhaps the socio-spatial gradient
is reverting to something more closely resembling the eighteenth century and
reversing the trend of the Victorian era when inner-urban areas became depleted of
professional residents because of the deteriorating environment.

Housing and land-use territories

An innovative model of land-use organisation with application to housing policy is
that devised by Alice Coleman (1969), based on findings of the Second Land Use
Survey of Britain. Faced with massively more data than Stamp had accumulated,
Coleman analysed field maps using five types of territory based on characteristic
mixes of land use. Recognition of these mixes was systematised by initially reducing
all land use to just three 'super-categories' termed 'settlement', 'farmland' and
'natural vegetation'. Where one super-category was locally dominant, the environment was classed as a 'scape' and where there was an inter-lacing of two or three
super-categories with none clearly dominant, the environment was classed as a
'fringe'. Implicit in the concept was the principle that scapes have relatively efficient
land use because of their compactness, while fringes are basically inefficient because
of fragmentation. Figure 2.4c shows the disposition of Coleman's five territories
using the concentric format adapted from earlier spatial models.

In England and Wales of the 1960s the compact 'townscape' occupied only
3.5 per cent of the country but contained one-third of the nation's housing and
commercial development; two-thirds of the townscape consisted of housing. By
contrast, the fragmented 'rurban fringe' occupied 6.5 per cent of the country but
only a quarter of it consisted of housing and commercial development, the rest
being a tangle of golf courses, utilities, motorways, abandoned fields, etc. Together
the two most developed territories (townscape and rurban fringe) covered almost
exactly 10 per cent of the country and accounted for 88 per cent of all its housing
and commercial development. Although these figures suggest a broadly compact
pattern of urbanisation in Britain, the relatively fragmented character of land use in
the rurban fringe hinted at inefficient planning (Coleman, 1977). Not only did agriculture show signs of decline through the extended interface with housing, but
housing areas themselves were rendered inefficient by excessive separation from
facilities and stress from unsympathetic riparian land users. While there are compen-
sations in rurban living in terms of interesting semi-rural walks, the environmental
uncertainties militate against them in many instances. Coleman's intervention in the
planning debate (1977) sprang from the premise that the rurban fringe, as mapped
by academic surveyors with no axe to grind, should be consolidated with a carefully selected array of compact and purposeful urban land uses, thereby taking
pressure off the coherent 'farmscape' territory (i.e. open countryside). This approach
was consistent with green-belt policy and anticipated 'urban capacity studies' by at
least two decades. Coleman's findings were heavily criticised by some planners

at the time who felt they had been unfairly blamed for a situation over which they had limited control. In the absence of a follow-up survey in comparable detail, no re-assessment of the extent of scapes and fringes has taken place, despite the methodology being entirely consistent with current thinking on urban regeneration and sustainable development.

Micro-environmental analysis

As Figure 2.4 indicates, the most celebrated spatial models have concentrated on land use patterns at the urban and regional scales. While useful for conceptual-ising housing development, the traditional approaches (Figure 2.4a–c) have a limited application to the design process where ground space utilisation at the domestic scale is pertinent. Figure 2.4d demonstrates an interpretation of surface differentiation within a hypothetical domestic plot, applying the principles of land competition and distance-decay at the micro-environmental scale. In practice, a dwelling is normally sited in the most accessible zone of the plot, near the road where 'economic' inputs (journey to work, deliveries of goods, etc.) occur. The concentric representation is thus schematic only and the model could be redrawn eccentrically (Barton *et al.*, 1995). Immediately surrounding the dwelling is a hard-surfaced area comprising a patio, yard, path or drive acting as a utility zone (for barbecue, dustbins, car parking etc.). The dwelling and its adjacent yard space may be likened to the central business district (CBD) and inner-urban industrial zone respectively, i.e. environments that generate the largest number of functions and highest density of movements. In a garden, the lawn (with cultivated borders) is normally the closest green zone to the dwelling, analogous to urban-fringe golf courses and playing fields, whereas the larger fruit and vegetable beds are located further away, comparable with the farmscape within a region. At the rear, and the sides in the case of large gardens, is the spinney plus compost heap, providing a semi-wild boundary zone acting as a micro-wildscape. This broad arrangement is observable in most gardens and reflects the diminishing impact of built forms, energy consumption and time spent with increasing distance from the dwelling. Where a good balance of these micro-environments is achieved in gardens, the development is more likely to contribute to sustainability. A problem for new dwellings with small gardens, designed to minimise land-take, is that the full range of micro-uses and ground covers is difficult to fit in, especially mature trees. Research by Best and Ward (1956) advocating more generous gardens merits re-examination in the context of the sustainability debate.

Interpreting density

No spatial measure causes more confusion than density. While density of popula-tion at the national and regional levels (Figure 2.3) is broadly indicative of urbanisation, the relationship between housing and land use depends crucially on design at the micro-environmental scale. The chief problems for both the developer and student of housing are definitional, stemming from the choice of ground units (acres or hectares), the range of site-occupancy measures (dwellings, habitable rooms, bed-spaces, persons), and blurred interpretations as to what ground area is defined as the residential unit (the plot only, plus estate roads, plus minor landscaping?). In the policy context Bibby and Shepherd (1997) refer to early concern among planners to restrict residential density by imposing upper limits, whereas recent debates revolve around achieving a minimum density of 30 dwellings per hectare (d.p.h.). However, it is rarely made clear in published discussion whether the 30 d.p.h. target includes ancillary land uses such as roads and landscaping. Moreover, figures quoted in the press are sometimes unclear as to whether the density relates purely to recent new-build or total land occupied by housing. It has long been appreciated by planners and developers that 'dwellings per hectare (or acre)' is an inadequate measure of density since sprawling properties such as bungalows can cover a high proportion of their plots while accommodating few people. A large single-household dwelling with affluent occupants is likely to generate a disproportionate number of motor vehicles whereas a multi-household block of flats with elderly occupants may generate comparatively little traffic. Plot ratio (floor-space relative to plot area) is therefore a more valid measure for assessing housing impact. In their research, Bibby and Shepherd (ibid.) have suggested that for every 1,000 housing completions in England roughly 40 hectares are urbanised, but this calculation is based on the premise that housing occupies about two-thirds of all land falling to urban use. Since that proportion is somewhat larger than suggested by other evidence discussed above, there is a need for further research into the composition of urban spread and the position of housing within that spread.

Conclusions

While much has been written on the intricacies of dwelling construction and design, the influence of demographic and social change on housing development is rarely elaborated in works with a technical or aesthetic slant. Similarly, while much research has been carried out on policy aspects of land availability and density, the overall picture in terms of housing's physical spread remains vague. The links made in this chapter between the physical evolution of the British dwelling, socio-demographic change and land-take to accommodate housing have revealed a number of key interfaces where more systematic research might prove illuminating.

Tracing the evolution of the British dwelling house provokes questions of residential density in the past and its relationship to life expectancy, quality of life, constructional challenges, statutory controls and the nature of ancillary space within domestic property. National figures are important for making comparisons with other nation states, hence the attention given in the chapter to historical data-sets. While the British Census is among the most robust in the world, its use in longitudinal studies has been dogged by changes in definition, enumeration methods, administrative boundaries and the format in which disaggregated data are made available. Electronic processing has assisted the public availability of data, but inconsistencies in presentation and a lack of clarity in the definition of urban and rural areas are a continuing constraint on housing studies. The perfect data-set would be a synthesis of the decennial Census and a site-by-site land use survey, spatially co-ordinated to provide small-area measures of housing density (Barke *et al.*, 1993). Despite the existence of GIS systems in many local authority offices, there is little evidence that detailed land-use information was gathered to coincide with the 2001 Census. It is possible that alternative sources of land-use information have been collected to throw light on the residential environment, but the scope and availability of any outputs are as yet unknown (Cassettari, 2003).

Research for this chapter has further highlighted the fact that the Ordnance Survey does not show land use per se and is therefore an imprecise guide to domestic space at any scale. This has implications both for students of past housing patterns and for modern researchers probing the distribution of housing within settlements. If we accept, in the absence of official guidance, that roughly 5 per cent of the UK is covered by homes, gardens and 'defended' ancillary space, the national average density of residential areas is roughly 20 dwellings per hectare. This benchmark figure is derived from an estimated footprint of 1.2 million residential hectares, a population of 59 million and an average household size of 2.3. From this crude calculation a whole set of variations at regional and local levels could in principle be computed, mapped and evaluated.

Forecasting is not simply a matter of projecting past trends. Changes in technology, social structure and consumer behaviour must be closely examined before making assumptions about the amount of space needed for housing in the future. Land requirements are calculated partly from population forecasts and partly on space yardsticks recommended by consumer groups and government. Derivation of those yardsticks is informed not only by past experience but also by a notion of environmental capacity as demonstrated in Coleman's land-use territory analysis. Although demographic forecasting and environmental analysis represent the demand and supply sides of the housing equation respectively, one analytical consideration they share is the importance of disaggregation. A key outcome of this chapter, therefore, is the realisation of the vital importance of understanding the basis on which phenomena are classified and recorded and the range of methods available for presenting information at different scales of enquiry. On a broad scale, demographic data are more plentiful than environmental data with respect to housing, but potentially field data are more easily updated at the local level. As yet there appears to be no official view on how to monitor the socio-demographic and physical texture of the residenial environment in a spatially comprehensive, integrated and consistent way.

Discussion points

1   Select either a small town, a large commuter village or a city ward accessible for investigation of its modern housing history. Obtain large-scale OS base maps depicting the place as it was around 1900 and at the present time. On each map

shade in all residential plots, being careful to exclude any land uses not strictly falling within residential cartilages. Using sample points, estimate the actual and percentage area under housing at each date, commenting on the scale of change over the past century.

2   Using information on the Internet compile a table of major land uses for the constituent parts of the UK (England, Wales, Scotland and Northern Ireland) highlighting the percentage area occupied by housing. Where data availability permits, indicate the pace at which housing's national footprint has been growing in recent times.

3   With reference to Figure 2.4, discuss the value of 'spatial models' in explaining housing development and suggest alternative terminologies more applicable to present-day living patterns.

Key reading

The scope of this chapter is such that no single existing work encompasses the same cluster of topics. For the historical context Hoskins, *The Making of the English Landscape* (1955) remains the definitive reference. Champion and Townsend, *Contemporary Britain* (1994) is helpful on the demographic side while Perkins and Parry, *Mapping the UK* (1996) reviews the many sources of data on housing's land requirement. Northcott, *Britain 2010* (1991) and Allmendinger and Chapman, *Planning Beyond 2000* (1999) offer useful scenarios.

Chapter 3
Housing need, housing demand and housing supply

Andrew Golland and Mike Gillen

Introduction: yesterday's solutions and today's problems

When we consider today's 'housing problems', it is all too easy to forget that they are the result of many years of 'housing development'. The housing problems we encounter today are very much a consequence of housing development decisions made in the past and in different political and economic situations. Indeed, to understand more about our current housing situation, it is necessary to understand the political and economic context in which housing development has taken place. Without doing this, there is a danger of blaming those directly responsible for housing development for all today's housing problems. This chapter aims to explain the context in which housing development companies, housing associations and local authorities operate.

Housing 'need' and housing 'demand'

Two concepts, housing 'need' and housing 'demand', are fundamental to an understanding of why, how and in what form housing development takes place. It is important to establish at the outset how these concepts impact on the volume of housing production, the tenure of new development, its location and the type of dwellings that are built.

'Need' and 'demand' are, in practice, difficult terms to differentiate. What developers know they can sell is often a completely different product from the one that local people (in the same area) think is 'needed'; there begins the practical difficulty of judging between 'need' and 'demand'.

In housing debates, however, there are clear distinctions made. Housing 'need' is conventionally associated with a more basic or fundamental requirement for housing, often related to the achievement of some form of minimal provision. This form of 'minimal provision' is often defined in terms of 'production targets', or in terms of some basic 'quality standard'. Housing 'need' has been defined as

> the quantity of housing that is required to provide accommodation of an agreed minimum standard and above for a population given its size, household composition, age distribution, etc, *without taking into account the individual household's ability to pay for the housing assigned to it.*

> (Robinson, 1979: 55)

Thus meeting 'housing need' assumes making some minimal form of provision but at the same time ignoring ability to pay. Taken in one way, there could be distortions to the housing system if households with an ability to pay for better housing were nevertheless subsidised up to the minimum provision level. However, it is usual in practice to ensure that subsidies which enable decent housing to be provided are targeted towards households in greatest 'need'.

Housing 'demand' is more usually associated with the requirements of individual households over and above the basic or minimum level of provision or 'need': whether, for example, the household requires an owner-occupied or a rented dwelling; whether it requires a semi-detached house or a flat; whether it requires a large garden and/or a garage, and so on. Housing demand is ultimately an issue which tells us more about the choices which households make in moving house or in gaining access to a new dwelling. Demand is strongly associated with 'effective demand', which is a demand supported by an ability to pay.

Indeed, housing choice is constrained by household income limits. As King states 'choice' is, in practice, not available to all:

> For a significant minority choice is deemed not to exist at all and thus housing is provided for them through either direct provision or subsidies. The reason for this, of course, is that certain households have insufficient means to provide for themselves.
>
> (King, 1998: 5)

Thus, income and ability to pay are the critical factors and it can easily be argued that those households with the highest incomes have the greatest housing 'choice'. In being able to pay for housing, households with 'effective demand' back up their housing choices and decisions with the necessary financial resources. These households have no need for state financial support. All other forms of 'demand' can be argued to be purely 'aspirational': households that would like to have a better or different form of housing, if they had the ability to pay for it.

The role of government and the market in meeting housing need and housing demand

The housing development policy challenge

The role of government in housing provision has changed significantly since the Second World War. European studies confirm that the UK is not alone in seeing important changes in housing policy. Boelhouwer and van der Heijden (1992) have 'mapped' the nature of housing policy over time in Western European countries. They show how the initial drive for production output was overtaken by a focus on policies aimed to improve the housing stock, and then with more recent policies targeted towards better housing allocation. In the UK, these policy shifts can also be observed with sometimes radical consequences for housing development.

The role of government in housing provision can be argued to have changed from one which was focused on meeting broad housing needs to one which is now focused more on addressing the specific demands of households. This theme will be developed in the sections that follow.

Housing development and housing need in the post-war period

In common with many other European countries, the problem of the UK's housing policy in the immediate post-war period was to overcome housing shortages. The need to produce a very high number of dwellings, both to cater for an increased number of households and to rebuild the war-damaged housing stock, were primary concerns of both Conservative and Labour governments throughout the 1950s and 1960s. Achieving high production rates was a necessary political goal and it was soon discovered that electoral success was balanced by success in housing policy. During the 1950s and 1960s, it was not unusual for 300,000 completions to be made each year, and this level of housing output can be contrasted with the recent past, where output has been in the region of 150,000 to 200,000 dwellings per annum. There has been much press coverage of the fact that in 2001 house-building completions fell to their lowest level since 1924. New housing production output has thus fallen significantly over time. Indeed, the most ambitious housing development programme was envisaged in the Labour Government's 1965 White Paper 'The Housing Programme 1965–1970'. With a commitment to 500,000 new dwellings per year, the government achieved nearly 80 per cent of this target in 1967.

The pressures on housing supply during the immediate post-Second World War period were great. As in the period following the First World War there was an expectation that not only would there be a sufficient number of homes but that the quality of the housing stock would be simultaneously improved. To assist the second of these objectives, there were slum clearance programmes, which aimed to provide a higher standard of housing, and these resulted in the temporary displacement of a large number of households. There was a rolling programme of demolition and new-build during the 1960s, and during the middle of the decade, the annual number of demolitions of poor quality and older housing was around 70,000. This annual volume has fallen significantly since then, although demolition of the very worst housing stock continues (see Plate 3.1).

Pressures on government and the house-building industry to meet such high development targets brought with them some radical solutions. Although the high-volume house-building programmes of the 1950s and 1960s were delivered to a large extent by private sector speculative development, it has been the subsidised local authority-building programme which has attracted most of the interest in housing development today. The main reason for this is the form of the housing, which was, to an important extent, high-rise construction.

There have been many texts written about the origins of the high-rise building boom, and about its subsequent problems, but there have been few books praising

Plate 3.1 Demolition of sub-standard council housing, Derby: R. N. E. Blake.

this form of housing. It is beyond the scope of this text to evaluate this particular housing development 'experiment', except to state that high-rise housing development appears to be making a re-appearance again, particularly in Greater London. For a full understanding of the issues three texts are, we feel, fully representative. Dunleavy's (1981) *The Politics of Mass Housing in Britain 1945–1975* deals with the political factors underlying the high-rise building boom; Coleman's (1985) *Utopia on Trial* evaluates the high-rise building solution from social, economic and design perspectives; and Power's (1993) *Hovels to High Rise* considers state housing development from an historical and European comparative perspective.

By the late 1970s general housing shortages were overcome as a result of consistently focusing housing policy on production and output. Data in the annually produced *Housing and Construction Statistics* (DoE, 1980) showed that the number of dwellings in the housing stock exceeded the number of households and thus it could be said that the policy had finally been achieved. Housing 'need' in its broadest sense had been met. A commonly quoted benchmark for this achievement is the government's Green Paper of 1977 which stated: 'we are better housed as a nation than ever before; and our standards of housing seem to compare well with those of similar and more prosperous countries' (Shore, 1977).

Since the beginning of the 1980s, the role of housing development within the political economy has altered significantly. Housing development is no longer first and foremost directed towards overcoming large housing shortages and is no longer purely an instrument to deal with housing need. The annual number of housing completions is more closely related to the annual increase in the number of households than was the case in the 1970s (Golland, 1998). This is explained in no small part by the fact that the number of dwelling demolitions has declined and hence additional new development need only keep pace with increases in the number of households.

The new housing need into the twenty-first century

It would be incorrect to assume that the political and economic debate about housing need has gone away. Indeed, the question of housing production and housing targets has resurfaced with some degree of controversy, not least because there is little consensus about the annual quantity of new housing development needed. The arguments are founded on a number of key policy reports. The House of Commons Environment Committee Inquiry into Housing Need (February 1996) concluded, for example, that around 200,000 dwellings would need to be built each year in England up to 2016; moreover, that between 1991 and 2016 there would need to be an extra 4.4 million homes added to the housing stock. This figure is broadly in line with the conclusions of a study by Holmans (1995) which suggested that about 240,000 new dwellings per annum would be needed over the same period. Other estimations are higher. Friends of the Earth (Rudlin, 1998) have calculated that the total need over the same period is likely to be nearer to 5 million. More recently, the DETR household projections (DETR, 1999a) suggest an additional need for 3.8 million households up until 2021.

Estimates of the overall need for additional homes vary mainly because the forecasting process is complex (see also Chapter 2). If housing need is considered at the national level, where no distinctions are made between the housing requirements for individual tenures, it will be evident that demographic trends are a key determinant. The main reason for building additional housing is the additional number of households which cannot be housed within the existing stock. Changes in the number of households in any given year will be broadly related to changes in the population. However, the population trend will not necessarily be reflected in the trend in household structure. The precise number of additional dwellings needed will be a function of the demographic cycle of births, marriages and deaths affecting the timing of household formation, as well as the level of household dissolution from separations and divorces. A very important emerging form of household demand and need is the single-person household. These are expected to constitute a very significant proportion of future housing demand.

Housing need and future housing requirements in specific housing tenures

In practice, when estimating the overall need for housing it is necessary to take account of preference and choice for individual tenures. In the study conducted by

Holmans (1995), the annual 'demand' for owner-occupied housing is estimated to be around 160,000 dwellings. The requirement for social housing is fixed as a 'residual' of total need. What this means is that the requirement for social housing is total need less the demand for owner-occupied housing. This approach is fine in as far as it is possible to accurately gauge the housing requirements for any particular tenure. Much depends on the performance of the economy and the availability of public subsidy to promote an affordable housing policy. Whilst the economy may be expected to grow, the rate of house price inflation, and with it the demand for home ownership, may not be so buoyant. Radley (1996), for example, has concluded that the scope for expanding home ownership is very limited.

Similarly, modest projections of housing need in the social sector exist. A research project carried out by Cambridge University (DETR, 1997) suggested a need of only 20,000 dwellings per annum, in contrast with Holmans' projection of a need of around 80,000 dwellings. The House Builders Federation (1997) have suggested that if social housing completions remain at the historic levels of the past few years, then the supply of private housing will have to increase significantly to keep pace with demand. This may be the case, although much also depends on levels of demand in the existing social housing stock; in particular, on the ability of policy makers and local housing managers to maintain this demand within specific 'problem' housing estates through renewal and community regeneration schemes.

It is above all important to recognise that housing need is not only driven by population trends but also by the affordability of housing. If housing is unaffordable in any particular sector, then this is likely to mean that households will not form in that sector, or that they will form in another sector. If the system of housing supply is not flexible enough to deal with this, then fewer households will be formed overall, leading to an inaccurate estimation of housing need.

Housing demand and housing choice

How does housing development provide choice?

The housing development process attempts to provide choice and to respond to housing demand. In particular, housing development attempts to meet:

*   the demand for choice in housing tenure;
*   the demand for choice in dwelling type and form;
*   the demand for choice in the method by which new homes are developed.

Of these three 'demands', the first two ('tenure' and 'type and form') perhaps create the most interest. There is also, however, an emerging recognition that housing development should provide an element of choice in the way that housing is acquired through the development process. This trend is recognised in modes of housing development such as 'self-build' (see also Chapter 13), where households can have their own specified input in the design and/or costing aspect of the dwelling. This method of developing housing is increasingly important although it remains undistinguished as a separate development option within the official housing statistics.

Housing development and tenure choice

New housing is developed in several forms of tenure. It can be developed for example, for the owner-occupied sector, for the social-rented sector and for the private-rented sector. The argument for providing tenure choice in housing development can be put on several grounds. Housing development might, for example, be able to redress imbalances between the effective demand, or ability of households to pay for housing, and an existing housing stock incapable of serving the prevailing demand. In other words, new development might currently suit demand better than the existing housing stock is able to do. It is argued that providing variety in housing tenure in new developments is necessary because access to home ownership is not universally available, and hence other forms of new housing ought to be built. This general approach to housing development has been consistently adopted by governments since the Second World War. However, it has only more recently (since 1990) become usual to include an element of social or affordable housing within (predominantly owner occupied) new estates (see also Chapter 5).

In practice, more pragmatic arguments tend to be forwarded for providing choice in housing tenure. One of the strongest of these relates to labour mobility and the capacity of new housing tenures to deal with the effects of economic change. It is clear that households will move between and within regions according to job or other opportunities and, as such, new housing should be made available accordingly.

In many respects, the housing development process in Great Britain has failed the most mobile households, catering mainly for owner-occupied or social-rented households in new (often suburban) estates. The private-rented sector has not been expanded via new housing development to such an extent, although some additional supply has been achieved via business expansion schemes, and more recently via 'buy-to-let' mortgages. As a result, this sector, which has the potential to cater for young, mobile and transient households, has not been fully realised. The nature of the market for this group is considered to be

> young, high income households, likely to enter owner occupation eventually; but with insufficient equity or wishing to retain mobility or freedom from the responsibilities of ownership . . . students . . . low income households, particularly single people, likely to enter social renting eventually and needing housing in the short term [and] . . . others made homeless (e.g. as a result of relationship breakdown) and needing housing in the short term.
>
> (Bailey *et al.*, 1998: 3)

Historically, it has been the existing housing stock which has absorbed this demand, and not new dwellings. Although new development has been realised by social housing providers with a specified target need group, mainstream and volume housing developers have avoided building housing for these groups.

The politics of tenure choice

While it is expected that housing development will provide tenure choice (for the reasons already given), it is unlikely that annual building output will be evenly distributed across tenures. The United Kingdom has a predominantly owner-occupied housing stock, at around 68 per cent (Radley, 1996). This position is explained not only by tenure transfers into owner-occupation from the older private-rented sector and local authority 'right-to-buy' policies, but also to a significant extent, by new housing development being consistently geared towards home ownership.

Two contrasting yet interesting explanations for the widespread development of home-ownership housing can be identified. One explanation is related to the demand or consumer side, the other to the supply or producer side. From the demand side, the explanation for the development of new owner-occupied housing is linked with the demand for owner-occupation more generally; owner-occupation is seen to have a number of inherent benefits which fulfil a household's ideal way of living. These benefits relate to both the consumption of housing – that is to say, the (largely intangible) benefits that are to be gained from living in an owner-occupied dwelling – but also to the financial, or investment benefits of home ownership, which can be converted into personal wealth. Saunders (1990) has explored both these forms of benefit in his text *A Nation of Home Owners*. In this book, home ownership is seen to appeal to the innate desires of households. Saunders suggests that two concepts are important: 'territoriality' and 'possessiveness'. He states:

> If we are by nature possessive creatures, then the desire to own our own homes would be readily understandable given the central role which housing plays in our everyday lives. [Likewise] if it can be shown that human beings are by nature territorial animals, then it could be argued that the desire to own a house is an expression of our nature.
>
> (ibid.: 70)

It is useful to note that when governments over the past 30 or 40 years have made a case for promoting home ownership, they have done so by appealing to similar instincts. As far back as 1951, Conservative Prime Minister Macmillan suggested that home ownership 'satisfies some deep desire' (Merrett, 1982: 119), while the Labour Government Green Paper (DoE, 1977) stated that to own a home reflected a 'basic and natural desire'. More recently, the Conservative Government stated:

> Clearly, the majority of people wish to own their own homes. This wish should in the government's view be supported. Home ownership gives people independence; it gives them a sense of greater personal responsibility.
>
> (DoE, 1987)

There has thus been a consistent policy in support of home ownership on ideo-logical grounds. However, support has been given for home ownership in more concrete terms. One method is direct, through the tax system, by way of mortgage interest tax relief. Historically, this has been a very important factor in helping to expand home ownership, although it now no longer provides any additional assist-ance. Perhaps more important has been house-price inflation, which has made alter-native housing tenures relatively less attractive in financial terms. Saunders shows (1990: 120–202) just how advantageous investment in owner-occupied housing has been. For the period investigated, it is suggested (ibid.: 203) that for the 'median home owner' a benefit of around £2,000 per annum was accruing. Another study (Golland, 1992) calculates that over the short run (two–three years), annual returns on capital invested in housing were sometimes in excess of 40 per cent for house-holds during the 1980s. The current housing market performance (1998 to 2002) is also providing very significant gains and returns to home-owners.

The policy promotion of home ownership has not escaped criticism. Political support for home ownership has been criticised where it is seen to be achieved at a cost to the stability of the economy. To some extent, the success of the 1980s housing policy, which expanded home ownership considerably, was at the expense of a stable economy; the collapse of the housing market during the early 1990s, along with the impacts of negative equity, provides evidence of that instability.

One of the continuing challenges for policy analysts has been to weigh up the effects of housing policy for the wider economy. Ball (1983: 11), writing prior to the housing market boom of the late 1980s, doubted whether the housing policy thrust could prevail over broader economic goals:

> To suggest that individual owner-occupiers control, via the ballot box, the limits of housing policy is to take notions of economic interest and representative parliamentary democracy to simplistic extremes. It would imply that governments never undertake actions against the short-term economic interests of the majority of people, Macro-economic policy, tax increases of any sort, price rises by any nationalised industry, and a whole host of state actions would similarly be 'politically impossible'.
>
> (ibid.)

It can however be argued that owner-occupiers, via the ballot box during the 1980s, did control the 'limits of housing policy'. Although governments did not make many short-term decisions against the economic interests of the majority, the result was the 'politically impossible', albeit very unsatisfactory, outcome of the early 1990s. Home ownership was heavily promoted during the 1980s, whilst at the same time, the economy over-heated. In a later study, *Housing Markets and Economic Convergence in the European Union* (Ball and Grilli, 1997: 47) it was concluded that the housing market destabilised the economy of the UK in the 'spectacular property boom' of the 1980s. More recently, government has provided itself with an alibi for housing market booms and slumps; in giving independence to the Bank of England to make decisions on inflation and interest rate responses it has effec-tively charged the bank with the task of controlling the housing market.

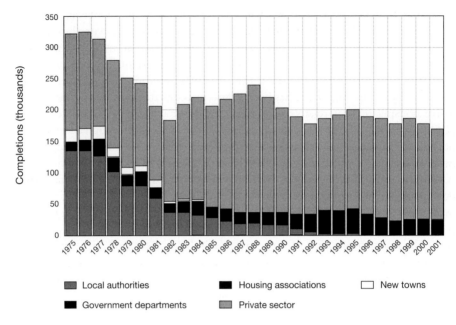

Figure 3.1 Housing production in the UK, 1975 to 2001.
Sources: DoE; DETR: Housing and Construction Statistics

The demand for owner-occupied housing has been met from the supply side by the private house-building industry. A detailed discussion of the industry and its operation is given in Chapter 4. Additional commentary is necessary here, however, as this discussion relates to the 'politics of tenure choice', and the private-sector housing building industry is, without question, the major player in the development of the UK's current housing stock. Figure 3.1 shows just how important the private sector has been over the past 25 years.

The importance of the private sector is immediately evident when looking at the number of completions in absolute terms, but also in terms of the private sector's proportionate contribution to overall output. The 'contribution' of the sector is almost entirely in the form of owner-occupied dwellings, although since the 1980s there has been some restructuring whereby the larger or 'volume' house-builders have carried out contracts for housing associations. This restructuring process is described more fully in Gillen (1995) and in Chapter 4 of this book.

Of crucial importance to understanding the issue of tenure choice in housing development is the association over time between private-sector output and Conservative governments, and between social housing output and Labour governments. Tenure choice in the UK has in the past been highly influenced by the political colour of government. It is not unfair to state, especially when comparing the UK with other European countries, that the UK's system of housing development has been highly politicised (see also Coles, 1993).

If the proportion of total output (Figure 3.1) is taken as a measure and related to the political party in power, then the following trends can be noted: a high proportion of private-sector output between the years 1970–73 (the Heath Conservative Government), and again between the years 1980–96 (the Thatcher and Major Conservative governments); and a much higher proportion of local authority housing output in the years 1974–79 (the Wilson and Callaghan Labour governments). From the aspect of tenure choice in new housing development, these political associations give cause for concern, not least because where the proportion of total output reaches over 70 per cent (as was the case for private housing during the 1980s), the alternative forms of housing tenure are severely reduced.

The reasons for the lack of choice in housing tenure are partially explained by the demand side; that is the support, both direct and indirect, which government has given to households wishing to own their own homes. The supply side, however, is also important. Ball (1983) makes a strong case for looking at the operation of house-builders in trying to explain the predominance of private-sector housing provision. There are many types of house-building firm which can be classified in terms of 'petty capitalist house-builders', 'small family house-builders', 'non-speculative house-building capital' and 'large capital house-building firms' (ibid.: 53, 64) (see also Chapter 4 for a fuller account). Different types of firm operate in specific ways, some looking for a high throughput of housing, some only building during buoyant housing market conditions, others speculating in the land market, some in the long term and some in the short term.

The private house-building industry is important for the political economy of housing provision in several ways. First, it operates on the basis of risk-taking and enterprise; it thus makes decisions about the timing of land acquisition and of house sales. In turn it influences the land market, land prices and, ultimately, the price of housing. Second, it provides the key source of new housing development in the country, and thus it regulates the level of housing affordability to a significant extent. Finally, it is the key lobby for the release of additional development land, and thus its actions affect the environment and landscape of Britain. In all these ways, the house-building industry is a potential source of political conflict and controversy.

Providing choice in housing type and form

Providing choice in housing development is not only about providing choice of housing tenure. Housing development aims to provide a variety of dwelling types and forms in order to meet prevailing demand. By 'dwelling type' is meant whether a dwelling is detached, semi-detached, terraced or a flat. Where 'flats' are analysed, there can be a further distinction into 'low-rise', 'medium-rise' and 'high-rise'. There are no hard and fast rules about these distinctions although 'medium-rise' within the local authority building programme of the 1950s and 1960s, for example, was considered to be between five and nine storeys (Dunleavy, 1981: 41). 'Flats' are developed as 'purpose-built', but are also developed through conversions of larger, usually former owner-occupied houses. Very often, these converted flats serve the private-rental market in Victorian inner-city areas where demand for owner-occupied dwellings has fallen over time.

By 'dwelling form' is meant the type of building which comprises the dwelling. This would be, for example, the 'low' and 'high' rise cases as introduced. 'Dwelling form' can be further considered in terms of the materials used to build the main structure of the dwelling, or the external envelope or cladding. 'Dwelling form' can also relate to the way in which housing is constructed, whether in the 'traditional' or in the 'pre-cast concrete' way. Most housing in the UK is constructed from traditional (brick and timber) materials where off-site work does not play a large part. Victorian terraced housing is perhaps the most well recognised 'traditional' building. By contrast, some of the housing constructed in the post-1945 period, particularly during the 1960s, utilised 'industrial' building methods involving significant off-site work to construct the main building elements. There is, therefore, a variety of type and form within the housing stock, although traditional building methods are mainly used.

Figure 3.2 shows the UK's housing stock, classified by housing tenure and house type. The graph shows that most owner-occupied dwellings are detached, semi-detached or terraced, whereas in the rented sector (including housing associations and smaller private landlords) the predominant dwelling types are terraced and (converted ('con') and purpose-built) flats. To make this analysis more meaningful, a comment is also needed about how the data in Figure 3.2 links with the age distribution of the stock. The following information is based on the 1997 Condition Survey (Joseph Rowntree Foundation, 1997): about 60 per cent of the

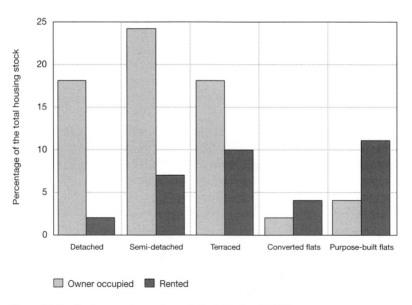

Figure 3.2 Dwelling types and house tenure in the UK in the mid-1990s.
Source: Department of the Environment National Housing Survey (1997)

detached housing stock was constructed post-1945, about 50 per cent of terraced pre-1945, about 50 per cent of semi-detached post-1945, while about 70 per cent of all flats have been constructed post-1945. The greater volume of detached housing has been constructed in the later (post-1945) period. These statistics show how varied the housing stock is; but, how has housing development produced these outcomes and what are the influencing factors?

There are a number of pressures on housing development to deliver dwellings of the right type and form. The pressures will vary according to the tenure with which we are immediately concerned, although they can be generally summarised in terms of demographic pressures, political pressures, economic pressures and consumer pressures.

The demographic pressures are very much those of housing need: changes in the population rate, the demographic cycle of births, marriages and deaths and other forms of household formation and dissolution. In order to ensure that local housing need is properly catered for, public and private sector agencies have to translate global housing forecasts to housing types, forms and designs within a specific development area. To do this, a number of different policy statements are considered, including local development plans, housing investment programmes and housing need surveys. This process is complex, and interested parties such as housing developers will try to influence the type and form of housing in order to maximise returns from their investment in land. New developments must provide an appropriate range of house types if long-run inefficiencies in housing allocation are to be avoided. Once new developments are sold to private households, there are very few mechanisms, other than market price and income effects, which can compensate for 'over' or 'under' occupation of a dwelling. In the rented sector, landlords can regulate occupancy levels and household densities more directly through rents.

It was argued in the preceding section that households' choice of tenure has been significantly affected by government policies. It is also clear, however, that governments have a significant influence over the type and form of housing development. In the 1980s, and arguably for much of the 1990s, the hallmark of new development was detached and semi-detached family housing in the post-modern style, that is to say, with traditional construction methods and layout. To a large extent, new social housing development has been built on similar lines. This is perhaps an inevitable consequence of local authorities taking a back seat in housing provision, and letting the 'market' solve development problems. House-building firms have taken advantage of the harmonisation of housing products across private and social sectors (see also Chapter 13 on Innovation in house-building). Research by Clarke and Wall (1996) showed that most of the larger firms have specialist companies within them for developing social housing.

Variety in housing form, if not in housing type as well, is being reduced across all sectors. A more cautious approach, based on tried and tested solutions to housing development, is now employed. This approach is a reaction to two trends: problem housing estates in the social sector and consumer taste in the housing market, although both trends can be viewed in turn as a reaction against more experimental forms of housing development. The results of recent government-funded research (Popular Housing Forum, 1998) suggests a very low demand for experimental housing. It was shown, for example, that builders and estate agents avoid the term 'architect-designed house' if this is possible, because of the connotations with irregular rooflines, unusual brickwork, steel structures, etc. (Kelly, 1998b). Experimental forms of housing are currently connected more with urban regeneration schemes; one such is Britannia Village at London Docklands, although more generally urban village schemes are concerned to restore traditional forms of housing within conventional street patterns.

Generally, social housing development has attempted bolder architectural solutions, the most experimental form of housing being evidenced in the local authority high-rise building programmes of the 1950 and 1960s. There were heavy resource commitments to these programmes. In 1965, for example, local authorities approved around 50 per cent of their total building programme in the form of houses, but also approved around 25 per cent in the form of low-rise flats and 25 per cent in the form of high-rise flats (Dunleavy, 1981: 40). High-rise was promoted by local authorities and the building industry as a way of solving a housing problem and government subsidies were a key policy instrument.

With hindsight, this form of housing development is now generally viewed as a failed experiment (see also Chapter 5), constraining the household's living experience, and creating a difficult living environment for households with children. Residents in high-flat estates are 'highly critical of their appearance. They dislike concrete surfaces, greyness, dark colours, car parks (especially multi-storey car parks), and an institutional or monumental appearance' (Dunleavy, 1981: 95).

The regional distribution of high-rise dwellings is also an important issue. Dunleavy (ibid.: 44) shows how unequally high-rise development was shared between regions. Between 1966 and 1971 the local authorities within the Greater London region granted 47 per cent of their total approvals in the form of high-rise dwellings, as against 12 per cent, for example, in the East Midlands. These regional inconsistencies might be explained by a number of factors including differences in land values, party politics or the role of individual planners and architects at the regional level. Whatever the precise explanation, however, the regional differences have significant repercussions for differences in housing choice.

The third key issue affecting housing form and house type is economic in nature. An important factor is housing densities. These will vary according to development plan policy and according to local housing development strategies. At the extremes very great differences are possible, where for example a large detached house is compared with densities in a tower block or row of terraced houses. Economics and politics confront each other over the question of density and land-use intensification. New policies, such as that engendered within PPG3 (DETR, 2000b), require local authorities and housing developers to increase densities to make development more sustainable.

Providing choice in the housing development process

Housing is developed for households in the UK mainly in two ways: through a speculative process of development or through a contract build method; the former, 'speculative' process is carried out by private house-building firms who buy land, construct dwellings and then market them for sale to owner-occupiers. Barlow and Duncan (1994) show that speculative housing development accounts for around 70 per cent of all production. The latter, contract build, is largely an approach used to develop social or affordable housing which is usually commissioned by housing associations. Unlike other European countries, in Britain there are few other ways in which housing is developed.

The approach arguably limits choice in housing provision. Historically, in both the speculative and the housing association development processes, the household is provided with a ready-made product over which it has very little direct input in terms of design or cost. It can be argued that the UK is in many ways out of step with other countries in these respects. In Germany, for example, and to some extent France, private households have a greater input to the planning, design and costing aspects of house-building (see also Chapter 12). In Germany, around 50 per cent of all housing output is procured by the 'self-build' housing development process (B.M.Bau, 1998). This approach can provide significant advantages in terms of cost saving, improved management of the building process and control over the layout and appearance of the dwelling (B.M.Bau, 1983).

Self-build is, however, becoming more widely adopted as a way of providing housing in the UK. Broome and Richardson (1991) suggested that there were around 13,000 annual self-build completions in Britain. The majority of these were in the owner-occupied sector. The motivation for developing these dwellings is for households to acquire a 'dream home' and to provide greater choice in the way in which housing is developed. In many cases a self-build project is supervised and managed by an architect, yet in other cases the term 'self-build' describes a method of development where the household has a significant physical input to the construction process.

Self-build is now also increasingly being adopted within the social sector. This is a focus of a recent research paper (Edge and Duncan, 1998) which concentrates on 'community self-build in the public and quasi-public sectors' (ibid.: 3). The paper examines the relative advantages of social self-build schemes against traditional methods and concludes that with self-build schemes in the social sector 'there is much that can be done to optimise the control of the design, organisation and construction of such schemes to ensure that they become a valid, pragmatic means of solving housing problems' (ibid.: 11).

Housing development and the demands on space

Where should housing be built?

The question of where housing should be developed is one which has never been far from the centre of the post-war housing policy debate. A key issue is that in the absence of some form of regulation, housing might be built in locations that are wholly unsuitable. 'Unsuitable' development might be housing built in environmentally sensitive areas, housing built in areas that are too inaccessible or housing built in already densely populated areas. Suggesting, however, that specific housing locations are in some way 'unsuitable' begs the question, 'from whose standpoint?' Are they 'unsuitable' from the planners' point of view, the developers' perspective, the housing consumers' standpoint or the business and environmental interest groups' perspectives? Once these questions are posed, it becomes easier to understand why the location of housing development is a political issue. We can summarise the nature of the problem in terms of:

- Land exploitation pressures: these are essentially economic demands, with land being viewed as a residual, or lowest common denominator, component of development. Where land is viewed in this way, housing is naturally in competition with other development uses.
- Land conservation pressures: these are essentially environmental demands to conserve land which assume that land has an intrinsic value in its non-developed state.
- Consumer pressures on land: these are essentially political demands, which come in several forms; for example, from individuals, from land conservation groups and from environmental interest groups.

These pressures each demand their own particular solutions and we will now describe each one in more detail.

Housing development and the competition for land

Where there are development pressures of any kind, there are pressures to exploit land. The use for which land is ultimately developed, however, will depend on a complex mix of factors including land-use planning, the housing market and markets for other types of property. Generally, theories of land-price determination assume that development giving the highest end-use value will create the highest land value. Thus, the land on which prime shops and offices in the city of London stand will be expected to be more valuable than farming land in the provinces. The profits or rents yielded by these different uses determine that land values will therefore differ. In housing, as well as commercial property development, developers calculate land values by deducting costs from the ultimate development value through what is commonly know as the 'residual valuation process' (see also Chapter 7).

The key point is that because of the economic factors determining land values, housing development will be in competition with other forms of development. In Von Thünen's (1826) model of land use, it was suggested that land around a central town would be used less intensively as distance increased from the city centre. A theory of 'concentric rings' was envisaged, with urban, and then agricultural uses further out, being the norm. Housing within many of the larger cities of the UK is indeed located either within a first (inner city) 'ring', or a second suburban 'ring'. In part, this is an historical explanation of housing location based on retail and business uses successfully pushing housing to the outer regions of city (see also Chapter 2, 'Spatial models of housing development').

A complementary approach is evident in the work of Alonso (1964). This work is perhaps best known for the relationship assumed between rental values and the distance of land from city centres. Alonso described a 'rent-bid' curve, whereby it was expected that central and urban locations would realise the highest rents. Today, because of the way in which the investment and property market operates, we can translate 'rental' values into capital values and, further, through the residual valuation process noted above, also estimate broad differences in land values at specific locations.

This cannot easily be done by employing the Alonso model alone. As Balchin and Kieve (1977: 19) point out, the model is general and

> it is necessary to consider separately the locational determinants of commercial and industrial use. To do so it is essential to identify the components of the cost and revenue gradients of business firms to indicate the basis of their profitability.
>
> (ibid.)

The inter-dependency of location and land value was recognised as long ago as the nineteenth century in Ricardo's (1817: 1971) analysis of the political economy. Land values were seen to have two components: 'transfer earnings' and 'economic rent'. The former is derived from the particular activity to which the land use is put (housing, commercial property, farming, etc.), while the latter reflects its scarcity value which derives from its unique location.

Scarcity value, a component of land value, is important for housing development because some locations are more 'scarce' than others. Although housing development cannot usually compete for land in city centres, this does not mean that it will not realise a higher value than commercial property in the suburbs or in the countryside. Retail or other commercial land uses may not always be the optimum use in terms of creating the highest land value. Housing may be able to compete, for example, where commercial sites are too inaccessible to be profitable.

The pressures to exploit land for specific end-uses are further affected by government policy measures. The division of land values into 'transfer earnings' and 'economic rent' is a conceptual one, but a separation which has created an ongoing case for specific forms of land taxation, particularly with the objective of taxing the scarcity element of land values. This approach has proved difficult to implement, and development land taxes are currently out of favour. However, it is important to say that with an increasingly buoyant housing and commercial property market, the question of re-introducing such a tax has not gone away.

Housing development and land conservation pressures

If there is no planning system to regulate land use, or if the planning system is weak or ineffective, then it will be difficult to conserve land in the face of development pressures. Many of the UK's major cities were largely established in their current development patterns before planning began to regulate land uses to any significant extent. One effect was for housing development to be extended into the countryside, alongside main transportation routes. A significant expansion of the housing stock took place during the inter-war years along these transport corridors. This was only really checked by the Restriction of Ribbon Development Act in the inter-war years, and more substantially, by the post-1945 planning legislation. A very significant proportion of the housing stock in the UK today has therefore been developed under conditions of only limited planning regulation; data from the English House Condition Survey suggests that in 1993, 46 per cent of the housing stock was developed before 1945 (calculated from Leather and Morrison, 1997: 21), the date at which the current land-use planning framework was about to be introduced.

The pressures to conserve land from housing and other forms of development can be argued to have been considerably stronger since 1945. There have been a number of planning and land-policy interventions from the immediate post-war period to the present day. A detailed exposition of these is not warranted here, although key issues are picked up and expanded later in the book.

Perhaps the most widely known planning constraint to be introduced in the immediate post-war period was the green belt, an urban containment mechanism (see Chapter 6). Ideally green belts were supposed to be 'several miles wide and in general it was assumed that developments of a non-agricultural or non-recreational nature would be refused' (Lawless and Brown, 1986: 120). Their functions were set out in government Circular 42/55: to check the growth of large built-up areas; to prevent neighbouring towns from merging and to preserve the special character of historically or architecturally important towns. The land-use principles underpinning green belts have been upheld, even through the 1980s, a period when planning came under attack from government; even Circular 15/84 indicated the 'permanent nature of sensibly drawn green belts' (ibid.: 121).

The effects of green belts on housing development are in the first instance quite obvious in that they restrict building on the outskirts of cities. They are 'no-go' areas for development. In theory, land values decline from city centres to the edge of the green belt in accordance with the theories of rent (see previous section). At the heart of the green belt, or at the mid-point between two urban locations, land values fall, in theory to a level around agricultural value. In practice, green belts provide a challenge to planners presented with housing targets to meet, and to developers looking to purchase land for building. In practice, land at the fringes of green belts becomes the subject of speculation and uncertainty; many developers do not see such land as being long-term agricultural. This has put tremendous pressures on green belts, particularly in areas of the South East and around London. Land values rise in areas subject to speculative activity, and if planning consent is given, unsatisfactory housing development outcomes can occur.

One conclusion about green belts is that although they provide the benefit of protecting rural areas from development, there are negative side effects, or externalities, arising from increased land values at the fringe areas. Harvey (1987: 250) suggests other 'defects' of green belts. These are in terms of 'adding to the problem of congestion by forcing developments in existing urban areas', 'failing to ensure that land is put to recreational use or even made accessible to the public' and failing to prevent development from bridging the green belt, thereby creating problems for effective village planning (ibid.).

The Labour Government of 1945, in addition to introducing the key legislation for green belts, also enacted legislation to enable the development of new towns, and since these are in practice an opportunity for development, rather than a land conservation measure, they should be mentioned here. The relevant legislation and history of the new towns are adequately covered elsewhere (see for example, Lawless and Brown, 1986; Harvey, 1987). The key point to note is that new towns were seen as satellites to the major cities. They had a number of functions, including the housing of overspill population from these cities. New towns were seen as being integral communities with complementary (employment and housing) uses. Via the twin policies of green belts and new towns, the existing major urban areas could function better, and rural areas be preserved.

Pressures to conserve land during the 1980s can be argued to be less significant. Planning was said to be 'developer led' (Healey, 1991), with Circulars 14/85 and 22/80 (DoE 1980c) providing the context for a 'presumption to development' in planning applications and planning appeals. This approach lasted only as long as the decade and the 1991 Planning and Compensation Act gave increased emphasis to development plans. The Conservative Government in power between 1992 and 1997 and now the Labour one elected thereafter have given re-emphasis to urban containment. For housing development this policy has major implications since regional targets are set for the proportion of total development to be built on 'brownfield' or 're-used' sites. The target at the national level is for 60 per cent of all housing completions to be built on 'brownfield' sites. This target will be difficult to achieve, especially at the regional level, due to the essentially 'rural' nature of some regions (see also Chapter 10).

The substantive challenge of the so-called urban housing capacity policies of the late 1990s relate to exploiting existing urban areas. This means seeking out a variety of opportunities, either working to an 'area based policy' approach, or to a 'portfolio solution' (De Montfort University and Entec, 1998). Many of these solutions do not involve new development, but renovation or re-development of commercial and industrial buildings. The urban housing capacity policy is reviewed in detail as a policy theme in Part Three of this book.

Consumer pressures and the location of housing development

Although government is responsible for conservation and environmental policy which restricts housing development, decisions are ultimately taken in the name of the public or the consumer's interest. As part of the democratic process of government, there is a raft of procedures through which people can make their views on development known. Within the planning process, the development control systems allows for objections to planning applications, for appeals to planning decisions, for call-in for planning applications by the Secretary of State, and ultimately, for recourse of an applicant to the High Court.

The political process of planning generally allows for interested parties to make a contribution to the debate on development. These 'interested parties' can be individual property owners or larger organisations. They can have an impact on any number of scenarios involving housing development; from objections to a neighbouring owner's house extension, to public inquiries on large housing estates on greenfield sites, to making a contribution to the consultation process on compulsory purchase schemes in inner-city areas. It is, however, the function of the planning system to make judgements about the value of these public and consumer interests. In many cases, objections are based on a fear that property values will be affected, the so-called 'NIMBY' ('Not In My Back Yard') factor; in more extreme cases objections arise because of neighbourly animosities. Often in these cases, the adverse impacts of new development are exaggerated. The local authority and parish council should always make a fully informed decision based on the planning issues.

Proposed housing development schemes are also subject to the scrutiny of organisations with specific environmental and/or sustainable development objectives. There are several of these interests; the CPRE (Council for the Protection of Rural England) and the Friends of the Earth are perhaps two of the most well known. They expended considerable effort during the 1980s, when the planning system was relaxed, in challenging both the need and the location of new development (Bramley *et al.*, 1995: 85). In the South East, fears raised about the effects of lax planning at the green belt fringes heightened awareness and policies 'enjoyed a degree of success' (ibid.). Friends of the Earth have emphasised not only the need for land conservation per se, but have built their policies on sustainable principles. This approach questions, for example, the effectiveness of government's latest polices on urban capacity:

> The debate about urban land capacity is . . . not a numbers game about the amount of land available and how much housing can be shoehorned onto it. It is rather about how we can influence urban trends that date back more than a century.
>
> (Rudlin, 1998)

This is an approach which recognises both the demand and supply side problems affecting housing development. Attempts to encourage housing back into the cities is a policy goal of other interest groups such as the Urban Villages Forum. The Forum encourages the planning of housing alongside other development, in mixed-use projects (Urban Villages Forum, 1995). This agency and other relevant bodies with planning and housing interests are considered later in the book.

Housing development and the demand for equity

The development of housing creates opportunities to achieve greater equity or fairness in housing provision. It can, and indeed it has been argued, that the housing development process *should* lead to fair or socially just outcomes and in particular, that the process of providing housing for the market via the planning system should yield some form of benefit to the wider community.

In the development process, the granting of planning permission is the key mechanism by which local authorities are trying to achieve these wider benefits. By granting planning permission, land is transferred from one (often agricultural) use to development of a different (built) form frequently with a significant increase in value. The increase in value can be regarded in two ways: on the one hand, it is seen as 'fair reward' to the land-owner; alternatively, the increase in value can be regarded as being an 'unfair reward' for the land-owner. It is deemed 'unfair' because the increase in value is not created by the land-owner, but by the general level of demand for the particular form of development.

These two ways of looking at the increase in land values due to the grant of planning permission (otherwise known as 'betterment') creates a problem which is common to other areas of taxation and public policy, namely, who creates the added value: the private individual, the organisation and the market, or the community or the state? There is no simple answer. Marxist approaches assume there is no value without state intervention, whereas free market explanations of development events do not associate added value with state interventions in any way. The policy solutions to the challenge of trying to achieve equity via the housing development process have been varied. The post-war government of 1945 adopted a very interventionist stance, with redistribution of land values as a central theme. This resulted in no small part from the Uthwatt report. Potentially more interventionist still, was the Community Land Act of 1975, which gave greater powers to the state beyond the existing development control system. The Act was, however, very complex to implement (Prest, 1981), and was abolished with the coming to power of the first Thatcher Conservative Government in 1979.

More relevant in terms of development activity have been attempts to tax development gains, and it is noteworthy that development land tax survived until the second Thatcher Government, only being abolished in 1985. Since the late 1980s, the main mechanism for realising equity and redistribution of gain within the process have been planning mechanisms. These have been variously called planning 'agreements' or planning 'obligations'. The key feature of these mechanisms is that local authorities can require developers to provide physical or social infrastructure as a condition of the grant of planning permission (see also Chapters 5 and 6). Developers may provide roads and services; they may also be obliged to develop social infrastructure in the form of affordable housing, schools, libraries, recreation or other community facilities. Although the development industry argued fervently for many years that social housing provision was not a real 'planning issue' (and this was upheld by the courts), local planning authorities are now normally considered to be within their rights (*intra vires*) where they require developers to provide a specified percentage of social housing within new developments.

The role of land-use planning and the development process in helping to achieve more equitable outcomes is dealt with in more detail in Chapters 5 and 6, which examine social housing development and the role of government.

Policy mechanisms: the changing role for state and market

A model for the political economy of housing development

The previous sections have outlined the needs, demands and pressures involved in the housing development process. The discussion focused on the underlying causes of development pressures but mentioned the nature of policy mechanisms mainly in passing. To understand more about the political and economic context, we should also look at the changing policy situation and the solutions adopted.

These 'solutions' include two approaches: the state, or government, as the solution to the (development) problem; and the market as a way of meeting housing development objectives. The relationship between solutions and development pressures is modelled in Figure 3.3. The figure provides a very simple approach to understanding the political economy of housing development, with the pressures for quantity, choice, space or location and equity being absorbed through the 'state' and 'market' mechanisms. At the centre is the housing object, which will vary in terms of tenure, type and location depending on the particular solution adopted. Under the headings of 'state' and 'market', it will be evident that there are a number of policy facets. These have been introduced by the previous discussion, where housing subsidies, land and planning policies are key aspects.

It is important to emphasise, however, that the relationship between 'state' and 'market' is in practice integral and it is unrealistic to suppose that governments can take policy decisions without there being some effect on housing and land markets. As Barlow and Duncan (1994) have suggested, it is not correct to assume that markets are 'good' and government are 'bad'. What matters (ibid.) is the 'state-market mix'. This point is significant, particularly where an evaluation of policies are required.

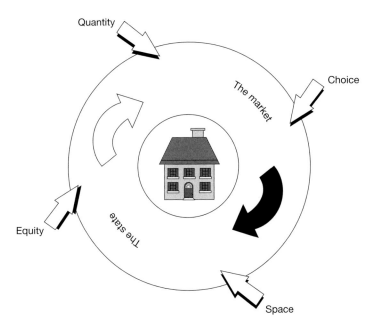

Figure 3.3 Conceptual model of the political economy of housing development.
Source: A. J. Golland

The changing significance of housing development problems

It is generally not disputed that the nature of housing problems change with time. This applies to housing development as in other aspects of housing and public policy. The emphasis given to particular policy solutions also changes with time. The way this has happened is set out in the European context by Boelhouwer and van der Heijden (1992: 273), who highlight in particular how housing policy problems have changed from 'quantitative shortages', through an emphasis on 'qualitative' and 'renewal' problems, through to a re-emphasis on specific quantitative shortages. It may be helpful to consider how the UK has fared in the light of changing pressures on housing development.

Quantitative pressures: 1945 and state intervention

The importance of government intervention in the immediate post-war period to combat severe housing shortages has been emphasised (ibid.). The UK's housing problems were part and parcel of these general European shortages and, as was outlined earlier in this chapter, government intervention was initially used as the key mechanism. However, it is important to state that before shortages could be fully overcome, a much broader range of agencies and mechanisms were used. To galvanise housing production across the range of private and social sector providers, a number of mechanisms were considered. These are tidily summarised in Ambrose and Barlow (1987: 111) and include 'direct state subsidies' (for social housing), 'indirect support for production and consumption' and 'profitability' in the private sector.

In practice, during the period 1945–70, although government did support housing production to a great extent through local authority building programmes, the private-sector house-building industry also played a significant role in meeting overall housing targets. 'Profitability' is the key to understanding the production function of the private sector, where house prices, land prices and building costs play an important determining role. The state of the housing market at times of severe housing shortages, as at other times, is thus very significant to housing policy makers who wish to know whether overall housing targets can be met.

Renewal and redistribution: development pressures in the 1970s

When it was generally believed that in the UK crude housing shortages were overcome, the housing policy emphasis changed away from a 'production' policy and focused on a number of different directions. This change of emphasis occurred around the late 1960s, and can be benchmarked against the ending of mass high-rise and social house-building programmes. In place of mass building programmes came a policy emphasis on renewal and housing rehabilitation. The specific policies, in the form of General Improvement Areas (GIAs, introduced in 1969) and Housing Action Areas (HAAs, introduced in 1974) were in practice 'location subsidies' aimed at improving specific older areas of the housing stock. The beneficiaries of these schemes were, to a significant extent, owner-occupiers who obtained benefits either directly or indirectly through local authority grants. Housing renewal grants, however, became less significant after the 1970s, when a greater targeting of state subsidies was required during the housing policy cutbacks of the 1980s.

Another important aim of housing policy during the 1970s was redistribution. This was particularly evident in efforts to intervene and to regulate the land market. Some of the most severe interventions of the post-war period were attempted at this time, and are associated with the Community Land Act of 1975, which effectively vested all development rights in the state. This policy had a significant stifling effect on the volume of land being brought forward for new house-building, and in the absence of the renewal policies being pursued at the time, might have led to large shortages in housing supply.

The private-sector new-build programme in the 1980s

The UK's housing development problems have not been the same as in other European countries. In the UK, the policy emphasis switched during the 1980s towards a policy focused significantly on housing tenure (see Malpass, 1986), whereby local authority house-building was cut back in favour of private-sector house-building development. This was quite a radical departure in housing policy, which had previously been aimed more at meeting quantitative shortages and ensuring a range of market and non-market housing choice. New private housing development became a logical consequence of the aim to expand the owner-occupied housing stock. The housing market, through improved trading conditions, would ensure increased levels of private-sector housing output.

What government did in the 1980s was to pass responsibility for housing output almost entirely to private developers. In this way, it would not be seen to be 'directly' intervening in the production process. The state was to withdraw from housing production. In practice, however, government gave significant impetus to the new-build market through its management of the macro-economy and through its deregulation of other areas of housing policy, particularly in housing finance and in land and planning policy frameworks. The emphasis on more open market solutions to economic problems was closely linked with housing market solutions, and the expansion of the owner-occupied stock can, from this angle, be viewed as a policy success.

The main objections to the development policies of the 1980s are based on location and equity issues. There were, for example, no planned expansions, as are evidenced in new town developments. Rather, new housing development tended to be located in an *ad hoc* manner, either by expanding cities in greenfield sites, or by building on 'windfall' or 'infill' areas. Further, new-build owner-occupied housing needed buoyant housing conditions, which in turn created pressures on land prices; many of the new housing developments of the 1980s were densely built. In many cases, households might have achieved a higher housing quality of environment in the existing housing stock, or even in the rented sector. In addition, the housing market boom which assisted the objective of increasing owner-occupied housing did not to any great extent increase the volume of social housing as a 'spin-off'. Whilst this was not an explicit aim of policy, it might be expected that more social housing could have been delivered as a result of improved housing market conditions.

Sustainable housing development: regulation and the 1990s

The pressures affecting housing development are at times more easily identifiable than at others. During the immediate post-war period and during the 1980s, the pressures were easily identifiable in terms of meeting quantity and (owner-occupied) housing tenure objectives. The mechanisms to deliver these objectives were state intervention and the housing market respectively. However, it is not always possible to identify so clearly the source of pressures, or the nature of policy responses.

During the 1990s 'sustainability' has been a key concept driving a number of policies relating to the environment. What is meant by 'sustainability' is by no means generally agreed upon. In the absence of such agreement, 'sustainability' is suggested to be a normative concept which discounts in some way future consequences or effects of today's developments. In the context of housing development, two key sustainability issues have arisen during the 1990s. The first relates to the housing market, and in particular the capacity of the market to increase the level of home ownership without creating severe financial and economic problems for the macro-economy; the second relates to the impact of housing development on greenfield sites. Both these issues arise to a significant extent from policies pursued in the 1980s.

Much of the policy and research effort in the 1990s has been directed towards trying to answer these questions. The Henley Centre (Radley, 1996) and Cambridge University (DETR, 1997), for example, have produced reports on the demand for owner-occupation, and hence the need for social housing. The Labour Government elected in 1997 has, on the other hand, focused efforts on minimising the effect of new development on land use. This policy is to some extent a continuation of the planning policy changes invoked during the early 1990s (towards a more prescriptive development planning framework), but is also more focused on re-using previously developed, or 'brownfield' sites. These policies are discussed in more detail later in the book. At this juncture, we can state that current pressures affecting housing development are focused broadly on issues relating to housing tenure and to brownfield site locations, but that pressures to achieve significant housing targets are also to the fore of the policy debate. These issues are expanded in further commentaries.

Discussion points

1   Identify and define the four main political and economic demands on housing development. Discuss the challenges facing government in meeting these demands.
2   Distinguish between housing 'need' and housing 'demand' and suggest how government and the house-building industry have sought to provide choice in housing development.
3   Evaluate the role of state intervention and market forces in post-war housing development in the United Kingdom.
4   Analyse the factors that may lead to disputes about the level of new housing development required at any given time.
5   Discuss the case for housing development as an equitable vehicle of housing provision.
6   Analyse the role of spatial and environmental policies in steering housing development (see also Chapter 6).

Key reading

For a basic economic interpretation of housing development, Harvey's *Urban Land Economics* (2000) is recommended. The political dimensions are well covered in Ball, *Housing Policy and Economic Power* (1983) and Dunleavy, *The Politics of Mass Housing in Britain 1945–1975* (1981). Saunders, *A Nation of Home Owners* (1990) examines the social and psychological aspects of need housing.

Chapter 4
The private house-building industry and the housing market

Mike Gillen and Andrew Golland

Plate 4.1 Private housing development, Sherwood, Nottingham: R. N. E. Blake.

Introduction to the house-building industry

When commentators speak of 'house-building' today, what they are usually referring to is a process largely dominated by speculative housing provision and
controlled by private house-building companies. In fact, in the UK some 70 per
cent of the housing stock is owner-occupied and eight out of ten new homes are
provided by the private house-building industry. The achievement therefore of
development plan housing targets depends largely upon the operation of the
housing market and the behaviour of private house-building companies.

Public-sector housing development is limited as we shall see in Chapter 5.
Today, that element of housing based upon need criteria is largely provided by

housing associations. The construction of these housing units however is often carried out under contract by private house-building companies. Consequently, when referring to the process of 'house-building', we are alluding to two distinctive types: speculative house-building and contract house-building. In speculative development the house-builder is responsible for both the procurement and financing of the land, along with the construction process and the sale and marketing of the dwelling units. The private speculative house-builder develops properties for a general market, where the purchaser is generally unknown until after completion of the dwelling. Only during periods of high demand will private house-builders sell dwellings from a plan, ahead of their construction. As far as contract housing is concerned, the house-builder enters into a contract with either a local authority and/or a housing association (the 'partner') to build a specified number of dwelling units. Here, there is no responsibility on the part of the house-builder for the acquisition of the land, nor a duty to find buyers or occupants for the dwellings. In essence, the latter process should effectively bear less risk compared with the speculative house-building process.

Private house-building is highly significant in the context of the wider housing market since the large number of units it develops form the greater part of annual housing supply. The effect of changes in supply, combined with changes in house prices are important both in terms of formulating the direction of government policy and in influencing consumer confidence (Nicol, 1994). Yet despite this, the private house-building industry has been comparatively under-researched. As a consequence, few either fully understand or appreciate the workings of this industry, its structure and its principal agencies.

This chapter provides an introduction to the private house-building industry in the UK. Drawing largely on research carried out since the 1970s, the discussion explores theoretical approaches to studies of house-building, the structure, output and product of the industry and in turn how these are affected by the prevailing structural aspects of the political economy.

Studying the industry: the theoretical perspectives

It is generally argued that there is a paucity of research examining the operation of the private house-building industry. This is primarily a result of the house-building process being peripheral to the interests of the established academic disciplines (Barrett and Healey, 1985). Most studies are descriptive, falling into two broad categories: the 'comparative statics' approach and the 'behavioural' model (after Monk, 1991). The former deals with the intention of house-builders to maximise profits and assumes, in essence, that all decisions can be readily explained in terms of achieving profit margins. However, this fails to address house-builders' actions during slumps, when profits are suppressed and the overwhelming necessity is to maintain a turnover margin in order to retain skilled labour and continue trading. The behavioural model on the other hand concentrates on the negotiating strengths of the agencies in the house-building process.

Despite the development of critically themed questions, few studies have placed their findings in a wider theoretical context. This is a problem, since it is necessary to understand how theoretical debates have moved in the field of housing studies if an adequate understanding of the private house-building industry is to be achieved.

The post-war tradition in orthodox British housing studies centred on the concept of consumption and failed to acknowledge the significance of the house-building industry. The main emphasis of research was on housing tenure, with state housing policy acting as an empirical focus (Ball, 1983). The two working concepts in this traditional approach were 'households' and the state, with the state possessing the power and means to deny or satisfy households' housing needs through housing policies. In these studies, housing provision is viewed as an issue of distribution, with households' consumption and costs accepted as given and compared with other households in order to evaluate the efficiency and equity of state housing policies.

Overwhelming focus on housing demand gave way to some extent, during the late 1970s and early 1980s, to the development of original research in the fields of Marxist economics (Ball, 1983), public policy implementation (Rydin, 1985 and Short *et al.*, 1986) and urban geography (Bather, 1976 and Barlow, 1990). The theories of housing articulated in this new body of research rejected the compartmentalisation of housing issues based on the state, consumers and tenure, which had been advocated in consumption orientated studies, for a behavioural approach which examined the relationship of social agents to housing provision and especially that of the house-building companies.

During the 1980s and 1990s, studies attempted to address what takes place 'behind the scenes' in the house-building process. This conceptualisation was necessary to examine effectively the contribution of house-building companies, the significance of specific events and the complexity of relationships that lead to housing development. Such a basis for research required the elaboration of several models, ranging from the simplistic 'equilibrium' and 'event-sequence' models to the more complex 'structure and agency' and 'institutional' models, adopted in the studies by Ball (1983), Healey and Barrett (1990), Lambert (1990), Healey (1991, 1992), Adams (1994) and Gillen (1995).

In these studies the term 'structure' is used to describe the socio-economic, political and cultural framework within which actors define and pursue their strategies, interests and actions (Adams, 1994). 'Structure', therefore, consists of the organisation of economic and political activity and of the institutional values that frame decision-making. 'Agency' describes the entire manner with which actors in the housing development process develop and pursue their strategies. Such an approach allows a detailed analysis of house-building companies, demonstrating that their strategies and actions are not automatically determined by the dominant social, economic and political forces (Healey and Barrett, 1990; Gillen, 1995). This approach contends further that the structural framework for development is neither fixed nor free from challenge, but that continuous 'interaction' occurs between structure and agency. This has allowed researchers an insight into the lobbying activities of the house-building companies and especially their pressure groups, such as the House Builders Federation and the Volume House-builders Study Group. Although described later in this chapter it is important to point out that the influence of these groups can be significant, with the lobbying of senior politicians and the ability to change policy and affect the broader economy.

The house-building industry and the housing market

The significance of the private house-building industry in the wider economy

In comparison with the total housing stock, the number of new houses built each year is relatively small. The total UK stock of housing in 1990, for example, was estimated at 22,800,000 dwellings. Private new housing starts for the same year totalled approximately 154,000, some 0.7 per cent of the existing stock (DoE, 1992b). However, it is not the quantity of new housing development that is of greatest importance in the housing market but the economic effects of this new supply (Ball, 1983). The significance of new private house-building to the economy is arguably greatest in the way the housing shortages feed through into volatile housing markets. This can make house prices too expensive in the short run, leading to instability in the wider economy. Political support and the promotion for home ownership have further exacerbated economic instability at times. The arguments and interconnections of the housing market, private housing supply and the economy are well explored in Maclennan *et al.* (1994), Meen (1994) and Clapham (1996). For the purpose of this chapter, a discussion of the political and economic policy framework for home ownership is sufficient for an understanding of the relationship between the house-building industry and the wider economy.

During the last three decades, the housing market has experienced two distinct cycles of boom and slump and associated smaller recoveries and declines. Such cyclical behaviour has resulted in significant structural changes to both housing production and also the composition of the house-building industry. Progressively, the effects of these cycles have been more pronounced, with the consequence that the last complete cycle, from 1984 to the mid-1990s, was the longest and most chronic in the post-war period.

As a consequence of the severity of the last housing market cycle, a growing body of research attempted to measure the nature of the interrelationship between the economy and the housing market (see for example, Adair *et al.*, 1991; Maclennan, 1994; Meen, 1994). This body of research has found that cycles of private housing output have occurred in tandem with wider economic cycles throughout since the early 1970s. Adair *et al.* (1993) claim that the promotion of free market principles by the Conservative Government of the 1980s impacted upon all sectors of the economy, but most acutely upon housing. The expansionist economic policies of the Conservative administration, aimed at reducing state intervention and increasing competition, were central to the economic consumer boom and rapid rise in housing wealth, measured by increasing housing production and house prices. Furthermore, allegiance to the policies of home ownership both reinforced the dominance of private-sector housing provision and raised this form of housing production to a central position within the national economy.

Fuelled by financial deregulation, wider credit availability and rising disposable incomes, the rapid house and land-price increases of the mid-to-late 1980s created inflationary pressures in the economy. By 1987 house price inflation was up to *five* times greater than the annual general rate or RPI. The industry's response was to increase production and maximise the potential profit gains from a demand driven market. However, the spectre of spiralling inflation was halted by the Conservative Government's decision to raise interest rates in August 1988 to 15 per cent. This action reversed the expansionist policies of the 1980s and made home ownership appear acutely onerous to many households. The ensuing widespread implications of these actions were evidenced throughout all sectors of the economy, but most especially in the house-building industry, where housing starts, completions and sales fell off dramatically. It is broadly agreed that the performance of the UK housing market not only intensified the 1980s economic consumer boom, but also accentuated the recessionary downswing and hindered any potential for recovery (Maclennan, 1994).

Trends in housing output

As was shown in Chapter 3, housing output has altered markedly under successive governments in the post-war period. The contribution of private housing output has grown considerably as a percentage of total output over this period, buoyed primarily by Conservative Government policies to support home ownership and reduce public housing programmes. Against this background, statistics show that total housing output, and especially private housing output, has declined considerably. Since the late 1960s, total housing output has more than halved and private housing output has declined from approximately 220,000 annual completions to around 150,000 completions today (DETR, 2001).

Figure 4.1 highlights the trend in UK private housing starts and completions. The fluctuating cycles are clearly evident in the peaks and troughs of the two series. Whilst both starts and completions shed light on the prevailing level of market demand, housing starts, in particular, are seen as a leading indicator of activity in the general economy.

The decision to start a housing development is a sensitive issue for a house-building company, and the timing of such development is critical. Failure to accurately interpret the housing market when commencing a housing development can lead to severe economic penalties. Once a house is under construction, it has to be completed. Therefore, much of the sensitivity to economic factors is

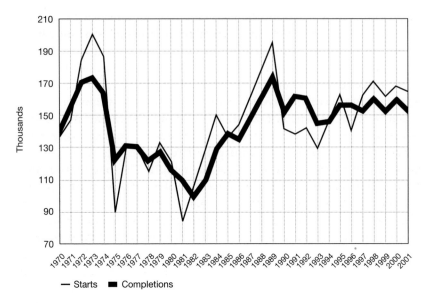

Figure 4.1 Private house-building starts and completions in the UK, 1970–2001.
Sources: National House-Building Council, *New House-building Statistics* (annual); DETR Housing and Construction Statistics

centred on this decision to start. Completions, on the other hand, can be tailored to come on stream when economic circumstances improve. For example, many house-builders will leave a foundation slab unfinished until a prospective buyer emerges, a practice which commonly occurred throughout the late 1980s and early 1990s recession and which fed through to less dramatic market trends for housing completion statistics. This is evidenced in Figure 4.1, where there is a relatively constant level of completions throughout the 1990s. The end result is long lag times between starts and completions, which effectively confuses the claim that both are a good indication of the levels of market activity.

Private house-building and the market for private housing

The emphasis of post-war house-building has switched broadly between policies aimed to maximise production and policies aimed to improve housing quality, where the nature of the policy has been dependent largely on the government in power. This political influence has been 'manoeuvred' by the broader economic, environmental and social climate. From a focus on meeting shortages in housing provision up to the 1960s, the emphasis changed to address renewal and rehabilitation in the late 1960s and 1970s (see also Chapter 3). Throughout the 1980s the political focus was firmly on the extension of home ownership and meeting rising consumer demand. During the 1990s the concern has once more been with meeting housing shortages, a policy driven by significant changes in the nature of household formation. At the same time, there has been growing environmental concern for development impact. The role of the private house-building industry throughout each of these distinct phases is marked by changes in company strategy and subsequently product.

Throughout the period from the 1940s to the 1970s housing shortages were largely addressed via government intervention, the principal form being local authority building programmes. The private sector played a small role in the provision of this form of housing, but a number of the largest companies constructed housing under contract arrangement for local governments.

Support for home ownership and a greater role for the market throughout the 1980s saw the rapid growth of the owner-occupied sector from 56 per cent of all households at the start of the decade to almost 70 per cent by the close of the decade. The rise in owner-occupation mirrored the growth and dominance of the private speculative house-builders, whose numbers and market share rose steadily throughout the decade. NHBC (National House-building Council) data show an increase of 45 per cent in the number of registered house-building companies for the decade of the 1980s. It is difficult to quantify exactly how many of the registered house-builders can be classified as private speculative companies, but the assumption is that most entered the industry to secure an element of the significant profits being made in the rapidly expanding private housing market (Wellings, 1993, 1994).

The restructuring of the major credit institutions and financial deregulation of the mid-1980s assisted the owner-occupied sector by opening up the avenues to mortgage finance. The resulting increase in income-to-mortgage ratios and affordability ratios accelerated the demand for owner-occupied housing, most especially in the private new-build sector, clearly shown by a rapid rise in output in Figure 4.1.

The 1990s were marked by a distinct oscillation between a qualitative and quantitative housing emphasis. At the start of the decade changes to spatial planning legislation, in essence a Conservative Government response to political pressures which had accumulated after a decade of market-led ideology, focused on escalating public concerns for the environmental impact of housing development. Following the 1991 Planning and Compensation Act, the increasing reliance on development plans to deliver housing supply in the most appropriate and sustainable locations altered house-building company strategies, actions and output. However, the release of the 1992 and 1996 based household projections saw a change towards a quantitative emphasis. Yet this time the quantitative issues were tempered by a growing research debate concerning the most appropriate forms of housing to meet projected demand and most acutely its location. Recent controversy concerning the suitability and capacity of previously developed urban sites to meet a projected 3.8 million increase in households up to 2021 has led to a series of contentious debates, articulated in URBED (1998), House-Builders Federation (1998a) and Healey (1998).

Structure and operation of the industry

The structure of the house-building industry

Beyond its economic importance, housing production has wider implications on land availability and the environment. It is not surprising then that housing production is a politically emotive subject area. Indeed, each political party has had a significant housing based agenda in their manifestos carried to the general elections of the last two decades. Consequently, it is rather surprising that relatively little research has been undertaken on the supply and production of housing in the UK, compared to the great deal of work on housing policy, housing markets and housing consumption. Further, the examination of the principal agents of production, the house-building companies, has been an area of relatively modest inquiry. This section provides an outline of the contemporary structure of house-building in the UK.

The UK house-building industry is, by comparison with other advanced manufacturing industries in the UK, comparatively antiquated. We explore the issue of innovation and house-building later in the book (Chapter 13). It is important to emphasise at this stage, however, the ease with which individuals and companies can enter the industry, compared to other advanced industries such as, for example, car manufacturing. Following the purchase of a plot of land with a residential planning permission, any individual may purchase the necessary building materials and either build the property themselves (subject to building and planning control legislation) or hire the essential construction skills from a wide range of sub-contractors and skilled craftsmen. This would be an extremely difficult process to manage in the motor industry. The ease by which firms can enter the house-building market is reflected in a large number of small companies with a low output. This phenomenon is also explained against the background of a rising housing market. Between 1985 and 1989, a 23 per cent rise in the number of registered NHBC housebuilders was almost exclusively due to entry by small house-builders with output below 30 houses per annum.

Many of the studies that include commentaries on the UK private housebuilding industry have been concerned with the investigation of size and organisational structure of individual firms. With the exception of Bather (1976), Ball (1983) and Fleming (1984), few studies have explored the wider house-building industry and the degree of oligopolistic power within the industry – a crucial indicator of the extent and significance of competition between house-building companies.

In order to understand better the broad structure of the UK private housebuilding industry it is necessary to adopt a system for classifying house-building companies. To do this, studies have tended to examine components of company size, in terms of annual output, profits, turnover and number of employees. Size provides a good measure of the various facets of a house-building company, as the aforementioned elements strongly influence modes of operation and internal organisation. Unfortunately, however, there is little standardisation in the way in which 'size' is defined and classified and thus it is sometimes difficult to be able to track changes in the structure of the industry.

House-building output, in terms of housing starts and completions, tends to be a favoured method of definition, due to their simplicity and ease of understanding. Annual housing completions tend to be preferred by city analysts when reporting on the industry, as these are considered to be a true representation of the finished product of the industry. However, economists sometimes favour housing starts, as these provide a better proxy for the intentions and thus the economic state of the industry.

Writing in 1983, Ball, in a seminal study of the house-building industry, provided a classification of house-building companies benchmarked against norms and availability of finance, stressing that this approximately relates to annual levels of housing output. While his study was carried out quite a long time ago and the data reflect a period before 1980, the classification remains robust and a close approximation to the contemporary industry. We would suggest one key amendment, however: more recently the large capital house-building firms have gained a greater share of the market. We set out below Ball's classification:

Petty capitalist house-builders These firms have an annual output of up to 20 houses. During difficult trading climates these house-builders may retract and build no houses for that period and are often vulnerable to bankruptcy, but responsible for up to 25 per cent of the industry's output.

Small family capital house-builders This group is dominated by local firms with long-standing ties in particular regions, building between 25 and 120 houses annually and again vulnerable to the consequences of bankruptcy.

Non-speculative house-building firms This group is characterised by firms whose main activities are not within the speculative house-building industry, who build between 120–300 houses each year.

Large capital house-building firms The large firms build in excess of 300 houses each year. These firms dominate the house-building industry's output. Usually this type of house-building company is a publicly quoted company, operating a two–five year land bank, where money can often be raised through periodical calls to the share market via rights issues. Despite their size and seemingly invulnerable position, firms have frequently been exposed to bankruptcy due to over-gearing at times of high interest rates and poor house sales (Monk, 1991).

Long term development capital This category consists of only the major house-building companies, building in excess of 500 houses per annum. This group of companies is typified by the ownership of several subsidiary companies operating on a regional basis and constructing a minimum annual output of between 150 and 250 houses. Take-overs and strategic acquisitions are common amongst this group of firms in order to sustain output levels (by acquiring the most critical of assets: land) and to retain membership of this select group of house-builders.

Ball focuses (1983) attention upon the last group of house-building companies in his study, whom he refers to as the 'volume house-building companies'. Implying that greater size enables the risks of market fluctuation to be minimised through the possession of a diversified market presence, Ball claims that these companies are relatively immune to the cyclical activity of the industry. Up to 1993 this was certainly the case in the recent recession, with no company failures amongst the volume house-building companies (Wellings, 1993). However, since 1993, the longevity of the recessionary period, along with the difficulties in obtaining both land and planning permission in the more prescriptive land-use planning regime of the 1990s, led to several volume house-building companies withdrawing from the industry.

The broad structure of the house-building industry today is remarkably unchanged from that of Ball's study period, displaying a pyramid composition, with a large number of small house-builders with a low output at its base, completed by a small number of companies with a large output at the top (see Table 4.1). The fluctuations over time, however, between the size of the industry and the differing size categories, provide an interesting illustration of company activity. Notable amongst the many illuminating features in the table is the significant role of companies building in excess of 500 housing units per year. A corresponding growth in market share of this group of house-builders is noted further on in this section. While there is relative stability in terms of the number of medium-sized house-builders over the period, this hides some prodigious developments by some of these companies, who have expanded into the volume categories.

The performance of the smallest house-builders, constructing fewer than 30 units per annum, is marked by a decline in registrations and related sharp decline in market share over the last 30 years. Despite the boom of the mid-to-late 1980s, the fortunes of the smallest house-builders have been modest by comparison with their larger competitors. An increasingly prescriptive planning regime, geared towards the development of previously developed brownfield sites, has increased the requirement for specialised housing development expertise. Furthermore, the increasing need to develop social and affordable housing (see also Chapter 5) in response to the mixed community agenda has put pressure on house-builders and smaller operators in particular. Despite these challenges, there are still opportunities for the smaller house-builders. The average size of land release in development plans continues to decline, assisted by small-scale infill developments prescribed in the principal planning and housing document PPG 3. Many of the larger house-builders are not geared up to deal with these smaller sites. The set-up costs necessary for the larger house-builders often mean that they require a minimum size of site and number of housing units. Estimates suggest that for the larger house-builders this is 2 acres and/or 20 housing units. Anything less than this is considered to be uneconomic.

Table 4.1 demonstrates that throughout the recent 20-year period 1980–2000, on average only 39 per cent of the total number of NHBC registered house-building companies were actively constructing housing units. At the height of the

Table 4.1 Number of builders by size of category, 1980–2000

Year	0 units	1–10 units	11–30 units	31–100 units	101–500 units	501–2000 units	2000+ units	Total
1980	12,327	6,945	688	228	101	13	3	20,305
1981	12,487	7,049	743	261	110	19	5	20,674
1982	12,971	6,907	33	320	122	23	7	20,383
1983	12,949	7,527	1,009	396	151	36	8	22,076
1984	13,385	8,190	1,013	395	152	34	11	23,180
1985	13,369	8,884	1,051	436	163	27	11	23,941
1986	12,859	9,526	1,190	501	184	31	13	24,304
1987	13,948	9,361	1,251	502	179	38	13	25,292
1988	14,418	10,112	1,500	603	215	46	13	26,907
1989	17,378	9,771	1,194	496	165	29	8	29,041
1990	19,998	7,671	901	353	130	24	8	29,085
1991	19,622	7,069	827	311	111	28	9	27,977
1992	16,150	6,257	696	329	128	22	10	23,592
1993	13,704	6,231	834	367	140	29	14	21,319
1994	12,498	6,370	827	379	140	33	17	20,264
1995	12,224	5,643	745	317	131	28	11	19,099
1996	12,032	5,098	658	283	105	25	12	18,213
1997	11,320	5,199	667	291	107	21	15	17,620
1998	11,179	4,712	618	271	92	23	14	16,909
1999	10,595	4,633	598	245	101	21	14	16,207
2000	10,157	4,313	559	205	101	22	15	15,372

Sources: adapted from National House-Building Council *New House-Building Statistics* (annual publication)

last housing market cycle in 1986, only 47 per cent of registered house-building companies were active. The majority of those companies that were not constructing were small house-builders (National House-Building Council, 2000). These small companies tend to enter and exit the industry on a regular basis depending on the oscillations of the wider market cycle, entering during boom periods and exiting during slumps. Small size affords some advantages to this ability to regulate entry and exit on such a frequent basis. However, the fortunes of one single site may dictate success or failure for these small house-builders. As such, many commentators regard house-building as a volume business, based on small margins and high turnover. This competitive situation was at its peak in 1986 (Gibb *et al.*, 1995).

As is the case in industries in which easy access and exits are possible, pace-setters tend to lead the way. In house-building the pace-setters are the volume house-building companies, defined as those building in excess of 2,000 housing units per annum. These large companies are often the industry's innovators and by consequence leaders in terms of production, land acquisition and marketing. While the house-building market is not controlled by the volume house-building companies, it is to a large degree conditioned by them. Such an oligopolistic tendency has been noted since the early 1970s in the research of Ball (1983) and Wellings (1993, 1994).

Ownership of house-building companies

The house-building industry is financed and organised by a broad array of investment interests, ranging from food conglomerates to international shipping and transport operators (Fleming, 1984). However, around one-third of the parent companies with house-building subsidiaries can, nevertheless, be classed as major construction conglomerates (Gillen, 1995). Ball (1988) noted the common association of construction conglomerates that invest in house-building, stressing that the latter's activities are easily subsumed into the construction conglomerates' divisional structures. Gillen (1995) noted that in a small number of cases, the transfer of labour and components between divisional subsidiaries, regions and even countries, helped support the house-building operations of construction conglomerates at the beginning of the 1990s. However, ease of integration in these ways has to be balanced against the operational difficulties associated with land speculation, the pursuit of planning permissions and product marketing. The subsequent difficulties endured by construction companies that diversified into the related, but very different, field of house-building in the 1980s and 1990s, is well documented in the work of Hillebrandt et al. (1995) and discussed below.

Each investor's reasons for investment in house-building differ. However, the common objective is a long-term profitable return:

> In order to be attractive, investment in house-building has to be large and long-term, use established expertise, and be based on money capital looking for a long-term profitable outlet. In this way, the risks of being caught in a downturn or over a misjudged land purchase are minimised.
>
> (Ball, 1983: 68)

The research of Gibb et al. (1995) and Gillen (1995) demonstrates a strong connection between public limited companies (PLCs) and house-building companies. In the research of Gillen (1995), of 31 leading house-building companies surveyed, 94 per cent were plcs, the remaining 6 per cent operating as private companies, two of whom were preparing to be floated on the stock market. Ball (1983) argues that this high rate of association owes much to historical circumstance, some of which may be external to the house-building industry, such as the potential alternative rates of return. However, the cyclical activity of the industry, particularly the boom period and resultant house price inflation and development profit growth, appear to offer the most influential investment conditions.

The legal status of a public limited company affords a number of advantages for house-building subsidiaries, in particular the ability to raise funds on the stock market via share placings and rights issues. Finance raised by these means assists in many ways: providing funds for land purchase (often via competitor acquisitions to gain access to land banks); redressing debt and gearing ratios; and strengthening share prices. To illustrate this point, the city analysts Crédit Lyonnais reported that during the period between February 1993 and June 1994 almost £2 billion was raised by house-building companies in share issues. Of this sum, the report claims that one-third was directed to new investments and the remainder to redressing weakened balance sheets following the recession of the late 1980s and imprudent land purchases at the start of the 1990s.

Operational coverage of house-building companies

For the private housing market the use of a site-specific resource such as land requires that the house-building company moves its location once this resource is acquired. Within the UK, the high degree of variability in the volume of land released at the local level tends to lead to the conclusion that the house-building industry must adopt a fairly flexible, even 'nomadic' approach to its operation. House-building companies are thus transient within (and even between) regions where they search for residential development land. This is particularly true of the smallest house-builders.

The desire of a house-building company to expand or concentrate in a specific location will encourage movement. Further reasons for a diversified operational structure include organic expansion and the incidence of lower input costs associated with sub-contracted labour and materials in distinct regions of the country. The medium and volume house-builders tend to operate across spatially linked regions.

Research undertaken by Fleming in the 1980s suggested that the operating areas of house-building companies were related to the time it would take to travel from a company's office to a potential development site (Fleming, 1984). In the research, Fleming found that a travelling time of one-and-a-half hours provided the limits to a company's operating area. For the largest companies, operating with several subsidiary companies, this often coincided with the spatial boundaries of another subsidiary company within the group. In this way, the UK could be split into regions governed by the major communication networks.

The size of the operational area is closely linked to the size of the house-building company. There is an expectation that the largest house-building companies will naturally operate over larger areas and, therefore, have a greater potential choice of sites than their smaller counterparts. A wide geographical coverage across the country also limits the vulnerability to regionalised supply constraints and weakened demand, allowing the transfer of resources across regions.

The largest companies achieve economies of scale, supplying extensive geographical areas. However, throughout the 1990s, many medium-sized house-builders concentrated their activities in only one region. While many of the larger house-building companies are multi-regional specialists, very few can claim to be national operators (Ball, 1983; Bramley *et al.*, 1995). The 1990s market slump and a resultant necessity to cut overheads may have contributed to this concentration into the regions. Additionally, the sale of divisions specialising in peripheral work, such as repair and maintenance, and the retreat from peripheral regions, was widespread in the industry following rationalisation programmes in the immediate period after the housing market collapse.

There is a degree of inter-regional dependence on the part of the house-building companies (Lambert, 1990). This relates to the structural framework provided by the land-use planning system. For example, region 'A' may experience expansion in terms of development activity, buoyed up by a leniency in the planning regime and quantity of allocated housing land, whereas an inflexibility in the planning regime in an adjacent region 'B', may prove to be the catalyst for growth in development activity in region 'A'. Short, Fleming and Witt (1986) identified such circumstances occurring to a certain degree in the counties of the South East during the 1980s.

Regional market trends in private house-building

The performance of individual regions in terms of housing output gives some indication of the way in which demand and supply vary. Generally speaking, the regions with the greatest demand for housing tend to be those that attract the greatest number of employment opportunities, and hence have the greatest level of house-building activity. The South East and the South West are good examples, where high demand is directly reflected in high house prices (see Figure 4.2). However, demand for new homes can only be met if the planning system is responsive enough to deal with the particular needs of the regional housing market in question. The constraints imposed by the planning system, in terms of non-development designations, and protected peripheral urban sites may reduce the ability of the industry to meet demand in some circumstances.

Figure 4.3 highlights the performance, in terms of housing starts, of eight English regions. The graph deals with the 1980s market boom and subsequent slump in activity throughout the 1990s. The period is marked by some important changes. Most evident is the decline in housing starts over the period for both the South West and South East. The falling fortunes of the south of England in terms of house-building activity are widely acknowledged by researchers and industry commentators. Whilst these regions experienced the greatest demand for housing during the late 1980s, due to demographic and economic advantages, the demand was considered to be of a pent-up nature, being fuelled by a favourable lending regime and significant price escalations. Adair *et al.* (1991) note that throughout the late 1980s the south of England experienced a severely distorted and imbalanced housing and land market. The subsequent collapse and rapid decline

Figure 4.2
Regional house prices in the UK,
mid-2002.
Source: Nationwide Building Society

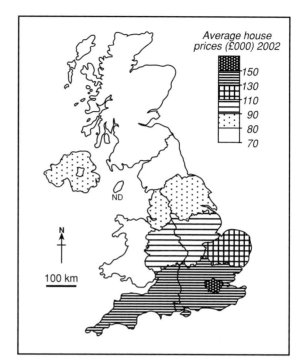

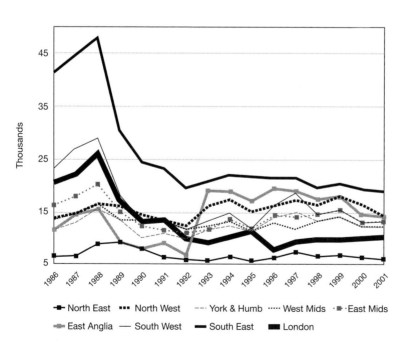

Figure 4.3 Regional house-building starts for England, 1986–2001.
Sources: National House-Building Council, *New House-Building Statistics*; DETR Housing and Construction
Statistics

in housing output represents a recorrection of these factors. The impact of this recorrection for house-builders is noted in Gillen (1998), with many companies finding themselves with high-priced land and fixed housing assets in a low-demand and low-price environment. The subsequent fall-out in terms of rationalisation and withdrawal from the southern regions was significant. In addition, many small house-builders experienced bankruptcy and some liquidation.

The 'northern' regions (comprising the North, the North West and Yorkshire and Humberside) display house-building activity ranging from relative stability to steady growth across the period. The pressures of housing demand in these regions were less significant than those on land in the south of England. While increases in starts occurred during the mid-to-late 1980s across the northern regions, the scale of demand and subsequent land and house price escalations were less marked than in the southern regions. This relative stability assisted house-builders across the northern regions, but in the post-market collapse period, many medium and large house-builders moved their operations into these more stable housing markets intensifying competition and, in certain locations, raising land prices to period highs.

The years 1988 and 1989 were the high point for starts in most regions for the period (see Figure 4.3). The North West and East Anglia were exceptions. In East Anglia, a steady rise is displayed for the period, but notably there is a high point during the mid-1990s around the time when nearby regions saw falls in activity.

Changes and recent trends in the house-building industry

Structural change

Over the last 25 years two significant structural changes have occurred in the house-building industry, each pronounced and having a major impact upon the composition of the industry. The first relates to the way in which housing development capacity is sourced. Here two 'sub' trends are important: the increasing propensity of traditional house-builders to develop housing for a range of client sectors which now includes home-owners as well as housing associations (up until the 1970s these forms of house-building were considered two segregated markets with distinctly different production agencies); and, the declining role of contracting firms (those involved in a wide range of activities including infrastructure projects) in house-building.

The second key structural change has involved the increasing concentration of housing output from a small number of now very large house-building companies. This industry transformation has involved a significant number of take-overs and acquisitions and a certain amount of rationalisation amongst the firms. In this section we will examine these two structural changes and identify the consequences for the house-building industry.

Sources of development capacity

As recently as the mid-1970s, house-builders working for the public and private housing sectors (characterised respectively by residential contracting and speculative house-building) operated separately. Today, at the start of the new millennium, many private house-building firms are directly involved in working for both sectors. The two separate routes for developing housing have, since the late 1970s, become less clear-cut. One key trend is the role of traditional house-building firms in the development of affordable housing, built under contract for housing associations.

Construction companies who traditionally avoided speculative house-building have gradually seen investment in the housing development process as a potential source of further profits, particularly where they can 'roll over' revenue made from contracting and engineering. Such companies tend to be publicly quoted companies, which see diversification as a means of attracting share capital and maintaining dividend payments, as well as keeping their large organisational structures and labour forces together. Economic changes which favour a particular construction market can be capitalised upon by these companies, through switching certain fixed-cost elements to the thriving sector, such as management, administration, plant and machinery and labour. Wellings (1994) maintains that contracting companies are often well placed to deliver speculative developments such as private housing. Indeed Smyth (1984) argues that speculative house-building was identified by contractors as a new market for the generation of profits as early as the 1950s when contracting workloads declined. The positive cash-flows generated from contracting were ultimately moved into house-building.

During the early 1970s, few house-builders switched their production between the public and private house-building sectors, and joint production on site was rare (Ball, 1983). Even the largest contractors, e.g. (Wimpey, Tarmac and Laing) established autonomous subsidiaries to undertake private house-building. Explanations for this situation are made in terms of the nature of capital investment, which differed for private and social house-building, and the demands of management, which also differed. Increased investment in the housing sector by traditional contractors occurred steadily however throughout the 1970s and 1980s as these operators saw an opportunity to exploit changes in the economic markets against a backdrop of declining central government support for public housing production.

Above all, the profit margins to be had, by timing output to coincide with house-price inflation, were an attraction significant enough to tempt contractors to diversify. Diversification was seen as a kind of 'natural home' for the cash reserves generated from contracting activities. Many contractors, however, entered the speculative housing development process when the housing market was at its strongest. This had the consequence that land and material purchases were very costly in relation the longer market cycle, leaving many with high costs in a low-demand and high-interest rate situation.

With hindsight, traditional contractors expanded their house-building activities too far. Even at the time, such operators could have been considered foolish for entering the market while land and build-costs were rising so fast. What is particularly astonishing is that the purchase of land continued unabated and without questions being asked of house-building divisions by their parent contracting companies. These issues are looked at more deeply in the work of Gillen (1998) and Hillebrandt *et al.* (1995), who focus on the irrational behaviour of firms during the boom period of the late-1980s. In particular, rights issues and provisions to offset overvalued land were common at the time. The fallout from these activities was a steady withdrawal by the contractors from house-building throughout the 1990s and the early 2000s. Hooper (2001) notes that in 1980 the list of top ten house-builders by output contained only four pure speculative house-building companies and six contractors, yet by 1996 the top ten consisted entirely of specialist house-builders.

As traditional contractors have gradually retreated from house-building, traditional house-builders have continued to develop speculative housing. However, they have increasingly done this at the same time as developing affordable housing on the same site. In part, this event has been forced on them via government planning policy, although very volatile historic housing market conditions may have caused some re-thinking to be done in the general approach to revenue maximising. It is now arguably much more clearly recognised that to survive the industry needs to focus much more on stock clearance and to equate today's selling prices with today's costs. During recession, house-builders are now more inclined to suppress profit margins in favour of maintaining a steady cash flow, thereby covering overheads and retaining some small profit allowance. Throughout the 1990s the combination of a slowly recovering private housing market and a steady increase in residential contract workloads undertaken for housing associations caused house-builders to consider alternative methods by which profits could be maximised.

Industry concentration

There was a marked trend at the beginning of the 1970s towards a consolidation of output in fewer, but larger, firms. This structural change in the nature of the industry continued apace throughout the 1980s and into the 1990s. For example, in 1983, 49 per cent of the total output of the house-building industry was achieved by companies building in excess of 500 houses per annum. This represented a mere 44 house-building companies out of a total of approximately 22,000 companies registered with the NHBC (National House-Building Council, 1993). In 1999 by contrast, the top 25 companies were responsible for 58 per cent of total market output (Hooper, 2001). As outlined above this concentration was assisted by the entry of contactors into the house-building sector, especially during the 1980s. Increasing concentration throughout the 1990s has been assisted by static levels of national housing production output, with total UK completions averaging around 150,000 from 1993 to 2000. The subsequent scramble for market share has resulted in significant variations in total volumes and market share over this period, as displayed in Figure 4.4.

The early-to-mid 1970s housing cycle is significant, in that since this cycle the house-building industry has witnessed considerable concentration. The 1973 oil

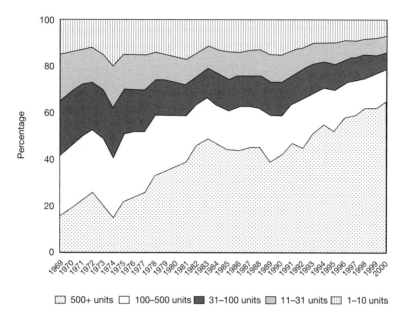

Figure 4.4 Market share of house-building companies in the UK by size of firm, 1969–2000.
Sources: Ball, 1983; National House-Building Council, *New House-Building Statistics*

crisis was followed by a severe economic slump throughout the UK business sector. This slump was particularly significant for the house-building industry in that it signalled a consolidation of capital investment in fewer, larger firms. The position of the largest house-building companies was becoming increasingly concentrated throughout the 1970s, in terms of both ownership and output, evident in the steep rise in output of the largest builders (see Figure 4.4).

From looking at Figure 4.4 we can begin to make a link between the housing market cycle and the nature of housing supply and the patterns of output. The graph provides one key conclusion: that during periods of housing market boom, more smaller firms enter the market, whereas in periods of tougher housing market conditions, demand is met by a smaller number of large firms. The largest companies lost the greatest proportion of market share during the booms of 1972–74 and 1986–89, falling from almost 25 per cent of the market to only 15 per cent and 45 per cent to 38 per cent respectively. Despite the scale of losses incurred, these companies successfully consolidated their position within the industry in a declining housing market.

The periods of depressed demand which follow the boom periods clearly show the increasing concentration of output by the largest house-builders, effectively regaining and substantially increasing their market allocation at the expense of the smaller builders. The smaller operators are exposed to a high incidence of bankruptcy and receiver administration during recessionary periods. The largest (volume) house-builders are cushioned to some extent against the effects of the recession, as they have been active in several regional markets; a diverse product mix and economies of scale also enable them to acquire the assets of their smaller counterparts when things have gone badly for the latter.

A new phase of concentration has emerged in the house-building industry since 1993. Continuing tight profit margins, low, and in some areas falling, demand, and a pessimistic outlook for market conditions has tended to encourage firms towards consolidation. This flight towards a safer position for many companies has resulted in widespread acquisitions, take-overs and mergers.

It was in many cases the house-building subsidiaries of larger contractors that withdrew from housing development in the face of the worsened market situation. The realisation by parent companies that demand was unlikely to alter significantly even in the medium (5 to 10 year) term, led to a reassessment of their commitment to the sector. There were notable 'exits' including the house-building 'arms' of Costain, Tarmac, Trafalgar House and Alfred McAlpine. Costain sold to Redrow in 1993, whilst asset trading between Tarmac and Wimpey in 1995 made the latter the largest company in terms of housing output. In August 2001, Wimpey further acquired the house-building assets of Alfred McAlpine. Trafalgar House, having found that house-building was perhaps not the best way to maximise returns on investment, sold its house-building arm to Persimmon. Taylor Woodrow actually acquired house-building capacity (from Bryant) in 2001, which demonstrates that some contractor-based companies remain committed to house-building. However, this transaction is very much the reverse of a trend allowing house-building to be increasingly dealt with by traditional housing development companies.

Housing development and the building product

As a consequence of the structural changes that have taken place over recent decades, medium and larger house-building companies have increasingly diversified their product range, with an emphasis upon achieving a broad portfolio of development sites, house types and housing tenures.

The Conservative Government's goal of expanding home ownership altered from a somewhat evangelical policy during the 1980s to a more moderate one to suit the more difficult market conditions of the late 1980s and early 1990s. There was a new emphasis on and commitment to affordable housing, referred to as 'social housing' development (see also Chapter 5). The 1995 Government White Paper *Our Future Homes* outlined the new emphasis that government intended to give to the affordable sector to meet wider housing policy objectives. This policy was to be supported by making changes to the planning and development control process (see again Chapter 5). In February 1989, the Secretary of State for the Environment announced that the planning system could be used to secure the provision of low-cost housing for local needs in rural areas (Bramley et al., 1995). This declaration provided the impetus for the current policy emphasis in PPG 3, which extends affordable provision to all areas and not just rural ones. PPG 3 also advocates that 60 per cent of the nation's new homes should be located within existing urban areas. The development of brownfield sites is a desirable environmental goal, but in practical terms the physical nature, levels of contamination and means of access to many of these sites represent a high risk for the industry. Nevertheless the industry has reacted positively to this changed emphasis, with many companies establishing separate divisions to develop brownfield sites.

A reliance upon affordable housing

As output stabilises, production tends to move upmarket in order to sustain profit growth (Crédit Lyonnais, 1995). During the mid-1980s, many house-building companies altered their product mix in this way in order to take advantage of the strong demand for properties at the higher end of the market. However, the onset of recession in 1989 signalled an end to this trend and, coupled with a new emphasis on affordable housing, house-builders looked to build homes at the less expensive end of the market. The strategy thereafter for many firms was to orientate production to first-time buyers and first 'trade-up' households, where demand was more sustainable. This policy was aimed to crank up activity by encouraging households on lower incomes to buy. Unfortunately, however, the profit margins realised from this type of product mix were a great deal lower than those enjoyed in the mid-to-late 1980s. Profits were also to be squeezed since building capacity would take place on land purchased at historically high ('boom') levels. Under these market conditions, housing developers had to plough ahead trying to maximise output as a way of maintaining some level of acceptable profit. Affordable housing provided some sort of platform in an uncertain market throughout the recessionary period.

The re-orientation of the private market in the 1990s created significant problems for the smaller house-builders. Not only unable to compete with their larger competitors for land in the private market, many smaller house-builders lacked the expertise to take advantage of the opportunities in the growing affordable housing sector. The rapid decline in NHBC-registered small builders over the period (shown in Table 4.1) demonstrates clearly the growing difficulty of market endurance and increasing competition from larger market participants.

In spite of the lower levels of profit margins generated from affordable housing, due to the absence of land speculation and marketing techniques, a number of medium and large house-building companies established separate affordable housing divisions, identifying this market as a provider of up to 25 per cent of future output towards the end of the millennium (Bramley et al., 1995). However, subsequent research undertaken by Gillen (1998) indicates that affordable housing is a temporary diversion tactic for developers waiting for better (speculative) housing market conditions. This is not least because house-building companies aspire not just to control the building construction process, but the entire planning and development exercise. Affordable housing provides them with only part of the equation. Barlow and Duncan (1994) affirm the view that it does not appear that house-building companies have changed their approach to maximising profits, and housing association development does not feature strongly in their plans. They conclude that house-builders view affordable housing work as a means of maintaining cash flow in the temporary absence of speculative gain. In support of this contention, Bramley *et al.* (1995) state that as the housing market recovers, the lower levels of profitability from affordable housing schemes dampen the enthusiasm for this development sector.

Emerging issues: the new housing demand and sustainable development

There are a number of emerging issues which are likely to affect the structure, operation and role of the industry going forward in this new century. Key factors are interlinked and relate mainly to the nature of new housing demand and its relationship with sustainable development policies.

It is clear that the nature of new housing demand is largely coming from smaller and single-person households. Whilst this form of demand does not necessarily mean building smaller homes, what it probably does mean is not building larger ones. Whilst interest rates (at the time of writing in 2002) are very low in historical terms, and thus financing a home is easier, there is nevertheless a limit to the amount of 'bricks and mortar' that can be funded from one person's income. Thus house-builders will have to be responsive to this situation.

Single-person households are, however, by no means a homogenous group and incomes will vary significantly across the range. House-builders thus need to target development in a fairly precise way if they are to prosper. One such market (for single 'professional' people) is an 'urban' one, where 'city living' is seen as being desirable. In developing for this market, house-builders can, in theory, build both profitably as well as sustainably. Indeed some major house-builders have already begun to put subsidiaries in place to deal with this emerging urban development market. Examples include Redrow's 'In the City' company, Persimmon's 'City Developments' and David Wilson's 'City Homes'. While the demands of urban development and urban regeneration can be more onerous than building on greenfield sites, the establishment of such subsidiaries provides the parent company with a much wider range of products to deal with more complex market demands.

Taking advantage of brownfield site opportunities nevertheless requires particular skills and often a quite different approach. Sometimes 'brownfield' site development will be new-build in traditional form on a cleared site. Under these circumstances the main consideration for the house-builder will be making the right offer for the site, given the fact that it may be contaminated or perhaps difficult to access. Other times a 'brownfield site opportunity' will be a conversion. This poses quite different problems for financing and marketing the development. Jones (2002) has studied the potential for developers on brownfield sites. In a survey, one developer highlighted the key issues in relation to 'traditional' forms of estate development:

> We are increasingly doing conversions for residential use. These schemes have a completely different effect on work in progress and available capital. With a traditional

housing estate, you are able to build and sell in phases – in blocks, allowing turnover to be generated at regular intervals. With conversions, you are simply working on one block all the same time. There is little scope for phasing work and releases to the market. You can't release one apartment for occupation while you are still working on the building as a whole. Work in progress is much higher on these schemes and turnover is more infrequent.

(Cited from Jones, 2002)

The problem of increased work in progress identified in the study leads naturally to a problem of increased cash flow requirements. This has knock-on consequences for the type and size of house-building company becoming involved in urban regeneration and brownfield site housing schemes. It will be inevitably more difficult for smaller companies to become involved since there will be a need for more 'up-front' funding because all units needs to be completed before any sales revenue is generated.

A question which might appropriately be asked at the end of this chapter is whether the house-building industry is necessarily bound to continue to consolidate with fewer, but larger firms. There is much evidence, based on the new challenges ahead, to suggest that 'big is best'. An experienced house-building industry commentator (Wellings, 2000) suggests, however, that house-building firms reach a best equilibrium point of output, beyond which expansion is not advisable. Wellings argues (ibid.) that unlike in manufacturing, there are no operational economies of scale as there is no house-building equivalent of doubling the size of a chemical plant to drive down costs. In contrast, there are diseconomies of scale in house-building in practice and there is a consensus among the industry's players that once an output of 400–500 units per annum is reached, it is prudent to form a subsidiary company. The thinking behind this is that, as production increases, there is a need for additional layers of management to control activities that were formerly overseen by fewer staff (Jones, 2002).

Discussion points

1   Discuss the key roles of the UK's private house-building industry and the different ways in which the term is understood.
2   Analyse the cyclical nature of house-building output by reference to the UK's economic performance and its housing market.
3   Distinguish between speculative house-building and contracting. Examine the role of each in meeting housing demand throughout the 1980s and 1990s.
4   Discuss the relationship between regional housing market performance and the operation of house-building firms.
5   What have been the key manifestations of structural change in the house-building industry? Examine their underlying causes.
6   Debate the implications of a sustainable housing development agenda for restructuring in the house-building industry.

Key reading

For an historical perspective Morgan, *A History of the NHBC and Private Home Building* (1987) is recommended. Theories of house-building are elucidated in papers, e.g. Healey, 'Models of the development process' (*Journal of Property Research*, 1991) and Hooper, 'The restructuring of the house-building industry' (House Builders Federation, 2001). Annual reviews by Crédit Lyonnais and monthly news in *House Builder* magazine provide a window on company activity.

Chapter 5
Social housing, affordable development and the role of government

Michael Oxley and Kathleen Dunmore

Introduction: what is 'social housing development'?

Criteria for definition

'Social' housing development is, in many ways, no different to other forms of housing development. It involves the construction of new housing units, or the rehabilitation of older ones. It involves providing housing of a sufficient scale and quality to meet the needs of the target household group. It involves achieving a specified return on the development such that the developer can continue to operate.

Social housing is however usually developed according to a different set of 'rules' from that in the market sector. Whereas housing for the market is usually developed to satisfy the demand for owner-occupation, social housing is normally developed for households to rent. This form of development caters for two main household circumstances: first, those households that cannot gain access to private housing finance, i.e. a mortgage; and second, households that wish to be more 'mobile', particularly smaller households with lower incomes who wish to adopt a more flexible approach.

Social housing is developed to meet housing 'need' (see also Chapter 3), whereas private housing is normally developed in response to what is thought to be 'housing demand'. The term 'social housing' is, according to Reeves (1996: 6), used to 'describe any accommodation which is provided for those who cannot compete in the marketplace to provide their own roof'. Social housing development, because it aims to impact on households outside the 'market', is directed towards lowering the costs of housing occupancy; normally this means developing social housing at rents below what might be considered 'market' rents. This situation triggers a requirement for two further conditions: first, housing developers who are prepared to accept less than a market rate of return on their 'investment'; and second, where these investors cannot accept less than the market conditions, some form of subsidy in order to deliver the social housing, or to make it affordable. In practice, the subsidy comes either from government, directly out of taxation, or indirectly from land value, where local authorities can obtain affordable housing quotas via the planning process.

From the point of view of those who commission and finance housing development, there are different objectives. For a private housing developer building speculatively, the main aim will be to sell the dwelling to an owner-occupier on a 'one-off' basis. Thereafter the dwelling falls into the second-hand housing market where its price and demand fluctuate according to market conditions. For a dwelling commissioned as 'social housing development' the objectives will be different. The 'social' dwelling will aim to meet housing need over the longer term with the goal of providing 'affordable' occupancy. For this reason, we need to take account of the management function when thinking about how to define social housing:

> The use of the term social housing is . . . generally understood to refer to housing provided and managed by local authorities – commonly called council housing – and (more recently) by housing associations and other organisations which together form the voluntary housing movement. These organisations are 'voluntary' in the sense that, unlike local authorities, they have no statutory obligation . . . to provide housing. In general, however, the essential characteristic of social housing is that it is provided by organisations which do not seek to make a profit.
>
> (Harriot and Matthews, 1998: 3)

Bramley (1993: 55) provides a further useful definition of social housing, which draws together all the elements of the related discussion. Social housing is defined as: 'housing provided for rent (or part-rent/part-buy) at less than full market cost by a socially responsible agency conforming to some form of tenant's charter or guarantee and allocating accommodation on a basis relating to need' (ibid.). This definition draws together both the means of provision and the issue of occupancy.

How useful is the term 'social housing development'?

The term 'social housing development' is a generic one, although one which is today arguably not entirely up to date. We use the term in this chapter as a way of making a link between the now outdated mode of developing housing for those in need, namely 'council house' development, which largely disappeared at the end of the 1970s, and the more modern version of development for households in need, namely 'affordable housing development'. The term 'social housing' is nevertheless significant when considering the historical perspective, which this chapter also deals with.

It is today important to consider the term 'affordable' housing development, which is arguably wider in its scope of definition than 'social housing development'. Affordable housing development is now the mode of providing housing for those on low incomes and those outside the market. Those organisations developing 'affordable' housing are not restricted to building housing for rent. They can, where local market conditions allow, develop low-cost owner-occupied dwellings. The government's Circular 6/98 makes this clear:

. . . planning policy should not be expressed in favour of any particular form of tenure. Therefore the terms 'affordable housing', or 'affordable homes' are used in this Circular to encompass both low-cost and subsidised housing (irrespective of tenure, ownership – whether exclusive or shared – or financial arrangements) that will be available to people who cannot afford to rent or buy houses generally available on the open market.

(DETR, 1998b)

This clause thus allows local planning authorities to develop housing for those on low incomes and other households in need to suit local market conditions. Where the housing market is very buoyant, and there is seen to be great pressure to provide an ongoing supply of affordable housing, local authorities may choose (via housing associations) to build 'affordable' housing for rent, so that this housing is controlled and maintained in perpetuity. Where the housing market is less strong, and where perhaps there is already a consistent supply of affordable homes coming via the owner-occupied market, then local authorities may think it more appropriate to develop low-cost home ownership or discount market products.

There has been a considerable change in emphasis and approach over time to the development of homes for those in need. The main change in emphasis has been from the 'ideal' to the 'pragmatic', from polarised policy positions advocating (either) the 'state' (or) the 'market' as a solution, to the situation now, which recognises the contribution to be made by both the housing and, in particular, the land market, as well as the role played by state subsidies in meeting housing need. By looking back at the history of social housing development, we can see how we have arrived at the current position.

Social housing development and its role before 1945

Early social housing development

Housing for those in need was, before the twentieth century, based on a fairly rudimentary and haphazard method of provision. The 'housing policy', if it could be called that, was, in essence a laissez-faire approach involving market solutions to problems of housing supply and demand:

Housing was seen in the nineteenth century as a simple, widespread commodity for which there was a fluctuating though on the whole growing economic demand; it could be, and was, bought, sold or rented in the marketplace. Despite the glaring disparities in housing provision between different social classes and the appalling housing conditions of the poorer groups in society, interference by government legislation in the housing market was strongly resisted.

(Lawless and Brown, 1986: 38)

Thus there was at the time a consensus against state intervention to alleviate housing need. Rather, the solution to the problems of overcrowding and poor housing were to be found in philanthropic activity or were to be achieved as part of wider initiatives associated with industrial investment:

> Housing, in the view of many, and in particular the numerically large, politically influential and economically powerful urban landlords, should not be subject to legislation. If the lot of the urban poor could not be remedied quickly or effectively by the forces of the free market in housing, then the philanthropy of private individuals or groups was a much more acceptable and in the end well-tried solution. This philanthropic approach to the housing problem took three very different forms: the 'model' village, the 'model' dwelling company, and the individual philanthropic landlord.
>
> (ibid.: 39)

The 'model village' is perhaps the earliest British example of 'social housing development'. The model villages, of which New Lanark in the Clyde Valley, Port Sunlight on the Mersey estuary and Bournville are perhaps the best known, were in many ways self-contained settlements. They were 'model villages' in that their design and housing layout were considerably advanced from contemporary housing. Importantly, housing developed in 'model' villages was occupied at rents which were strictly controlled, usually so as to provide households working at the local factory or mill with an affordable means of putting a roof over their heads.

'Model dwelling companies' were set up during the Victorian age in the form of trusts and companies whose aims were to develop housing for poorer households. Two of the most remarkable were the Metropolitan Association and the Peabody Trust, which focused their activities in London. These organisations in many respects pointed the way for the modern housing association movement. The model companies were instrumental in developing new affordable housing at a time when there were few other initiatives of the kind. However, as Lawless and Brown (1986: 42) have suggested, the model dwelling companies failed in many cases to accommodate the very poorest households as even the low rents required to reward investors were well above what many households could afford.

The social housing development programme and the advent of state subsidies: the inter-war years

Although poor housing conditions can be understood as the main justification for state intervention to support social housing development, the trigger for government action was the aftermath of the First World War. At that time, there was a strong feeling that housing should be built to reward the home-coming servicemen:

> An election was fought on the slogan 'Homes Fit for Heroes' and in 1919 the first 'national' housing programme was introduced. The new programme can be simply summed up as an intention to build 500,000 houses for the working classes in three years.
>
> (Nevitt, 1966)

Several important pieces of legislation were produced in the aftermath of the First World War to promote house-building for those in need: the Addison Act of 1919, which gave powers to local authorities and public utility societies to develop new housing, but whose housing development programmes were financially underwritten by central government; the Chamberlain Act of 1923, which placed a much greater emphasis on local authorities to develop successfully, yet expanded subsidies also to private builders; the Wheatley Act subsidy of 1924, which raised subsidies for a period of 40 years. Later on, the 1935 Housing Act provided subsidies for dwellings built on highly priced land. The details of the provisions of these pieces of housing legislation are extensive; they are well covered in Malpass and Murie (1990: 54–9) and Nevitt (1966: 76–91). It is mainly important here to appreciate the key features and objectives.

Perhaps the most significant change from the pre-1914 period was the acceptance that the state, either in the form of direct subsidies paid by central government, or via local authority rate grants, should help promote new housing development. A number of mechanisms were used; annual subsidies, or one-off grants, which were normally paid direct to the developer (whether local authority or private); subsidies to reduce the cost of land acquisition; or subsidies to reduce the cost of borrowing. The housing development policy of this period was broadly to meet the needs of the 'working class'. However, housing need generally was so great, partly because the Addison Act failed to meet its targets, that the private sector was brought in and its production subsidised. This had important consequences:

> A lump sum of £130 to £160 was given to any builder who built a house for sale or rental. The subsidy was restricted to houses with a maximum floor area of 1,250 square feet but was not restricted to houses below a certain price, and no regulations were laid down as to the occupants of these houses.
>
> (Nevitt, 1966: 81)

Thus, government subsidies, aimed to meet the needs of the poorer household sector went into the construction of housing for owner-occupation under some circumstances. Later legislation cut back on these general subsidies and ensured that all future subsidies for new dwelling construction could only be accessed where households were to be re-housed from slum dwellings. In this way

> central government took the effective measure of stopping the general needs subsidy as a way of imposing the view that the function of public housing should be to rehouse the poor, leaving the private market to provide for the rest of the population.
>
> (Malpass and Murie, 1990: 57)

At the same time, the building societies had expanded their lending activities quite considerably, with the result that the owner-occupied sector, rather than the rented sector, grew.

Models for social housing development since 1945

Context

Social housing has been developed since the Second World War with government playing a number of varied roles. In this section, we distinguish the key approaches, or models, of social housing development since 1945. In these models, we see social housing development: first, as a product of the welfare state; second, as a planning and development experiment; third, as a residual process; and finally as a product of planning gain in a market economy. We now explain how these models have worked.

Social housing development as product of the welfare state (1945–55)

In many ways, the role of government in the promotion of social housing development was well established by the end of the Second World War. The key Housing Acts of the inter-war years had set in place a framework for subsidy and taxation for council housing. However, a significant proportion of the housing stock, some 450,000 dwellings, had been destroyed in the war, creating a substantial new housing need. The incoming Labour Government set out a highly planned programme for many areas of social and economic policy. The National Health Service and the Town and Country Planning Acts are good examples of the 'dirigiste' approach adopted by that particular administration. Very much in line with these initiatives was the continued role for local authorities as developers of social housing.

The continued subsidisation of housing could be justified at the time by a government concerned to establish a welfare state in a market economy; indeed, this is still the case today. The subsidisation of social or affordable housing can be justified on several grounds according to arguments relating to welfare economics. The first justification is the assumption that there is 'market failure', and hence a need to provide for those not able to access housing at a cost determined by the market. This assumption provides an argument, for example, for regulated rents to make housing costs affordable. A second justification is the assumption held in welfare economics that not all goods consumed in the economy are 'private', namely that some should be considered 'public'. A strict distinction between these two forms of goods suggests that private goods are those which 'if consumed by one person cannot be consumed by another', whereas public goods are those that 'even if consumed by one person, can still be consumed by other people' (Begg *et al.*, 1989: 340).

The term 'public housing', often used instead of 'council housing', begs the question as to whether housing provided by the state, be it 'social' or 'affordable' in nature, should be considered a 'public good'. Strictly, a house lived in by one household cannot usually be lived in by another at the same time. The same applies for private or owner-occupied housing. However, because social or council housing is allocated according to a measure of housing 'need', it is in some senses a 'public good'. Once one household has left the dwelling, it can be re-allocated according to the same principles, by the arbiter and definer of 'housing need' (the state) so that another household can enjoy or experience housing shelter. This process does not occur in the private owner-occupied sector, or indeed in the private rented sector, where decisions about housing allocation are mainly 'private' ones left to individuals, relatives or trustees. The idea of 'public' housing, to be continually occupied by those in housing need, is nevertheless a key tenet of the housing policy set up in the immediate post-war period.

The third justification for subsidisation is the welfare economics argument that some goods can be considered to be 'merit goods'. These are 'goods that society thinks everyone should have [or in the case of merit 'bads', not have] regardless of whether they are wanted by each individual' (Begg *et al.*, 1989: 343). Perhaps the best examples of merit goods are health and education services. Many people will not pay for these unless the benefits are completely transparent to them. However, it can be argued that the benefits, or 'beneficial externalities' to society, outweigh the costs to the individual, with the result that the state takes the relevant action via taxation and subsidy policy to ensure that the services are available to all. In this way, social, public or affordable housing can be seen as a merit good. Some households might not actually want to occupy the dwellings allocated to them (perhaps preferring private housing), but not to provide social housing at all would be entirely unacceptable to society. From a highly practical point of view, if no social housing were to be provided, and homelessness and mass overcrowding accepted, an intolerable burden would be put on the health service and it would be exceedingly difficult to justify extensive spending on such things as education.

The establishment of the welfare state in the immediate post-war years was important for housing development in that it bolstered, or underwrote, housing policies directed towards social housing provision established during the inter-war years. A huge local authority building programme was set in place. Dwelling output rose from some 25,000 units built in 1946 to nearly 225,000 units completed in 1953 (DoE, *Local Authority Housing Statistics* (annual)), almost a tenfold increase. Over the same period, private sector production rose from 30,000 units to only around 60,000 (ibid.), only doubling output. This focus on quantity of social housing output was complemented by a focus on quality in the development of council homes. Malpass and Murie (1990: 71) describe the key features of post war social housing: 'one of the most visually striking features of post-war housing is its variety. Compared with pre-war estates there is much greater variation in layout, form, density and finishing materials.' In addition, space standards were high, a consequence of the Dudley Report, published in 1944. This set out a minimum dwelling size of 900 ft^2 for a three-bedroomed house, which was 'comfortably exceeded during the whole period of the Labour Government up to 1951' (ibid.).

The establishment of the welfare state can be argued therefore to have had several important impacts for social housing development: the provision of housing intended to serve households in housing need, in sufficient quantity and of a high standard. These outcomes can be argued to reflect a desire by government to obtain a maximum return for society by its intervening actions.

Social housing as a planning and development 'experiment' (1955–75)

Why the 'experiment' in social housing development?

The Second World War provided an opportunity to change significantly the way in which social housing was provided. The pressing housing shortages meant that government and local authorities would have to look at alternative and possibly radical means by which affordable homes could be built for the very extensive numbers of households in housing need. To some extent, the 'opportunity' was missed in practice. The mode of social housing development continued in much the same vein as before: on new greenfield estates at the urban fringe and in the form of mixed low-rise dwellings. However, some policy makers and professions, particularly the planning and architectural ones, saw an opportunity to provide much more innovative housing development solutions, making a break with past practice:

> The twentieth century in Britain has been split in two by a great revolution in housing. The first half of the century was dominated by the age-old system of natural selection, which left people free to secure the best accommodation they could. The second half has embraced the Utopian ideal of housing planned by a paternalistic authority.
>
> (Coleman, 1985: 6)

Indeed social housing was to be 'Utopian' and high-rise development in particular was to be the mechanism. This form of living was thought to encourage a sense of 'community', and because there was a relatively low land take-up, to provide a very high proportion of (communal) recreation area. The model for this was the architect Le Corbusier's 'Radiant City' (ibid.: 7). Although this idea was first conceived during the 1920s, it had no role to play in Britain until after the Second World War, where it was considered more seriously as a way of alleviating housing shortages.

The social housing development 'experiment' in the form of high-rise living is today commonly explained in three main ways. First, as a product of a very real housing problem, the need to build a very large number of dwelling units in a short time, where 'industrial' building methods could be applied more appropriately than with traditional low ones. Second, it can be seen as a response to the enthusiasm of planners and architects to break a trend with the past and do something different to provide people with a better way of life. Sometimes this belief was very strongly held as the following extract shows:

> We really believed, in a quasi-religious sense, in the perfectibility of human nature, in the
> role of architecture as a weapon of social reform . . . the coming Utopia when everyone
> would live in cheap prefabricated flat-roofed multiple dwellings – heaven on earth.
>
> (Johnson, P.; from Coleman, 1985: 3)

A third important factor was the local authorities themselves who often saw the role
of high-rise building not only as being a solution to housing shortage but also as
providing an enhanced image of their area:

> Architects have always been tempted to build high buildings, even when they were inap-
> propriate. Tower blocks were part of the architectural and municipal prestige – a desire
> to make a mark on the landscape, to display technical proficiency, and to announce the
> arrival of a new age.
>
> (Nuttgens, 1989: 18)

The high-rise social housing development boom could not, however, have taken
place without the support of central government, who were responsible for a major
part of the subsidy programme and associated building targets that were to be
achieved. The mid-1960s has been described as the 'birth, life and death of the
national housing plan' (Merrett, 1979: 13), a response to the policies of the time.
From 1956 onwards, central government put into place a subsidy system aimed to
reward and encourage the developers of high-rise dwelling construction. Under the
new finance system, the subsidy available for a flat in a six-storey block was 2.3 times
higher than the basic subsidy paid on a house; if the flat was in a block of 15 or
more storeys then the subsidy was three times that of a house, and above 20 storeys,
3.4 times (Dunleavy, 1981: 37). The approach to subsidising high-rise housing
continued until 1965, when the increments to the progressive storey-height subsidy
above six storeys were abolished (ibid.: 38).

The importance of high-rise development to social housing provision

Having looked at the background to the high-rise development boom, it is
important to look at its significance in the broader picture of social housing provision. Figure 5.1 provides an overview of house-building in the social sector from
the early 1950s to the mid-1970s. Whilst dwellings commissioned by local authorities were to a significant extent built in the form of houses for the period, flats and
high-rise homes made up a very significant proportion of local authority output.
The output of high-rise dwelling blocks increased steadily from 1953 to 1966, and
between 1964 and 1968 high-rise dwellings made up around one quarter of all local
authority approvals. Dunleavy (1981: 40) has further analysed how the output of
high-rise dwellings was made up:

> Within the high-rise category there was a marked trend towards increasingly tall blocks.
> From 1955–65 blocks of five to nine storeys, often termed 'medium rise', made up
> between 4.3 and 5.6 per cent of all public housing, varying without any apparent pattern

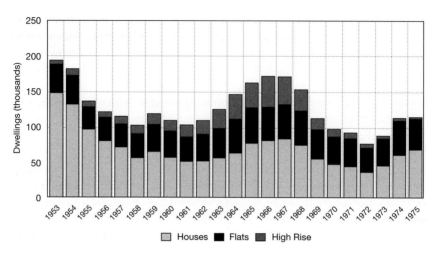

Figure 5.1 Local authority approvals by building form, 1953–75.
Sources: Government Housing Statistics (1966); DoE Housing and Construction Statistics (1976)

from year to year. Taller blocks, on the other hand, were an increasing proportion of public housing during the period. Blocks of 10–14 storeys expanded from 0.7 per cent of public housing in 1955 to 8.4 per cent in 1963. Blocks of 15–19 storeys expanded from 0.1 per cent of public housing in 1956 to 8.3 per cent in 1964. The tallest blocks, of twenty storeys and over, expanded from 0.3 per cent of public housing in 1959 to 4.5 per cent in 1967.

(ibid.)

In turn, there was significant inequality in the distribution of high-rise homes across the country. Between 1966 and 1971, almost half of all dwellings approved for local authority building programmes in London were high-rise; in contrast, for example, only 3 per cent of all approvals for the same period in Wales were high-rise homes (ibid.: 44). Thus high-rise development fell disproportionately between regions.

Did the experiment work?

Perhaps the most well known evaluation of the social housing 'experiment' is that by Alice Coleman (1985). Her book *Utopia on Trial* is a detailed evaluation of the impact of high-rise social housing development on its occupants and their environment. There is little scope here to deal fully with this highly detailed study which is particularly valuable with respect to the relationship between housing form and the social pattern of behaviour of households in high-rise homes. Based on a number of case study estates, the conclusions of the book were ground breaking and although the problems of high-rise housing are today well known, it is this text that will be remembered as one of the first to point the way to appropriate development solutions in the future. The conclusions found, for example, that levels of social breakdown were far higher in flats within high-rise estates than in houses occupied by people from a similar background, and that litter, vandalism and graffiti and other problems of estate management were more likely to be found in the high-rise areas. Not surprisingly, the final conclusion rejected the development of any more such flats (ibid.: 171).

Moreover, the role of high-rise flats in housing provision was seen to be limited, mainly because of the narrow 'market' which they appeared to serve:

> The abandonment of high-rise flats as a major housing type seems to have been broadly in accord with the weight of public opinion. The attitudes of users towards flat-dwelling depended largely on the composition of their families, surveys in the late fifties indicating that while many single persons and childless couples positively liked living in flats, the overwhelming majority of families with children disliked them on the grounds that they were too noisy, too small, and 'not the right place' to bring children up.
>
> (Burnett, 1978: 288)

Thus whilst high-rise was seen to be acceptable for smaller households, it was not so for larger households, particularly those with families. There is little evidence to suggest that this is also not the case today, although with household structure becoming smaller, and land prices remaining high, there is in some quarters a renewed call for high-rise flats, particularly in London and in the private sector.

The decline of the high-rise housing solution can also be linked with two further events. First, there was a reduction in the preferential treatment given in subsidising high-rise blocks. This occurred during the mid-1960s and was a response in no small part to the suspicion that high-rise was an inefficient way of developing homes; whilst it was important that there was an 'even playing field' with respect to the development of houses versus flats, there was little point in providing subsidy if the effect of that subsidy was to push building costs beyond an economic limit. Second, and arguably the most important factor in the decline of high-rise building, was the partial collapse of a tower block, Ronan Point in the London Borough of Newham in 1967. The image that high-rise development might be technically flawed was of sufficient concern for government and local authorities to turn back to more traditional forms of social housing development during the 1970s.

Social housing as 'residual' development (1979–90)

From the end of the 1970s, social housing development was relegated down the policy agenda, and today this policy choice has led commentators to see social housing as 'residualised'.

Social housing development can be regarded as 'residual' in two main ways. First, social housing output is seen as a residual or 'mopping up' process in housing supply, where the purpose of building social housing is simply to deal with market failure; i.e. to provide housing units not provided by the private sector. Second, social housing development can be 'residual' in the sense that it aims to provide for a residual group of households, who are in some way 'beyond' the mainstream housing system.

There need not necessarily be a link between these two concepts; in practice, it may be sound housing policy to increase the proportion of social housing output (relative to the private sector) at a time when the demand for housing by those at the margins of society is falling. Developing more social housing may allow those directly above the lowest group to improve their housing standards. Conversely, relatively less social housing may be built at a time when housing demand amongst the poorest households is growing. Whether these policies are 'right' or 'wrong' depends on the way in which housing 'need' is interpreted, and the wider subsidy arrangements governing support for different housing tenures.

The term 'residualisation' (see also Clapham and English, 1987; Emms, 1990; Malpass and Murie, 1990) appeared in connection with social housing development very much as a result of the right-to-buy policy of the Conservative governments of the 1980s. This policy initiative allowed council house tenants to buy their homes from the local authority. The term thus considers not only housing development, but also what is happening in the housing stock. The objective of social housing development was, very much in this context, seen as being directed towards those households at the very margins of society. As many tenants of council homes were in practice able to exercise their 'right-to-buy', 'affordable' housing supply fell in the absence of a compensating new build programme. Where new affordable homes were built, they were increasingly focused on the very poorest households, meaning that the social housing stock became increasingly residualised.

This approach had the potential to reduce the level of government subsidy at the beginning of the 1980s, particularly as the Thatcher Government was promoting owner-occupation and private house-building to a great extent. However a reduced subsidy burden depended on a number of other factors. One consideration was the extent to which revenue from rents lost due to council house sales would affect local authority finance. Another, arguably far more significant factor, was the future performance of the housing market, important for the expansion of owner-occupation. As we now know with hindsight, the policy worked well up until the late 1980s, when the housing market crashed spectacularly. The aftermath of this event demanded that policy makers looked rather more optimistically at the potential role of the social sector. Today, in relatively buoyant housing market conditions, the need for affordable housing development over and above those marginal or 'residual' households is fully recognised. This is particularly the case in London and the South East, where affordable housing is targeted at professional households on the lower income scales. The 'residual' social housing development programme was to be delivered, not by local authorities, as had been the case in the 1970s and beforehand, but by housing associations. Local authorities were still to be involved in social housing development (Plate 5.1), although only via an 'enabling' or facilitating role. The third Conservative Government produced a White Paper in 1987 (DoE, 1987) setting out how they saw the future role of local authorities:

> The future role of local authorities will essentially be a strategic one identifying housing
> needs and demands, encouraging innovative methods of provision by other bodies to

Plate 5.1
1980s social
housing
development,
Beaumont Leys,
Leicester:
A. J. Golland.

meet such needs, maximising the use of private finance, and encouraging the new interest in the revival of the independent rented sector. In order to fulfil this strategic role they will have to work closely with housing associations; private landlords; developers; and building societies and other providers of finance.

(DoE, 1987, para 5.1, Meeting Housing Needs)

Housing associations were to build social housing using a more entrepreneurial approach to financing development. This would take place in the context of a private rented sector which was increasingly being deregulated:

The Housing Corporation and some individual housing associations have been developing alternative financial possibilities with the encouragement of the government. These arrangements have involved two key elements. First, schemes are being developed using assured tenancies rather than Rent Act tenancies. Second, private sector sources of finance have been available on an index-lined or low-start basis. With higher repayments in later years when rental income has increased. The combination of these two elements is making it possible to develop viable schemes with more private sector and less public sector involvement. This facilitates improved efficiency and allows public resources to be used more effectively.

(DoE, 1987, para. 4.5, 'The Independent Rented
Sector: Housing Associations')

These changes allowed housing associations, supported still to a significant extent by central government subsidy (first HAG (Housing Association Grant), and then SHG (Social Housing Grant), to negotiate 'top-up' private sector funding and to let their units on rent levels closer to those in the 'private' (landlord) rented sector. This essential approach to social housing development has prevailed since the beginning of the 1980s, although the subsidy element from central government has been gradually reduced, putting pressure on rents and on the housing associations to find ever more cost-effective ways of financing development.

Social housing development as planning 'gain' (1990 onwards)

As governments have increasingly scrutinised public expenditure on housing, so policy makers have had to find alternative ways of funding social housing development. Since the beginning of the 1990s, an important new model of social housing development has emerged; that which develops social or affordable housing via the planning system.

'Via the planning system' covers many complex and difficult issues, and it should be emphasised that the use of the planning system does not obviate the need for government subsidy. Fundamental to the development of social housing using the planning system is the concept of 'planning gain'. In its very simplest form, planning gain is the bundle of benefits, both physical and financial, that a local authority, acting on behalf of the community, can obtain from a developer wanting to obtain planning permission for a site. In practice, planning gain usually involves developers making some form of contribution to physical infrastructure, for example, roads or landscaping, as well as to some form of amenity of social or economic benefit, for example, affordable housing, schools, libraries or recreational facilities. The extent of the contribution (by the developer) and the gain (to the local authority) depends upon the specific circumstances of the development. Under very buoyant housing market conditions, for example, local authorities can ask for more than under conditions where land values are very low.

The process of developing and subsidising social housing through the planning system is controversial. The planning 'gain' or 'deal' is normally agreed through what are known as 'Section 106' agreements. These are legal agreements, attached directly to the grant of planning permission, which stipulate matters relating to the development site in question; with respect to affordable housing, the agreements typically set out the proportion and quantity of affordable housing to be built, its nature (whether social rented or low-cost home ownership, for example) and the phasing of the building (in line with the private sector completions). The agreement is often based on a lengthy negotiation process in which both developer and local authority test each others' strengths and weaknesses. The whole process raises a number of important questions, some of which relate to practical matters, and some of which concern the broader philosophical debate about the rights and wrongs of land taxation. Perhaps the most important of these questions concerns the right, per se, of local authorities to ask for planning gain in the form of contributions from private sector interests such as housing developers.

Is it right that local authorities should 'gain' from the planning process?

If the planning and development control process impacts on house prices and land values, then it can be argued that planning has dynamic impacts, impinges and controls markets and has an ability to affect the affordability of housing. The house-building industry tends to see the planning system in this way, usually arguing for the release of more land to meet housing demand and to make new homes more affordable for people.

An interpretation of a simple supply–demand model would seem to back up this argument. As more land is released to the housing market, so the price of housing can fall. Taking an extreme stand, the house-building industry might, on the basis of these arguments, refuse to provide any planning gain in the form of affordable housing, since the problem of expensive housing would all be to do with a 'lack of land'.

A different way of approaching the problem of developing affordable housing is to begin from the standpoint that it is not the planning system that is at fault, but the wider housing market itself. From this standpoint, one sees the planning system as a mechanism for recouping some of the benefits created by the housing market. This argument can be supported on the basis that house prices are predominantly driven by what happens in the second-hand housing market, which is not immediately affected by planning. House prices more broadly are, it might be argued, determined by the strength of the economy based on the efforts and enterprise of its people.

One argument for planning gain being required of developers and (in practice, land-owners – since costs are passed from the former to the latter), can be based on the assumption that the planning system is not responsible for increasing or decreasing land values, but is responsible only for re-distributing them. Oxley (2003) provides an example of how this argument runs:

> If planning permission for housing development exists for plot A, but for other plots B, C and D only permission for agricultural use is forthcoming, it is likely that A will be developed for housing, whilst the other plots will not. The owner of plot A will see the land value increase from its agricultural use to its residential development use value. The owners of plots B, C and D will not receive any gain. In the absence of any planning restrictions, it is the owner of plot B that is most keen to sell to the residential developer. This owner will accept a lower price than the owners of the other plots. The housing

developer finds that higher bids are necessary to secure plots A, C and D and thus buys plot B and builds houses. The other plots remain in agricultural use.

Without planning, the owner of plot B sells to the residential developer. With planning, the owner of plot A sells to the residential developer. An effect of planning is to redistribute wealth between the owners of plots A and B. Both the pattern of land use and the pattern of wealth distribution are affected by planning.

(Oxley, 2004)

Under these circumstances, Oxley asks, 'If the owner of plot B has lost wealth and the owner of plot A has gained wealth as a consequence of planning, should the former be entitled to some sort of compensation and the latter a "betterment tax?"' The scope for penalising land-owners with a 'betterment' tax, or for asking for planning 'gain' on the increase of the land value consequent on the planning process, is a matter for extensive debate. We consider here the essential 'bones' of the debate.

A starting point is to consider first the hypothesis that whilst the planning system may not change the aggregate (overall level) of land values in the country, it does change the economic position of individual land-owners significantly. If this standpoint is accepted, then a case can be made for local authorities to ask for planning gain. The key question which then however arises in practice is, 'How much?'.

How much planning gain?

The approach to dealing with this question is often dealt with by referring to the economic concepts of 'transfer earnings' and 'economic rent'. The distinction between these two 'returns' to land is made in the following:

Land can be viewed as a factor of production. Classical economists divided the rewards to factors of production into two elements: transfer earnings and economic rent. Transfer earnings according to their analysis are necessary to ensure the supply of a factor for a particular use. They are the minimum payment necessary to stop a factor being used for the production of some alternative commodity. Thus if the farmer can sell a plot of land for £100,000 to another farmer, he will not sell for less than this to a residential developer. The residential developer will need to offer the farmer at least £100,000 to secure the land.

Economic rent is a payment over and above transfer earnings. It is a payment above that which is absolutely necessary to secure the use of a factor for a given productive purpose. Assume that the residential developer offers the farmer £500,000 for the land and this sum was accepted. As long as an offer above £100,000 was made, the farmer would have accepted. If £500,000 is received, a large part of this is economic rent.

(Oxley, ibid.)

The implicit task of the local planning authority under the current approach to affordable housing development is to achieve some planning gain, either in the form of physical improvements to the site, or in the form of social infrastructure. What it does, in negotiating a developer agreement, is to try to 'capture' some of the economic rent that will be 'generated' by the change in land use. This process is complex not least because of the difficulty in trying to establish how much of the economic 'rent' to try to capture. If its demands are too onerous, then the land-owner will leave the land in its current use (returning only 'transfer earnings'); if its demands are not onerous enough, it then leaves itself open to the charge of not having recouped enough benefits for the community. Most importantly, to what extent should the economic rent generated 'contribute' to the development of affordable housing. We consider now this question.

To what extent should the planning process and planning gain contribute to affordable housing development?

The broader principles of the arguments for local authorities seeking planning gain have been discussed. A strong case for developers making a 'contribution' in some form as a result of the increase in land value of a site can be made. A more difficult question is, perhaps, in what 'form' should this gain be?

The case for affordable or social housing being included in a local planning authority's planning gain 'shopping list' is arguably more controversial than the case which suggests that some form of contribution should be made per se. The Joseph Rowntree Foundation's *Inquiry into Planning for Housing* stated rather strongly the case against the principle of affordable housing development as a manifestation of the planning process: 'We do not think that it any more reasonable to expect the suppliers of new private housing to house the homeless than to make farmers responsible for feeding the hungry' (Joseph Rowntree Foundation, 1994: 33).

On this basis, there is an argument that affordable housing should never be allowed to be included as part of an authority's planning gain 'package'. The limits of what can and cannot justifiably be asked for is, however, by no means well defined. Healey *et al.* (1993) concluded that it may be reasonable for the planning system to require development schemes to provide a contribution under two main circumstances: first, in relation to the costs of necessary additional infrastructure; and second, in relation to the costs of adverse impacts on the community. It was concluded to be unreasonable, however, 'to require a developer to contribute on an ad hoc basis to wider community objectives, such as social housing, unless it can be justified in terms of the specific development' (ibid.).

The demand for a contribution towards affordable housing provision, either in the form of land, or in the form of a payment in lieu (where developers can pay authorities directly instead of building social housing) is particularly controversial in the light of the changing role of local authorities from developers to strategic enablers. The problem is well highlighted in the case of *Tesco Stores* versus *Secretary of State for the Environment* ([1995] 2 All ER 636). In this case the judge pointed out that his predecessors would have had an entirely different situation when faced with planning gain scenarios: he suggested that 20 years ago judges would have expected the public sector to provide most of the infrastructure (roads, etc), where the developer was in effect a free rider on the public purse (Fordham *et al.*,

1998: 267). Now, however, the position had entirely changed, and the developer would be expected to pay for the full impact of his scheme upon the existing community and its facilities. This situation begs the question as to whether a developer should be expected to find funds or a contribution, in some way, to affordable housing development, as well as to the very fundamental physical infrastructure needed at site level.

There is an irony in the historic development of the relationship between social housing and the planning system. For many years at a time when local authorities could more justifiably have asked for social housing contributions, they were debarred from doing so by the courts. Thus local authorities could not use the planning system to fully integrate housing and planning policies. In the case of *Royco Homes* versus *Hillingdon LBC* (1974 QB 720), it was held that local authorities should never try to control tenure, price and ownership by means of their planning powers. This was because (at the time) local authorities gained their powers from separate housing and planning statutes and thus it would be ultra vires (acting outside their powers) if a council were to try to act on housing matters under its planning powers (Fordham, 1998). Thus local authorities could grant planning permission for 'housing' (use) but not control what happened on the site with respect to the tenure of housing built. This and other similar rulings clearly constrained the development of social housing to sites owned or leased by local authorities themselves.

More recently, however, as developers have been gradually asked to provide more by way of physical infrastructure contributions, the legal rulings governing the planning and affordable housing question have been balanced more favourably towards local planning authorities. In a landmark case, *Mitchell* versus *Secretary of State for the Environment* (1994 2PLR 23), Lord Justice Saville stated:

> I cannot accept this argument [that 'cost or type of tenure' cannot form part of a planning purpose]. To my mind there is no discernible distinction to be drawn between a need for housing generally, and a need for particular types of housing, whether or not the latter can be defined in terms of cost, tenure or otherwise.

This type of argument has been influential in determining the thinking behind government policy on the role of the planning system and affordable housing today. Circular 6/98 consolidates to a significant extent, the legal precedents of the 1990s. This states: 'A community's need for affordable housing is a material planning consideration which may properly be taken into account in formulating development plan policies and deciding planning applications' (DETR 1998b, para. 1).

In principle this allows local authorities to include an element of affordable housing in planning policies, although the Circular does not provide authorities with the ability to prescribe housing tenures in an overt way:

> Planning policy should not be expressed in favour of any particular form of tenure. Therefore the terms 'affordable housing' or 'affordable homes' are used in this Circular

to encompass both low-cost market and subsidised housing (irrespective of tenure, ownership – whether exclusive or shard – or financial arrangements) that will be available to people who cannot afford to rent or buy houses generally available on the open market.

(ibid.: para. 4)

Implementing the Circular requires local authorities to take great care. If they overtly prescribe housing tenure then they are acting beyond their powers and developers are not bound to accept their plans. However, they can, via the inclusion of affordable housing in their plan and the use of the findings of a robust local housing needs survey, nevertheless ensure that a range of suitable types of affordable housing become developed.

More recently, DTLR have reviewed the planning and affordable housing question and have suggested a system of 'tariffs' that might provide a more flexible approach to social and economic regeneration. The tariff approach is outlined in the government Green Paper on Planning Obligations (DTLR, 2002b), and is currently under discussion at the time of writing.

Affordable housing development and the role of housing associations

The role of housing associations

Affordable housing in the UK today is predominantly provided by registered social landlords or housing associations. As we have seen earlier in the chapter, this has not always been the case, as local authorities were the main providers and developers up until the mid-1970s.

In practice, the 1974 Housing Act encouraged housing associations to become involved in developing social housing and provided public funding through the Housing Corporation, its governing body. The incoming Conservative Government actively supported this initiative, particularly as it meant that public subsidy could be reduced, and the autonomy of local authorities in housing development be cut. By the early 1990s, housing associations in England were completing 15,000 units per year compared with 8,000 local authority completions. By the end of the decade, housing associations were completing around 20,000 units per annum as compared to only around 300 local authority dwellings.

There are currently over 2,000 housing associations in England, managing around 1.45 million homes. However, about three-quarters of all housing association properties are owned by just 7 per cent of associations (around 150 in total). These associations are also the main developers of new affordable housing, although specialist associations providing for minority groups and those with special needs also play an important part in meeting the full spectrum of housing need. Locally based housing associations can also play a vital part in assisting community regeneration, revitalising run-down estates and meeting specialist local need. Over the past decade around 120 new 'stock transfer associations' (also known as LSVT) have been formed to manage and develop homes transferred to them by local authorities, and more stock transfers are expected in the years ahead with a further number of authorities currently seeking to transfer their stock.

The role of the Housing Corporation

Housing associations are voluntary, 'not for profit' organisations. Some are charitable bodies, others are Industrial and Provident Societies, but there are also trusts, co-operatives and companies. Housing associations are funded and regulated by the Housing Corporation, a non-departmental public body, sponsored by the Office of the Deputy Prime Minister. The Housing Corporation's key aims are to 'regulate and promote a viable, properly governed and properly managed housing association sector, to invest for the creation and maintenance of safe and sustainable communities and to champion a resident focus in the housing association sector' (Housing Corporation, 2002).

Effective regulation by the Housing Corporation is essential both to ensure prudent management and safeguard the £25 billion of public money which has been invested in housing associations since the Corporation was set up in 1964. Its regulatory role is, however, highly significant in helping to lever in private finance, because since 1989 housing associations have been increasingly reliant on private sector finance to complement the subsidies they receive from central government for affordable housing development. Each scheme is financed by a grant from the public purse and a mortgage backed by rental income. The Housing Corporation collects and analyses financial and managerial information on all housing associations, concentrating particularly on those with the largest number of housing units and those with the greatest potential scheme risks.

The Housing Corporation publishes a range of performance indicators for the larger associations. These show their annual performance measured in terms of rental income, vacancy rates, rent collection and target times for responses to repairs. The Corporation also has powers to intervene if an association is believed to be in financial difficulty or if there are serious disagreements within the board or between the board and the executive team. Steps taken range from the replacement of some or all of the board members with personnel nominated by the Housing Corporation to a forced merger of the association with another.

The Corporation can also advise on the level of risk which it believes individual associations should be exposed to and can block projects without Housing Corporation funding if it believes that the risks are unacceptable. Housing associations, therefore, although quasi-independent bodies, are in reality quite tightly controlled with regard to their activities and areas of operation.

The Corporation funds a range of different types of affordable housing development through the associations. These include social rented housing (89 per cent of its programme for 2001–02) and then various forms of low-cost homes for ownership, sheltered housing and supported housing for people with special needs. Funding can be for new-build or purchase and renovation development. A major part of the housing association programme consists of regeneration initiatives (65 per cent in 2001–02) particularly on existing social rented estates. Larger associations owning over 2,500 properties received 64 per cent of the budget programme in 2001–02 and small associations owning fewer than 500 properties received 11 per cent. Black and minority associations received 15 per cent of the rental programme (Ujima, a leading Black and Ethnic Minority (BME) association received £39.1 million, the largest single grant to any association). Total provision in 2001–02 was expected to be 22,850 units (including both new-build and regeneration) and within this total 1,100 units were expected to be in villages with a population below 3,000 inhabitants.

Financing and funding

Housing association development is usually based on a mix of public and private finance. The Housing Act 1988 introduced a system of 'mixed funding'. Prior to this Act, social housing had been wholly funded from the public purse. Under the present regime the housing association raises a mortgage against rental income which covers part of the cost of provision of the dwelling, with the remainder financed by a combination of a grant from either the Housing Corporation or the local authority (commonly known as Social Housing Grant) and possibly an element of subsidy from the housing association's own reserves. The maximum price that the housing association can pay for the property is set by the Housing Corporation using a system of Total Cost Indicators (TCIs). TCIs are set on a borough-by-borough basis and are reviewed annually. A simple worked example of a development costing using the TCI mechanism is given below:

Example of development costing for a two bed 65 m² flat at TCI band B (2000–1)

1   TCI framework

Total Cost Indicator for the flat*	**£85,000**

2   Rental calculation for the housing association

Gross rent per week	£68	
(Therefore) gross rent p.a.	**£3,536**	
Less Management (@ 10 per cent gross rent)		£354
Maintenance (@ 12 per cent gross rent)		£424
Repairs reserve (@ 15 per cent gross rent)		£530
Voids and bad debts (@ 5 per cent gross rent)		£177
Total	**£1,485**	
Net rent therefore	**£2,051**	
The net rent will fund a loan or mortgage of:	**£20,000** **	

3   Capital funding reconciliation:

Grant rate (set via government policy)	
@ 49 per cent of TCI	£42,091
Plus capital loan	£20,000
Total	**£62,091**
Deficit to be funded from registered social landlord (RSL) (£85,000–£62,091)	**£22,909**

* It is important to note that the developer will not normally receive the full TCI cost. It is usual for housing associations to deduct around 10 per cent of the TCI to allow for their own internal costs and overheads.

** £2,051 net rent p.a. would be the amount charged by a private sector lender for a loan of £20,000 at an interest rate of 9 per cent over a period of 25 years.

Land for social housing and social housing providers

Over the past decade, but particularly since 1998, when Circular 6/98 *Planning for Affordable Housing* clarified the use of the planning system to provide afford-able housing, an increasing proportion of the overall supply of land for social housing has come through planning gain (see also previous discussion). It is diffi-cult to assess the full extent of land provided this mechanism. DTLR Housing Investment Programme (HIP) data returns suggest that around 15,000 units per annum are being 'approved' via this route. Not all such approvals will be for social rented housing; some will be for low-cost market sale, and not all approvals will translate into completions in the same year. However, this represents a significant change from previous methods of land procurement which typically involved housing association purchase of local authority land, often at a discount price. It also requires local authorities, housing associations and private developers to work in partnership in an attempt to develop mixed and balanced communities as recom-mended in Circular 6/98 (paragraph 1) and this can at times prove difficult and contentious (Entec UK and Nottingham Trent University, 2001).

Social rented housing is required to be provided to Housing Corporation scheme development standards. These seek to ensure that properties are robust, low maintenance, energy efficient and cost-effective to run. These standards differ from those prevailing in the private market, particularly in terms of floor space (social rented properties tend to be larger than housing sold for sale at the lower end of the market) and quality of fittings and finish (social rented properties tend to be more durable and less visually appealing). Low-cost home ownership properties are not covered by scheme development standards.

Housing association, regeneration and community development

Housing association development takes place against a highly varied regional hous-ing market backdrop. The absolute level of house prices varies greatly and at the

Figure 5.2
House price increases in the UK by
standard region, mid-2001 to mid-2002.
Source: Nationwide Building Society

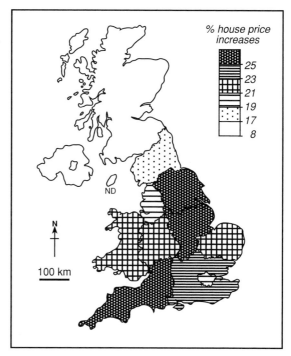

time of writing (2002), house price growth is moving ahead at a far faster rate in some regions than others (see Figure 5.2). The decline of older working-class areas in the North and the Midlands in particular has brought problems for housing associations who had invested heavily in these areas. Low demand is a problem for about two-thirds of housing associations and directly affects 8 per cent of the English housing stock (about 87,000 homes). Although the bulk of the properties affected are in the North and the Midlands, problems of low demand can also be found in the south of England and in parts of Wales and Scotland. Symptoms can include high levels of voids, crime litter, vandalism and anti-social behaviour (Ford and Pawson, 2001; Bramley, 2000). Low demand is a problem for both housing associations and local authorities. Housing associations have sought to address these issues by working in partnership with local authorities and other public sector agencies to develop a range of regeneration initiatives including skills training, provision of small workshops, mixed-use development and provision of additional leisure facilities as well as improvements to properties and the overall environment. The Housing Corporation (2001) has produced a sustainability 'toolkit' which provides guidance on effective methods of renewal and how to gauge their success.

The role of the NHF (National Housing Federation)
Housing associations are represented by the National Housing Federation which provides good practice guidance, undertakes research on housing related issues and

produces annual data on lettings and sales by registered social landlords. This is carried out via a monitoring system known as CORE, administered for many years by the Centre for Housing Policy at the University of York.

Social housing development and provision in Scotland, Wales and Northern Ireland

Housing associations are also the main providers of social housing in Scotland, Wales and Northern Ireland. In Scotland, the regulatory and funding body is Communities Scotland (part of the Scottish Executive). In Wales, social housing is the responsibility of the National Assembly for Wales. In Northern Ireland, social housing development is supervised by the Northern Ireland Housing Executive.

The scale of social housing development is much smaller in Scotland (*c.*5,500 dwellings completed in the financial year 2000–1). In Wales the number of completions is also relatively low (950 dwellings in the same financial year). Over the same period 1,150 units were completed in Northern Ireland.

Developing affordable housing into the future

It is clear from the foregoing discussion that the processes and means of developing housing for those in need have changed significantly since 1945. We have moved from the archetypal 'council housing' through 'social housing' to what we now call 'affordable housing'. This shift mainly results from two key factors. The first factor is a re-interpretation of the concept of 'housing need', where social or affordable housing is now much more highly targeted towards those on low incomes or in greatest need, rather than being built to alleviate mass housing shortage; the second factor is a shift in policy focus towards reducing state subsidies for the development and construction of affordable homes. This latter policy has been implemented to a large extent through the role given to housing associations who have successfully raised significant private finance through the capital markets.

There is now a dilemma in affordable housing development. Using the planning system to intervene in the development process to build affordable housing is not a welcome policy for many people since it represents a return to a form of land taxation which has in the past created many inefficiencies and inequities in the land market. Yet, in the absence of such planning policies, affordable housing will not be developed on a wide enough scale since government is not prepared to put in the level of subsidies that it has done in the past. It is thus important that the problem is attacked from several directions:

> The potential demand for social housing (low-cost for sale and subsidised rented) across the UK over the next 20 years is likely to be considerable – or, at least, exceed the level of current and recent supply. The planning system will play a pivotal role in meeting demand both through effective land assembly and the creation of land subsidy where appropriate. However, it is widely acknowledged that, given the weight of demand, land use planning is no substitute for adequate funding. This must come in the form of

contingent subsidy for planning-led policies and more general funding for a wider social-housing strategy.

(Gallent, 2000: 142).

Since the market will not provide for all households, government is currently left debating the merits of bolstering the planning for affordable housing policy thrust and/or devoting more taxpayers' money into new affordable development. Many of policy problems might be solved via a better understanding of the supply–demand relationships between the new and existing 'markets' for affordable housing. In many areas of the country, the level of voids is very high, and housing is falling into disrepair. Much of the most recent policy thrust has instead been directed towards those areas of the country, and in particular London and the South East, where housing surpluses hardly evidenced.

Nevertheless, there are still pockets of over-supply and voids even in areas of high demand such as the South East and Greater London. This makes it even more important that policies are in place to allow local authorities and developers to select appropriate solutions for specific locations. There remain, however, significant problems with leading policy guidance: the exhortation to develop mixed communities in PPG3 is not easily reconciled with, for example, Circular 6/98, which does not encourage payments-in-lieu, having the capacity to re-direct funding between new and existing affordable housing schemes and locations. Threshold policies create particular problems on smaller sites for achieving a balanced development mix and there are still reservations about the workability of a tariff system.

Against the backdrop of these issues, the debate about how best to develop affordable housing is likely to rage for some considerable time to come.

Discussion points

1   Define what is meant by 'social housing' and describe its main forms in the light of changes in government policy.
2   Outline the major reasons for the failure of high-rise social housing development. Evaluate the possibilities for a return to this form of house-building.
3   Discuss the case for using the planning system to deliver affordable housing.
4   Explain the roles of the Housing Corporation and its relationship with the housing associations.
5   Discuss the hypothesis that the approach to social housing development has become more efficient and more equitable over time.

Key reading

The definitive government document is Circular 06/98, *Planning and Affordable Housing* (DETR, 1998b). Recent text books exploring subsidised housing include Reeves, *An Introduction to Social Housing* (1996) and Harriott and Matthews, *Social Housing: An Introduction* (1998). A key article from the development perspective is Gallent, 'Planning and affordable housing' (*Town Planning Review*, 2000).

Part Three

Steps in the Housing Development Process

Chapter 6

Planning and land acquisition

Ron Blake and Paul Collins

Introduction

This chapter deals with two activities crucial to the release of land for housing: the statutory regulation of land use, and the business of acquiring sites to build houses on. In the house-building industry these activities are known respectively as 'planning' and 'land-buying' (or acquisition). Together they represent a pivotal stage in the development process where 'floating' demand for homes is systematically 'shifted' into specific geographical spaces through professional decision making. Traditionally, planning and land acquisition were fairly distinct activities, involving local government officials and private-practice surveyors in a frequently adversarial relationship. Planning was characterised as excessively bureaucratic and surveying as unashamedly commercial. With the maturing of each profession there has been positive convergence, creating a more seamless process in which land acquisition and land-use regulation are mutually reinforcing. It is now widely accepted by planners that the creation of a good built environment requires a grasp of market behaviour, while developers have come to appreciate that commercial success depends on an awareness of public infrastructure, environmental capacity and social capital. In reviewing each sector in sequence, emphasis is placed on the historical drivers of change, current professional responsibilities and the key techniques employed to bring land forward and make it ready for housing development.

Fundamentals of planning

Ideological, philosophical and visionary perspectives

To the developer 'planning' means 'town and country planning' as defined by successive Acts of Parliament. Planning's distinctive focus is on the use of land and buildings, including intensification of use and changes in appearance. Developers habitually use 'planning' as shorthand for 'planning permission', as witnessed in advertisements for building plots 'with planning' or 'subject to planning'. The employment of planning methodologies by manufacturers and business corporations has provoked town and country planners to adopt the more specific term 'land-use planning', although this rarely appears in the titles of statutes, departments or reports. 'Environmental planning,' with connotations of global and rural issues, is popular in academe but tends to be avoided in the context of house-building operations. The continental alternative of 'spatial planning' has been slow to gain acceptance in Britain although it now figures in 'joined-up' strategies for Greater London and Wales. In defence of their role planners have long made the point that one householder's environmental gain from a new or improved dwelling may well signify a loss of amenity for neighbours. This hypothetical situation has connections with chaos theory, whereby small incremental changes reverberate through a system with disproportionate and unpredictable results. The certainty provided by a publicly accountable land-use plan, supported by consistently applied development controls, may be seen as a social freedom outweighing the traditional right of the individual to develop land anywhere and in any manner.

Since the Second World War British planning has been concerned overwhelmingly with rectifying the negative effects of the two most massive waves of development in modern times: Victorian industrialisation and inter-war suburbanisation. While propelled by economic growth, and adding many positive features to the landscape, both waves were achieved in the absence of strategic land-use policies and only limited controls over the quality of building. Moreover, despite the fact that post-war planning has adopted an increasingly pro-active agenda, a preventive role dedicated to avoiding a repetition of past mistakes still figures prominently in its philosophy today. Planning is thereby 'interventionist' in spirit, using land-use regulation as a mechanism for shifting power from commercial, corporate and landed interest to the general community, not least to the economically and socially excluded. Redistribution of opportunity can be achieved through taxation, levy, licensing and the statutory protection of amenity, all of which carry penalties for non-compliance. Planning's re-distributive stance redefines the urban and rural environments as a 'public good' for all sectors of the community to enjoy. A well designed individual dwelling and a conveniently laid-out housing scheme differ only in scale and may be seen as microcosms of a well structured town or region. 'Transferability' of skills between spatial scales is stressed in planning education and is pertinent to house-building practice.

As well as being socially re-distributive, planning has always endeavoured to facilitate the provision of infrastructure so that the industries and businesses upon which society depends can thrive. In addition to water, power, transport and telecommunications, housing itself can be considered as infrastructure. The sustainability of London's present economy depends critically on the availability of land for appropriate and affordable housing delivered through the planning system. At a deeper level, public support for town planning lies in the fear of civil unrest that has haunted British politicians for two centuries. Thus while planning can take some credit for facilitating the general rise in living standards, its may also be seen as a plank in the upholding of democracy, social cohesion, culture and tradition.

Since the early 1970s British planning has become enmeshed in global debates concerning the Earth's diminishing natural resources and threatened habitats. 'Spatial comprehensiveness' – the synthesis of town and country and their constituent land uses – is fundamental to the holistic design advocated by Ebenezer Howard and carried forward in the 1930s by L. D. Stamp and others who used field evidence to highlight threats to agriculture, wildlife and the countryside. This dimension of planning has now been incorporated into the wider goal of sustainable development (World Commission on Environment and Development, 1987). A final key characteristic of planning is its co-ordinating role. Planners today have to consider a range of concerns of almost infinite complexity and challenge. This explains the widespread misunderstanding of, and occasionally hostility towards, planning's key endeavours and its apparent tardiness in making decisions.

Public health and municipal engineering origins

The close association between planning and housing began in the 1830s as a response to epidemics of cholera, a water-borne fever that claimed tens of thousands of lives in English industrial cities. In 1842 a Manchester lawyer and poor law commissioner, Edwin Chadwick (1800–90), produced a report on the sanitary conditions of the labouring population including a call for reforms in the design and construction of mass housing. The resultant Public Health Act of 1848 set higher standards for drainage, ventilation and lighting in new dwellings although it was advisory and not universally adopted. Several decades passed before significant further legislation was enacted, the most notable being the Public Health Act of 1875 which required rear gardens to be provided and roads to be of certain minimum widths. The latter act signalled an important progression in thinking from the dwelling as simply a built form to being one element in overall living space inclusive of the external ground environment.

These improvements applied almost exclusively to new development, leaving existing areas in a generally poor condition. Thoughts therefore turned to more radical ways of preventing urban problems from occurring in the first place. Howard's garden city model provided one possible solution, based on the allocation of green space around each individual dwelling. The high-rise designs of the Swiss architect, Le Corbusier (1887–1965) offered a radical alternative whereby residents could enjoy stunning views across parkland and have access to many of their daily necessities under the cover of a large 'unitary' building. Though polar opposites, both visually and in terms of their micro-environmental organisation, these two approaches to towns of the future were driven by a similar missionary zeal to provide communities with an infinitely more habitable living space than was available to the mass of the population around the close of the nineteenth century. The problem of how to acquire land for new urban settlements was common to both scenarios, while the differences in design revolved around the question of whether residents would be better served by having green space directly attached to their homes, or provided as roof gardens and sweeping parks served by rapid public transport (Hall, 1992).

In practice most urban improvements during the late-nineteenth and early-twentieth centuries consisted of municipal parks, suburban railway extensions and progressively lower-density housing lacking the community facilities and integrated management envisaged for garden cities. The post-Second World War new towns programme created a number of 'balanced' communities with a planned relationship between housing and jobs and exemplary road design, landscaping and neighbourhood centres. In existing urban areas the principal municipal legacy of visionary planners has been the residential tower block together with its notoriously undefended ground space (see Fig. 2.2, p. 24). It is in this area of social provision that planning, housing and municipal engineering have the least creditable record, although critics rarely mention the strict cost yardsticks imposed by government on local authorities to meet house-building targets.

Evolution of town planning and related legislation

The first statute to bear the word 'planning' was the Housing and Town Planning Act 1909 which permitted local councils to draw up 'schemes' for areas under pressure from new housing development. This provision was not obligatory and most councils were reluctant to take advantage of it for fear of having to compensate unco-operative land-owners. After the First World War (1914–18) the Housing and Town Planning Act 1919 extended the scope of planning by allowing councils to prepare schemes for land under pressure of any kind, making it compulsory for all boroughs and urban districts with more than 20,000 inhabitants to do so, and enabling two or more local authorities to prepare schemes jointly. Interim measures were introduced to minimise bogus compensation claims, but a lack of trained staff combined with cuts in public expenditure prevented much progress being made. Because district councils (the designated planning authorities throughout the inter-war period) were slow to draw schemes up, the Local Government Act 1929 gave powers to county councils to perform the planning function on districts' behalf. The Town and Country Planning Act 1932 then extended the scope of planning to land already developed and to land unlikely to be developed, heralding a commitment to spatially comprehensive plans, case-by-case development control and planning agreements. While this hinted at a more systematic approach to land-use problems, national responsibility for planning policy remained with the Ministry of Health while locally the town clerk and engineer dealt with planning matters.

The greatest impetus to the creation of a comprehensive planning system was the Second World War (1939–45). During the campaign resource allocation of every kind was tightly regulated by a coalition government, but fewer than three-quarters of local authorities in England and Wales had resolved to prepare a planning scheme and most lacked the experience to administer development control. To address this deficiency the Town and Country Planning Act 1943 allowed for the appointment of a special minister 'charged with the duty of securing consistency and continuity in the framing and execution of a national policy with respect to the use and development of land throughout England and Wales'. A parallel statute, the Town and Country Planning (Interim Development) Act 1943, extended controls over the whole county, thereby incorporating areas that had not been part of any local planning scheme on the eve of war.

When peace returned in 1945 the newly elected Labour Government embarked on an historic programme of reforms that included agricultural subsidies, a national health service, nationalisation of the railways and numerous other measures that were to shape British life in the early post-war decades (Hennessy, 1992). Among the enabling legislation was the Town and Country Planning Act 1947, arguably the most far-reaching statute in the history of development control anywhere up to that time. Key differences between the 1947 Act and its pre-war counterpart were that planning was now obligatory everywhere in Britain and no local authority could delay submitting a plan indefinitely. The new-Act incorporated essential ideas from the Barlow, Scott and Uthwatt expert reports and the seminal 1942 report *The Control of Land Use*. Development plans defined in the Act were required henceforth to reach Whitehall (national headquarters of the civil service) within five years of the 'appointed day' (1 July 1948) and would be scrutinised against common guidelines drawn up by staff at the planning ministry. Local authorities were required to conduct a range of surveys before formulating their plan and to allocate land in five-year phases over a twenty-year period. Ministerial approval was required for the plan to become operative and provision was made for modifications based on local objections.

Allocations in the 1947-style plans conferred no automatic right to build on land, or change its use, as the state now owned that right. Fulfilment of the plan had to be via individual planning permissions that the relevant local authority could either grant or refuse using the plan as a benchmark. To this end the Act was amplified with special instruments defining the parameters of 'development' and, unlike the pre-war situation, no compensation was payable for a refusal of planning permission. Ownership of land was not affected and its existing use was protected in law, unless a new activity caused nuisance. Where land was rendered incapable of beneficial use because of the plan, e.g. on the line of a proposed road, the owner could serve a purchase notice on the authority. The 1947 Act also empowered councils to declare Comprehensive Development Areas (CDA) for dealing with war damage and obsolete structures holding up reconstruction, including powers of compulsory purchase.

Within 20 years the 1947 system had already become unwieldy. In 1964 a Planning Advisory Group (PAG) was set up to explore possible modifications and concluded in a radical report (Ministry of Housing and Local Government, 1965) that existing development plans were ill-equipped to deal with the challenges of population growth, rising motor-car ownership, new leisure patterns and the property boom. Accordingly, the Town and Country Planning Act 1968 introduced a two-tier framework of land-use regulation, distinguishing between strategic and tactical issues. This idea was consolidated through the Town and Country Planning Act 1971 in anticipation of a major organisation of local government.

The ensuing Local Government Act 1972 created a two-tier pattern of councils with planning represented at both levels. The mid-1970s saw an unsuccessful attempt to recoup profits from land deals to pay for infrastructure (Community Land Act 1975). Symptomatic of the Conservatives' return to power in 1979 was the Local Government and Land Act 1980 which introduced Urban Development Corporations (UDC), a controversial area-based policy that allegedly undermined local accountability while failing to deliver affordable housing (Ambrose, 1986). As part of a general assault on local democracy, the Local Government Act 1985 abolished the Greater London Council (created in 1963) and six Metropolitan County Councils (created in 1974), depriving conurbations of a strategic level of planning. The Housing and Planning Act 1986 introduced 'simplified planning zones' in an attempt to stimulate regeneration by lifting the so-called 'burden' of planning.

One of the unforeseen consequences of reducing the role of strategic planning during the 1980s was an increase in the number of appeals lodged by private housing developers who found themselves in conflict with local councils hamstrung by out-of-date plans. An overhaul of planning legislation was therefore put in motion by the enlightened environment secretary, Michael Heseltine. This change of mood resulted in two new Acts that have remained the basis of plan-making and development control. The Town and Country Planning Act 1990 preserved the spirit and structure of the 1947 Act and with its two parallel acts – the Planning (Listed Buildings and Conservation Areas) Act 1990 and the Planning (Hazardous Substances) Act 1990 – acknowledged the rising importance of environmental concerns. Matters left out of this trio were swiftly incorporated into the Planning and Compensation Act 1991, stipulating that all land-use decisions should be 'plan-led' and that 'executive agencies' such as English Heritage should have a stronger involvement in plan and policy formulation.

The implication of planning's core provisions being divided between several Acts is one factor in Labour's current perception that the planning system requires a further overhaul after 30 years of tinkering. Proposals for a change were published in 2001 but put on hold in May 2002 due to a Cabinet re-shuffle that reallocated responsibilities for transport, planning, housing and urban regeneration. Specific issues in the reform of planning will be reviewed later in this chapter following a discussion of the status quo.

Current responsibilities for planning

There is still a deep-seated confusion among the general public about what planning is and who is responsible for it. Development, particularly house-building on open land, is widely attributed by the media to 'the planners' without differentiation between those who commission, finance, provide land for, approve, construct or purchase it. In reality the character of any building activity is the product of socio-economic demand, entrepreneurial initiative and public services engineering, duly moderated by all kinds of pressure groups with contrasting motives for supporting or opposing development. It is important therefore to identify the centres in which planning's key functions are carried out, to summarise how these centres operate within the overall process of land-use regulation, and to elucidate how housing issues relate to the aims of planning.

British planning's multi-layered and hierarchical structure is crucial to the understanding of housing development. There are five levels at which building and land-use activities are administered, ranging from the supranational to the civil parish. Transfers of responsibility have occurred between these tiers, involving both upward and downward movements for planning and housing. When Labour regained power in 1997 planning was assigned to a new Department of the Environment, Transport and the Regions (DETR). Following the party's re-election in June 2001 DETR became part of the Department for Transport, Local Government and the Regions (DTLR), losing its rural and global functions to the former agricultural ministry now expanded under the acronym DEFRA (Department for the Environment, Food and Rural Affairs). Many in the land-based professions regretted this split, and the lost opportunity to restore the words 'Planning' and 'Housing' to Cabinet. In May 2002, responsibility for local government and regional affairs was transferred to the Office of the Deputy Prime Minister (ODPM), a significant loss of identity.

Supranational government

There is much concern in Britain about surrendering monetary policy to the European Union (EU), the influence of the US and Japan over manufacturing and the general effects of globalisation on the nation's way of life. The extent to which these external influences make their mark on the environment is mixed. Farming bears the clear hallmarks of the Common Agricultural Policy (CAP) but is counterbalanced by a host of environmental directives, e.g. the challenge to major road proposals designed to relieve town residents of heavy through traffic. The doctrine of sustainability propounded at the Rio Earth Summit in 1992 is now implicit in construction standards, employment law, transport policy and much else. There is an EU directive requiring that an Environmental Impact Assessment (EIA) be carried out for certain major development proposals. Under the Treaty of Maastricht 1992 the principle of 'subsidiarity' declared that public functions should be carried out at the lowest appropriate level consistent with efficient management. While agriculture, habitat protection and pollution control are acknowledged as transcending national boundaries, the provision of non-linear infrastructure such as housing and community facilities is considered to be best achieved at local level. Town and country planning, with its site-specific and negotiating culture, is not therefore a primary focus of supranational administration. As an island nation Britain is less likely to be affected by cross-frontier economic planning issues than Scandinavia or the Low Countries for example. It remains to be seen whether convergence or divergence in planning systems becomes the predominant trend as the European Union grows in extent and moves towards a regional structure. Either way it seems improbable that either land-use planning, housing provision or design control will assume a more supranational character.

Central government

Neither housing provision nor land-use planning has ever been a primarily central government function in Britain. Despite advocacy for a 'central planning agency' parliament in wartime conferred the responsibility for plan-making and development control on local authorities. This reflected a political consensus that democracy and social stability were best served by leaving decisions about property in the hands of locally elected councils. To avoid the problems inherent in a patchwork of unco-ordinated and potentially conflicting plans, the 1947 Act secured a basic consistency of approach by carefully framing regulations, guidelines and inspection regimes. However, planning problems such as coastal erosion are best tackled when local authorities are informed about the wider picture in other areas. A crucial function of central government is therefore the framing of common guidelines on recurrent planning issues based on collected experience. By this mechanism councils are spared unnecessary legal and research costs while their communities gain a better environment through the incorporation of 'best practice' into planning decisions. Central government has a dual responsibility of ensuring that wasteful practices are minimised and that no local authority is forced to react in ignorance to challenges that could have been predicted and prevented.

Equally important, central government has an overarching role to ensure that every planning procedure conforms to the law. The term 'central government' comprises three elements: parliament (elected members and peers), civil servants and the boards and officials of centrally appointed agencies. Each element requires a grip on relevant legislation and is responsible for scrutinising the performance of all local authorities and other agencies. New and amended acts must be steered through both Houses of Parliament which involves inputs from planning lawyers. Recent governments have tended to introduce legislation through explanatory 'green papers', followed by the more traditional 'white paper' that sets out the parameters of the proposed reform. The purpose of this sequence is to give plenty of time for consultation and feedback, although the rigid distinction between green and white papers has become blurred (Cullingworth and Nadin, 2002).

The history of post-war planning abounds with government circulars (e.g. DoE, 1980c), advice notes, orders, statutory instruments and commissioned studies on all manner of environmental issues. Over the past two decades the core content of these documents has been consolidated into a suite of Planning Policy Guidance Notes (colloquially abbreviated to PPGs) that now constitute the government's definitive body of advice on land-use matters. By far the most influential guidance for house-builders is PPG3 *Housing*, first published in 1992 and revised in 2000 to incorporate rapidly evolving ideas on living space. There are now more than twenty different PPGs, those most closely related to housing being PPG2 *Green Belts* (1995) and PPG25 *Development and Flood Risk* (2001). There is also a suite of Minerals Planning Guidance (MPG) that indirectly affects the residential environment because mineral reserves can constrict housing expansion while mineral extraction can threaten visual amenity, air quality, rural tranquillity, road safety and riparian property values. A third suite of government advice notes, Regional Planning Guidance (RPG), contains the government's future allocation of new dwellings for each region.

Inspection is a long-standing role of the planning civil servant and takes place in three key arenas: (1) the adoption of plans, (2) the framing of planning policy guidance and (3) development control. In the first arena, an inspector is appointed to preside over each local development plan inquiry, hearing objections and gathering information before recommending to the Secretary of State whether the plan should be approved or amended. In the second, because of the volume of housing allocations, inspectors have presided over inquiries into RPG and PPGs. In the third, an inspector acts as an arbiter where planning permission has been refused and the developer elects to appeal to central authority for reconsideration. In the context of development control, a major application may be 'called-in' by the minister to ascertain whether it conforms with PPG and other material considerations. A plan itself may also be called in where a local planning authority appears to be in breach of government guidelines.

A final role of central government relevant to housing and planning is the Commissioner for Administration, or 'Ombudsman' (a Scandinavian tradition of grievance resolution). Under the Local Government Act 1974, a Parliamentary Commissioner for Administration may investigate cases of maladministration allegedly caused by a planning inspector, while a Local Commissioner for Administration may investigate allegations against a local government official. Grounds for compensation must relate strictly to the administrative aspects of the matter, e.g. unreasonable delay, poor communication or misleading advice.

Regional government

Britain still has no effective tier of regional government. The rationale for regional planning is the disparity in economic success between those regions experiencing intense development pressures and those suffering the effects of structural decline. From a housing perspective the regional problem is manifest in acute shortages of accommodation in 'pressure' areas and embarrassing surpluses in 'problem' areas. The 'planning' solution has traditionally been to divert jobs and infrastructure projects to regions where labour and housing are in abundance, for example by issuing or withholding industrial development certificates (Distribution of Industry Act 1945). There was no post-war provision for elected regional councils and all subsequent measures for reversing regional imbalances have been administrative compromises by one or other of the two main political parties. Regional planning focused on the redistribution of opportunity *between* regions and the redistribution of opportunity *within* regions. Abercrombies's *Greater London Plan* used new towns and the green belt to redistribute housing development within the metropolitan region.

Regional thinking has never been completely abandoned however. As early as 1962 the Conservative Ministry of Housing and Local Government set up a

Manchester office to administer the massive slum clearance programmes for the north of England. On re-election in 1964 the Labour Government of Harold Wilson embarked upon a programme of legislation to assist industry to relocate in disadvantaged regions with inducements such as advanced factory units, subsidised training places and grants for the reclamation of derelict land. Major economic studies were produced for each English region, although specific housing requirements were not included in any of the reports. By the late 1970s it was widely felt that the multiplicity of regional funding regimes was making little impact and that market-led regeneration of the inner-urban areas was a more important strategic goal. It was partly on that premise that the Conservatives were re-elected in 1979 and have remained ideologically opposed to giving additional power to the regions. Another decade passed before a comprehensive assessment of housing needs at a regional scale was undertaken.

In 1989 Regional Planning Guidance (RPG) was given separate identity, reversing the flagging commitment of the first two Thatcher administrations to macro-spatial housing policy. Government Offices for the Regions (GOR) were established in 1994 to co-ordinate the various civil service departments and facilitate the levering in of European and private sector funds for regeneration. In the remaining years of the Conservatives' long stint in power the Department of the Environment, under secretary of state John Gummer, showed increased commitment to a co-ordinated approach to regional problems, but still fell short of advocating regional elected councils. New Labour's return to power in 1997 marked the beginning of the current political agenda to strengthen regional planning. The creation of a Scottish Parliament and assemblies for Wales (and Northern Ireland) established a precedent for devolved government in the UK, and subsequently the Greater London Authority (GLA) has assumed executive responsibility for planning and housing in the capital. Pressure for elected regional assemblies seems to be strongest far away from London, particularly the North East and Cornwall. Predictably, enthusiasm for regional government is weakest in southern, eastern and central England where voters tend to resent the prospect of an additional tier of control paid for out of income tax.

As an interim measure Regional Development Agencies (RDAs) were set up under legislation in 1998, with a remit to improve business efficiency, manage EU financial assistance and consolidate existing development programmes in rural areas. The eight RDAs are currently answerable to the secretary of state for Trade and Industry and received an increased annual budget of £2 billion in the Chancellor's July 2002 spending review. RDAs are centrally appointed bodies comprising members co-opted from industry, local authorities and education. The fact that they are not democratically accountable has attracted widespread criticism, reinforced by allegations that they duplicate the role of the GORs and county structure plans. An argument deployed in the RDAs' favour is that their functions will be transferred down from central government and not wrested from local authorities.

A number of moves have been made to popularise regional planning at grassroots level. East Midlands Development Agency (EMDA), for example, is poised to take over some of the housing, planning, transport and economic assistance responsibilities from the Government Office for the East Midlands (GOEM) and has facilitated cross-fertilisation of policy by co-locating with several other agencies in a Nottingham office complex. More widely, RPG notes are to be drafted by consortia of the relevant local authorities, GORs and RDAs and an Examination in Public (EIP) is to be held along similar lines to those for structure plan adoption. Planning strategies for emergent sub-regions such as the Thames Gateway (bringing together east London, south Essex and north Kent) should in principle be easier to frame through a regional approach.

Local government

As indicated, the principal focus of land-use planning and housing provision in Britain is the local authority (also referred to below as municipal council or simply 'council'). For the student of housing development this tier can be confusing because there have been several re-structurings of local government over the past two centuries, involving changes to local area boundaries, county and district names, administrative terminology and the level at which particular roles are performed. As well as being interesting from an historical perspective, the fluid nature of British local government has had a particular impact on housing and planning. In England there are three types of local authority: county, district and unitary. In Wales and Scotland there are only unitary councils while in Northern Ireland there are only districts. These differences make it difficult to generalise about planning arrangements across the UK, although the basic philosophy and approaches to land-use control are much the same everywhere. This mixed pattern is the fruit of comprehensive local government re-organisation in the 1970s, the abolition of the Greater London Council and six English metropolitan councils in the 1980s, and the twin political agendas of devolution and increasing the number of unitary councils in the English shires in the 1990s (see Cullingworth and Nadin, 2002). A chronology of important local government changes is embodied in Appendix A of this book.

Over the past two decades the general two-tier system of local government crystallised in late Victorian times has been reduced to a single-tier system except in England's more rural shires. A few county councils such as Norfolk have remained unaltered since the mid-1970s and continue to provide transportation and education services for their whole geographical area including the County town. Most county councils however lost one or more of their urban areas to unitary status as an outcome of the 'English review' started in 1996. Unitary councils perform all local government services within their area, including strategic planning, even where a tight administrative boundary would make a county-wide approach more logical. For this reason various *ad hoc* arrangements have been put in place locally to address planning issues that straddle boundaries.

County councils, with depleted but specialised planning staffs, frame strategic land-use policy and deal with planning applications for minerals, waste, countryside and recreation matters. District councils, of which there are typically about half a dozen per shire county, are responsible for drawing up a district-wide land-use plan and dealing with all other planning applications. District councils are also building control, housing provisions and environmental health authorities – three functions closely allied to planning. Because of their experience of small-scale case-work, the districts have recently been made responsible for community development initiatives required by government as part of the urban regeneration programme. This function could lead to the formation of more unitary authorities as districts are amalgamated.

Finally, the role of civil parishes deserves mention. Although parish councils have no statutory powers in planning or housing, they have the right to be consulted on planning applications, on the formulation of development plans, and in the preparation of their own village plan. 'Town councils' (not to be confused with the pre-1974 borough councils and urban district councils) have the same set of rights and responsibilities in the urbanised communities. The residents of Wollaton, a former village now engulfed by Nottingham's suburbs, recently voted by a large margin against having a separate council because they preferred planning matters to be handled by their elected members on the City Council.

Executive agencies and ad hoc bodies

There are more than a thousand other agencies that perform functions relating to land use, housing developments, housing provision and the environment. Though indirectly accountable to ministers, these have a degree of independence that distinguishes them from civil service departments. Names familiar to the planning practitioner include the Countryside Agency, the Environment Agency, English Heritage, English Nature, English Partnerships and the Coal Authority, all of which are 'statutory consultees' in plan-making and the development control processes. A wide range of research institutes in receipt of government funding, e.g. the Building Research Establishment and the Centre for Ecology and Hydrology, also fall within this category. As politicians have striven to reduce the size of the public sector the number of quasi-autonomous, non-governmental organisations (quangos) has increased. Their advice is essential to the resolution of planning problems and their effect on housing development is considerable. National organisations not in receipt of regular government funding also play an important part in framing environmental policy relevant to housing. These comprise well known charitable bodies such as the Civic Trust, the National Trust and the Royal Society for the Protection of Birds. Pressure groups such as the Council for the Protection of Rural England and the Town and Country Planning Association are routinely consulted on housing matters, as are professional bodies such as RICS and RTPI. In the construction sector there are independent bodies such as the House Builders Federation and the National House-Building Council who serve the industry on a semi-commercial basis, sustained by subscription and reputation. Around the country there are hundreds of civic societies and wildlife trusts that are also self-financing and operate under the umbrellas of national federations. It is customary for local planning authorities to consult these bodies during plan-making and development control, and many practising planners and employees of house-building companies are private members.

Consultancy

An increasing volume of planning work is carried out by private consultants working either for companies, as individuals or in academic institutions. In the early days of planning it was customary for new towns to be designed by architectural consultants, for example Sir Frederick Gibberd (Harlow), because there was then limited design expertise in the public sector. The celebrated economist-planner Nathanial Lichfield specialised during the 1960s in cost-benefit analysis for town expansion schemes. Today, major reports are more likely to be concerned with social policy analysis in support of government initiatives. The universities are playing an increasing part in consultancy of this kind and regularly provide expert witnesses before parliamentary committees. This increase began in the 1980s when the Conservative government's attempts to reduce the influence of planning on the housing and property markets led to an escalation in the number of planning appeals simultaneously with reductions in staffing levels in council planning departments. As a result a sizeable proportion of the planning profession became skilled independent consultants and there are now many more companies doing planning consultancy than was the case 30 years ago. Much of their casework is concerned with obtaining planning permission and lodging appeals on behalf of frustrated developers, but there is an expanding sector specialising in pro-active research concerned with urban conservation, regeneration, sustainable development and housing needs.

Development plans

A 'development plan' consists of a group of statutory and non-statutory documents setting out the future land-use framework for a local area. Due to changes in planning legislation and the structure of local government, development plans are currently of three types: Structure Plans (SP), Local Plans (LP) and Unitary Development Plans (UDP). The operational relationship between these is complicated by the fact that local government is structured differently across the UK. In areas where two-tier administration survives there is a vertical relationship between plan types, whereas unitary plans can only have a horizontal relationship with structure or district plans. For the achievement of a coherent national land-use framework special planning arrangements between individual counties and unitaries are increasingly the norm.

Structure plans

In England and Wales the two-tier planning system requires a County Structure Plan to set the strategic framework for local plans. The Lake District and the Peak District National Parks are also Structure Planning (SP) authorities. 'County matters' to be included in SPs include population distribution, employment location, communications, recreation, tourism, natural resources and countryside protection. An SP must also contain a minerals plan and a waste treatment plan as these are regarded by government as strategic issues. The literal plan is limited to a 'key diagram' containing no specific land allocations other than broad zones such as green belts and heritage coastlines. The SP acts as a filter by which housing allocations handed down to each county by the GOR are distributed between the constituent districts. All SP policies are spelt out in a 'written statement' which has to justify the proposed scale of growth and restraint in terms of external socio-economic trends, government guidelines and geo-environmental events such defence base closures or flooding.

Since 1991 Structure Plans have no longer had to be formally approved by the secretary of state. County councils are now responsible for adopting their own plan but must hold an Examination in Public (EIP) where the Secretary of State can intervene if necessary. The status of the SP has not been diminished by this change and the quality of input from government departments and agencies remains high, particularly in expansive counties such as Devon where co-ordination of the districts is difficult because of distance. House-builders have a special interest in SPs because county matters set parameters for strategic land-buying and marketing. A practical problem of SPs is that they take a considerable time to review because of their wide scope and need for constant research. It is therefore common for a county strategy to be out of date when local districts are embarking on their own plan reviews. Hampshire and West Sussex have repeatedly challenged central government over the high numbers of new houses they are expected to accommodate, with inevitable repercussions for the district councils.

Local plans

Since the 1991 Act every district, borough or city council is required to prepare a single district-wide 'local' plan. Previously many second-tier authorities had concentrated their efforts on 'action plans' covering specific sub-areas. Under current arrangements a local plan comprises a 'written statement' covering all matters pertinent to the improvement of the physical environment including management of traffic, and a 'proposals map' based on the Ordnance Survey (OS). No particular scale is prescribed, but for built-up areas a 1: 10,000 base (akin to the old 'six-inch' Town Map) is normal while for peri-urban areas the 1: 25,000 (Pathfinder scale) is appropriate. In extensive rural areas the 1: 50,000 (Landranger) scale is more appropriate because any larger scale would make the maps unwieldy. To facilitate the depiction of detailed proposals it is standard practice to include a number of 'inset' maps at an appropriately larger scale than the district-wide map.

Regulations concerning content are embodied in PPG12. In outline, a local plan must be in broad conformity with the current Structure Plan, all detailed proposals must be supported by reasoned justification, and all sites earmarked for new development or redevelopment must be given an alphanumeric code e.g. H1.7 (see Figure 6.1). Stylistically, it is practice to show extensive use zones in pale tones and key sites in striking colours for legibility. Areas where no significant changes are envisaged are left uncoloured, provoking the observation that local plans are not spatially comprehensive in the strictest sense. Local plans are not meant to be master plans, and 'blank' areas may well yield sites for development as a consequence of socio-economic change. In these circumstances the planning authority can invoke written policy to find an acceptable successor use.

Allocating sufficient land for housing, employment and recreation involves forecasts derived from the structure plan and space standards embodied in PPGs. 'Allocated' housing sites are quantified in the written statement by hectarage and number of units. However, a proportion of the overall target provision is 'unallocated' in anticipation of 'windfalls', i.e. sites that become unexpectedly available due to industrial and institutional change beyond the control of the local authority (Council for the Protection of Rural England, 1988). Statistics presented in local plans can therefore be rather confusing as they also include completions and current commitments that must be deducted from the overall 'plan period' allocation.

Adoption of local plans involves two formal stages to give maximum opportunity for public participation. Initial draft proposals are sent out for consultation to key bodies identified in PPGs. The draft plan is then deposited for public inspection at municipal offices and libraries for six weeks during which time written objections and comments are received and considered. Negotiations take place with objectors, and a revised plan is drawn up incorporating reasonable amendments. To resolve outstanding disagreements a public inquiry is held and presided over by an inspector appointed by the Secretary of State. In due course the inspector's report is also placed on public deposit and the local authority must make necessary modifications before formally adopting the plan. Members of the public have a right of appeal to the High Court where a major planning principle has been left unresolved, and the Secretary of State may 'call in' the plan where he perceives an issue with wider implications. While required by statute, local plans in themselves are not legally binding documents and are always negotiable in the light of 'other material considerations' relevant to land use and the environment. In practice the 'plan-led' system ensures that the local community exerts a strong influence on the location, siting and character of housing development.

Unitary development plans

In single-tier authorities no physical policy framework is imposed from above. To solve this problem a Unitary Development Plan (UDP) must include a Part 1 devoted to county matters such as transportation and waste disposal and a Part 2 dealing with the more site-specific issues found in a district plan. Because most unitary authorities in England are fairly built-up the mapping conventions are similar to those in a district plan. UDPs have existed in London and the six metropolitan counties since 1985 but the creation of many more unitary authorities in the late 1990s has complicated inter-authority relationships, e.g. in Berkshire where the new UDPs have an extensive rural component. In Nottingham, which has a tight administrative boundary and is ringed by a two-tier system, the current Plan Review is being conducted in close collaboration with the Nottinghamshire Structure Plan to eliminate possible conflicts of policy inherent in a mixed-mode administrative framework (Nottingham City Council, 2001).

Development control

In a mixed economy with a strong market sector, the great majority of building operations and land-use changes are initiated by private and non-governmental agencies (Brotherton, 1992). With the exception of sensitive military installations, all development proposals come under the scrutiny of planning authorities who are obliged to make clear decisions on a case-by-case basis. Development control is the process whereby local planning authorities ensure that any new building, extension to a building or change of use is acceptable in terms of location, design and impact on the environment. Local authority consent to develop is known as 'planning permission'. Applications are decided by a committee of elected councillors, or by officers with delegated powers where proposals are simple and straightforward. Because every plot of land or building is geographically unique, the scope for making decisions on a completely routine basis is limited. Development control is therefore characteristically time-consuming due to the need to inspect sites, consult neighbours and consider wider issues. All decisions are taken on individual merit, guided by the development plan and other material considerations.

Definition of 'development'

Since its inception British planning has been bound by a legal interpretation of what is and is not 'development'. This distinction is articulated in the General Development Order (GDO) which identifies certain land use changes and building operations as 'permitted development'. Exemptions from control in the housing development sector include loft conversions, small extensions, porches, outhouses, low boundary fences and dish aerials below the roofline. In other land-use sectors there are exemptions that may also influence the quality of residential environment, most notably agricultural and forestry practices, temporary road works, demolition and small outdoor advertisements.

Planning applications must be submitted for all significant building operations, including extensions that add more than 15 per cent to a dwelling's volume, new garages closer to the road than the existing dwelling, alterations to historic buildings and changes of use between certain specified categories. In specially

Plate 6.1 Attractive porches protected by an Article 4 direction, Blackburn, Lancashire: R. N. E. Blake.

protected areas the local authority can lower the threshold of control via an 'Article 4 direction' which effectively turns permitted development into statutory development for planning control purposes (Plate 6.1).

To establish the thresholds where 'change of use' officially takes place a Use Classes Order (UCO) has existed since 1947, the last revision dating from 1987. There are about a dozen use classes, e.g. B1 (Business) and C3 (Dwelling-house), plus a *sui generis* class covering miscellaneous uses, e.g. petrol filling stations. So long as there is no significant building operation, a minor change in activity within these classes does not normally require planning permission; but where, for example, a house-holder wants to run a hairdresser business from home, planning permission is required (and would probably be refused in a wholly residential street). Sub-division of large dwellings into flats is also classed as 'development' for planning purposes.

Planning applications

A formal planning application must include a range of information including ownership, proposed use, plans and drawings. A fee is payable on a scale related to the size of the proposal. In many cases the application is drawn up and submitted by an architect, planning consultant or land agent experienced in presenting information in a manner that will assist the planning officer and committee in making a fair and correct determination. Planning permission involving new building operations is normally granted in two stages: (1) outline and (2) detail. This procedure is particularly relevant to housing development where the applicant needs to know that the principle is acceptable in terms of land use, location, density and access, before commissioning detailed dwelling and landscape designs. The two-stage approach may be likened to the structure plan/local plan relationship operating at the higher spatial scale. Planning applications should rightfully be determined within eight weeks, beyond which the applicant is entitled to appeal against a 'non-determination'. As part of 'best value', planning authorities are ranked according to the percentage of applications they resolve within that time-frame. It can be appreciated that some authorities have more complex issues to deal with than others and that there is a temptation to meet government targets by sacrificing rigour. Developers sometimes submit identical applications for the same site in quick succession (a process known as 'twin-tracking') in order to get in the appeal queue. Caseload is therefore not a precise indicator of demand or land-use change.

A productive stage in the development control process is the informal discussion between developer and official. This enables the developer to discover pitfalls in his scheme and incorporate modifications before submitting the application. By this means both sides gain: the developer is more likely to get permission for an enhanced proposal while the authority adds to its stock of good-quality housing. Minimising the number of appeals is a further incentive to enhance designs by prior negotiation.

Rights of objection and comment are facilitated through the public consultation process. A register of planning applications is kept at town halls and libraries while advertisements are posted on sites, published in local newspapers and mailed to neighbours. Civic societies and residents' associations may subscribe to lists of applications so they can lobby councillors to promote their views. Since 1992 local authorities have responded to government pressure to raise public awareness of their activities and to liaise with neighbouring authorities on development applications likely to have an impact across municipal boundaries. Since 1998 it has also become standard practice to carry out an environmental assessment of any application for major development with unpredictable impact. This clearly implies a time-frame longer than eight weeks and illustrates the tension in development control between prompt determination and the responsibility to secure on the public's behalf a safe and attractive environment in the long term. Where any proposed development appears to depart from the plan, the local authority must notify the Secretary of State and wait to see whether the departure is deemed serious enough to be 'called in'. In such cases the government is in effect requiring the local council to take *longer* than normal in determining a matter in the interests of quality.

Agendas and officers' reports are also placed in the public domain and thereby become available for any interested party to consult. Members of the public can attend council committee meetings to object or offer support to a proposal (Darke, 1999). Since the 1991 Act the principle that decisions should be led primarily by the published developed plan has focused debates on strictly planning matters and discouraged the political free-for-all that was beginning to taint planning's reputation for detachment. There are however recurrent issues regarding planning's link with social and economic trends. Traditionally, planning committees were loath to refuse development on the grounds of over-provision, steering clear of commercial judgement. From an environmental perspective, however, a professional planner could legitimately argue, for example, that vacant apartments are likely to attract unlawful occupancies and thereby depress the neighbourhood. Increasingly, such considerations are being accepted as 'material'. Before Lord Rogers' campaign for an urban renaissance the underlying message from central to local government was that councils should avoid being over-prescriptive in design matters. This was intended to reduce the number of appeals and help speed up the determination of applications. Thus another balancing act has emerged, between the public's desire for a more agreeable built environment and more affordable accommodation through accelerated supply.

When a planning officer draws up a recommendation relating to a particular application the two guiding criteria are: first, the plan and, second, other material considerations. Though formally adopted, the plan on its own is not a legally binding contract between developer and authority, and while the plan is the principal guiding factor, it can legitimately be moderated by non-spatial forms of guidance. In practice most planning control decisions are soundly based on government policies articulated in PPGs and embodied into the structure and local plans. Design matters are normally addressed through 'supplementary planning guidance' (SPG) drawn up by the local authority to enhance development control. Carefully drafted SPG strengthens the hand of the authority at appeals and is a creative focus for pre-application discussions.

Planning permission is expressed in one of three formats: outright approval, outright refusal, or conditional approval. A refusal must be accompanied by reasons so that the applicant can decide whether it is worthwhile appealing. Conditions comprise 'reserve matters', which are particularly apposite to the design stage of residential schemes, and planning obligations that relate more to provision of infrastructure. All conditions should be precise, necessary, relevant, reasonable and enforceable; otherwise the scope for appeal and further litigation is open-ended. Typical planning conditions in housing development include access to the highway, effective landscaping, phasing to reduce nuisance during construction, and maintenance following occupation. Conditions applicable to other forms of development that often affect residential neighbourhoods include the height of buildings, hours of operation and access facilities for disabled people. A general condition states that any development should commence within five years of the permission, primarily to discourage long-term site vacancy and the attendant problems of squatting, fly tipping and vandalism.

Appeals

Because development control decisions involve a high degree of interpretation, the planning acts allow disappointed applicants a right of appeal to the secretary of state against refusal, conditions and non-determination. Approximately a third of appeals are successful. The appeals process may be seen as a restraint on over-restrictive planning committees and a form of quality assurance imposed on local authorities by central government. In the 1980s the volume of planning appeals became problematic due to the Conservatives' deregulatory agenda and the fact that many structure and local plans were still incomplete. 'Planning by appeal' came to characterise that decade. High-profile dismissals such as the abortive applications by Consortium Developments at Tillingham Hall (Essex), Foxley Wood (Hampshire) and Stone Bassett (Oxfordshire) paved the way for the plan-led system in the 1990s.

There are three ways in which an appeal may be dealt with: by written representation, by informal hearing before an inspector and by public local inquiry. In the written-only method the inspector normally visits the site and makes a decision within about six months; some 90 per cent of appeals are dealt with in this way. Hearings involve discussions between applicants and local officials, led by the inspector; there are no cross-examinations or third-party objections, a code of practice is used rather than a formal procedure, and decisions typically take about nine months. Inquiries can take over a year if the Secretary of State is drawn in. The vast majority of decisions are reached in under a year by the inspector alone, except where green belts and very large residential developments are involved. Third parties cannot themselves lodge an appeal against a planning decision but they may raise objections at inquiries. Where the Secretary of State dismisses an appeal the developer may take the matter to the High Court on strict matters of law. Third-party objectors can appeal to the High Court and request a judicial review where a major travesty of planning principles is alleged.

A final aspect of the appeals process relevant to housing developers is costs. No costs are normally payable to either party, except where one side can prove time wasting; this is a useful disincentive to litigation purely for financial gain. However, where an owner feels that land has been rendered incapable of beneficial use by a planning refusal, or by a consent given on adjacent land, he can serve a 'purchase notice' on the local authority, which must then buy the site at the price it would have fetched had the planning decision been otherwise.

Enforcement

Whereas the appeals mechanism offers the developer some prospect of more favourable treatment through independent re-examination, enforcement gives the planning authority power to reverse development after it has been started through ignorance or wilful disregard. Development without planning permission can be made lawful if the developer is prepared to submit a retrospective application that is ultimately successful. Unacceptable development must however be removed and a substantial fine is chargeable. A developer may appeal against an enforcement notice but has only a one-third chance of success. The 1991 Act gave local authorities increased powers to investigate suspected contraventions of planning law up to ten years from the start of the alleged infringement. A 'stop notice' may be served in urgent cases, for example the impending demolition of an historic building. The scope for enforcement is also of interest to any householder who is the innocent victim of riparian 'development', for example where a neighbour is using a garage for motor repairs. Failure to comply with an enforcement or stop notice is a criminal offence. Government is currently considering higher fees for retrospective applications and penalties commensurate with the benefit derived from infringement to fund the extra staff needed to keep up with contraventions.

Planning obligations

As a form of planning condition 'planning obligations' involve a developer agreeing to provide infrastructure such as a new road or open space as compensation to the community for a loss of amenity or a strain on local facilities (Cornford, 1998). Planning agreements have long been an integral part of town centre redevelopment but their use in housing development, though originating in the 1930s, increased significantly in the 1970s when government resourcing of public services first came under serious review. The 1991 Act replaced the idea of gain by agreement with 'obligations', which can be used as material considerations in planning appeals although strictly they do not rank as normal planning conditions. One aspect relating specifically to house-builders is pressure by the planning authority on the developer to provide an affordable housing element in schemes where, from a purely commercial angle, this would not be viable. There are ethical questions if a developer is seen to be 'buying' a planning permission with a promise to provide affordable homes. It is also contentious whether developers should be expected to include in a planning application matters that are not strictly to do with land use or the environment (the old debate about 'social engineering'). Finally, there is the controversial question of 'commuted payments' whereby a developer makes a financial contribution towards affordable housing or other off-site infrastructure, e.g. a library or arts centre, in return for planning permission (Ennis, 1994, 1997).

Special policy areas

In planning for housing development there are six areas of land-use policy that can be singled out for discussion beyond the general review of plan-making and development control presented above. These are: (1) green belts, (2) new and expanded towns, (3) urban regeneration, (4) urban conservation, (5) rural settlement and village planning and (6) countryside planning. In each policy area the basic planning processes apply but the strength of intervention is greater because of special socio-economic or environmental factors.

Green belts

Arguably the best-known of all planning policies, 'green belts' have figured prominently in debates over housing development because they are a cause of frustration among house-builders, they are fiercely defended by existing house-holders for the positive effect they have on property values and the amenity they confer. Planners, characteristically, are divided on the merits of green belts, which some regard as a trusty instrument of development control and others as an inflexible anachronism. Strictly, green belts are a policy zone requiring formal designation, and are not synonymous with unspoilt countryside; indeed, many areas with green-belt status have no scenic distinction. London's green belt pre-dates comprehensive land-use controls and initially had to be pieced together incrementally by land purchases (London and Home Counties Green Belt Act 1938). Eventually, a government circular enabled planning authorities to establish green belts regardless of land-ownership, and several provincial cities ranging in size from Birmingham to Cambridge are now 'contained' by this device. Green belts are not, however, compulsory and certain other cities, for example Leicester and Norwich, have elected not to have one (Elson *et al.*, 1993).

There are five key purposes of green belts: (1) to check the sprawl of large built-up areas, (2) to safeguard accessible countryside from urban encroachment, (3) to prevent the coalescence of neighbouring town and cities, (4) to preserve the special character of historic towns, and (5) to encourage urban regeneration. Intriguingly, protection of agriculture is not one of the primary stated aims and a growing percentage of green-belt land is now devoted to quasi-rural enterprises such as golf courses and riding stables. The prevailing policy is to permit only small changes of land use that do not involve significant built forms. Problems arise when large institutions such as hospitals and air bases are decommissioned and the land-holding authority comes under pressure from the Treasury to dispose of the site for the highest obtainable price. In these situations it is now common practice for local authorities to permit redevelopment within the 'footprint' of redundant installations, especially if the site has high-grade infrastructure enveloped by mature trees. Where a council wishes to reduce the extent of a green belt to promote development, the government normally intervenes to keep the green belt intact. The 1991 White Paper *This Common Inheritance* contained a specific commitment to the green belt concept.

New and expanded towns

Like green belts, new towns are a descendant of Howard's garden cities and Abercrombie's Greater London Plan. While accounting for barely 5 per cent of the national population, new towns and their offshoot, expanded towns, have had a disproportionate influence on civic design, housing layout and thinking about urban planning in general. As part of the post-war agenda to restructure damaged and decaying inner areas, the New Towns Act 1946 created a New Towns Commission with unprecedented powers to acquire land compulsorily and to develop integrated communities independently of local councils. Architect-planners were given a blank canvas to prepare 'master plans' catering for populations in the 50,000–100,000 range. Design innovations such as segregated cycle ways, pedestrian shopping precincts and 'radburn' (car-free) housing layouts became hallmarks of the British New Towns programme.

Some 30 new towns were built under the 1946 Act. London's ring included Harlow and Stevenage which controversially took prime agricultural land, although Basildon helped consolidate under-utilised plotlands. In northern and midland England a secondary aim was to reclaim industrial wastelands, e.g. Telford, Shropshire. Despite generous allocation of public open space, compact design ensured that overall land-take was economical compared with 'organic' urban expansion (Best, 1964). The Town Development Act 1952 was a Conservative contribution to decentralisation that encouraged small towns in stagnant rural areas to accept overspill population from congested boroughs in the conurbations. Successful examples include Thetford (Norfolk) and Swindon (Wiltshire) and may be seen as a prototype of development by partnership. Flows of 'newcomers' (the theme of a 1960s sit-com on BBC TV) were on a more modest scale and compulsory land acquisition more limited that in new towns proper. A proposal to expand Barnstaple, in north Devon, was abandoned because local employers feared destabilisation of the wage structure.

Milton Keynes was the last new town to be designated (in 1965) and differed in being conceived as a cluster of mainly private-sector communities. With a target population of about 250,000 it served not so much as a satellite of London but as a prime economic location based on the trunk routes of England's affluent heartland. By the 1980s new towns in general were at variance with government's policy to regenerate run-down cities by the market-led approach. The programme was effectively wound up during the 1990s and planning responsibilities transferred, as originally intended, to the relevant local authorities. English Partnerships have since inherited the property assets but these are not being fully used to maintain the housing stock, much of which is showing its age. At a more strategic level, the economic base of new towns has been badly affected by factory closures especially multinational companies that were originally attracted because of the efficient industrial estate layouts provided. Increases in outward commuting, youth unemployment and lack of big city attractions have exacerbated the deterioration of a public environment designed on the assumption of regular maintenance (Thomas, 1996).

The success of Milton Keynes as Britain's only 'new city' is evident in plans for major 'urban extensions' that adhere to the principles of PPG3 relating to density and its relationship to public transport corridors. A linear city between Cambridge and Huntingdon, involving the reopening of a disused railway, redevelopment of redundant military sites and possibly a new relief airport on the former United States Air Force base at Alconbury, is one imaginative idea for coping with pressures on the rim of the South East (Hall and Ward, 1998). The government's current planning reforms include major sub-regional growth points near Stansted airport (Essex) and Ashford, near Eurotunnel, in addition to Milton Keynes and the Thames Gateway.

Although plans for private-sector 'new settlements' were wisely quashed in the 1980s, two innovative 'new villages' at New Ash Green (Kent) and Bar Hill

Plate 6.2 A General Improvement Area in Blackburn, Lancashire, illustrating traffic calming and landscaping: R. N. E. Blake.

(Cambridgeshire) built in the 1960s should not go unmentioned. For housing historians these are worth visiting and are interesting because they were sociologically analysed from the start (Thorburn, 1971). The case for new settlements generally is a matter of ongoing debate (Hall, 1989).

Urban regeneration

Early post-war 'reconstruction' was dominated by the CDA approach which sadly involved the premature demolition of many fit dwellings to make way for commercial use. Until recently building societies were inclined to refuse mortgage applications in such areas on the grounds that the properties might become unsellable. Small businesses also fell victim to rigid zoning, eroding local employment and townscape diversity. Blight caused by road widening schemes and protracted negotiations over compensation turned many inner-urban areas into residential deserts (Ambrose, 1986). Mass clearances of sub-standard inner housing was justified at the time by the creation of outer estates and satellite towns, but despite generous provision of local open space and community facilities, the 'outer areas', too, lost social and economic cohesion. By the end of the 1960s, it was already evident that other action was needed to tackle low achievement, racial tension, crime and poor environment. In 1969, for example, 'General Improvement Areas' (GIA) were introduced as an alternative to demolition (Plate 6.2). A sequence of initiatives ensued, including the Urban Programme, the Inner Areas

Act 1978, Urban Development Corporations (UDC), City Challenge and the New Deal for Communities. Being mostly time-limited these initiatives have led to 'scheme fatigue' whereby local authorities and other public service providers feel they are on an endless treadmill of applications for funding that merely adds to uncertainty and sometimes runs counter to the normal plan-making process (Bailey et al., 1995).

Urban regeneration came of age in the mid-1990s with the establishment of the Single Regeneration Budget (1993) and English Partnerships (1994) which extended funding to depressed mining and rural areas. The emergence of private–public sector partnerships as a normal mechanism for achieving urban regeneration was a significant product of the decade, culminating in the report of the Urban Task Force (1999) and the *Urban White Paper* (2000). Local plans now routinely include 'mixed-use' land allocations with the express purpose of promoting the 'urban renaissance' through a synergy of housing developments and employment gener-ating activities. These spatially explicit allocations usually involve the publication of a development brief with carefully articulated goals (see Chapter 7).

Urban conservation

The protection of buildings and townscapes for 'heritage' reasons is a relative newcomer to town planning. While most of the built environment currently enjoying special protection comprises civic, industrial and transport buildings, there are a significant number of domestic buildings that echo their period and place and are accordingly earmarked in local plans as a constraint on, and increasingly an opportunity for, future development. 'Protected' dwellings, whether freestanding or integral to the 'street scene,' have exacting maintenance requirements and they may affect the value of adjacent properties, positively and negatively, by virtue of their age. Old buildings have delicate structural relationship with adjoining prop-erties, hence the attention being paid by residential developers to their attributes as the volume of infill development increases. Much of the thought put into residen-tial design guides stems from an appreciation of the qualities of older buildings found in the centres of towns and villages (see Chapter 7).

Powers to preserve individual historic buildings were given by the Ancient Monuments Act 1882, but affirmative action depended on the good will of land-owners. Furthermore, only structures pre-dating 1700 were considered worth recording, so few dwellings other than mansion houses figured at this stage. In 1908 Royal Commissions were set up to compile inventories of historic buildings meriting protection but effective action was delayed until after the Second World War when destruction resulting from enemy bombardment presented a compelling case for safeguarding what remained. The 1947 Planning Act provided a means whereby 'listed buildings' could be protected from demolition or defacement as part of general development control. Grants for repair were subsequently made available under the Historic Buildings and Ancient Monuments Act 1953 and eligibility for listing was gradually extended to include more ordinary residential buildings. As a consequence, London's Centre Point, a redundant 1960s office block recently converted to residential use, is now listed as a fine example of its era. There are over half a million listed buildings in the UK but English Heritage have no record of the proportion that are residential.

Listed buildings are graded into three main categories, as explained in the relevant government guidance (PPG15 *Planning and the Historic Environment*, 1994). Grade I are rated as 'outstanding or exceptional,' Grade II* as 'more than special' and Grade II (unstarred) as 'special.' Under the Planning (Listed Buildings and Conservation Areas) Act 1990 a local planning authority must notify English Heritage of any Grade I or II* building that becomes the subject of a planning application, and any Grade II building where either demolition is proposed or grant aid is needed. There is also a Grade III category of 'locally interesting buildings' that a planning authority can invoke as a material consideration in development control. National and civic societies such as the Georgian Society, the Victorian Society and the Twentieth Century Society are routinely consulted. Listing is co-ordinated by the local authority in conjunction with English Heritage and its equivalents in Wales, Scotland and Northern Ireland. Where an unlisted building of heritage importance is threatened by redevelopment a Building Preservation Order can be served on the owner until listing is formalised. An aggrieved owner may serve a purchase notice where 'listed' status precludes beneficial use, while compulsory purchase by the local authority is possible where deliberate neglect by the owner threatens public amenity. A government minister may 'call in' a planning application relating to a listed building in cases where the local civic society feels that the planning authority has taken insufficient account of heritage factors. Particular difficulties are occurring with large abandoned country houses where planning discourages conversion to multi-occupation residential use because of isolation. The price of PPG3 can be irreversible deterioration.

Urban conservation came to the fore when modern architecture became widely unpopular following the first wave of post-war redevelopment. The Civic Amenities Act 1967 enabled the designation of 'conservation areas' comprising groups of building not necessarily listed, plus walls, railings, trees and other feature of townscape value. While the spotlight initially fell on the centres of historic cities such as Bath and York, scores of market towns and villages have since gained new protection of their street scene and backlands, including many modest but charming residential properties. In 1974 Nottingham's Lace Market quarter became the nation's first Industrial Conservation Area but is today dominated by tasteful ware-house conversions to residential use. The Article 4 direction has been widely invoked to protect buildings from inappropriate modifications in areas not meriting full conservation area status. Since 1997 urban conservation has been administered centrally by the Department for Culture, Media and Sport and is seen as consonant with the goal of sustainable development.

Rural settlement and village planning

Approximately one in four Britons currently lives in a village, hamlet or small town. Put another way, an estimated 10–15 million people are not direct beneficiaries of urban facilities or affected by the urban renaissance. Since the 1950s the population living in rural areas has generally been growing, although certain remote districts are still registering net out-migration (Shucksmith, 1990). A number of defunct mining villages were controversially demolished altogether when they lost their economic raison d'être. At the opposite extreme many former agricultural villages were so greatly expanded that they now resemble the worst type of suburb (Brett, 1965). Pre-PAG development plans represented rural settlements by symbols and lists containing minimal information. Despite declining traditional employment, the rural economy and way of life were assumed to be stable and of low priority as a planning issue. It must be acknowledged in retrospect that planning then lacked the expert staff to address specifically rural problems. Policies for individual settlements consisted of schedules of infrastructure to be provided, e.g. a sewage disposal works, health centre, or by-pass. Realisation during the 1960s that housing development for non-locals was likely to become the principal driver of change led planners in many counties to draw up a 'classification of settlements' which distinguished between small villages with low capacity to absorb development and 'key' villages where existing and planned infrastructure made housing expansion a viable proposition (Ambrose, 1974). With mass rail closures, highway improvements and calls for stricter conservation in the built and unbuilt environments, a more discerning approach to rural development began to be reflected in plans. Modern structure and district plans have absorbed this methodology, providing more explanation of the rationale for differential growth than was required in the old-style plans (Cloke and Shaw, 1983).

District plans now contain 'insets' for all growth villages. These are physical plans at an enlarged scale showing the allocations of land to meet development needs and sites to be conserved in an unbuilt state. A device with 1960s origins is the 'village envelope', a line in a village plan defining the physical limits to growth and by implication the surrounding fields to be protected. The envelope approach has been criticised because it implies that any site inside is developable while nothing outside can be developed. For this reason many village plans are based instead on the 'environmental capacity' approach which sacrifices the rigid principle of containment for a looser but more subtle framework of control. A fundamental criticism of the entire concept of growth restraint in villages stems from the issue of affordable housing (Gallent *et al.*, 2002). It has long been alleged that young people on low incomes have been effectively squeezed out of their native area by wealthy interlopers who buy up scarce building plots or renovate cottages at high cost. Provided that a key village or small town is close at hand it can be argued that 'rural gentrification' does not necessarily dislocate poorer families and that affordable housing is best provided in growth settlements. To an extent general car ownership has undermined the argument for an affordable housing provision in every single village.

In terms of fuel economy, any dispersed population may now be regarded as unsustainable as comprehensive public transport provision in rural areas is unviable.

Countryside planning

One of the most powerful constraints on housing development is the protected countryside (Burton, 1992). This is especially so in Britain because of its high overall population density and variety of cherished landscapes (see Chapter 2). Whereas green belts are geographically specific, the countryside in general extends from the edge of the built-up area to the shoreline and inevitably encompasses precious natural resources. The fact that almost all housing development has traditionally involved displacement of green fields means that countryside issues cannot be decoupled from the housing development process. Even if land recycling targets are met, 40 per cent of all houses are destined to be built on greenfield sites.

Notwithstanding the CPRE's laudable vigilance over the irreversible erosion of rural tranquillity, the spread of housing has long been evaluated by planners in terms of its impact on agricultural production, wildlife habitats and the hydrological cycle. These constraints are integral to land-use policy and graphically portrayed in statutory development plans (see Figure 6.1). As well as reiterating green belts and areas of outstanding natural beauty (AONB) shown in the county structure diagram, local plans also show a wide range of protected sites such as areas of biological importance, scenic value, archaeological significance and washland. Key pieces of legislation for countryside planning are the Countryside Act 1968 and the Wildlife and Countryside Act 1981.

In certain circumstances countryside policies can prove an asset for housing development. Proximity to country parks is one of a number of environmental criteria by which a house-builder might decide to buy land in an area. Properties that follow design guidance and echo the local materials and building styles are more likely to get planning permission and retain their value. Dwellings are part of the countryside and any new-build development should give the impression of having grown organically within it. The politically tinged question of holiday and second homes has, however, clouded the countryside planning debate. Renovation of a fixed stock of older dwellings undoubtedly pushes prices up, leading to the exclusion of people who cannot compete. At the same time it is probable that low-income groups would not necessarily wish to renovate older properties and widespread abandonment and decay would doubtless ensue without newcomers. It is significant that the former Countryside Commission (formed in 1968) was redefined in 1998 as the Countryside Agency with an expanded brief to address the social and economic challenges of rural areas. This is a further manifestation of the growing influence of mainland Europe on British planning.

Land development questions

Land-ownership, land values and land acquisition were major impediments to the establishment of garden cities and a general system of land-use control during the first half of the twentieth century. Despite the enactment of a far-reaching planning system in mid-century, decisions concerning the development of land have been overwhelmingly made in response to market forces. Even under austerity conditions the Labour Government of the late 1940s was restrained in the amount of land it could legally confiscate for public works. In keeping with Britain's traditionally mixed economy, there has been a continuing debate concerning how the rights of the private land-owner to maximise value can be reconciled with the rights of the local community to adequate housing, good facilities and an orderly environment. A perennial question therefore is how development land, particularly for housing, can be 'brought forward' in requisite quantities to satisfy both the commercial interests of the market and public need.

Land values

The eternal debate over land values stems from the principle that any decision to sell a piece of land entails a loss of opportunity to derive a future income from it (Ratcliffe, 1976). Value, expressed as selling price, provides a measure of the potential advantage to the existing owner of disposing of land rather than holding on to it. In a regulated land-use system the effect of development plans is to modify the pattern of winners and losers, in as much as certain potentially lucrative sales may become pointless because of restrictive zoning. While there have always been advantages conferred on some land-owners by the accident of a favourable location, the imposition of statutory plans has compounded differences in value between sites. Two neighbouring farmers with aspirations to sell off fields for housing can expect different reactions from the planning authority if one lives in the green belt and the other in less protected countryside. Similarly, the costs incurred by a home-owner building an extension are likely to be higher if the property lies within a conservation area where higher design standards are required. Because planning makes development land scarce, acquisition of land accounts for a larger proportion of overall housing costs in Britain than is the case in less regulated countries, except where special legislation allows the government to subsidise the cost of land. The question of land values cannot therefore be de-coupled from house prices. Regional inequalities in property values generally act as a deterrent to social mobility and in prosperous regions with strong environmental protection policies they force land values still further upwards with a knock-on effect on housing production and affordability.

Since 1945 there have been three attempts to increase housing output by intervention into the free market in land. The Town and Country Planning Act 1947 kept values down by levying a 'development charge' on planning permissions, but this levy was abolished by the Conservatives in 1954 who felt that the charge acted as a disincentive to bring land forward for housing. An anomaly whereby local authorities could acquire housing land compulsorily at agricultural values (while private developers had to pay 'development' value) was ironed out in 1959. When Labour returned to government they set up a Land Commission (in 1967) with powers to assemble land compulsorily where fragmented ownership or 'hoarding' were perceived as impeding the attainment of housing targets. A levy on profit from land deals was included to fund land assembly, but when the Conservatives were returned to power in 1970 they abolished the whole idea. On re-election in 1974 Labour set up a Community Land Scheme which gave local authorities the power to acquire land for broadly similar purposes, but this too met an early demise when Margaret Thatcher became premier in 1979 (Thornley, 1993).

Compulsory purchase and land assembly

In a number of circumstances the 'reactive' nature of the British planning system has failed to achieve an important planning objective. This was especially the case with mass housing renewal schemes where local authorities had to assemble sites of considerable size using powers of compulsory purchase. While housing development is now overwhelmingly a private-sector industry, housing associations and public–private partnerships still require land to be compulsorily acquired on their behalf, particularly in inner-urban sites where access is often impeded by the obdurate owners of adjacent properties. Compulsory purchase powers are available to local authorities under the 1990 Town and Country Planning Act to acquire land for disposal to private house-builders, although this facility has been used sparingly. Exceptional is the Land Authority for Wales (LAW) which has been able to accelerate housing output in the principality by acquiring a number of large sites. Acting independently, the LAW has also won a number of appeals on behalf of housing developers through the normal planning process. Transferability of property rights by compulsory purchase is thus an essential ingredient of the development process (Ratcliffe, 1976). The most frequent use of compulsion is in connection with highways where land outside the strict operational requirement can be acquired to ensure that residents are protected from noise. Human rights legislation has deterred wider use of compulsory purchase, so negotiated mechanisms for ensuring land availability continue to be preferred. There are, however, provisions in the current Planning and Compulsory Purchase Bill to strengthen powers in order to speed up the process of urban regeneration.

Land availability studies

Traditionally, land for housing development became 'available' at the behest of land-owners responding to market opportunity or parochial need. Before comprehensive planning regulations came into effect any plot was, in principle, available so long as the price offered exceeded the perennial yield from its current use. In practice most land did not enter the housing market because of remoteness, traditional farming patterns and low demand. The rationing of development opportunity to achieve the twin goals of urban containment and rural conservation profoundly altered the concept of land availability in the 1940s. Large tracts of land considered worthy of protection were abstracted from the housing market by legislation with the express aim of protecting the natural environment in the public interest.

Recent focus on questions of land availability must be examined by reference to deficiencies in the planning system (Adair *et al.*, 1991). During construction booms the supply of allocated sites has started to run out, sending alarm signals through the industry. In slumps the amount of unused land has embarrassed planners charged with maintaining an efficient and attractive environment. Responding to these oscillations, local authorities have taken a cautious line in the amount of housing land they allocate in plans. In consequence, many districts have found themselves with as little as two years' supply in a plan that is not scheduled for immediate review. The origin of specific action to increase land availability lies in political pressure to create a better match between housing demand and the plan-review cycle (Hooper, 1979, 1980). As a planning concept 'land availability' first emerged in 1970 when the Ministry of Housing and Local Government (MHLG) issued Circular 10/70 asking local authorities to ensure a five-year supply to prevent shortfalls in housing output. To assess the scale of the crisis a research report covering the West Midlands region was soon commissioned (Shankland-Cox Partnership, 1972). Follow-up circulars in 1972 and 1973 focused on land with planning permission and further research revealed that many of the sites allocated in plans were not actually available because of ownership, infrastructure and marketing problems. The debate culminated in a study of Greater Manchester conducted jointly by the DoE and the House Builders Federation which established a general methodology for assessing land availability (DoE and House Builders Federation, 1978).

When the Conservatives returned to power they issued Circular 9/80 (DoE, 1980b) which made housing land availability studies mandatory and required them to be more closely attuned to planning and market considerations. The methodology then became embroiled in a wider government agenda to downgrade the status of plans and development control. However, DoE-commissioned research by Roger Tym & Partners (1987) on the South East showed that much land being developed for private housing was not allocated in statutory plans and therefore cast doubts on the efficacy of land availability studies as a tool for enhancing plans. By the early 1990s the debate had shifted to definitions of 'availability' and the fate of non-implemented sites. A turning point came with a report by the Joseph Rowntree Foundation (1994) in which the vexed question of 'windfall' sites was considered in relation to regional guidance on house-building targets. PPG3 *Housing* (1988) had already introduced the concept of regenerating brownfield land as a priority and subsequently the land availability study as a methodology has evolved into the 'urban capacity study' (see Chapter 10).

Land acquisition strategy

Thus far the role of land in house-building has been examined principally in terms of a publicly managed natural resource. In a mixed economy the acquisition of specific parcels of land for housing development falls predominantly to the private sector, involving both in-house land-buyers employed by the large house-building companies and independent surveyors and valuers engaged by smaller developers. Public authorities also have estates departments employing staff with similar qualifications to those working in the private sector. In both sectors it has become increasingly common to adopt a strategic approach to the compilation and management of a land and property portfolio.

Area reconnaissance

Private house-building companies normally operate within a defined geographical area. The larger companies typically have regional divisions enjoying a fair degree of autonomy in defining its product. 'Area reconnaissance' describes the first stage in an exhaustive analysis of the territory in which a company operates. Surveys at 'area' scale rely heavily on the techniques of town and country planning, with important inputs from corporate strategy and marketing. The right area is acknowledged as being as important to successful housing development as the right site, and intangible factors such as quality-of-life and sense-of-place can also be critical in arriving at the right product mix (Rogerson, 1997).

There are two vital elements in an area reconnaissance. The first is a scan of the main physical attributes such as urban spread, industrialisation, accessibility, scenic quality and environmental protection policies. These attributes represent the supply side of the development equation and provide a basic yardstick for comparisons with adjacent areas and national averages. The second element is an estimation of demand to live and work in the area, based on recent build-rates, infrastructure programmes and marketing intelligence. All this precedes any consideration of particular sites and is similar in many respects to structure planning, with the obvious difference that a commercial house-builder's land acquisition reconnaissance can be at any level of detail and abandoned if the area targeted reveals low market potential. A useful planning methodology for testing the housing market was devised by Coopers & Lybrand Associates (1987), using the percentages of planning permissions taken up before expiry, houses sold prior to completion, and house-buyers from outside the survey area as key measurers of buoyancy. Hampshire County Council (1990) adopted this methodology and discerned a special need for starter homes in the area.

Desktop surveys

The search for development sites involves a comprehensive survey of the targeted area so that no valuable 'niches' are overlooked through generalisation. A 100 per cent field-by-field survey yields the best results but is expensive in human resources if attempted on a scale larger than the neighbourhood. Air photography provides a useful alternative for estimating land use over wider areas but is limited because it cannot read signs or record attitudes. Desktop surveys usually begin therefore with published maps and small-area census data. A tried and tested methodology is the 'sieve map', whereby a series of mapped variables are overlaid to reveal zones of opportunity and constraint (Figure 6.1). Standard variables include land-form, geology, hydrology, soil type, agricultural productivity, vegetation cover, subsidence, contamination, air pollution, and noise. Each variable can be expressed in gradations to reveal land that is either difficult to build on (e.g. steep slopes or

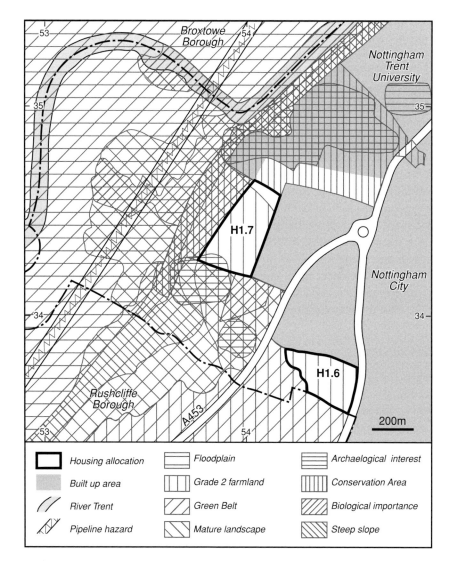

Figure 6.1 A 'sieve' map illustrating the effect of multiple constraints on land allocation for housing in the rural–urban fringe of Nottingham.
Source: Nottingham Local Plan Review (First Deposit Draft) 2001

floodplains), would be environmentally damaging if it were developed (e.g. wood-land or downland pasture), or a health hazard to future residents (e.g. factory waste or low-flying aircraft). Added to these constraints are policy zones such as green belts and conservation areas, and institutional constraints such as defence establishments.

Normally a sieve map contains only the most problematical land for each variable (e.g. top-grade farmland, nature reserve, 50+ decibels), leaving significant 'blank' areas where development might be possible because of relatively low build-costs or low impact. One key advantage of a sieve map is that areas of multiple con-straints quickly emerge from the overlaying process. Figure 6.1 demonstrates the limited scope for new housing in a section of Nottingham's urban fringe. An elabo-ration of the sieve technique called 'potential surface analysis' was employed in the 1960s to give credence to sub-regional growth studies such as that for the Coventry-Solihull area. Using OS grid squares, the land surface was scored not by the presence of constraints but by their absence, so that the blank 'solution spaces' yielded by the sieve map were depicted as peaks of relatively high 'developability' while the areas of multiple constraint formed troughs. Problems encountered trying to quantify potential beyond what the humble sieve had attempted led ultimately to the decline of potential surface analysis. Both methodologies are worth retaining as desktop tools for land acquisition. In conducting a desktop study it is also fruitful to carry out a systematic search of planning registers held at council offices. A complete record of residential planning decisions in recent years up to the latest council meeting is an important adjunct to the sieving process and may provide invaluable insights into how developers and home-buyers are responding, knowingly or other-wise, to environmental constraints and opportunities. Wilcon Homes is one company to have developed a site assessment procedure along these lines.

Saturation surveys

In business, the question arises as to whether detailed and spatially exhaustive surveys can be justified in cost terms. Large companies with established land-buying teams may be able to afford staff to work permanently on land resource monitoring but for smaller organisations the pragmatic solution is to target niche markets in sub-areas with high perceived growth potential. However, to achieve focus it is necessary at some stage to have carried out a 'saturation' survey of the wider market area in order to ascertain where the promising niches and sub-markets are located. This principle is akin to that which characterised land-use planning in its early days when spatially comprehensive, all-purpose ground surveys were regarded as an essential complement to the decennial Census. Such surveys have regrettably become a rarity in council planning departments but increasingly common at the divisional offices of leading house-building companies. A saturation survey does not have to be spatially comprehensive in every respect. There are other relevant data that can be mapped symbolically from sources not requiring field visits.

Socio-economic data, e.g. on household composition, car ownership and income at postcode level, can be superimposed on environmental zones and transport networks to produce valuable market intelligence on residential preference and demand. A further dimension of commercially driven saturation surveys is the trawling of professional, trade and local journals for opportunities to acquire land. Combined with inter-professional networking, this technique enables any site to be assessed from a developmental and environmental perspective. Information technology (IT), and particularly geographical information systems (GIS), have crucial parts to play in matching the supply and demand perspectives on land acquisition.

Field work and base maps

While strategic land searching is conducted primarily on a sub-regional or even broader scale, fieldwork ('shoe-leather research') is still important. 'Ground truth' surveys are already embodied in many published data sources (e.g. the Census, Ordnance Survey, geology) but are not routinely employed when searching for development niches above the neighbourhood scale. There is nevertheless a place for 'fast-track' fieldwork in the form of targeted site visits in order to confirm the suitability or otherwise of sieved land. Another type of field-based survey, usually carried out by motor car with a passenger as observer, is 'sign spotting' where details of market activity are recorded from estate agents' boards positioned on sites. Geotechnical and geo-environmental analysis of particular sites once they have been brought forward for development will be dealt with in Chapter 7.

Before considering procedural aspects of land acquisition at site level, a brief mention should be made of base-maps as surveying tools. For more than two centuries the Ordnance Survey has provided a consistent basis for identifying and measuring land resources and assets (Oliver, 1993). For strategic surveys a scale of 1: 25,000 (2½ inches to the mile) is apposite as published sheets covers a sizeable area while still showing garden and field boundaries. The next larger scale, the 1: 10,000 (6 inches to the mile) is better suited to surveys of big cities and their suburbs as individual plots are easier to pick out and coloured annotations easier to apply. For submitting planning applications and keeping asset records, the larger OS scales are more appropriate. Maps (sometimes referred to a 'plans') at 1: 2,500 (25 inches to the mile) and 1: 1,250 (50 inches to the mile) are especially useful in property transactions as they accurately show the footprint of individual buildings and road width. In preparing planning applications a 'blow up' to 1: 500 scale is normal in order that notes about the site and associated buildings can be written on the map itself. Finally, thanks to digitisation, large-scale OS maps can now be purchased for any territory required by the user up to a certain paper size. Customisation of area is however, significantly more expensive than standard sheets lines.

Land buying procedures

Types of site

While all building sites are ultimately unique because of their geography and history, there are several perspectives from which they may be categorised to assist the development process. Apart from variable ground conditions (see Chapter 7) there is a situational distinction between freestanding, peripheral and infill sites that has potential implications for design. Another typology is based on size whereby small sites are better suited to independent local builders preferring a succession of short-term contracts, and large sites to satisfy volume builders with longer-term business development objectives. Sites may also be categorised according to their planning status: allocated or unallocated, with or without planning permission, and covered by or free from restrictive policies. Infill sites might usefully be sub-divided into those located in a suburban or village setting and those lying within an inner-urban regeneration zone. These sorts of distinction are usefully fed into the company's database, so that those tasked with acquiring or disposing of sites can feel confident that the decisions they make are rational and sound.

Proactive and reactive approaches

There are two generic approaches to the identification of land and property for development and both apply to house-building. Proactive identification describes the desktop, saturation and fieldwork approaches and is akin to the preparation of statutory plans in being spatially comprehensive. Reactive identification describes the incremental acquisition of sites from market intelligence. Ultimately both information streams should be integrated into the company's database. The rationale of the proactive approach is to keep ahead of competitors, a secondary advantage being that it enables the property team to gain familiarity with the marketing area. Apart from gaining a structured overview of the environmental and socio-economic factors influencing regulatory behaviour, the 'trawling' of planning departments and estate agents' offices is an excellent way of building up inter-professional networks. The reactive approach involves intercepting, sifting and keying in information about land or property that has already been placed on the market or is ready to be marketed. It is the role of the land-buyer to monitor all published sources, including the electronic web. Most sites are advertised in the principal property journals and are handled by professional agents who keep particulars governed by the Property Misdescriptions Act 1991 and enforced by the local authority trading standards office. Changes of government policy, e.g. the pressure on local education authorities and hospitals to release their under-utilised playing fields for development, is another sector where a reactive approach on the part of the commercial land-buyer is apposite.

By tradition, many sites are offered on an individual basis and there is no 'equal opportunities' requirement to advertise. The reasons for confining the offer to a single potential purchaser or a small group of competitors range from satis-factory past transactions, recommendation by a third party, company reputation, and rapport between particular buyers and sellers.

Negotiation

There are two main methods of buying land through commercial transaction: (1) where property is advertised for sale on the open market, and (2) where developers have identified sites not on the open market but where the owner(s) might be willing to negotiate a sale. In either situation the sale may be by private treaty, tender or auction. Private treaty is a method whereby the vendor can choose the buyer and the agent plays a large part in matching both sides of the transaction. Where land is sold by auction any bid from the 'floor' is a legal offer and a formal contract becomes binding on the fall of the hammer. It is vital that every aspect of a planning, techni-cal and legal character has been researched and evaluated before the event. The advantage for the vendor is the quickness of the transaction but he cannot select the purchaser. For the purchaser there is the advantage of speed but careful prior checking of records at the Land Registry and local authority is essential.

Tenders can be formal and informal. In sales by formal tender potential buyers are invited to submit bids to a named person, at a prescribed place, by a prescribed date and time. Advertisements are usually placed in the *Estates Gazette* or *Property Week* and sometimes in local newspapers. One great advantage to the vendor is that selection can be on criteria other than price; the great disadvantage for the buyer is that bids are 'in the dark' and he does not know that lower bids may have been placed. With informal tenders a guide price is often given by the vendor. A dis-advantage for the purchaser is that the vendor can play one purchaser off against another (known as gazumping). Sales by public sector organisations, even where there is a motive to raise capital for the taxpayer's benefit, rarely use private treaty because it could provoke allegations of corruption.

Options are a mechanism particularly germane to housing development. An option to purchase arises where a land-owner enters into an interim contract with a potential buyer allowing that buyer the right to purchase the site at an agreed date in the future. This typically involves sites with development potential but which do not yet have planning permission, are hemmed in by ransom strips, or are occupied by tenants whose leases have not expired. To secure the option, a devel-oper normally pays a 'consideration' and registers it in the Land Charges Register. A conditional contract requires some act or event which triggers a legal obligation to complete a full contract. Conditions might, for example, involve the acquisition of an adjoining plot or the involvement of a funding partner as the condition for clinching the sale at some time in the future. Where land has been defined as having potential, but the owner is not willing to sell outright or by option or conditional contract, the buyer may be able to agree a right to pre-emption. This amounts to a binding agreement that if the parcel is to be offered for sale, the potential buyer gets first refusal without obligation. Because this type of arrangement does not create a legal property interest, it is not entered in the Land Charges Register.

In summary, private treaty is the most flexible sales method but depends on the highest negotiating skills. Auctions are the fairest but least flexible, and tenders are the most advantageous to the seller. Outright purchase is ideal for swift realisation of potential but depends on ready access to cash, while options and conditional contracts are more appropriate for the longer term and require more delicate negotiations. Within a company it is essential that the land-buyer has the approval of head office or executive group before clinching deals (Stratton, 1983).

Tenurial and legal encumbrances

Decision to purchase depends in part on the anticipated additional costs associated with existing ownerships on or surrounding targeted sites. A common encumbrance is the 'ransom strip' which can be defined as any land that separates a potential site from an existing adopted highway on to which access would be essential. Acquiring such a strip can be expensive and involve protracted negotiations with the owner. Other tenurial encumbrances are outstanding leases and licences. Agricultural tenancies can be problematical for land-buyers as there is a strong measure of protection for tenants under the Agricultural Holdings Act 1986. Residential tenants likewise have protection under the Leasehold Reform Act 1967 and the Housing Act 1988. Residential licences are more easily extinguished if an owner wants to sell for redevelopment. The Criminal Justice Act 1994 enabled squatters to be evicted more easily.

Legal encumbrances consist mainly of easement and covenants. Easements are legal rights enjoyed by one owner over another, such as rights of way or access to drains and light. In order for an easement to exist in law there must be a 'dominant tenement' (the land enjoying the right) and a 'servient tenement' (the land subject to the right). On transfer of ownership the rights and obligations pass to the new owners but easements can be extinguished by negotiation. Sites with access rights over adjacent open space are an excellent prospect for new housing. Covenants are a control over activity for the benefit of adjoining properties and can be both positive and negative. Positive requirements do not remain enforceable on new owners but negative requirements, e.g. cutting down specified trees or blocking a view, 'run with the land' and may involve recourse to the Law of Property Act 1969 to modify or revoke them. Lands Tribunal proceedings can be expensive and claims should be based on public interest. For the land-buyer the short-term inconvenience of a covenant may enhance a site's ultimate desirability. Most developers sensibly consider sites on a two-stage basis to filter out encumbrances before purchase and thereby avoid unnecessary work.

Land-banking

To ensure there is sufficient land to meet housing demand, house-builders have increasingly resorted to 'land-banking'. This provides an insurance against oscillations in the market and restrictive planning regimes. In post-war boom years companies in the more prosperous regions came close to running out of developble land and responded by establishing their own portfolio of sites by progressive acquisition.

Definition and scope

A 'land-bank' may be defined as the amount of land held in stock by a developer at any point in time, excluding sites already under construction. The size of this resource is routinely kept up to date because it has to appear as a costed asset in the company's annual account. It can be a key factor in precipitating mergers and take-overs. Quantification includes total extent (in hectares), number of separate parcels (in hectarage bands), number of building plots (in density bands), number of years' stock (assuming current production rates), and overall valuation (£). Further relevant information might include the land bank's geographical distribution by local authority, the balance between brownfield and greenfield sites and the proportion with planning consent (either allocated or unallocated in local plans). Geo-environmental data such as contamination and flood risk are increasingly relevant as will become clearer in Chapter 7. Land-banks need to be constantly topped up or sites disposed of depending on market conditions.

Interim site management

Sites forming part of a land-bank require systematic management from the time of purchase up to the time that construction begins. Plots can lie idle for more than ten years and deterioration may affect saleability. With the emphasis on recycling brownfield land the presence of buildings on vacant sites is an increasingly important consideration. Reasons for positive management include:

- Duty of care to visitors, neighbours, children, and even trespassers. Under the Occupiers Liability Act 1957 there is a responsibility to secure buildings and boundaries and to post 'danger' notices.
- Mothballing of historic structures, including unblocking of drains, temporary roof covering, removal of expensive materials such as lead and mouldings.
- Pest control.
- Securing easements such as neighbours' right to light.
- Maintenance of fencing to deter squatters.
- Checking on the legality and licensing of temporary uses, for example car parking, car boot sales.
- Opportunities for land swops, and elimination of ransom strips by negotiation.
- 'Topping up' planning consents by carrying out preliminary ground works.
- Reviewing valuations.
- Tidying up to improve marketing image.

Asset or liability?

In bullish market conditions (booms) land-banks are viewed as an asset whose value increases faster than house prices (White, 1986). During slumps, the most recent of which was in the early 1990s, millions of pounds worth of land value can be written off in balance sheets and company shares (see Chapter 9). In addition to their long-term advantages, land-banks are useful to companies because they enable rapid response to market opportunities, switching operations from problematic sites, land swops and joint ventures with other developers. Land-banks also provide collateral for borrowing and a saleable asset when cash is urgently needed to sustain production. On the negative side, land lying idle may fail to achieve appropriate planning consents or legal agreements with adjoining owners and public authorities. Sites can be blighted by adjacent developments post-dating the acquisition, by a new restrictive planning policy or through the activities of local opposition groups. There are instances where development sites have been de-allocated from plans following revised estimates of housing need. Fly tipping, squatting, vandalism and arson are ever-present problems.

Conclusions

The importance of planning in Britain reflects the country's high density of population, intensive land utilisation and popular regard for urban and rural amenity. This chapter has emphasised the close historical link between housing policy and planning policy, highlighting the evolution from concerns about human health to matters of location, accessibility and design. Compared with most other countries the British planning system is complex due to its multi-layered administrative structure and frequent modifications; yet its flexible, negotiating and interpretive culture is much admired. From the housing developers perspective the principal obstacles to commercial success are a shortage of building land exacerbated by planning restrictions and the complexity and unpredictability in the system itself. Since part of planning's raison d'être is to accommodate the needs of all sectors of development, there are legitimate questions regarding the discipline's effectiveness in matching the demand for, and the supply of, land. From the house-holders perspective there is much to be gained from an orderly and well designed environment in which development is constrained by the conservation of heritage and natural resources. This requires public servants and private citizens to acquire a sound knowledge of environmental issues, placing a unique responsibility on planners as co-ordinators. Planning at its best seeks to minimise risk for the whole community by creating a framework that is transparent, legible and fair. Lingering doubts revolve around the questions: who wins, who pays and who decides? All aspects considered, planning's key objectives have not radically altered in a hundred years and the delivery system through physical plans and development control is much the same as it was half a century ago (Davies, 1998). The one policy area that stands out as radical is sustainable development, although many of its tenets were implicit in urban containment policies of the pre-Rio era. Current government proposals for reforming the system are focused primarily on creating a more effective regional allocation of housing land, facilitating the implementation of major infrastructure projects and speeding up the processing of individual planning applications. This ambitious agenda differs in emphasis from previous reforms but, true to the evolutionary tradition of British planning, its underlying mission is to supply an orderly land-use pattern and decent homes for all.

Discussion points

1   Consider a scenario in which all physical plans and development controls are removed to eliminate bureaucracy. What immediate impact might this have on the quality of housing development?

2   With reference to the latest published version of a local plan, select three 'allocated' housing sites for field inspection. Investigate the previous use and current state of the land, noting the number and type of dwellings where the development has already been implemented.

3   Examine a current housing proposal that has aroused public controversy. From local press coverage summarise the market or social need of the proposed development and the basis upon which objections have been raised.

4   From the 'Casebook' section of *Planning* magazine (weekly) create a concise typology of housing development applications based on proposed use. Construct a bar chart comparing the incidence of the main classes of application over a 12-month-period.

5   In the role of a developer's land-buyer, draw up a priority list of documents and databases that the company should subscribe to in order to maximise the effectiveness of its land bank.

Key reading

The definitive references on planning are Cullingworth and Nadin, *Town and Country Planning in the UK* (2002) and Duxbury, *Planning Law and Procedure* (2002). Rydin, *The British Planning System* (1998) and Greed, *Introducing Town Planning* (1996) provide more critical insights into the discipline. Numerous articles on specific aspects of land-use control are listed in Cullingworth and Nadin, e.g. Adams, 'The role of landowners in the preparation of statutory local plans' (*Town Planning Review*, 1992) and Gallent and Bell, 'Planning exceptions in rural England' (*Planning Practice and Research*, 2000).

Chapter 7
Site appraisal and residential estate layout

Ron Blake and Andrew Golland

Introduction

The ground on which housing development takes place is rarely a blank canvas. Britain's high population density, combined with the fact that most development is concentrated within or close to already built-up areas, ensures that houses get constructed predominantly on sites with a long history of human occupation. This is not a new phenomenon, for the older parts of historic towns indicate successive rebuilding on sites first occupied as agricultural land (Hoskins, 1955). There are several reasons why the appraisal of sites is essential to the housing development process. From a cultural perspective the obliteration of historical features is unpopular and provision has therefore been made in planning law for investigations to rescue artefacts. From a marketing perspective the preservation of landscape features can be both a selling point for developers and a source of contentment for users. From an engineering perspective the configuration of the ground has an effect on build costs and influences the design of estate roads and services. Lastly, development has an enduring impact on the surrounding area and there is a responsibility on developers and public agencies to ensure that the new fits in with the old not just visually, but ecologically and socially.

This chapter focuses on the main considerations in preparing sites for housing development up to the commencement of dwelling construction (see Chapter 8). Clearly, some notion of dwelling type will be in the mind of the developer at outline planning stage and indeed may also be reflected in the company's marketing strategy during the local plan review. But before the construction of individual dwellings can start a range of key issues must be addressed by the developer, including density, ground conditions, drainage, vehicular and pedestrian circulation, and conservation. These may well determine whether or not a developer decides to buy a particular site, which introduces questions of market demand and viability touched on earlier in the book. The present chapter thus provides a link between the broader land-use aspects of the housing development process and the more publicly visible process of constructing houses. Before outlining the practical routines of site investigation and estate layout, a series of policy issues relating to estate development are reviewed. The opportunity is also taken to consider aspects of viability at different spatial scales within this 'open ground' stage of the development process.

Policy and market drivers of residential estate layout

Development layout: from Constable to kerb appeal

Key changes in highway design

Important changes have taken place in recent decades in the policy and practice of estate layout for new housing developments. These changes relate in particular to highway design where there has been a clear shift away from the somewhat rigid and severe style of road layout that was a feature of housing development in the 1960s, to the more informal, almost casual, present-day criteria for road design. The essence of new highway thinking, as established originally in Design Bulletin 32 (DoE, 1992a), is for the previous 'prairie' estates of wide, straight roads to be replaced by a hierarchy of roads that quickly diminishes the need for speed by de-scaling the road size and classification dependent on the number of dwellings served. In the light of present-day fashion for 'joyriding', the conventional 6–10 metre building lines for frontage dwellings has encouraged high-speed motoring and is a priority for replacement. Thus it is now the case that the main collector road soon reduces to lesser-width feed roads and eventual access road or access ways serving a maximum of 15–20 dwellings where even the footpaths may be dispensed with for a joint (normally paved) road/pedestrian way. The thinking here is that each cul-de-sac's house-owners will drive at a cautionary speed for the safety of their neighbours or family members.

Much of the praise for the return to traditional design in both highways and dwelling standards must be given to the legendary 'Essex Design Guide' first published three decades ago (Essex County Council, 1974). This guidance thoroughly and clinically analysed the deficiencies of the contemporary problems of housing design and estate layout. The Guide energetically encouraged the return to traditional design and informal layout emphasising that the typical idyllic village setting occurred by genuine innovation and almost casual evolution well before the emergence of formal planning control as engendered by the Town and Country Planning Act of 1947.

Despite the excellence of an extremely well presented and qualified publication with many examples of typical layouts and preferred solutions for a whole range of densities, the immediate reaction from most developers (and many architects, it should be said) was rejection and outrage on the grounds of increased costs due to more expensive materials and a general reduction of density caused by the need to provide households with a greater degree of privacy and improved space standards. Developers argued that these changes would lead to higher sale prices and, they believed, a decline in the demand for their products.

Such pessimism, however, proved unfounded, as developers and architects gained confidence in their ability to respond in an innovative way to the emerging design policy agenda. They became gradually more enthusiastic about the policy and the Essex landscape began to be returned to the indigenous vernacular style for which it had long been recognised in, for example, the paintings of John Constable. The growing reputation of the Essex Guide and its clear call for new thinking also gained the attention of the house-building industry. Many local authorities produced their own version with an emphasis on a return to traditional design and sensible traffic speed reduction; the guides for Cheshire, Hampshire, Lincolnshire and Suffolk are among the most practical and well illustrated examples.

The 'new urbanism', density policy and PPG3

As developers have embraced the principles of more effective estate design and planning for the larger, speculatively built developments, a number of other important changes have been taking place. Perhaps the most important of these is the move towards more effective planning of housing within existing urban areas. This has been encouraged by government policy aimed at more efficient use of land (see Chapter 10), as well by an emergence of 'urban design profession', taking its ideals to some extent from the 'new urbanism' movement and the spirit of PPG3. We deal now with these issues in more detail.

It was recognised as late as the mid-1990s that local planning authorities were failing to achieve the densities in housing development that would be needed in order to deliver the sustainability agenda linked to greenfield land-saving and urban land regeneration. A study by the University of Reading (Breheny, 1997) provided a number of interesting findings. The study looked at 'numerical' density standards (for example policies on dwelling per hectare) as well as 'non-numerical' standards. When looking at the numerical standards, it was found that in more pressured development areas, average achieved densities fell in the range 30–36 dwellings per hectare, while in non-pressured areas, densities stood as low as 18 dwellings per hectare. While these standards are all relative on a regional basis, they fall well below those standards which are now being sought via current policy. The analysis undertaken by the Reading academics of the non-numerical criteria for deciding density policy was perhaps even more enlightening. First, it was found that most authorities would focus mainly on the 'character of the existing area' for deciding non-numerical density standards. The study also found that 'far from being keen to promote higher densities, local authorities [were] often resisting further intensification, and [were] using density standards to do so' (ibid.). Further, the study concluded that:

> For advocates of urban compaction generally, and higher residential densities in particular, all this evidence must make depressing reading.
>
> Clearly many authorities do not use density standards at all, and where they are used it seems to be in a rather half-hearted, pragmatic fashion.
>
> Where quantitative evidence on standards exists, it shows no discernible trend to higher standards. The qualitative evidence shows a remarkable lack of interest in PPG13 – given that it is very much the Government's flagship guidance on planning for sustainable development.'

> (Breheny, 1997: 87)

These findings were applicable to the situation in the mid-1990s. Since then, central government policy makers and urban designers have taken steps to encourage better use of land and more ambitious density standards. We comment now on some of the key initiatives and sources of information.

The report of Lord Rogers' Urban Task Force (1999) considered in some detail the relationship between density and urban design. It concluded that:

> . . . the message [was] clear; the lower the density (say, 20 dwellings per hectare), the larger the amount of area that is occupied by buildings, roads and open space . . . this form of layout promotes excessive car use and makes it difficult to justify a bus route. As density levels are increased – even to moderate levels of 40 or 60 dwellings per hectare – the land-take diminishes rapidly. People are close enough to communal facilities to walk, and an efficient bus service can be made viable.
>
> (Urban Task Force, 1999: 60)

Thus the focus on new urban developments in particular is now on increasing densities, although new housing layout more generally should also seek to increase densities and reduce reliance on the car.

A research study commissioned by the Department of the Environment, Transport and the Regions (Bartlett School/Llewelyn Davies, 1998) focused on the use of density in urban planning. Considering a wide range of issues relating to density, the publication is particularly useful in setting out the historical density policy that has been applied to housing layouts (ibid.: 9–17). The research also highlights lessons from international practice, with a particular examination of the US and Europe. In terms of the relationship between development form and density, the report considers (ibid.: 53–7) how different ways of specifying density standards affect the form of the built environment. Using six case studies representing different levels of density ('low' to 'high'), the report finds that the way in which density is specified is highly significant for the character of the eventual built form. More specifically the report finds that:

> The measures of dwellings/area and habitable rooms/area will tend to have different effects. By defining the maximum number of dwellings, developers are encouraged to build the largest dwellings possible (i.e. large family houses) on a given site up to the maximum permitted density.
>
> Conversely, by defining the maximum number of habitable rooms, developers are encouraged to build more smaller units (i.e. one bed or studio flats) to provide the largest development area per habitable room. In either case (sunlight to local market conditions) developers interpretation of the density standard will seek to achieve the maximum amount of building floor space.
>
> (Bartlett School/Llewelyn Davies, 1998: 55).

The effect of different density standards on the built form in terms of its relationship with open space, gardens, parking and so on is determined in large measure by the relationship between the achievable selling price and relevant building costs for each particular dwelling type. Developers may not wish to build smaller units, but faced with a density standard based on a number of habitable rooms (per hectare), they may find building smaller units the best way to maximise land value and thus come up with a competitive price for the land-owner. The report also looks at the use of plot ratios, more popular abroad, and concludes that this standard, where applied, can 'directly determine' the amount of built development on a site. Plot ratios, which 'express the total amount of floor space in relation (proportionally) to the site area', are said to be able to 'facilitate more innovative design solutions', be useful 'in respect of mixed developments' and are 'effective at all density levels' (ibid.: 58).

Estate layout and the marketing of new homes

'Kerb appeal'

Perhaps one of the most significant and lasting effects of the changing emphasis of design guidance for estate layout has been to increase awareness amongst developers of the need to achieve 'kerb appeal' for new dwellings for sale. 'Kerb appeal' is a difficult concept to define although vitally important for developers to achieve when trying to market new homes (see Plate 7.1). There is no set 'standard' for 'kerb appeal' yet it can be achieved via improved design, materials, the siting of dwellings and, most importantly, hard and soft landscaping.

Present-day values, therefore, in terms of design and layout, are now firmly established with all developers paying great heed to innovation of design coupled with essential 'Sunday afternoon – George get your cheque book out, we're having it' appeal (Rogers, 1996). Traditional materials are back with a vengeance even down to the greetings card thatched cottage and duck pond setting. It is instructive to note the way in which developers now strive for a complete individuality or uniqueness of dwelling. Whilst a dwelling will always be 'unique', simply because of its location, developers tend to go further and try to provide developments in which no two homes are exactly the same. This approach may, however, be counterproductive to the aim of building 'traditional' homes:

> . . . a detailed study of some national developers' latest styles suggest an exaggeration and bastardisation of traditional design in the name of competition coupled with the desperate quest for originality which, if considered is an obviously contrived and a contradiction of terms, with the inevitable consequence that tomorrow's styles are in danger of becoming an amalgam or pastiche of classic styles that could well ridicule or deride the original intention for revival of traditional values.
>
> (Rogers, 1996)

The shift towards greater individuality of dwelling design and estate layout can be seen as a shift towards the trend in some other European countries; in particular

Plate 7.1 'Kerb appeal', or a lack of it? Popular house types fronted by an unadopted road at Herne Bay, Kent: R. N. E. Blake.

Germany and France, where new-build dwellings for home ownership are very clearly aimed to 'individualise' the occupant.

The marketability of new estates: an industry viewpoint

The House Builders Federation (1998b) recently published, on behalf of the DETR and the Planning Officers Society, a research report examining the way in which estate layout might improve or detract from quality development. The report had at its heart the key question: 'What makes a well designed housing layout?'

The answer, it was concluded, lies largely in the context in which the new housing is being developed. Individuality and distinctiveness that makes the most of the site and its landscape and townscape setting is at a premium. 'The most criticised designs are those that introduce housing which could be in any suburb, regardless of its context' (ibid.: 4). While the report acknowledges that planners and developers are often at their most innovative and most responsive on difficult brownfield sites, it nevertheless emphasises the importance of good planning in more favourable suburban and urban fringe locations:

> . . . a well-designed housing layout, especially on suburban sites, introduces variety and contrasts within the scheme so that the spaces between the houses are not merely standard

streets and cul-de-sacs, but avenues, squares, crescents, mews, courtyards, lanes, alleys, greens, and all the other words that our language offers to describe the traditional variety of spaces.

(ibid.: 6)

Barriers to a well designed housing layout were identified in terms of 'rigid highway standards', 'standard house types' and 'planning standards'. In these respects, high-quality housing layouts can be hindered by what is known as a 'highways engineering' approach to urban design, where 'road form is considered before space', and where the responsibility for the design of the estate lies with people not fully trained in the art of urban design.

Housing layout and estate quality could also be improved if developers were to approach site layout in a completely different way. What developers tend to do (ibid.: 8) is to use standard house types that they have developed elsewhere for each new site, irrespective of the particular circumstances on the ground. A better way ahead, it is suggested (ibid.) would be for developers to plan housing form based on the particular site circumstances. The practical objection is that this approach makes the land acquisition process much more complex; using standard dwelling types, the market revenue and anticipated build-costs (see later in this chapter) can be estimated, and hence a reasonably robust land bid offer made.

A further obstacle to well designed layouts are planning standards. These are often rather reductionist, applying minimal standards best suited to responding to the developers' initial ideas, rather than being proactively promoted towards a sound design solution. The HBF report makes the assertion that:

It is unlikely that revised standards alone would improve the quality of layout design. Different standards would result in different solutions, but the fundamental problem remains that it is not possible to measure design quality against standards rules . . . lifting the quality of housing development requires that we should devise a way of setting a bold and ambitious target with a site-specific response that establishes an urban design concept.

(ibid.: 11)

The implications of estate layout: a design perspective

The focus on improved dwelling layout and the aim of achieving higher urban housing development densities has led to increasing concern that new developments should function properly. The recent report on urban design (Llewelyn Davies, 2000) focuses on 'urban structure' as a concept for future development:

The term 'urban structure' refers to the pattern or arrangement of development blocks, streets, buildings, open space and landscape which make up urban areas. It is the inter-relationship between all these elements, rather than their particular characteristics that bond together to make a place.

> Urban structure does not imply any particular kind of urbanism: it applies equally to the centre and to the suburb, and everything in between; and of course it applies equally to the city, the town and the village.
>
> (Llewelyn Davies, 2000)

Thus, the need in all new developments is to ensure that not only is the built form aesthetically pleasing and provides a safe environment, but that built form and space interact in a successful and sustainable way.

Development viability

What is 'development viability'?

As indicated in Chapter 6, allocation of land in a plan does not automatically ensure its development to a pre-ordained specification. In a reactive planning system sites are brought forward in a generally logical order, but each has to be made 'viable' through a scheme that is both profitable to the developer and acceptable to the planning authority in terms of its layout, design and impact.

Assuming that planning permission is in place, development viability needs to be considered from two angles:

- Economic viability; this largely reflects the local housing market supply and demand conditions.
- Layout viability; this largely reflects the nature of the development brief which sets out the key opportunities, constraints and tolerances governing any scheme that might be devised, and in particular, the density and dwelling mix envisaged.

A brief of some kind normally precedes the granting of planning permission, especially for large sites with a mixed-use designation. Smaller sites may not involve this intermediate stage, although a 'feasibility study' is a normal part of the two-stage planning application process (see Figure 7.1). Site valuation and planning permission can be obtained in either order but increasingly a valuation is known before an application is submitted.

Assessing economic viability

The viability of a development scheme depends on a number of key variables, some of which are within the control of the developers, and others of which are less so. In very simple terms, the viability of a housing development scheme depends on the ability of the site in question to generate a required land value for the land-owner.

For the land-owner, some questions will be more clearly apparent than others. Paramount is whether the site in question will provide a competitive housing land value, and whether the housing land value will exceed other possible commercial uses. However, other factors will be less transparent, for example the effect of density policies on land value, and the associated planning regulations that govern density. Ultimately, a positive and competitive land value and one that provides some 'return' to the land-owner is what matters and what underlies the decision to sell to a developer.

From the developer's point of view, the concern is primarily that revenue from the site exceeds development costs in such a way that a surplus can be generated in order to pay for the land. This can be expressed:

$$S = MR - DC,$$

where: S = surplus, MR = market revenue and DC = development costs.

As long as MR is greater than DC, then some 'surplus' will be generated. We say 'surplus' because it is quite possible that the developer does not pay the full residual value (market revenue less development costs) in acquiring the land, but manages to keep some of the value back for himself either to invest directly in the scheme or to invest, perhaps, in another site.

Basic viability appraisal

The textbook approach to assessing the viability of a site for housing development is known generally as the 'residual development valuation' approach. This approach is outlined in texts such as Millington (1988), Baum and Mackmin (1989) and Britton *et al.* (1989) and it can be summarised with a simple example:

A developer wishes to acquire a site to build one detached house. The developer believes that the house can be sold for £100,000, and that the base costs for building the house will amount to around £50,000. The question facing the developer is how much to pay for the land?

Residual development approach:

Market revenue (known also as 'gross development value' (GDV))	£100,000
Base build costs	£50,000
Ancillary cost allowance (5 per cent base build costs)	£2,500
Finance costs (@ 8 per cent base build costs + ancillaries)	£4,200
Sub total	*£56,700*
Developers normal profit allowance (@ 15 per cent of GDV)	£15,000
Total costs	*£71,700*
Surplus amount to pay for land (£100,000 less £71,700)	**£28,300**

These figures are exemplary only, although they are not unrealistic. In practice, there would be other modifications to the appraisal process. These relate to the anticipated time taken to acquire the land, to build on it and to sell the house. In the example, a year is anticipated with finance costs for building the house at 8 per cent. If, however, the developer needed to borrow funds to finance the land purchase, then an additional amount would be required to make allowance for this fact. Under those circumstances, the residual value for the land would fall to reflect the additional costs borne by the developer.

Another factor to take into account is the expected level of profit, or return required by the developer. For a small operator, or building company, the appropriate measure of return may be a simple net profit based on the sale value of the house. Some of the larger housing developers, however, particularly those listed as public limited companies, operate on a 'return on capital employed' basis. In these circumstances, the decision to purchase land is based on the per cent return that the development will yield over a specified time period taking account of the amount of finance tied up in the scheme: labour and materials. If this benchmark is not satisfactory, then land will not be purchased.

The nature of the site will also influence land price. Very often developers cannot know before acquiring the site what difficulties may be present for the building process. For difficult brownfield sites, the only method of reflecting the anticipated risk may be to increase the required profit level. This has the direct effect of lowering land values, hopefully (for the developer) alerting the land-owner to the need to lower his 'horizons'. In practice, of course, this is a game of 'cat and mouse'. Where all land bids are unexpectedly low, the land-owner can simply assume there is a problem with the site, or, on the other hand, be suspicious and hold out for another time.

Planning policy effects on housing development viability: density, development mix and affordable housing policies

In order to operate most efficiently, a developer will strive to obtain the optimum estate layout and development mix. A development that is heavily 'weighted' towards smaller housing types is less likely to yield the best land value unless densities can be increased significantly. Developers have, over time, increasingly tended to build more detached housing at the expense of semis and terraced/town house types. One reason for this is that development costs do not rise commensurately with sale prices. While larger, more expensive housing tends to be better finished (with fewer 'standard' fittings) the extra cost is normally considered an investment producing a very robust selling price.

In the example below, we show how development mix impacts upon the amount that the developer might pay for the land. Let us say that detached houses sell for £150,000 each, semi-detached homes for £95,000 each and terraced/town houses for £70,000 each. Furthermore, development costs are £600 per m^2; detached houses are built to 140 m^2; semi-detached houses to 100 m^2 and terraces to 70 m^2. In Table 7.1, it can be seen that Site One, which has the largest proportion

Table 7.1 Housing mix and development value

Dwelling type	Site 1	Site 2	Site 3
Detached	5 units	3 units	3 units
Semi-detached	3 units	5 units	3 units
Terraced/town	3 units	3 units	5 units
Gross development value	£1,245,000	£1,135,000	£1,085,000
Development costs	£726,000	£678,000	£642,000
'Surplus'	£519,000	£457,000	£443,000

Source: Authors' example

of detached housing, produces the highest 'surplus'. Site Three, at the other end of the scale, has a significantly lower surplus, largely because of the greater proportion of terraced housing.

In practice, one way of increasing the land value of Site Three, for example, would be for the developer to insist on the local authority allowing one or two additional dwellings on the site via a 'relaxation' of density policy. However, the developer would do this only if a changed development mix produced an increased land value. Under some circumstances, adding smaller homes to the site may simply produce a more crowded estate without adding significantly to the land value. What matters is the relationship between development values and development costs for each house type at specific locations. This relationship is not at all transparent and is usually gleaned by developers' market research at the local level. It is often noted that developers push for detached housing because it can be produced at much the same density as for semi-detached housing, but at significantly increased margins.

Affordable housing impacts

Whether affordable housing is included in an estate depends on where the developer is located in the country and the size of the site. Circular 6/98 (DETR, 1998b) sets out the relevant 'thresholds'. These state that outside Inner London, the site must be more than 25 dwellings or be greater than one hectare for local authorities to be able to enforce an affordable housing quota. In the Inner London boroughs, the threshold is 15 dwellings.

The effect of affordable housing on the viability of a scheme can be considerable. Developers usually emphasise that the positioning of the affordable housing within an estate is critical. Developers normally prefer affordable housing to be placed together, often in a 'corner' in order that it does not 'stigmatise' or otherwise affect the rest of the development. Local authorities are often equally keen to see affordable housing 'pepper-potted' around the new estate in order to achieve some social 'mixing'. The irony of this situation is that housing associations, who are usually in the management role for the affordable housing, prefer to have all the affordable together in order that their role can be made easier.

In practice, developers will often try to sell all the private housing before the affordable homes are built or at least occupied. In this way, there is usually very little detrimental impact on sale price. Local authorities, however, can now force developers to build and sell on affordable housing in tandem with private housing; this can be tied up through Section 106 agreements.

Of much greater concern to the developer of affordable housing is the form of tenure. If this is social rent, for households on benefit rather than low-cost home ownership, for example, the developer is likely to want to reflect this fact in the bid for land. Also of concern is the extent to which affordable housing will be subsidised via the Housing Corporation. The effect of affordable housing on development viability is extensively analysed in a recent case study of Greater London (Oxley *et al.*, 2001).

The impact of estate layout on viability: the role of the development brief

Development briefs are non-statutory documents. There are no official regulations specifying their role or format and hence virtually no mention of them in books relating to planning law. Briefs are used to facilitate dialogue between developer, planners and other regulators, and are consonant with the collaborative and conciliatory culture that characterises housing development today. The terminology of briefs can be confusing as there are up to 20 variants. Four variants in common use are:

- 'Development brief' is a generic term covering any assessment of a site that amounts to a land-use plan in miniature irrespective of authorship.
- A 'planning brief' is produced by the local authority or its consultant to artic-ulate what the authority would like to see happen to the site and to attract market interest.
- A 'developer's brief' is produced by a prospective developer or its consultant to initiate dialogue with the local authority, to attract investors and thereby increase the likelihood of obtaining planning permission with favourable conditions.
- A 'design brief' or 'design statement' is normally drawn up by the developer's agent and focuses on landscape, townscape and other aesthetic aspects of a scheme once the land-use factors have already resolved.

Financial and management briefs written by or for a developer, and agreements between neighbouring planning authorities on *ad hoc* issues, are other variants.

In essence, a development brief provides a framework against which different development options can be assessed with regard to environmental capacity, build-costs, and impact on the ground. Supported by adequate research it can be invoked as a supplementary planning guidance and as a material consideration in develop-ment control, particularly where the local plan is ambiguous. The brief is also a means of co-ordinating the views and standards of other public bodies which may have conflicting remits. Exact requirements and specifications should be kept to a minimum and the guiding principles emphasised instead, unless covenants and by-laws represent important development constraints.

Indicative layouts and sketch designs are appropriate items to include, so long as alternative solutions arising from discussions are given a hearing and a chance of being incorporated. Influences outside the site and opinions elicited from local people should also be taken into consideration when codifying opportunities and constraints. In particular, any off-site works that might be required by the local authority as 'gain' should be spelt out so that costly *post hoc* negotiations can be avoided. Where a particular developer is not yet identified an expert market appraisal is advisable for larger sites.

Briefs, whether they are prepared by a planning authority, a developer, or a consultant acting on either's behalf, should cover the same basic range of issues. Convergence in the training of planners, architects and surveyors renders this increasingly likely. Public participation is equally desirable, although under current regulations formal consultations are not required. Development briefs should cover the following range of issues:

- reason for developing
- location of the site
- size of the site
- current tenure and disposal
- market interest
- planning status
- planning history
- land-use options
- surrounding area
- adjacent land uses
- features to be retained
- features to be added
- features to be removed
- terrain and ground conditions
- highways and rights of way
- utility services
- community facilities
- views of local people
- design scenarios
- list of involved organisations.

Site appraisal and housing development in practice: a case study

To illustrate how urban infill sites can be viably developed while meeting planning and design objectives, a real-life case study is presented here. Figure 7.1 shows a small area of 'backland' in Ilkeston, Derbyshire, where the site owners and the local authority are in agreement that a small addition to the housing stock would be beneficial to the neighbourhood. A point in favour of the proposed development is the fact that the site is destined shortly to become vacant and is therefore likely to degenerate into an eyesore. Valuation has not been disclosed although financial viability is positive in this case.

The site lies behind a row of houses built in the inter-war period and was originally an allotment garden. Its eastern boundary is formed by a local distributor road with Victorian terrace houses on the opposite side (Figure 7.1a). Among the inter-war houses is a social club with an associated 'beer garden' to the rear. In 1995 the owners of the club received outline planning permission for five dwellings on the 0.24 hectare site (Figure 7.1b). Consultation between the planners and British Coal confirmed that there was no record of faulting or weakness in the ground and the Environment Agency raised no objections relating to flood risk. Derbyshire Highways stipulated visibility splays at the proposed vehicular access point, plus at least two car-parking spaces per dwelling. Incorporating these conditions into the planning permission, the council required that all vehicular surfaces should be of solid-bond material, no dwellings should be occupied until the road and visitors' parking facility were ready, tree planting and landscaping should be carried out during the first season following construction, and the existing bus stop shelter should be moved for safety some distance from the access. On design, there was a condition stating that the houses should be 'domestic in style and not out of scale in a suburban location'.

Subsequently, it emerged that a market gardener operating from the adjacent allotment was also proposing to sell up his business. This presented a golden opportunity for the club owners to enlarge their site by 0.11 hectares to form a potentially more viable development of 0.35 hectares (Figure 7.1c). Accordingly, during 2001 a feasibility study was drawn up for ten dwellings. On considerably less that twice the area, the residential scheme density could be increased from 21 dwellings per hectare (d.p.h.) on the initial site to 28 d.p.h. on the enlarged site. This enhanced density is very close to the 30 d.p.h. advocated in the government's PPG3 (2000) and there is, therefore, optimism that the revised layout will also get detailed planning permission. In their correspondence with the planning consultant, the highways authority expressed concern about the effect of ten new dwellings on traffic flow. The consultant responded by pointing out that cessation of truck movements in and out of the market garden would compensate for any additional danger caused by the development. Accepting this balancing principle, the development control officer is minded to recommend approval of the expanded scheme when all 'reserve matters' have been resolved.

This case yields a number of interesting lessons with regard to development at the site scale. First, there has been no serious objection from neighbouring households, most probably because the abandoned site could attract fly-tipping and provide an assisted passage for intruders into back gardens (Figure 7.1a). A positive use for the site with maintained boundaries is thus likely to enhance rather than

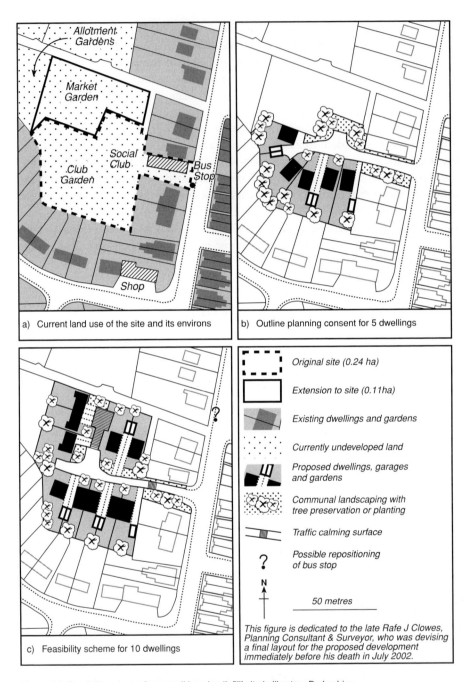

a) Current land use of the site and its environs

b) Outline planning consent for 5 dwellings

c) Feasibility scheme for 10 dwellings

Original site (0.24 ha)

Extension to site (0.11ha)

Existing dwellings and gardens

Currently undeveloped land

Proposed dwellings, garages and gardens

Communal landscaping with tree preservation or planting

Traffic calming surface

Possible repositioning of bus stop

N

50 metres

This figure is dedicated to the late Rafe J Clowes, Planning Consultant & Surveyor, who was devising a final layout for the proposed development immediately before his death in July 2002.

Figure 7.1 Feasibility scheme for a small housing 'infill' site in Ilkeston, Derbyshire.
Source: Erewash District Council, R. J. Clowes and author's fieldwork

depress riparian property values. Second, the acceptability of the scheme has been dependent on a skilful increase in density on what amounts to a land-assembly exercise in miniature. A comparison of layouts (b) and (c) in Figure 7.1 demonstrates that the initial scheme had 'dead' space on the north side of the estate road, consisting of a turning bay surrounded by generous landscaping. In the revised scheme more of the roadside has been allocated to individual gardens, enabling higher density to be achieved with no sense of cramming. This solution also highlights the principle that on infill sites with a capacity for fewer than ten traditional dwellings there is an irreducible need for road space that only becomes economical when both sides are developed. The original site in this case study was awkward because it was narrow, but 'fattening' enabled more effective utilisation.

Site investigation and appraisal

Terms and definitions

Investigation of sites prior to their development or redevelopment involves a wide range of professional operations at different spatial scales. As intimated in Chapter 6, development sites can vary from tens of hectares to a fraction of one hectare, depending on the type of allocation in the local plan. The current accent on compact housing development, due to the shift towards recycling of brownfield sites, plus the parallel tendency for large site to be developed by several house-builders, has made it increasingly necessary to analyse the ground in order to satisfy an expanding range of safeguards required by legislation and customer-care guarantees.

Insofar as the term can be defined, 'site appraisal' involves the systematic investigation of the physical surroundings, ground condition, engineering problems and anticipated environmental impacts of proposed construction and maintenance projects. Because of the need to meet environmental safeguards, all site appraisals must consider not only the viability of the engineering operations but also the impact of the development on nature, the surrounding buildings, the local community and wider society. With many sites containing re-usable structures in urban settings, the concept of site appraisal can no longer be seen purely in terms of open ground and must embrace the challenges of refurbishment, conversion and extension within more constricted sites.

Geo-environmental assessment

As the range of factors to be considered in house-building continues to expand, the term 'geo-environmental' has been coined to encompass everything that relates directly and indirectly to the natural environment. In this sub-section a short review of those factors is presented in the style of a traditional geographical account.

Landform

Topography and aspect are fundamental to developability. The former influences build costs while the latter influences microclimate, particularly in high latitudes (see also Chapter 8). High-density housing becomes prohibitively expensive on gradients steeper than 10 per cent and low densities housing on gradients above 25 per cent. (Barton *et al.*, 1995). Hillsides facing north achieve lower solar gain than those facing in other directions, affecting both the dwelling and its garden. Drainage is influenced by a combination of landform, climate and the composition of rocks. This in turn influences the configuration of watercourses, standing water and vegetation, each crucial to landscape texture and character. Agricultural and forestry practices, while no longer relevant to sites which have been brought forward for housing development, may nevertheless have bequeathed features that merit separate conservation or incorporation into developments, for example iron fencing.

Archaeology

Archaeological investigation is now a normal practice in site appraisal, signalled in local plans by designated areas based on the advice from local and national experts. Housing developers are conscious of their heritage responsibilities as, for example, was Bellway Homes who recently (2002) unearthed Roman industrial artefacts in Cheshire. Television programmes such as Channel 4's *Time Team* have helped public and professional understanding of ancient mounds, ditches and foundations plus the geophysical and cartographic techniques used to identify these features. Conservation of past environments is an important corrective to present-day technocentrism

Derelict land

The legacy of human occupation in more recent times finds expression in underground voids and ducts for which there may be no accessible records (Fleming, 1991). As well as being of direct importance to geotechnical engineers, the presence of obsolete infrastructure below ground is of considerable interest to industrial and military archaeologists (Blake, 2001). Abandoned earthworks, emplacement and drainage systems are increasingly being investigated as part of site appraisal before new housing development takes place, for the benefit of the contractors, future residents and the historically minded citizen. Derelict land (now referred to as 'brownfield sites') has been conventionally defined as 'land so damaged by industrial and other use that it is incapable of beneficial use without treatment' (Ministry of Housing and Local Government, 1963).

Treatment often requires specialised engineering operations but effective re-use can be achieved by designs that ingeniously place new buildings where disturbance to the surface and substructure has been minimal.

Contaminated land

Contamination is not always visible, although experts can usually discern it from the absence or discoloration of plant species. A key aspect of contamination is the fact that dangerous chemicals can migrate laterally from one site to another along open watercourses or through the water table. Thus in site appraisal for housing development it is necessary to ensure that all toxins are safely removed before construction begins in order to avoid costly disruption of residents should a source be later discovered on the estate. Equally, toxins can migrate into a completed development from an external source after the residents have settled. Trigger values are set to establish when a contamination 'event' has taken place. Sites that have been remediated are sometimes deemed unsuitable for any housing at all because of suspected residual contaminants in the ground that could damage the health of gardeners and children. Sites with aggressive ground conditions are best zoned for industrial and commercial use provided the surface is capped with concrete or bitumen (Nathanail *et al.*, 2002).

Air pollution

Atmospheric conditions affect developability in a variety of ways. On sloping sites the higher land is most exposed to wind and driving rain, a fact that has to be balanced against increased solar gain and superior views. Buildings erected downwind of heavy industry, quarrying and motorways are more likely to experience air pollution as well as vibration and noise. In housing development grit and dust falling on windows, drying linen and plants are the most obvious form of atmospheric pollution, but chemical attack on the dwellings' fabric is also a hazard (see Chapter 8). A related hazard of topical concern is the alleged effect on human health of overhead electricity transmission lines and telecommunications masts. Again, intelligent site planning can help to minimise these risks.

Hydrology and biodiversity

Hydrological analysis is important whatever the site's size. Large developments will probably have watercourses traversing them that should be altered as little as possible consistent with public health and safety. The configuration and flow characteristics of watercourses provide clues to geological structure and ground disturbances, and should be checked for signs of pollution and irregular flow. For small sites knowledge of the hydrology of the surrounding land is crucial in designing drains. Finally, vegetation and soils need to be assessed. In the past it was customary to bulldoze sites with little regard for their 'biological capital'. Today, thanks to pressure from conservationists, it is standard practice to assess the implications of new development for the local flora and fauna. However, this is a two-way process, and planners are also concerned to capture the benefits of the local natural environment for new housing occupants. The science of ecology has demonstrated, for example, that mature trees can provide shelter against inclement weather, arrest soil creep and maintain 'biodiversity' by providing niches for rare species. Trees also help absorb air pollution and noise, while ponds and stream banks offer oases for wildlife and human recreation. Soil conservation is important for land restoration following construction.

Flooding and flood prevention

There are approximately 2 million homes and businesses sited in river-based or coastal floodplains, involving about 10 per cent of Britain's population. Traditionally, these areas had the economic advantage of good communications and in present times watersides have a high aesthetic appeal. Planning policy has discouraged the building of homes on floodplains but the lure of flat sites and the established settlement pattern have conspired to continue to attract developments in these potentially hazardous zones. The sudden floods of autumn 2000 cost £946 million in 200,000 insurance claims (Howe and White, 2001, 2002). The effect on hypothetical capital value when insurers exclude household items from cover is reason enough to discourage development in such locations. The Environment Agency, within the framework of the Environmental Protection Act 1990, has promoted the idea of 'sustainable urban drainage systems' (SUDS) whereby any development that is susceptible to flooding or prolonged rainfall is designed with maximum permeable surfaces to assist natural absorption and restrain catastrophic flow (Environment Agency/ Scottish Environment Protection Agency, 1999). A 'seller's pack' proposed for introduction by 2005 will require a statement of flood risk in all property transactions.

Geotechnical investigation and appraisal

The civil engineer and engineering geologist have long played key roles in making sites structurally sound for urban development. 'Geotechnical' investigation is part of broader environmental assessment focusing on the cost implications of disturbed ground, constructional challenges and the technologies needed for effective engineering and remediation. Low-rise housing is a comparatively straightforward form of development because its weight does not place a great stress on the ground, although when failure does occur it affects a lot of people acutely. High-rise housing requires higher standards of engineering to achieve basic stability, but is less sensitive to minor irregularities in the ground because the residents are distanced and shielded by car parks and other hard surfaces. Whatever the density, housing development on previously used land must clearly be preceded by a thorough physical investigation carried out by qualified engineers.

Basic geology

A perfect dwelling substructure consists of a robust geological material plus a smooth, almost-level surface at a comfortable elevation above the water table. Since these desiderata also hold good for agriculture, it is no surprise that 'greenfield' sites are generally preferred by house-builders. In sites that have not been previously built over, the basic geology is the usual starting point of an investigation. The best materials are gravel and sand, which are permeable and have a high bearing capacity. Chalk and limestone are also robust but may be compromised by solution holes. Silts and clays are less robust, less permeable and prone to freeze-thaw and shrink-swell cycles. The worst natural ground is peat because of its compressibility and high water retention.

Made ground

Worst of all for building on is so called 'made ground' or 'fill'. This artificial environment is associated with past landfill activities and former industrial premises where 'land raise' was necessary to achieve an even surface. Made ground is also an unpredictable material. Fill can be 'engineered' to produce a fairly reliable building surface but 'non-engineered' fill is prone to collapse and would constitute a 'geo-hazard' beneath a residential estate. Organic and metallic content contributes to the instability of fill and renders it problematical from the house-builder's standpoint. Engineering of fill involves crushing the inert material to minimise the proportion of voids between particles that contribute to settlement under weight. Vegetative waste is the source of methane which is combustible. The importance of a geo-technical input to site valuation can thus be appreciated.

Subsidence and erosion

Other practical considerations dealt with by the geotechnical engineer include subsidence, erosion and deposition. These processes all occur naturally, but their incidence has been increased by uncontrolled building, mining and tipping. A key aspect of site investigation therefore is to examine old maps to ascertain the position of faults, voids, landslips and other geohazards, and to assess the risk of ground failure beneath proposed development. Plate 7.2 is a reminder of the problem of coastal erosion in eastern and southern England, exacerbated by plot-land style development from the inter-war period.

Plate 7.2 Development on unstable ground. Cliff-top recession due to the sea and rainwater action has eroded the garden of this bungalow at Herne Bay, Kent: R. N. E. Blake.

Implementing design and layout: key issues

Just as housing development sites must be appraised for their geo-environmental and geotechnical attributes to meet the increasing array of guidelines on structural, microclimatic and ecological integrity, so must they be appraised in terms of their design potential for agreeable and effective living spaces. Estate layout has long ceased to be a mechanistic exercise confined to the drawing board, and is now an art-form equivalent in complexity to the applied science of site investigation. In this concluding section we return to the end-product and review the key design variables of residential estate layout, suggesting how landform vegetation, density, orientation, road hierarchy, car parking, non-vehicular circulation, style, security and safety can be synthesised into realisable schemes.

Design concept

For any housing development scheme it is first essential to express the key elements of the proposal in a conceptual diagram. This may already have been done as part of viability assessment at development brief stage, in which case the designer will be fully aware of the land-use planning context. The job of the architect or planning consultant is to 'work up' the proposal from basic principles that tie in with the adjacent urban or landscape structure in such a way that the 'environmental capital' of the locality is maximised for the benefit of the new residents and any negative impacts of the development on the host community are minimised. While every site is unique in its geographical setting, the common aim of all residential development is to retain established flows across the site so that the development adds something to the community and is not perceived as intrusive. A key principle, illustrated in Lincolnshire County Council's (1994: 18) design guide, is that development should contain a range of densities with the higher-density dwellings located closest to the main entry point while the properties with the largest gardens should be sited to the rear abutting onto the countryside. The logic of this distribution is to place the majority of the residents near to a bus stop on the assumption that the more affluent residents will require fewer visits by social service vehicles on a daily basis. Where the site is surrounded by existing development this arrangement may be problematic, especially if there is an affordable housing element that the developers prefer not to flaunt. Linkages into adjacent sites harnessing natural corridors and 'desire lines' that break the proposed development into manageable 'cells' is a design approach geared to ultimate user-satisfaction.

Road hierarchy

Even on small infill sites the relationship between new dwellings and the highway is critical. Whatever the socio-economic status of the residents, vehicular access arrangements must be incorporated into the design to admit emergency and utility vehicles. At the same time roads must be designed to maximise safety, minimise pollution and have the least impact on visual amenity. Modern road systems are hierarchical and as a general principle the wider and busier the road, the further back dwellings should be sited from it. In central urban situations this may not always be possible and compensating measures such as sound-proofing and rear courtyards are used to re-orient dwellings away from heavy traffic flows. In suburban and growth village layouts residential properties are best accessed from secondary roads to avoid the debased amenity experienced in pre-war ribbon development (see Chapter 2). The faster the traffic, the greater the distance between junctions, hence the practice of minimising the number of vehicular access points into estates. Motorists should progressively reduce speed as they approach their residential destination, time loss being a small price to pay for safety, tranquillity and neighbourliness. To assist planners and designers, Design Bulletin 32 (DoE, 1992) classified roads into three main levels: district distributors, local distributors and access roads. District distributors carry the flow around town, have roundabouts and traffic lights and should not give direct access to homes (remember ribbon development). Local distributors are the veins of residential zones and typically feed off a controlled junction. They are often flanked by a planted strip to soften the impact of traffic noise on homes, and junctions with access roads are designed to serve a maximum of 300 dwellings. Access roads are best looped to facilitate movement of emergency and large delivery vehicles, although 'dead ends' with turning space are unavoidable in most estates. Culs-de-sac serving more than 50 dwellings should have sidewalks strong enough to support heavy vehicles in exceptional circumstances, but those with fewer dwellings are increasingly being designed with 'calmed' surfaces where the rigid distinction between vehicular and pedestrian use is blurred (Lincolnshire County Council, 1994: 94).

Road and parking environment

Roads and parking areas within residential areas are part of the total living space. As length and width are reduced by design, so the social importance of the vehicular environment increases. The conventional 30 mph limit remains the norm on local distributors but on access roads devices such as raised junctions, and narrowed carriageways (chicanes) are being introduced to bring speeds down below 20 mph. Physical restraints can be as close as 40 m apart on minor access roads. Estate road design is meant to discourage through traffic ('rat runs') by means of curvatures that impose time penalties on drivers looking for short cuts. Because on-street parking by visitors is difficult to prevent without ugly yellow lines indicating penalties, normal carriageways have a minimum width of 5.5 m. Where a road passes between two buildings to reach a rear parking area this standard may be relaxed. To prevent the residential landscape becoming dominated by parked cars, spaces between, beneath and to the rear of dwellings are now advocated in some design guides (e.g. Surrey Local Government Association, 2001).

Energy and water efficiency

Estate layout can play a significant part in meeting international targets for energy conservation. Over half of carbon dioxide (CO_2) emissions in Britain come from energy use in buildings. Reductions can be effected directly by more efficient dwelling construction and indirectly through the use of materials that have been manufactured in low-energy and non-toxic environments (see Chapter 8). The embodied energy and transport costs of mass-produced building materials can be reduced by substitution of local materials in favourable circumstances. The role of estate layout in energy saving focuses on three areas that have come to the fore on the last three decades: solar gain, walking, cycling and public transport, and water recycling. Passive solar gain is achieved by orienting the key living space of dwellings within 30° of south (in northern latitudes), also maximising daylight and wind-assisted ventilation. If all dwellings were identically oriented southwards estates could be monotonous, which places a responsibility on the designer to snake the road layout around clusters of dwellings. Detached houses are the least energy-efficient form and great ingenuity is required to achieve privacy and architectural interest in the semi-detached form. Minimisation of movement by means other than the motorcar can be achieved by integrating footpaths and cycle-tracks into the developments and minimising gradients and detours. Regarding water-use efficiency, there is the opportunity for rainwater and 'grey water' harvesting (see Chapter 8) and water treatment outside the home but within the estate. SUDS permit rainwater to filter into the ground rather than flooding across concrete and bitumen to the detriment of residents and the environment. Estate design should incorporate passive water conveyancing such as detention ponds and reed beds within the development.

Surveillance, safety and security

The dominant concerns of estate residents are pedestrian safety, burglary and mugging. Pedestrian safety is achieved first, by strategic segregation of road and footpath systems and second, by speed restraint of motor vehicles on access roads leading to dwellings and community facilities. Personal safety can be increased by main entry doors facing onto visible space and by eliminating rear alleys from the design altogether. Open car parking should be visible from owners' and neighbours' downstairs windows. Pedestrian and cycle routes should be well lit and have no niches where criminals can hide. This has introduced a dilemma for the designer, for extensive planting of shrubs to create desirable biomass also creates precisely those lairs from which assaults can be mounted unobserved. The preferred planning strategy therefore is trees, preferably behind walls. Bright lighting can be a nuisance to householders and destroy the sense of night-time tranquillity, especially in select suburbs and villages. Children's play areas emphatically should not be sited in secluded places for obvious reasons. The police architectural liaison officer plays an important part in 'designing out crime', counselling for example that a labyrinth of narrow pathways linking culs-de-sac offer ready escape routes for criminals. CCTV cameras among dwellings are an admission of insecurity and passive 'designed-in' measures are always preferable.

Land economy and density

There is a general assumption in estate layout that building density should be maximised to reduce land-take. A design-led approach enables this to be done by providing a mix of dwelling types, some of which are of higher density than conventional family dwellings to reflect changed demand. As indicated in the previous sub-section, high densities (50 or more dwellings per hectare) can be balanced against those below 25 d.p.h. in the more peripheral locations. A case for comparatively low density is the retention of local distinctiveness. High density has traditionally been achieved by high-rise, a form regarded as alien to suburban and village estates. A device increasingly used in three-to-four storey, mixed-density developments is the terrace with rear car parking accessed via an arch formed by the upper floors of one property. Provided parked cars are visible and enclosed by a wall, this is an effective environment. Reduction in parking standards can increase site density, releasing land for amenity.

Local distinctiveness and vernacular style

One of the major criticisms of conventional housing estates was their drab, monotonous appearance. This was chiefly due to repetition of a limited number of house types over large areas and the imposition of geometric road patterns and unnecessarily large gardens (see Chapter 2, Figure 2.2d). Local character was ignored by erasing landscape details and accepting materials and designs produced by builders and local authorities from the drawing board rather than by multi-disciplinary teams in the field. Local distinctiveness resides in two key legacies: the vegetation and building tradition. The vegetation defines the basic structure of the site and should be protected wherever possible to help absorb the new development into the general texture of the area. Mature trees have a powerful and cradling effect on new dwellings. Local building materials and construction methods are important because they reflect local geology and craftsmanship. Boundary walls and outhouses should be designed compatibly with local tradition. Developers marketing new homes can increase sales by emphasising specific association with the area, but the longer-term social benefit is a development that quickly settles into the local landscape.

Conclusions

Site appraisal and residential estate layout are both comparatively recent specialisms within the housing development process. Builders traditionally have appraised the ground by intuition and received experience, largely to avoid obvious hazards such as flooding or to maximise solar gain. More thorough site investigation to anticipate contamination and collapse is essentially the result of recent de-industrialisation and the government-led agenda to recycle as much vacant land as possible to accommodate residential growth. Estate layout design using systematic environmental analysis techniques is the product of an affluent society with ever-rising expectations of its home environment, the growth of expertise in the urban design professions, and the global agenda for more sustainable forms of development. It is this last consideration that unites the geotechnical and design dimensions of site analysis. While site investigation works from the premise that the space *below* development is crucial to its viability, estate design follows the principle that the space *between* dwellings is every bit as important as the dwellings themselves. This chapter has taken the housing debate on a circular journey, starting with the goals of estate layout, reviewing means, pitfalls and challenges, of development and ending with a practical framework for design. In the next chapter we shall focus on the individual dwelling as a micro-environment and living space.

Discussion points

1   Discuss the key changes in the practice of private housing estate layout in Britain during the post-war period.
2   What is meant by development 'viability'? Highlight the key factors impacting on residential site viability and demonstrate the key financial inputs using worked examples.
3   Examine the concept of 'kerb appeal' and suggest how customer taste could be reflected in estate layout.
4   Define the term 'site appraisal'. What steps would a residential developer normally be expected to take to ensure a site had been correctly 'appraised' prior to the construction of dwellings.
5   In the role of a planning consultant, draw up a checklist of possible ground problems on behalf of a house-builder looking for sites to develop.

Key reading

For modern thinking on urban design the Final Report of the Urban Task Force, *Towards an Urban Renaissance* (1999) and DTLR/CABE, *By Design: Better Places to Live* (2001) are essential. Site planning and landscaping with particular reference to conventional suburban and village infill are articulated in several county design guides: Essex (1974), Suffolk (1993) and Lincolnshire (1994). Techniques of land appraisal can be found in: Clayton *et al.*, *Site Investigation* (1995); Nathanail *et al.*, *Contaminated Land Management* (2002); and Syms and Knight, *Building Homes on Used Land* (2000).

Chapter 8
Dwelling construction and design

Gavin Tunstall and Ron Blake

Plate 8.1 A well proportioned house with defensible space at Herne bay, Kent: R. N. E. Blake.

Introduction

The dwelling house represents one of modern society's more interesting paradoxes. As a major component of the UK's built environment, the experience of living in houses is of fundamental importance to the lives of the whole population and yet few people play any real part in the creation of their own house. They create a home by making personal, but essentially cosmetic, alterations to a building designed and constructed according to the values and standards of earlier times. To a large extent, therefore, residential conditions with respect to comfort, convenience and economy are not entirely satisfactory to the present-day occupants. Customisation of new dwellings is being introduced by the more innovative developers but so far this only benefits a tiny minority of house-holders.

While the house is for private, personal use, it also functions within the wider community and environment of which it is a part. Designed to satisfy the needs of the individual occupant, every dwelling by default has an effect on its immediate neighbours and others nearby. The public/private balance evident in the rich variety of house types and groupings throughout the UK has evolved through continuous experimentation, as those charged with designing, constructing and managing the housing stock search for 'better ways to live'. Alternative ideas about the function and the appearance of houses are devised, regularly amended or even radically changed as a result of the influences of diverse pressures, including the advance of technology, the dictates of national politicians, the preferences of leading practitioners and, increasingly, as a result of onerous commercial targets and market forces.

House-builders are faced with resolving apparently conflicting design issues as they attempt to respond to the challenge of generating ever increasing 'numbers'. On the one hand, they are under local pressure to achieve expansion and regeneration through new construction, while on the other hand they are expected to encompass conservation, promote sustainability and minimise the wider environmental impact. This chapter reviews the main technical and aesthetic challenges faced by the producers of housing at the level of the individual dwelling.

Links between construction and materials

From tradition to innovation

Forms of construction and selection of materials in the UK fall into one of two categories. Traditional methods of load-bearing construction, originally developed through the use of locally produced 'raw' materials such as bricks, slates and plaster achieve guaranteed satisfactory results when used in the 'correct' way. Periodically however, innovations have been introduced using concrete, steel and timber frames, and glass, plastics and fibres as attractive, economical or practical alternatives. Statutory controls influence innovation, prompting designers and manufacturers to develop new products and systems through research and development in pursuit of improved performance.

Innovation is a continuing source of debate in today's house-building industry. Key questions concern the relative merits of:

- load-bearing brick-and-block walls versus timber framing;
- on-site 'wet' construction methods versus off-site factory prefabrication;
- traditional crafts and trades versus new skills and methodologies;
- technological advance versus pastiche design.

More broadly, the aim of building construction is to create closed environments through the selection of appropriate materials and assemblies. The resistance to water penetration and the retention of warmth, for example, relate to the inherent characteristics of the materials and forms in which they are used. Historically, the simple mass of materials ensured they withstood the forces imposed on them. Stone, clay, timber and thatch, for example, gave some limited protection from the elements, but inevitably these materials and systems deteriorated. The introduction of glass, glass fibre, plastics and other synthetic materials to resist rising damp and prevent wasteful heat loss has helped to prolong the useful life of all modern buildings.

The selection of materials used for building houses is inextricably linked with methods of construction (see Cook, 1984; Barley, 1986). Most of the built environment, especially houses, was, and to an extent still is, constructed from local, readily available materials, selected originally because of an understanding of local geology, ecology, climate and soil structure (see Plate 8.2). Skilful techniques in the handling and detailing of stone, slate, clay, limestone, iron and timber developed in response to the constraints and limitations of each material, and throughout the UK recognisable vernacular styles of building reflect local features and characteristics (see Brunskill, 2000).

Surviving houses from the sixteenth century onwards exhibit strong regional variations, some of which are still reflected in the construction of new houses today. Periodic disasters such as the Great Fire of London prompted changes in the use of materials and construction systems, but generally house-building has remained

Plate 8.2 Detached garages in Norwich, rendered with flint in keeping with local building traditions: R. N. E. Blake.

rooted in traditional methods. The boom in demand for economical mass housing from the mid-nineteenth century onward was accompanied by the exhaustion of local resources which, linked with the extension of transportation systems, and changes in manufacturing processes and economic controls, brought about a decline in genuine 'vernacular' construction.

The development of 'materials science' as a discipline led to the invention of new synthetic materials, but the design and construction of houses displayed a reliance on 'pastiche' designs and 'pseudo' construction methods associated with previous systems. Consequently, both design and construction failed to satisfy demand. Recent failures in some systems can be attributed to the incorrect application of materials and ignorance about the constraints which our building predecessors rigorously observed. The decline in the designer's and craftsman's understanding of the properties of materials (see Lyons, 1997) has seen the introduction of extensive control systems, regulations, codes of practice, standard specifications and testing procedures with an ever-increasing reliance on site supervision for quality assurance. The chief technical controls in force today are: British Standards Institution (materials), Codes of Practice (workmanship), Agrément Certificates (products), Building Research Establishment (digests of test results), NHBC Standards (house-building guarantees), Building Regulations (construction requirements) and European Technical Specifications (CEN harmonised standards).

Raw materials, manufactured components and assembled structures are each influenced by the constraints of the design brief, desired quality, cost and the methods of handling, fixing and anticipated use. The scientific properties of materials and the specifications for their detailed assembly are well documented, but technological advance, revisions to the manufacturer's recommendations and changing building regulations periodically demand re-assessment of construction practice, changing understanding of best practice, or even 'good practice' at any particular moment in time.

Materials, components and assemblies

Building construction combines basic materials with manufactured components (see Stroud Foster, 2000). Sand, cement and aggregates are used in a 'raw' state whereas stone, slate and timber are 'worked', creating components with attractive, durable finishes. Clay, plaster, glass and plastics are moulded or cut into units, creating bricks, blocks, tiles, sheets and boards or into special shapes for pipes, extrusions and sanitary ware. Various fluids are used for gluing, jointing, protecting and decorating. A typical house will contain the following range of materials:

Cementitious: cements, lime, gypsum, aggregates for concrete and blocks, sands for mortar, screeds and renders.
Burned-clay: bricks, roof tiles, ceramic and terracotta floor and wall tiles.
Stone: aggregates, hardcore, random rubble, ashlar, slate.
Gypsum products: plaster, plasterboards boards, coving.

Glass: windows, doors, mirrors.

Timber: softwood, hardwood, processed boards, t&g floor boards, chipboard, hardboard.

Steel and alloys: rolled, stainless, galvanised, iron, reinforcement, structural members, nails, screws, fittings.

Aluminium and alloys: Door and window frames, ironmongery, rainwater goods.

Copper and alloys: brass, bronze, cupronickel.

Lead: flashings, damp-proof courses.

Plastics: upvc, polythene, sheet vinyl, rubber, laminates.

Glass fibres: insulation, canopies.

Porcelain: enamelled sanitary goods.

Asphalt and bitumen: dpcs, roofing materials.

Joints and seals: mastics, neoprene gaskets.

Paints and coatings: glues, paints, stains.

Paper: linings, wall coverings.

Materials, components and assemblies can be defined and assessed at a number of stages in the life-time of the dwelling: design specification; manufacture; delivery; handling and manipulation; assembly; fixing; finishing; in use.

Factors which shape performance levels include the location and degree of visibility, and the extent of exposure to aggressive forces within the completed construction. Traditional practice is a guide to performance, but 'innovative' or novel solutions to building construction cannot alter the basic characteristics of the materials. In many cases, performance is related to the intrinsic features, composition, method of manufacture, size, shape and cross-section. Cohesiveness, response to compression, tension, bending, shear, impact forces, resistance to permeability, absorption, expansion and contraction, and the smoothness or abrasiveness of finished surfaces are all matters of fact which influence the selection of materials as well as determining how they may successfully be combined (see also Everett, 1994).

Design requirements present a range of choices which can be stated as being essential, desirable or preferable, and which demand assessment in advance of deciding how construction may be achieved. For example, the need for the finished construction to be strong and stable, able to withstand imposed loads without moving and cracking is an essential aim, which can be achieved in a variety of alternative ways. Other aims include resistance to the hostile effects of the climate, water, frost, wind, sunlight and atmospheric pollution so that deterioration, weathering and normal wear and tear can be reasonably controlled by occasional or regular cleaning and economical maintenance over a planned lifetime. Construction may be permanent or may offer flexibility permitting partial or complete dismantling and reassembly.

Construction must be safe and comfortable, minimising the risk of injury through fire damage, structural collapse and the spread of dangerous fumes. Damages may be caused too by abrasive chemical and biological attack, and by unwanted fungi and insects which can be extremely destructive if undeterred or undetected. The control of excessive heat loss, humidity, solar gain and sound transmission have a bearing on acceptable comfort levels, and construction should generally be seen as producing a comfortable as well as an attractive and aesthetically pleasing environment. All of the above factors are further influenced by availability of materials, time programming, skill levels, economical capital cost, maintenance costs and depreciation, and personal perceptions of quality.

On site, consideration must be given to the implications for labour and plant, wastage, theft and vandalism, testing, inspecting, delivery and storage. Supply issues such as sourcing, packaging, conditions of delivery, continuity of supply, solvency, factory testing and guarantees, technical support and quality assurance are all pertinent to the selection and specification of materials, components and assemblies. For some materials and components, the process of manufacture causes unavoidable variations in dimensions and colouring, which may be regarded as inherently attractive if handled correctly by careful selection, mixing and anticipation of tolerances. Tolerances at junctions between materials and components are affected by ease of cut and fit, fragility, protection of exposed surfaces, simplicity of shape, repetition of patterns, ease of handling, laying, fixing and fitting, time and skill.

The anatomy of the dwelling

In construction studies it is conventional to make a primary distinction between substructure, superstructure, services and microclimate. This approach stems from the fact that buildings are fixed into the ground and therefore cannot be readily compared with other manufactured products. In certain respects the dwelling can be interpreted as a 'machine for living' (Le Corbusier, 1923), but the organic nature of its evolution also provides comparison with the human body in terms of anatomy, physiology, circulation, metabolism and life-cycle. The anatomy of a dwelling house is an extensive subject for which there is a range of important texts (see for example, Salvadori, 1990; Levy and Salvadori, 1994; Riley and Howard, 2002). Here we summarise the issues pertaining to the key elements. Figure 8.1 provides an overview of the key structural elements and environmental concerns which the designer and builder of dwellings have to take into consideration.

Substructure

In the previous chapter emphasis was placed on ground investigation to test the feasibility of developing sites for housing. While it is unusual today for planning permission to be given on grossly impractical sites, the integrity of the ground must be checked for possible hazards even after construction has begun. Substructure includes the ground below the dwelling but in this context comprises more importantly the layout of foundations and footings.

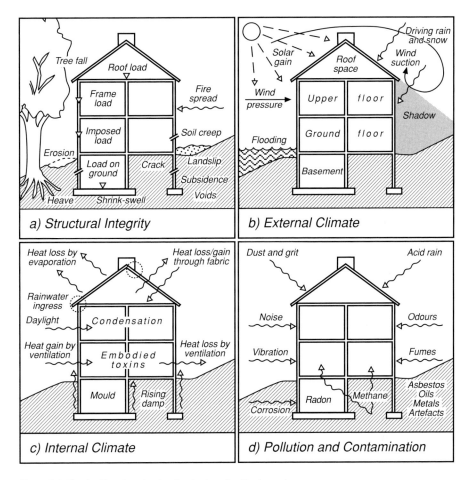

Figure 8.1 The dwelling: key structural and microclimatic elements.
Source: Simplified from a variety of construction and environmental science texts

Foundations

Foundations are designed and constructed to provide a secure, level platform upon which to build the superstructure of the dwelling and resist movement induced by imposed loadings (Figure 8.1a). Under normal conditions, ready-mixed *in situ* concrete is poured into excavated trenches below external and internal wall positions at a depth of approximately 1,000 mm where it will be unaffected by temperature variations. Specially designed foundations, incorporating steel reinforcement are used for sloping sites and in weak or disturbed sub-soils where ground movement may be anticipated. In exceptional cases, the potential for ground movement dictates the use of a reinforced concrete raft or a form of piling. Variation in ground water content, particularly in association with large trees and clay sub-soils is a major cause of damage to foundations. Subsequent settlement and cracking is one of the most costly causes of building failure.

Footings

The space between the foundations and the ground floor provides an opportunity to create a basement or semi-basement (Figure 8.1b), particularly on sloping sites, although generally perimeter brick footings built off the foundations restrain a compacted hardcore platform which supports the ground floor, and provides a level base for all walls above. Walls below ground level are strong enough to resist soil and ground water pressures, and at ground level, damp-proofing and insulation are detailed into the construction to resist water penetration and minimise heat transference. Drainage outlets and ducts are built into the substructure in advance of connection of service feeds from external mains.

Superstructure

Ground floor

The ground floor is constructed to resist rising damp, is insulated to minimise heat loss and is strong enough to support anticipated imposed loads (Figure 8.1c). Traditional construction takes the form of an *in situ* concrete slab over the compacted hardcore base, laid on a polythene damp-proof membrane. Alternatively, the floor is constructed with concrete beams and blocks suspended off the perimeter footings. Both options are insulated and covered with a sand cement screed finish. Suspended timber joists and floor boarding or decking provide a potential alternative but with an increased risk of rot damage. Enclosed voids are ventilated to minimise dampness and special ventilation measures are required to deal with the presence of methane or radon gases (Figure 8.1d).

Walls

There are two main types of wall: structural and partition. Structural or 'load-bearing' walls support floors, ceilings and roofs, and cannot be easily altered or removed. Partition, or non load-bearing, walls simply infill the space between other structural elements, and can be removed without causing structural damage. A structural wall can be either continuously load-bearing, constructed in horizontal courses of bricks and/or concrete blocks, or built with vertical posts and horizontal beams or ties in the form of a frame. Traditional load-bearing masonry walls are widely used in the construction industry, but alternative methods of construction are becoming increasing popular. Timber or steel framed houses, and other forms of prefabrication offer economies in manufacture and erection, and can more readily accommodate improvements in insulation values (expressed as SAP ratings). Traditional construction is relatively labour intensive, subject to delays resulting from 'wet' trades and dimensionally erratic. Although such construction has a high embodied energy content, the massiveness of this form of construction can be used to advantage for thermal storage, for example, via trombe walls (see glossary). However, off-site, factory-made components associated with framed systems offer better quality control and dimensional accuracy, and 'dry' site construction improves speed and quality of the finished work.

The shell of the building is designed so that there is structural integrity through all floors, to ensure stability. The external inner leaf, or framing system, runs full height to support all floors and the roof. Some internal walls are continued up to roof level to add stiffness, and to support floor joists and parts of the roof. Party walls between separate occupancies (semi-detached, terraces and apartments) are designed to reduce sound transmission. Doors and windows punctuate the external elevations for access, natural light and ventilation.

Roof

The principal function of the roof is to exclude rain, which was achieved tradition-ally through the use of pitched roofs built with timber purlins and rafters, creating a void which, though accessible, was often not habitable. Prefabricated roof trusses, developed as a matter of economy after the Second World War, filled the roof void with timbers, preventing use by occupants. Recent developments are reverting to the concept of utilising the roof void, a significant potential floor space available at little additional cost, provided that the form of construction and headroom are appropriate. A 'cut' roof design with lowered eaves and dormer windows is a common solution to utilising roof space, although space must be found on the landing below for a staircase (see Figure 8.3 later in the chapter). Pitched roofs offer the opportunity for installation of solar panels, which may become commonplace in the future. The use of flat roofs has been limited by resistance to their appear-ance and regular failure of both materials and systems, offering a limited lifespan.

Fixtures, fittings and finishes

All dwellings contain a variety of fixtures and fittings which are 'built-in', perma-nently fixed and not easily moved or changed. Staircases, fireplaces and drainage installations are permanent fixtures, expected to last for the life-time of the building, whereas others such as bathroom and kitchen fittings are semi-permanent with a finite lifespan and can be changed if desired. Other fittings and finishes, including doors, ironmongery, light fittings and wallpaper, can be easily changed to suit the occupier's desired decor.

Building services

Structural integrity, as important as it is, does not alone make a modern building habitable. Services in the form of water, heating and power are essential in completing the domestic environment. Foul waste from bathroom, cloakroom and kitchen fittings is collected through internal plastic wastepipes and taken out of the building to external manholes and underground sewers. Rainwater from roofs passes through plastic gutters and downpipes to separate manholes ensuring that foul and surface water are not mixed. Cold water from incoming mains and hot water from boilers is distributed through pipe work to outlets, including storage tanks, cisterns, radiators and taps. Plumbing and drainage outlets are normally grouped closely together as a matter of economy, using relatively short, convenient connections.

Electricity, gas and telecommunications services provide power, lighting, heating and communication facilities. Incoming mains, meters, distributions boards, boilers, radiators, cooker points, mechanical vents, television aerials, telephone outlets and some general lighting are normally installed as standard fixtures and fittings to satisfy typical needs. Installations are designed to achieve standard performance levels for internal temperature, illumination and ventilation. Additional outlets are spread around the building in anticipation of user demand.

Microclimate

The purpose of a dwelling is to create an artificial climate that is either warmer or cooler, drier or moister, than ambient conditions outside as dictated by the season or weather. In Britain and other countries of the northern latitudes the predominant objective is to create a microclimate that is drier, warmer and less windy than the 'mesoclimate' of the locality. Pressure on buildings by driving rain, for example, is greater in the hilly north and west than in the inland parts of the south and east with implications for build-costs and domestic comfort (Figure 8.2).

The importance of services in regulating temperature is easy to appreciate. The integrity of the substructure is also crucial in preventing heat loss, ingress of moisture and other negative 'flows' affecting the energy balance. Dwelling microclimate is thus dependent partly on the materials and construction methods, partly

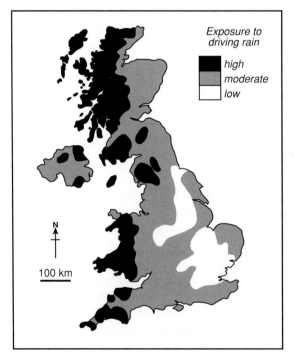

Exposure to driving rain

high
moderate
low

N

100 km

Figure 8.2 Exposure to driving rain in the UK.
Source: Simplified from research data collected by the Building Research Establishment

on the provision of special services (cabling and ducting), partly on fuel supply and partly on gifts from the natural environment. It is also important from an environmental perspective to appreciate that the dwelling is a place of embodied energy in terms of the manufacturing processes that go into the materials used, and as a source of toxic emissions into the atmosphere from fuel consumption and effluents (Figure 8.1d). Good design and sensible estate layout can assist passive solar gain and thereby reduce some of the effects of exposure. A whole area of 'green architecture' has emerged concerned with the twin goals of reducing energy use and minimising global warming through prudent dwelling design.

Design, function and the home

The function of dwellings

At the simplest level a dwelling provides a secure, sheltered environment for its occupants. The walls, floors and roof that make up their home is commonly subdivided into discrete spaces catering for specific physical, emotional and cultural needs. Cooking and bathing are essentially practical activities, whereas others such as eating and entertaining have the added psychological and social connotations of image, style and displayed status. These functions vary in importance with the age of the individual. The individualistic nature of relaxing, studying, and even sleeping confound a unitary definition of 'needs', complicating possible design solutions. As the very idea of a house and its contents is based on personal experience, designers anticipate solutions which may or may not be appropriate or correct, and which may limit the occupant's realisation of other possibilities (see also Lambert, 1993). Advantages may be missed, and disadvantages ill-considered.

The fundamental purposes of the typical dwelling are broadly as follows:

- to withstand and give protection from the elements: wind, rain, damp, cold and heat;
- to use reliable construction techniques and materials at appropriate cost;
- to cater for and withstand the effects of normal usage without the need for undue maintenance and repair;
- to eliminate health and safety hazards under normal usage;
- to permit safe evacuation in the event of emergency;
- to enable control of the internal environment to currently acceptable minimum standards for air supply, temperature, humidity, lighting and acoustics;
- to minimise wasteful energy consumption;
- to minimise deleterious environmental impact on, and from, neighbours;
- to maximise the potential of the site by exploiting positive features and alleviating negative ones;
- to conform with the requirements of interested authorities;
- to be visually pleasing internally and externally.

Most houses contain a broadly similar range of accommodation, with inter-linked spaces in recognisable patterns. Plan types vary according to the size and number of spaces and their configuration results from their orientation to salient features on each site. The design of a new housing development containing numerous properties is often based on generic floor plans, modified to suit local constraints and varied to introduce elements of individuality. The accommodation and appearance of individual dwellings commonly displays a consistency with the general style of the whole development. Historically, this can be seen in the spacious elegance of the Georgian terraces in Bath (see also for example, Binnen, 1998) the grimy claustrophobic Victorian terraces in Nottingham, and even in the ubiquitous concrete deck access blocks of the 1970s, each type of development a collective of individual, yet similar dwellings. This remains true of current development, ranging from 'standard house-type' greenfield solutions in estate layout form to 'one-off' individually designed, inner-city apartment blocks. Such developments, together with large properties, single dwellings on extensive sites, or houses designed to 'infill' gaps between existing buildings, all fit the one-off description and are unlikely to be suitable for direct reproduction elsewhere.

Typical standard dwelling types of today include: bed-sits, flats, apartments, maisonettes, loft conversions, terraces, semi-detached houses, detached houses and bungalows. The present-day demand is for smaller properties, not only as a matter of economy, bearing in mind land values and construction costs, but also to provide 'starter homes', or 'affordable' housing. Other significant forms of residential development include bed-sits for students and housing for the elderly. These homes are usually designed in the form of easily managed, small-scale self-contained flats or bungalows for those who wish to retain their independence. Purpose-designed warden aided accommodation is also important for those who need personal and medical assistance, or for those with special needs or disabilities.

Activity and flow

Although buildings are three-dimensional, the design of the dwelling house can be illustrated in two dimensions by combining individual spaces into a layout or 'plan form', with specific or relatively loose definitions of function. Traditionally, spaces within dwellings are called rooms, and given titles such as lounge, dining room, kitchen and bedroom (see also Allen, 1995). The current trend for smaller households with more rooms able to support the concept of cellular living supports the notion that members of the household are seeking to pursue their own interests throughout the day, increasing the need for flexibility in both layout and form of construction.

The activities of daily life are largely predictable, and while it is difficult to determine categorically the behaviour of every occupant, common patterns will be apparent. Defined activities rarely take place in isolation. They mix together, demanding movement or 'flow' from one to another, leading to other demands or desires. For example, the principal activity of arriving at the house can be elaborated to include: easy, safe access into the site for vehicles and pedestrians; acceptance of deliveries including milk, papers and mail; protection from the elements while unlocking the front door; dealing with visitors; and presenting an image to neighbours. Once inside, there is a need to remove and store wet clothing and use the toilet before proceeding to other parts of the house, possibly without disturbing other members of the household. There are other links to parking spaces and/or garaging, to storage and private external space. Each activity suggests other possible connections with advantages, disadvantages, limitations and compromises, building up a framework of spatial organisation which resolves into the plan arrangement.

Design and functional space considerations

There are several important design considerations to take into account if residential development is to have functional appeal (see Ching, 1996). These range from issues concerning the external appearance and siting of the dwelling on its plot, right through to the layout of individual rooms within the dwelling. As we shall see in Chapter 9, both external and internal factors are crucial to marketing, selling and customer satisfaction.

Public access and approach

The external 'kerb appeal' characteristics of any building are often of greater importance to potential purchasers than the subsequent detailed exploration of the interior. The apparent size, spaciousness, importance, image and style can dictate the purchaser's attitude to the property. For example, a wide shallow plot is perceived as being larger than a narrow deep plot. The quality of the design and use of materials for the front elevation may determine whether or not further investigation takes place at all. Perceived elevational variation is significant, maximised when houses are on sloping sites.

The definition and detailing of the boundaries to the frontage of the property should recognise the need for 'defensible space', a term used to help to explain the significance of the intangible boundaries between public and private occupation (Newman, 1973). An open-frontage style of development creates feelings of greater spaciousness, but generally at the expense of individual privacy and control. In the absence of walls, fencing and planting, a demarcation line is required, clearly indicating the point at which 'strangers' are intruding into private territory. The extent to which occupiers are provided with a genuinely usable front garden, the quality of outlook (the view) directly away from the building and the ability to accommodate the 'car', or cars, are all current issues for debate (see Plate 8.1).

Main entrance

The main/front entrance is the principal public and focal point for visitors. It is 'public' in the sense that it is where strangers are controlled or received, without their intruding into private spaces beyond. It is a point where shelter is useful before the door is opened, and where a porch, lobby or hall can offer protection from cold draughts when the front door is opened and members of the household enter the house and pass through to other living areas.

Secondary entrance and private approach

Other entrances into the building are usually private, for use by the occupants only, linking internal and external spaces in a less formal way, for example, having break-fast on the terrace in the early morning sun or enjoying a garden party barbecue in the evening, as well as removing rubbish, hanging out wet washing and feeding the cats. These 'utility' functions tend to be associated with the kitchens, but should in any event avoid the need to pass through living rooms, with consequential intrusive effects of unwanted noise and smells disturbing other living activities.

Circulation space

Circulation space is the space needed for the flow between activities. It can be precisely defined as a corridor linking two other spaces together, or it can be more amorphous and less specific. Expensive corridors can be wasteful and unattractive, and unlit, dark passages, halls, landings and stairs can be dangerous to use, espe-cially for elderly occupants and small children. Larger, naturally lit spaces such as an inner hall or a library landing, which cater for necessary movement and separate major activities from one another, may also usefully contain visitors, assist work-ing from home and provide additional storage space. Circulation space defines and separates the conflicting activities of different age groups, including work/play, educational study/musical practice, privacy/communal activity, access, noise and smells.

Living space

Activities such as sitting, resting, TV watching, listening to music, reading and entertaining are undertaken in different ways by different people, determined by their lifestyle preferences. Floor size, orientation, outlook and privacy substantially affect the quality and potential for occupants' use, and the flexibility to modify the function of living spaces from time to time, or alter them radically as the nature of family life changes. The design of any dwelling can be arranged to support poten-tial future extensions to create the additional living space that is most needed. For all but the smallest of starter homes, more than one living space is essential to accommodate conflicting activities at the same time.

Food preparation

Traditionally, food preparation was at the heart of the dwelling. The 'farmhouse kitchen', warm and large enough to accommodate the whole family, encouraged a communal approach to living, which is diminished by the reduction of space to satisfy food preparation alone. A sufficiently large space can accommodate cooking, eating, children's play, recreation and other aspects of family living. Natural light and attractive views enhance this space which, when correctly linked to external spaces, permits outdoor living and convenient, safe supervision of small children. Food preparation is a practical activity demanding a space where health and safety is paramount. The 'working triangle' between cooker, sink and worktops should be self-contained to avoid risk of injury when hot pans are being moved, and should not contain circulation space leading to other areas in the house. Kitchens are normally well-ventilated to minimise the spread of water vapour and smells to other areas of the house.

Eating spaces

The activity of eating is subject to considerable personal variation, from the formality of dining with important guests to the informality of quick snacks taken anywhere inside or outside the house. Formal dining requires sufficient space to accommodate the necessary furniture, located to give convenient access to entertain and impress visitors. The concept of a dedicated dining room is changing with present-day attitudes to eating, as meals are taken in other places such as the kitchen, or in front of the television in the living room. Formal eating is an important activity, but one which is becoming less frequent, potentially releasing the 'dining room' for other family activities. Barbecues in sheltered locations outdoors, breakfast on the terrace or parties in living rooms should be anticipated and incorporated into the dwelling and garden layout.

Utility and storage space

There are activities associated with all households which create 'mess', including washing and ironing clothes, storing dirty shoes and wet clothing, mending broken equipment and accommodating pets. Integrated into other spaces, any of these activities may cause inconvenience and conflict. It is useful to have a space which can be used for working, which can be closed off from other areas, and which is closely linked with external spaces for deliveries and removal of waste. The extent of storage space needed by occupants is generally underestimated in the design of most houses. Typically, a family stores coats, shoes, clothes, linen, prams, brooms, vacuum cleaners, food, crockery, pans, books, wine, tools and much, much more. Storage space can be provided in the form of store rooms and built-in cupboards, but in any house plan, sufficient space is made available for free-standing fittings to be added by the purchaser/occupier. Storage space can be generated by thoughtful planning and sensible construction, taking advantage of roof spaces or under-stair voids for example. External storage space is needed for refuse containers.

Sleeping spaces

Sleeping places, the most private spaces within any dwelling, are usually allocated to individual members of the family. The main or 'master' bedroom normally accommodates parents while smaller rooms are for children and a guest or 'spare' bedroom is provided for occasional visitors. Traditionally, bedrooms included clothes storage, and bathrooms were separate and communal. Recently, the inclusion of dressing rooms and en-suite bathrooms has reinforced the self-contained nature of this aspect of living. Creating additional bed spaces is the most common reason for extending dwellings in order to accommodate 'newly arrived' children, growing teenagers and/or elderly grandparents, who in some cases may need to occupy suitably adapted ground floor space.

Toilet and washing facilities

The demand for toilet and washing facilities is related to the number of people in the household. Older houses with a single bathroom containing a bath, basin and WC can only satisfy the needs of one member of the family at a time. Nowadays, multiple bathrooms and toilets are commonplace, and all new houses are required to include a separate ground-floor toilet/cloakroom.

Private amenity space

Space around the dwelling provides a 'buffer' zone against the activities of neighbours and opportunities for outdoor living. Some space should be private, secure and sheltered, safe and attractive for all members of the family, ranging from play space for small children to quiet sitting areas for the elderly. The relationship with adjacent buildings and the nature of boundary walls and fences determines the extent of privacy, overlooking and overshadowing. The treatment of landscaping and planting is generally a matter of occupier preference, but design decisions establish a framework for storage, surfacing and planting possibilities.

Space standards

The basic requirements of 'activity and flow', derived from anthropometric and ergonomic data, determine *minimum* space dimensions. Creating the floors, walls and ceilings for rooms or 'open-plan' arrangements introduces additional constructional constraints that limit dimensional possibilities. Practicality and economy influence clear spans, maximum wall heights and practical sizes for door openings, windows and staircase risers. Worktops, baths and sinks are designed to suit human dimensions, while other installations are governed by the demands of economical 'work', as for example in the layout of the kitchen based on the working pattern: work top (food preparation); cooking; worktop (food serving); work top (clearing away); washing up; worktop (storage).

The Public Health Act of 1875 was the first attempt to provide guidance on minimum space dimensions for new houses. The Parker Morris report *Homes for Today and Tomorrow* (1961), was adopted to ensure that new houses complied with minimum standards for room sizes and storage space both to satisfy occupier demand, and as a mechanism for cost control of public housing through the 'housing yardstick', relating capital expenditure to defined floor areas. Development today commonly provides accommodation below Parker Morris standards for single occupants, starter homes or for the elderly, but above Parker Morris for family dwellings, specifically geared to market forces.

Aesthetic principles in dwelling design

Dwelling form

Positive and negative features are also seen in the volumes of the three-dimensional building, and in spaces between buildings and other features in the landscape. The image of the building presented to the eye is a collection of forms, sometimes interlinked or overlapped, complicated by the effects of perspective which can lead to the perceptual ambiguity and optical illusions as mentioned earlier (see also Prizeman, 1975). This can be avoided if the forms remain 'visually determinate' so that each can be identified in its own right as part of the overall composition. Described as 'articulation', this enables the viewer to see how the elements or constituents of the composition fit together. A composition that is 'visually indeterminate' appears incomplete and unsatisfactory, and can create feelings of restlessness. A composition can avoid dualities by careful articulation of forms and by co-ordinating 'similarities' making forms appear to belong to the same family, referred to as 'unity': the intentional harmonisation of shapes, tones, colours or backgrounds.

An element of logic leads the brain to make certain assumptions as, for example, that the front elevation is the most important of the four, and that the front entrance door should be prominent. Main entrances located on side elevations are aesthetically confusing as well as difficult to find. The roofing of square-plan buildings causes ambiguity when the eye and brain are unable to decide which way the roof should span, and hence cannot determine which is the most important elevation. There is an aesthetic logic applied to the apparent suitability of structural supports, the nearness of openings to edges of walls and the relationship of solid to voids (masonry to openings) when support systems may appear too weak for their task. Elements or whole buildings can appear to be falling over even though they may be perfectly stable. The visual balance of any elevation is centred around imagined axes. A symmetrical gable wall for example has a central, balanced axis. Other features such as windows create additional axes, which alter the balance and visual stability.

There is an aesthetic logic too in the use of materials, both in the sense of using a material in its natural state, and also to announce the separation of forms by visual boundaries. Natural, self-coloured materials are honest and logical whereas decorated materials deny the material's basic characteristics. Arbitrary changes in materials unrelated to form boundaries can destroy the logic of the forms or volumes. This is pertinent in the design of extensions to existing buildings, where incompatible materials can impact on the visual integration of new and old to the detriment of overall composition (see Figure 8.3).

Proportion

The relative height to width of any particular form, or the relationship between one form and another, is not only governed by the technicalities of construction and

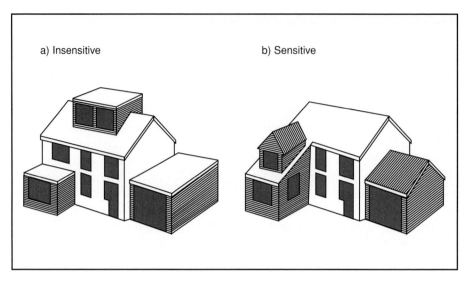

a) Insensitive

b) Sensitive

Figure 8.3 Two design approaches to the extension of a hypothetical dwelling.
Source: Adapted from various local planning control leaflets

the performance of components and materials, but also by perception and scale. Scale, as opposed to size, is a relative measure of a form judged against other familiar reference anchors, notably the dimensions of the human body. Perception of scale depends upon the location of the dwelling, the character of surrounding buildings and the relative juxtaposition of elements on the elevations, including the effect of shadowing caused by projections, overhangs and recesses. Designers from Pythagoras to Le Corbusier have invented mathematical systems which are claimed to offer designers principles for relating dimensions to achieve 'perfect' proportions. The best designers (see also Lawson, 1997) are able to blend forms together in a sympathetic manner without vulgarity. Interestingly, some psychological effects have been demonstrated, including the fact that tall buildings are generally perceived as being exciting because they represent 'being awake', while low buildings are seen as passive, associated with resting or 'lying down'. Where dwellings are extended it is important to retain basic proportions by echoing the roof pitch and not breaching the ridge line (see Figure 8.3). In this illustration the same additional accommodation can be achieved either (a) insensitively with flat-roof cubes or (b) sensitively with tiled projections that preserve the original design concept.

Detail and colour

The use of materials and components in a simple and unadorned form has been the basis for much architectural design, arguably at its most successful when expertly detailed. Detailing should not be seen as incidental decoration, but rather the handling of materials, components and assemblies in such a way that visual interest is maintained down to the smallest component. For example, the detail surrounding a window with feature brick sills, jambs and articulated heads defines and emphasises the opening, reinforcing the visual balance which creates interest through additional texture and richness. The sub-division of the lights within the opening, the nature of ironmongery and even the patterning of the glazing are details which either enhance or detract from the visual experience. Inclusion of extra details such as porches, bay windows and conservatories can be used to add detail to the appearance of identical plan-type dwellings.

Colour can unify the appearance of a building, harmonising disparate elements or introducing interest through 'contrast'. This is an important factor in the selection of materials, which may be inherently self-coloured, or which may require applied decoration. Natural colours in most materials used in the UK are relatively limited, but offer subtle tonal variations. Some forms of construction create strong visual images, as for example with strong brick and mortar joint contrast. The effects of weathering through staining, streaking and algae growth will inevitably affect the visual appearance of the building as materials either deteriorate or mellow in time, depending upon the severity of exposure to climate or other aggressive forces.

Visual perception, aesthetics and style

Satisfying occupant need within the constraints of construction is achieved in many different ways in terms of both layout and appearance of 'the house'. For any plan layout, changes in systems, materials and details are used to modify the style and appearance of the finished building. Equally, variations in appearance are achieved through changes in construction and plan layout as function and appearance are interrelated. Every building is a combination of function and appearance and changes in one always affect the other (see Smithies, 1981 and Tunstall, 2000).

The appearance of any image is detected through the eye and assessed by the brain. Whilst eyesight is a tool for receiving light waves reflected off the surface of objects (a relatively simple mechanical process explained by the science of optics), perception depends upon the interpretation made by the brain, which is influenced by memory and previous experience. The eye and brain subconsciously process raw data into 'meaningful' images, concentrating on elements which are new or unexpected. Images containing familiar clues are recognised and understood with minimal effort by comparing them to images stored in the memory. As long as there are sufficient clues, the brain will revise its perception of an image in accordance with expectation rather than reality. In fact, in some circumstances, the brain's conclusion is nowhere near the reality, as illustrated by simple optical illusions, which deceive the brain, causing interest, uncertainty or irritation.

A part of the house can be seen as an image, or more correctly as a series of changing images, as one moves around and through the structure. The composition may be extraordinary, unique and worthy of close scrutiny, or it may be so easily recognised and so comfortable that it goes unnoticed. Without being extravagant, designers are able to create interest and excitement through the addition of subtle variations which stimulate and attract attention or require onlookers to investigate and explore. Of course, they are also able to create confusion, discomfort and monotony, either by deliberate intent, or more commonly by default.

There are two significant driving forces in any composition: the forces that tend to create order, including harmony, balance and rhythm which are comfortable, relaxing and easy to live with; and the forces which tend to introduce disorder or variation, including vitality, contrast and discord. These are the forces of light and shade, which help to determine the extent to which some images are regarded as attractive while others are not and, importantly, why there may be little consensus about the quality of the appearance of a building, which may be regarded as excellent by some but derided as a 'monstrosity' by others. Individuals will tolerate variations to familiarity and expectation up to a point but, faced with the challenge of working hard to understand new images or complex variations, may conclude that the work as a whole is unsatisfactory and dismiss it as unattractive.

Principal elements of aesthetics with respect to buildings thus include the 'form' of shapes and volumes, their 'proportions' as individual components and in relation to the whole construction, the quality of detailing of components and the colouring of materials. The descending hierarchy of scale applies to the visual composition of the house from the view of the whole building in its context, seen against neighbouring buildings or landscape, to the shape and size of the front elevation, the proportions of the front door, the quality of the detailing of the door leaf, even of the keyhole escutcheon. At each level, additional information is added by the designer to enrich or impoverish the viewer's experience of the building.

Elements of composition

The structural elements of any composition are points, lines, planes and volumes, seen either as positive objects, or by default seen negatively in between and around other objects. The rectangular shape or 'form' of a wall is defined by the lines around its perimeter, and the shapes of windows and doors contain visible points, lines and planes at their corners, edges and faces. These are positive elements, but others are created by the spaces and voids between them, which have significant visual force in their own right. For example, a symmetrical elevation has a strong point at its centre, even though it is not marked, and a row of windows is a strong visual line leading the eye from side to side or in a particular direction towards another point. Subconsciously, the eye tracks from point to point, along lines, around planes and through volumes, searching for clarity and for a resting or 'focal' point, a centre of visual attention. Competing focal points can create stimulation and interest, but if they are of equal value they can cause a 'duality' a conflict of centres of attention. The eye, unable to rest in one position, flits back and forth, creating unease and fatigue.

The influence of the site itself

The dwelling house can be viewed in the same way as most commercially manufactured or exchanged goods, except that it is anchored in a location, referred to as the site (see Chapter 7). Traditionally, the site is an area of land with a legally defined boundary: around all four sides of a detached building; on three sides of a semi-detached building; and to the front and rear only for terraced properties. Multi-storey flats or apartments share whatever open space is available on a communal basis. The site and its surrounding environment possess both positive and negative characteristics, imposing influences on the potential design and construction of any building placed on it. Marginal differences between apparently similar plots can have a significant impact on commercial viability as well as the potential quality of life for future occupants.

The site's characteristics can be categorised as its physical features, the prevailing environmental conditions, socio-economic activity in the area and legal constraints. A visual inspection (walkover) reveals obvious features and conditions on, above or around the site which influence decisions about the nature of construction. Topography, existing structures and trees are easily noted, but other influences are not so evident, including the accuracy of boundary markers, possible legal constraints and the intentions of adjacent developers, which can only be determined by research or enquiry addressed to interested parties or sources of authority and control. Other information is obtained through field measurement, recording dimensions, levels and the location of services. Specialist investigations examine underlying geology and possible soil contamination.

Environmental factors affect decisions about the nature of design, and particularly about the way in which the building can be used by its future occupants. Conditions on, around and beyond the site boundary, such as means of access, adjacent development and views, determine the orientation of the building to its site, minimising overshadowing and maintaining privacy. Market research and analysis of local trends are used to justify commercial decisions while study of local facilities and amenities assists marketing strategies (see Chapter 9).

Orientation

Designers and developers seeking commercial economy through the use of repetitive house types may deprive potential purchasers and occupiers of significant amenity value by ignoring a site's inherent advantages and disadvantages. Means of access, views and the effect of sunlight on both external and internal spaces depend on the way in which the building is positioned on its site. For example, sunlight illuminates external spaces and penetrates internal spaces in the early morning, benefiting bedrooms and kitchens placed on the east side of the plot. The hot, mid-day sun creates glaring light in summer, requiring shade and protection to south-facing rooms, although in winter the same rooms will benefit from weaker, passive solar gain throughout the day. The late-afternoon sun, setting in the west, gives a pleasant light and warmth to living spaces and for sitting outside in the evening. Dwellings orientated on this basis offer a much more attractive living environment than those which are not. The orientation of adjacent properties to one another also helps to create or deny privacy. Houses can be designed so that infrequently used spaces such as garages, hard standings, cloakrooms, stairs and dining rooms are adjacent to one another, whereas frequently used living spaces are located away from each other. Potentially noisy kitchens, lounges, living rooms and external 'sitting-out' spaces require greater individual privacy from their neighbours, and generate greater noise and potential sources of annoyance to neighbours.

The design process

Thinking about design

Much has been written about design and the way in which designers think. In any discipline, designers attempt to resolve complexity into rationalised simplicity on the basis of their knowledge, expertise, ability, talent, inspiration, perspiration and, sometimes, sheer good fortune (see Tunstall, 2000). Dwelling design is essentially concerned with organisation, with the analysis and synthesis of relevant factors pertinent to the construction and the basic physical and emotional needs of its future occupants. It encompasses:

- the whole development – the design of a number of dwellings grouped together;
- the individual dwelling – the design of the single house;
- discrete spaces – the design of the single room;
- materials and details – the design of the components within each room.

Every design factor can be considered as an 'element'. Each element must be examined and understood both in its own right and in the way in which it combines with other elements. Subsequent integration into a 'whole', or rather more accurately a series of 'wholes', is based on the hierarchy of perception. Seen in this way, design is coherent and pleasing when experienced from a distance, becoming more practicable, satisfactory and interesting as a greater level of detail is revealed. This concept applies to the physical workings of the house, its layout and its amenities as well as to its appearance. It applies to cost, marketing, energy efficiency and maintenance, which can always be seen in the context of the large 'picture' as well as the smallest of details. There is no definitive route towards the creation of a workable design, but a common approach often involves:

- *Analysis*: of an element, or a set of elements to understand what they are, what they mean or can mean.
- *Synthesis*: of a selection of elements which meet specific objectives while subject to constraints or controllable variables.

- *Appraisal*: of system performance including comparison with alternatives.
- *Feedback*: to make improvements based on findings.

This strategy is 'analytical' and proposes that a solution comes from the results of detailed examination of the elements. Alternatively, and partially in reverse, synthesis, appraisal, feedback and analysis is an intuitive approach, proposing a solution in order to elicit a response which can subsequently be analysed for validity. Designers work in either or both of these ways, but it is generally common to find that initial design proposals are refined by further analysis and synthesis, repeated in a spiral fashion until the best proposal is reached, or until a deadline is imposed. The possibilities for the design of a house are very numerous, and ideas can be changed and improved almost infinitely.

The designer's essential objective is to resolve requirements and constraints in such a way as to establish an optimum solution for the given conditions. The parameters for the design of the estate, the individual dwellings or the apartment block are defined by the 'design brief', which includes the development variables, modified by subsequent discoveries. The design resolves or accommodates apparent conflicts such as townscape and highway treatment, the developer's profit and social need, public access and residents' privacy, retention of mature trees and provision of useful gardens. Design is concerned with decision taking in an informed and logical manner, but also occasionally intuitively or speculatively. It is sometimes described as being about taking risks, making choices to do with correctness, appropriateness or suitability, and decisions that can affect the future lives of occupants for many years to come.

Developing the design

Proposals for the design of individual dwellings and the estate layout are usually illustrated on drawings and described in written specifications, developed to a suitable level of detail for the purposes of communication demanded at the time. Initial sketch drawings exploring ideas are simple, showing two-dimensional shapes and three-dimensional forms in approximate outline, developed later in more detail for costing and construction purposes. Typical drawings produced to illustrate proposals would include:

- *Site plans*: overall configuration of dwellings, technical details for roads, sewers and services layouts, landscaping and planting.
- *Floor plans*: ground and upper floor plans for construction, services, fixtures, fittings and furniture.
- *Elevations*: showing the appearance of the dwelling from all sides.
- *Sections*: showing vertical 'cuts' through the dwelling to elaborate construction details.
- *Details*: large-scale assemblies of materials and components in the overall construction.

The design period and stages

The design stages generally follow the sequence of the sections which now follow here, although the precise content will vary with the size and complexity of the development and the specific relationship of the designer to the client.

Inception

This marks the beginnings of the project, establishing links and relationships between the developer's design team (consultants), the contractor's construction team and the statutory authorities. Initial investigations to assess the site conditions determine the principal issues of the development and reveal the potential for satisfying the developer's brief. Preliminary consultations and feasibility studies confirm viability, or lead to an understanding with regulatory bodies that a marketable design solution is a possibility.

The process of building procurement has received much recent attention, notably through the Latham (1994) and Egan (1998) reports, which focus on relationships between the parties involved. Both reports called for greater co-operation and less confrontation in the process of designing and constructing buildings. In volume house-building the developer is client to both architect and contractor, acting for future home-buyers unknown. Legal responsibilities are formulated and Construction (Design and Management) Regulations (CDM) requirements must be addressed at inception.

Sketch proposals

Assuming development is practicable in principle, design intensions are illustrated on sketch drawings showing an idea or a number of alternative ideas for the layout and appearance of the house. Sketches are based on measurements taken during site survey and information researched as part of the design brief. Discussions take place with the planning authorities, particularly where any development may affect neighbours, or where design is important, as for example within a conservation area. The drawings at this stage could form the basis for an outline planning application once the principle of development is established. Sketch drawings are sufficient for preliminary costings, established by specialist quantity surveyors or obtained from builders in the form of estimates. Other authorities are consulted for advice on drainage, highways, services, fire safety and crime prevention (Secured by Design).

Schematic design

The preferred idea from those considered in the previous stage becomes the focus for more detailed design work. Initial sketches giving a flavour of the final scheme are developed and checked against the original intentions in order to ensure that requirements, site conditions and statutory controls are incorporated, or can satisfactorily be incorporated in due course. The aim at this stage is to test that the framework for the building or estate design is practicable when considered from all points of view, even if some questions remain to be answered. For the individual house, drawings of all the floor plans and elevations are prepared to investigate the workings and the appearance of the new building.

Planning application

The schematic design drawings can be submitted to the local authority for approval in the form of a planning application, which together with written supporting information indicates construction intentions, including dimensions, room titles and specification of all visible materials. The application must include a current Ordnance Survey plan and certificate of ownership. The planning process empowers the local authority to scrutinise and if necessary modify design proposals. The authority's officers consult interested parties and agencies before making recommendations to their planning committee, which is made up of elected Council members. The planning function is essentially concerned with the principle of the development, with its appropriateness and appearance in its surroundings and with the way in which adjacent owners and residents might be affected. Almost all building work is subject to planning approval, which must be obtained before work can commence on site.

Building control

The local authority building control function is concerned essentially with the detailed construction and subsequent use of the dwelling, focusing on the nature and quality of materials, construction detailing, workmanship and certain environmental impact measures. Proposals are required to comply with current Building Regulations, which are set out in the form of Approved Documents including both mandatory standards and useful guidance.

The areas covered in the current Building Regulations are:

A   Structure (1992)
B   Fire safety (2000)
C   Site preparation and resistance to moisture (1992)
D   Toxic substances (1992)
E   Resistance to the passage of sound (1992)
F   Ventilation (1995)
G   Hygiene (1992)
H   Drainage and waste disposal (1992)
H   Drainage and waste disposal (2002) and Sewers Protocol (2002)
J   Heat producing appliances (1992)
J   Combustion appliances and fuel storage systems (2002)
K   Protection from falling, collision and impact (1998)
L   Conservation of fuel and power (1995)
L1 Conservation of fuel and power in dwellings (2002)
L2 Conservation of fuel and power in buildings other than dwellings (2002)
M   Access and facilities for disabled people (1999)
N   Glazing – safety in relation to impact, opening and cleaning (1998)
O   Materials and workmanship (1999).

The schematic design drawings are progressively developed to show intended construction in detail, in compliance with each relevant section of the regulations. Changes are implemented from time to time in the light of experience and political direction. For example, the structural design of multi-storey buildings was revised following the Ronan Point tower block collapse in London (1967), and current concern for minimising energy waste will undoubtedly lead to changes in the design and construction of floors, walls, roofs, openings and ventilation systems. The building control system also functions as a check on construction. The authority's officers are required by law to inspect and approve fundamental elements such as foundations, structural work and drainage. A similar quality assurance can be achieved through the services of the National House-Building Council (NHBC), which is available to the Council's members.

Pre-contract administration

The pre-contract stage involves continued development of drawings and specification information in advance of commencing building construction on site. All elements of construction are defined, described and in some cases 'measured' by a quantity surveyor. Bills of quantity facilitate competitive pricing and support supervision of construction on site. Appropriate contract documents are exchanged to suit the prevailing legal relationships of all parties involved in the development.

The extent of detail provided or required depends on the nature of the understanding between the parties as to what is to be provided or created. For example, the construction of a wall may be shown and described generally as 'brickwork', to be constructed in a manner suitable for its purpose. This loose definition places responsibility on the builder to construct a 'suitable' wall, which could lead to a result which is unsatisfactory to both designer and client. Alternatively, requirements can be elaborated, describing precisely how the wall should be built, including full specification of materials and workmanship. This method establishes a standard which can be used to assess fairly the completed work. Of course, any innovative use of materials or deviation from manufacturers' recommendations must be very carefully documented to correctly define responsibility in the event of failure. Commercial house-builders who adhere to design guidance are unlikely to get into this kind of trouble.

The construction process for a single dwelling normally begins as soon as the design has been finalised, formal approval obtained, and contract conditions agreed relating to costs and programming.

Post-contract supervision

As building work proceeds, pertinent information is made available. Materials are ordered and delivered, plant and labour secured in accordance with a construction programme. Construction is checked against drawings and specifications, and valuations prepared for interim payments to contractors, sub-contractors and suppliers.

Changes to documentation may result in costly 'variations', either by client choice, revisions to design intentions or the discovery of unknowns. The design and construction teams work together to complete the contract as planned, on time and on budget. Everyone involved should be concerned with health and safety matters on site.

Completion

Completion is achieved when the new building is handed over to its owners or occupiers free of 'snags' (known defects), in full working order and including all instructions and guarantees. Completing the development includes confirming fulfilment of statutory requirements and duties, preparation and settlement of final accounts, production of 'as-built' record drawings and specifications and eventually making good latent defects and learning about how to implement potential improvements for the future.

Conclusions

Consumer demand for comfort and convenience continually raises perceptions of what is 'normal', and yet developers are constrained by the need to improve energy efficiency, reduce pollution, use land more intensively and construct dwelling that are 'affordable', particularly to 'first-time' buyers. The 'escalator theory of desire' is nevertheless driving the market to cater for an ever more discerning clientele. Provision of complex equipment and additional facilities such as en-suite bathrooms is difficult to reconcile with the concept of low-cost housing. The economics of generous room sizes, useful gardens and accommodating the motor car are therefore playing an increasingly large part in shaping residential design. What has not changed to the same extent is the crucial need for developers to understand the substructural, superstructural and microclimatic elements of the dwelling and how these inform the design process.

Building construction and design must integrate 'general principles' with specifically identified 'local' variations. Knowledge of building techniques, the behaviour of materials and aesthetic appearance, combined with an understanding of daily human behaviour, are essential to the creation of an effective domestic environment. The characteristics of the site, the requirements of occupiers and the community's interests are ultimately unique to each location. Historically, developments with qualities that are valued both by occupiers and by the wider community have proved to be the most viable. Others, deemed appropriate in their time (for example pre-fabs or deck-access flats), became genuinely redundant and were eventually demolished to make way for 'new' ideas. Perhaps professional designers, developers and controlling authorities can do no more than produce residential developments that seem appropriate 'at the time', and there are in fact no perfect answers which resolve all conflicts in a sympathetic and even-handed manner. It will always remain to be seen whether a particular development is truly sustainable and can be judged as 'better'.

Discussion points

1   Explain with examples how the availability of local materials has influenced construction methods and the visual appearance of dwellings in Britain.
2   Summarise in text and diagrammatic form the key structural elements of a modern dwelling.
3   Discuss ways in which generic design principles are reflected in the production of British homes.
4   Analyse by reference to key texts the relationship between function and design in the home.
5   Assess the impact of recent legislation and government guidance on the quality of housing development in Britain.
6   Explain the distinction between local building control and planning control. To what extent are the two functions converging in their objectives?

Key reading

Dwelling construction is well documented in a range of texts, e.g. Stroud Foster, *Mitchell's Structure and Fabric* (2000). Particularly informative are Marshall and Worthing, *The Construction of Houses* (2000) and Riley and Howard, *House Construction* (2002). Powell-Smith, *The Building Regulations Explained and Illustrated* (1999) addresses matters of inspection and control. Dwelling design from an historical perspective is reviewed in Quiney, *The Traditional Buildings of England* (1990) and Nuttgens, *The Story of Architecture* (1998). The question of standard house-types is covered in a substantial article by Hooper and Nicol, 'The design and planning residential development' (*Environment & Planning B*, 1999).

Chapter 9

Finance, procurement and marketing of housing

Paul Collins and Ron Blake

Introduction

To conclude the 'procedural' part of the book, this chapter examines how house-builders, housing providers and home-seekers acquire the financial wherewithal to engage in the housing development process. Consideration of these aspects intro-duces an important commercial dimension to the study that so far has been confined to the macro-organisational review of the house-building industry presented in Chapters 3, 4 and 5. Mindful of the environmental, constructional and design aspects summarised in Chapters 6, 7 and 8, the discussion now moves forward to address the complex web of financial relationships that exist between the producers, financiers, promoters and buyers of residential accommodation. Before examining the funding, solvency and efficiency of private house-building companies, an oppor-tunity is taken to summarise how people procure and pay for housing across a spectrum of tenures. With the emergence of buy-to-let, housing associations and municipal stock upgrading as alternatives to the buoyant owner-occupied sector, the field of promotion and publicity has become an important facilitating activity in housing development. The chapter therefore concludes with a review of strategic marketing and promotional techniques in housing provision.

Basic considerations in housing finance

Definition of housing finance

In the public-sector professions, 'housing finance' is generally understood to mean government provision for housing through subsidised house-building and sub-sidised rent (Malpass and Aughton, 1999). In the private development sector, finance is concerned with the identification of sources of capital funds for constructing dwellings and with the provision of private (mortgage) finance for housing consumers. It is therefore useful to draw a preliminary distinction between 'housing finance' and 'house-building finance'. Much of the debate on housing as social provision centres on the availability of finance raised though taxation and its deployment in the form of subsidy to assist those unable to pay market prices (King, 2001). From the occupant's point of view subsidised housing has already been partially paid for at the production stage and requires only the payment of rent to secure access. For many people their rent is also subsidised. Housing offered for rent by commercial landlords has similarly been financed in advance and the costs of purchase have to be paid back using the income from market rents. However, a simple distinction between tenants in the public and private sectors is complicated by the fact that some private tenants can also receive housing benefit to help them meet the cost of rent. The picture is further complicated by the fact that housing associations can now raise capital finance from both public and private sources. Registered social landlords (RSLs) provide accommodation under arrangements with local authorities who regulate the letting business (see also Chapter 2). Within the wholly private sector a fundamental distinction has to be drawn between renting from a commercial landlord and personal borrowing to buy a house on a long-term repayment basis. Tax relief on mortgages (MIRAS) was phased out at the end of the 1990s. Finally, there is an industrial distinction between house-building companies that construct entirely for sale on the commercial market and those that engage in the production of affordable housing on behalf of local authorities and housing associations.

Two perspectives on housing finance

Housing finance is therefore best considered from two broad perspectives: (1) consumption and (2) production. Put simply, consumption finance can be defined as the resources available to families or individuals to obtain living accommodation, whether they are council tenants on low incomes, first-time professional buyers or wealthy pensioners in spacious apartments. Production finance, by contrast, represents the capital needed to acquire housing land and to design, construct, equip and market dwellings, whether on an exclusively commercial basis or with subsidy. While these two financial areas tend to involve different professions, one important factor unites them: housing production (the supply side) can only be sustained if there is local housing need (the demand side). As the mechanisms for producing houses and the personal opportunities to raise funds to enter the housing market diversify, the financial relationship between producer and consumer draws closer. Private house-builders, and to an increasing extent social housing providers, are now becoming directly involved in the sourcing of finance on behalf of their 'customers'. We therefore preface the discussion of production finance with a brief review of consumption finance. Consumption issues will resurface later in the chapter when the marketing techniques used by house-builders are explored.

Consumption finance

In the public sector the key financial challenge has long been how to fund adequate housing for the lower-paid (Gibb and Munro, 1999). When municipal housing was first provided in large quantities in the 1920s, the rents charged were generally higher than for privately rented accommodation because the tenants selected for the new estates were skilled manual workers in regular employment. Local authorities could borrow funds to be repaid over a period up to 60 years using the receipts from rent. After 1945 council estates increasingly became associated with social breakdown, vandalism and noise. Labour councils gained a bad reputation for constructing tower blocks with poor estate layout, but successive governments of both persuasions continued to endorse 'modern' design solutions for mainly financial reasons. Before 1979 local authorities built many more dwellings than they disposed of, but when the Conservatives returned to power in that year they introduced the right-to-buy initiative in order to extend owner-occupation and win voters by reducing taxes. While amplifying the privately owned housing stock should logically have reduced the demand for new-build, it successfully freed up the market by adding cheap family-size dwellings to the tradable stock. The principal negative effect was to leave the high-rise, poorly constructed and run-down accommodation in municipal hands to be upgraded later at the taxpayer's expense.

The Conservative reforms of the 1980s and early 1990s shifted home procurement firmly into the private and quasi-governmental sectors. Local authorities have since become 'enablers' rather than direct providers, and several cities, e.g. Glasgow, have disposed of their entire stock to housing associations. The Housing Act of 1988 introduced Housing Action Trusts, which gave council tenants the option of running their own estates – a provision that did not meet with widespread enthusiasm. The Housing Investment Programme (HIP) was refined around this time to encourage neighbourhood enhancement by systematic renovation of the stock. The Local Government and Housing Act 1989 cast housing associations and private landlords as the chief providers of rented accommodation while council rents were raised to market levels to reduce the need for subsidy. Since 1997 Labour have stabilised rents and ensured that a proportion of capital receipts are diverted to stock renovation. The Conservative strategy of downsizing the municipal housing estate has not been reversed.

Since 1988 housing associations have been able to set their own rent levels but they are required to transfer 80 per cent of net income into a repair fund. In their last year in office the Conservatives, through the 1996 Housing Act, empowered the Housing Corporation to lend money to organisations other than housing associations to help reinvigorate the private rental sector. From an historical perspective, this contrasted with Conservative deregulation under the Rent Act of 1957 and the resultant extortions (known as 'Rachmanism') that Labour had to check through the Rent Act of 1965. The poor image of private renting in that era took decades to reverse; for example, when the poll tax was introduced in 1990 landlords were widely suspected of not passing on all they had collected from tenants (Malpass and Aughton, 1999). There is still an ongoing debate concerning whether subsidy should be paid to the housing provider to keep rents low or whether the tenant should pay full market rent with the aid of housing benefit.

Over two-thirds of the UK's housing stock is now owner-occupied as a result of sustained output of new-build and council sell-offs. 'Home-ownership' is supported by all three political parties because the vast majority of voters aspire to it. Originally the key sources of finance were inheritance and savings, but during the twentieth century the mortgage became the primary mechanism for stepping onto the domestic property ladder. A century ago there were over 2,000 professional lenders in the form of regionally based mutual building societies with no shareholders to pay and exclusive commitment to their borrowers. The number has now dropped to fewer than 100, some famous names such as the Halifax having become de-mutualised banks. Insurance companies, local authorities and other institutions have also entered the lending arena. The key issues for borrowers over the past two decades have been the method of repayment, the level of individual debt and the value of equity relative to interest rates. Traditionally, it was customary to borrow up to four-fifths of the sale price of a dwelling, the amount agreed being equivalent to 2 or 2.5 times the borrower's annual salary. Since financial deregulation in the 1980s, this ratio has grown to almost 5, due mainly to low interest rates and the increase in dual-income households. Catastrophically, in 1988 the housing boom came to a sudden end in the wake of general economic downturn. Falling house values, insufficient to meet outstanding debt, gave rise to the phenomenon of 'negative equity' and thousands of homes were repossessed by the banks and building societies. This had a depressing effect on house-building as there was a temporary surplus of properties until markets steadied in the mid-1990s.

Over the past decade interest rates have fallen to a post-war low, yet house prices have rocketed, allegedly because of flagging output caused by land shortages and planning delays. The spectre of plummeting house prices has so far been kept at bay by politicians haunted by vivid memories of 1988–93. There is a current tendency for home-owners to re-mortgage their property to release equity to fund home improvements, holidays and cars on the assumption of continuing high levels of employment and earnings. However, an unexpected concern of many home-owners is the reduced value of endowment policies which were over-sold in the 1980s on the promise that the value on maturity would be more than sufficient to pay off the capital sum borrowed. Disappointing dividends from the stock market have left many home-owners short of funds close to their retirement and wishing they had taken out a straight repayment mortgage. Surrendering an endowment can entail a loss of up to 20 per cent of the value; increased repayments to cover a basic mortgage are found to have a negative effect on spending in the high street. These turbulences in consumption finance will inevitably be reflected in falling demand for certain types of dwellings and the profits of those house-builders who specialise in the worst affected sectors of construction or improvement.

Production finance

Britain's housing stock of about 25 million units grows by less than 1 per cent a year and by far the greatest number of domestic moves take place between second-hand properties. Nevertheless, between 150,000 and 200,000 new dwellings have been constructed annually over the past decade plus a growing number of conversions and renovations. Like consumption finance, the funding of housing construction is multi-faceted because it involves a widening range of operations affected by economic and fiscal change. Key changes during the twentieth century were the re-organisation of labour, the intervention of government and the role of the stock market and financial institutions. Between the two world wars the massive expansion of both private and municipal housing was achieved by general contractors, e.g. Costain and Wimpey, who as a consequence of their flexibility developed separate house-building arms. In the post-war period, specialist house-builders have increasingly operated as independent companies with direct access to banks and other lending institutions. Large municipal councils created direct labour organisations (DLO) until their wasteful practices were stopped by compulsory competitive tendering (CCT) during the 1980s. Major capital funding of municipal housing departments and new town corporations has come to a virtual standstill. Much of the public renovation work is now handled by 'arm's-length' agencies with the freedom to employ house-builders and sub-contractors as appropriate to the particular location and job. While funds are still allocated by central government under various acts and initiatives, housing production finance is increasingly dispensed in an entrepreneurial, rather than a bureaucratic, environment.

Financial practice in house-building

Company financial statements

Every public limited company is required under the Companies Act 1985 to publish an annual statement of their results. This statement usually contains three types of account plus a commentary on recent achievements and prospects. The critical accounts are: (1) profit and loss, (2) balance sheet and (3) cash flow. Where a house-building company is part of a larger concern, the balance sheet may be presented as two accounts: company and group. In addition, the annual statement contains statistical highlights, including pre-tax profit, earnings per share, operating margin, legal completions, turnover, land-bank and dividend per ordinary share. Further 'non-statutory' information includes average selling prices and gearing. The latter expresses debt as a percentage of assets and therefore companies with low gearings of, say, below 30 per cent, tend to impress investors and lenders.

Profit and loss account

This is a statement of the company's trading over a year or half-year period. House sales are first balanced against land and production costs for each site and aggregated at company headquarters to produce 'gross profit'. Administrative and marketing costs are then deducted to derive 'operating profit'. Subsequently interest payments and tax must be deducted and separately disclosed by law to enable investors to see the full picture. 'Retained profit' (following all deductions) is crucial to pure house-builders who otherwise must rely on share capital and bank borrowings to sustain their cash flow and achieve profitability.

Balance sheet

This presents the company's financial position in terms of assets, liabilities and capital at the end of the financial year. Assets are categorised into 'fixed' and 'working' and it must be specified how each has been financed and whether the assets are owned or otherwise controlled. Fixed assets include machinery, offices, land-banks and stakes in other companies and are normally sold off only in a reces-sion, e.g. as Barratt Homes did in 1991–92 following their record corporate loss. Working assets are those purchased with the intention of resale within the current trading year, e.g. part-exchange stock. Liabilities are categorised into short, medium and long term. Short-term liabilities (to be paid in one year) include builders' merchants and plant hire bills. Medium-term liabilities (to be paid between 1 and 5 years) include company acquisitions, e.g. Westbury's take-overs of Clarke Homes in 1996 and Prowting in 2002. Long-term liabilities (to be repaid after 5 years) normally include major capital investment where the lender holds an interest, e.g. a land-bank, as collateral. In summary, the balance sheet shows where finance comes from and what the company owes, balanced against where finance is employed and what the company owns.

Cash-flow statement

This statement fills in what happened to money during the company's last accounting year. Public limited companies must specify where funds have been obtained and the use to which those funds were put. Key sources of funds include operating profit, business disposals and share issue. Uses of funds include acquisi-tion of companies and the payment of interest, dividends and taxes. Cash flow is a measure of liquidity, measuring the company's ability to pay all creditors while continuing to purchase land, materials and labour to sustain operations. A number of high-profile companies have ceased trading due to poor liquidity, including the Standen Group (construction) and Polly Peck (textile and hosiery). All information for the cash-flow statement is derived from the profit and loss account and balance sheet, the additional function being to highlight whether the company's long-term finance is sufficient to meet long-term commitments and whether there is an over-reliance on short-term finance to sustain operations. Annual accounts present the evidence which lenders, investors and home-buyers are entitled to see before associating themselves with particular house-builders.

Stock market rating

House-builders' ability to raise cash is influenced by their rating on the City of London stock market. Only the top 50 or so house-building companies have 'listed' status, so the following remarks exclude the many smaller companies who pro-duce houses for sale using other forms of finance. City fund managers are gener-ally reluctant to include house-building in their clients' investment portfolios because of the industry's poor image gained during the housing 'crash' of the late 1980s. Despite good profit margins over the past decade, house-builders feel aggrieved that their trading performance is not highly regarded by the City. From an investment perspective the market still needs convincing that housing pro-duction is a sustainable source of earnings, yet until confidence in the industry has been secured its financial status will remain low (Thompson, 2002). A stock market rating is based on the price/earnings (p/e) ratio, where a company's share price is divided by its earnings per share. A company's share price reflects market trading, which in turn is heavily contingent on broker expectations. In 2001 the average p/e of all companies traded on the London Stock Exchange was 17, yet house-builders averaged about 9. Wimpey, perhaps the most widely known house-building name, was rated close to this average. The case for re-rating has been repeatedly made by leading house-builders (e.g. Alan Cherry of Countryside Properties) but City analysts remain unconvinced that the risk of another profits downturn can be averted.

The House Builders Federation points to the pressing need to raise national housing output above 200,000 units per annum and recognises the industry's difficulties gaining access to finance (Thompson, 2002). Within construction generally the contracting sector has achieved comparatively low profit margins yet most of its leading companies are rated in the p/e range 10–16, with Alfred McAlpine (no longer a house-builder) rated at 27. The City argues that despite high margins, house-builders eat up most of their profits in maintaining land-banks. These land-banks are susceptible to interference through central government planning and environmental policies. All in all, shareholders tend not to reap dividends commensurate with the risk. Moreover, contractors see long-term projects funded by the Private Finance Initiative (PFI) as a more robust area for investment. The perception of City analysts is that house-builders' profits are not being cascaded back through the economy sufficiently. Currently, land-banks are regarded as a fairly sound asset because of low interest rates and a buoyant demand for new homes, but falling house prices could see big write-downs in company balance sheets as occurred a decade and a half ago. Finally, low City rating is compounded by the perception that house-building companies are not big enough. Taken together, all the UK's publicly quoted house-building companies only approximate to the size of some individual multinational companies. Indeed, the entire UK construction industry (contracting and house-building) represents only 2 per cent of the financial market and is smaller than Vodaphone's global value. House-building firms thus often find it difficult to attract development finance. Consolidation (see Chapter 4) has been one response to the low rating problem.

Cash flow and the developer's loop

The way cash flows through the house-building cycle is illustrated in Figure 9.1. This diagram includes 31 movements of cash in and out of a hypothetical company focused on six key stages of the development process.

The stages (represented as ovals) and flows (as arrows) are purely indicative and have no precise relationship with the formal accounting process. Schematically, development proceeds in a clockwise movement starting with finance at the base (six o'clock). Finance comprises four main sources: loans, shares, retained profit and grants. Key financial outgoings are dividends to shareholders, bank interest payments and maintaining the land-bank. In practice, finance raising and repayments occur throughout the cycle. In the early stages of construction the emphasis is strongly on outgoings as sites are prepared, the only income being infrastructure

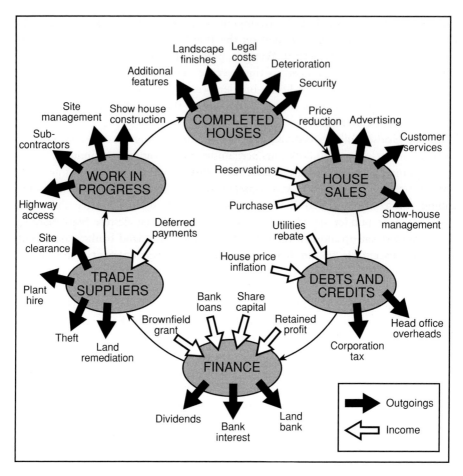

Figure 9.1 The 'Developer's Loop' – a schematic cash flow for the housing development process.
Source: From an idea by Ron Biggin (W. S. Biggin & Sons Ltd)

accumulation for which deferred payments are normal. Work in progress (WIP) is entirely an outgoing, although it counts as an asset in the balance sheet because it would be cashed in if the company were taken over. Once houses are completed there are still at least five costs relating to enhancement and protection prior to their sale (top of the loop). As sales begin there is a positive cash flow from reservations and purchases which, in a successful scheme, should outweigh the combined costs of land, production, security and publicity. In a sluggish market, price reductions may represent a late outgoing while incentives such as carpets and finishes are offered to retain a competitive edge. In an appreciating market, house-price inflation may represent income but this will be partly offset by head office administrative costs and tax responsibilities. When all creditors have been paid and debtors have rendered what they owe, a successful company will retain sufficient profits to feed into further purchases of land, equipment and materials. Certain other types of business operate on a similar 'tread-mill' basis, but house-builders are particularly vulnerable to short-term cash-flow problems and that compounds the industry's generally brittle image.

Sources of capital

Because house-building is predominantly speculative, a typical developer will need working capital in excess of £150 million to produce 1,000 medium-sized homes for sale at average current prices. The object therefore is to secure sufficient funds to sustain production until proceeds start to exceed build and finance costs. Any funding obtained must also take into account unforeseen circumstances such as poor weather and slow-downs in legal completions. When housing developers commence trading as independent businesses, their initial funding is derived from the parent company's own resources. Most house-building companies originated as arms of building contractors, a good example being Redrow Homes in 1974. In the first instance banks and other lenders will not normally provide start-up capital unless it is personally underwritten by the developer, e.g. by offering a home as collateral. To encourage efficiency and place greater responsibility for risk on the developer, banks now normally lend a maximum of 50 per cent of the purchase value of land unless the developer's trading record merits more favourable terms. Working capital (for short-term and medium-term purchase of materials and labour) is normally restricted to two-thirds of anticipated build costs and is released on a draw-down basis, i.e. the bank dictates the programme. Expansion capital (for head office development, land, plant and machinery and acquisitions) is more problematic because of its long-term nature. When Westbury Homes purchased Prowting Homes in 2002 the enlarged group had to increase its capital base by around 85 per cent to ensure continuation of its operations.

To simplify a complex business it is useful to distinguish between internal and external sources of finance. Internal sources comprise retained profits and sale of assets. External sources comprise bank borrowing and share issue. As indicated in the discussion of published accounts, retained profits after taxation and dividends may be regarded as the corporate equivalent of personal savings. In large successful companies retained profits provide a large proportion of the overall capital base, e.g. Westbury Homes at the beginning of 2002 recorded that 40 per cent of its capital came from profits. Retaining profits is cost-efficient because it keeps interest payments down, reduces management time in chasing external funds and raises credibility in the market place. Under-utilised assets that can be traded include land options, plant yards and non-core activities. In a reverse move, Costain Homes sold its entire house-building operation to Redrow to bolster its contracting and overseas mining operations.

Borrowing from banks and other financial institutions is commonplace in house-building regardless of company size. The term 'debt (or loan) capital' is used to indicate borrowing that is time-limited, tax deductible and re-payable whether the company is profitable or not. In broad terms, short-term borrowings (e.g. bonds) are sourced from high street banks while medium and long-term borrowings (e.g. business expansion) are sourced from merchant banks and other more specialised financial institutions. Interest changes are deducted from profits before taxation but nevertheless show up in the accounts as an indicator of reliance on external support.

An alternative source restricted to publicly listed companies is 'share capital' or 'equity'. Share issue averages 25–35 per cent of listed companies' capital base – in Westbury's case about 40 per cent (similar to its retained profits). Share issue involves a risk for the investor and is therefore strongly influenced by the company's reputation for paying dividends. Share capital is important at the time of management buyouts, take-overs and expansion projects, and is vital as a shock absorber in recessions when retained profits and loans are less forthcoming. The primary investment market (the FTSE 250) includes only a handful of house-builders with market capitalisations above £500 million, e.g. Barratt, Persimmon and Westbury. Many house-builders operate on the secondary or Alternative Investment Market (AIM). Ordinary shares are relatively risky but the shareholders have voting rights. Preference share are less risky because dividends are fixed but shareholders have no voting rights. House-building companies often issue shares with a reserve price for which the general public and institutions can bid under specific tendering procedures. Rights issues of new shares to established shareholders are generally in proportion to existing holdings and at a discount as an incentive to maintain investment levels. To illustrate the value of share capital to a house-building company, Westbury Homes have current share capital totalling £11.3 million.

Procurement of housing development

In other sectors of construction there is a fairly clear relationship between client and contractor (Morledge and Sharif, 1996). The client, say a university or car dealership, will engage an architect, quantity surveyor or civil engineering consultant to prepare a design brief, obtain planning permission and procure construction from a contractor. Importantly, payments are made at key stages of the work so that the contractor is not wholly dependent on whether the project is ultimately profitable. Private house-building is significantly different in that no income is usually received until the work is complete. In the speculative house-building process, the home-buyer is unknown until the product is ready for sale. While this situation is akin to the retailing of consumer goods, the closest parallel to house-building is speculative office development where revenue is not initially guaranteed; but it is easier to drop rents to attract commercial tenants than it is to slash the price of homes. The one area of house-building where risk can be minimised is social housing. In this sector the housing association is funded to make stage payments to the house-builder who is in the role of contractor rather than developer. Low profit margins for the 'contractor' are the price for the comparative safety of a subsidised contract, which is why regeneration partnerships are emerging as an attractive route for house-builders in a time of market uncertainty. In small-scale 'design-and-build' projects the ultimate householder may have a closer involvement in the project, dealing with the contractor from the start and bypassing the architect and quantity surveyor.

In volume house-building and residential regeneration a more important procurement relationship is that between the developer and its contractors, as it is no longer customary for large house-builders to carry out work using their own operatives. There is also a relationship with materials suppliers who have an interest in long-term agreements with main developers based on a reputation for reliability. Westbury Homes, for example, sources the bulk of its bricks from Moore Scott and its timbers from Jewsons, but more importantly the company has achieved greater 'upstream' control by opening its own 'Space 4' components factory. Westbury's site managers exercise quality control by signing a 'green card' which the sub-contractor cashes in according to a regionally agreed scale. Within house-building companies generally there is increasing focus on site managers as co-ordinators of the procurement process.

Marketing and housing development

Market monitoring

In terms of neo-classical economics houses represent an asset in demand for the flow of services they provide over time (Maclennan, 1982). Because no two houses are identical, the market in housing is a place of complex exchange involving life-style choices based on size, type, design, standards and fashion. Housing is also immobile, therefore demand for it in one locality cannot be automatically met by supply elsewhere. For this reason, housing markets are essentially local in character and broadly coincident with travel to work and schools catchments. There are never-theless wider 'niche' markets in which the more socially mobile groups participate, e.g. retirees from Midland conurbations choosing whether to move to south west England or north Wales. Access to housing services therefore depends heavily on macro-economic policy and the finance market, and house-builders need to under-stand wider patterns of supply and demand before considering how to market their product. This knowledge has been of growing importance since the mid-1980s when municipal provision of housing resources was dented by right-to-buy. With two-thirds of Britain's dwellings now owner-occupied, plus increasing choice available in the form of housing association and privately rented properties, the role of marketing in the residential sector has never been livelier. As average household size continues to fall, additions to the housing stock through commercially pro-vided house-building increasingly involves house-builders searching for purchasers and tenants and prospective house-holders searching for ideal accommodation. Marketing is the professional activity whereby producers seek precise information on their customer base and the customer is provided with precise information on the availability of alternative products.

Market research by house-builders

Given the localised character of the housing market, commercial house-builders have developed their marketing skills largely from intuition and informal networks within their parent industry. However, the larger companies today have created specialised sales and marketing departments using techniques adapted from manufacturing and retailing. Market research and promotional/selling techniques require different skills, the former feeding back to land-buying and the latter to design. To arrive at a commercially successful product-mix, house-builders need to acquire and evaluate a wide range of data for their geographical area of operation. Coopers & Lybrand Associates (1987) defined five kinds of data that should figure in any housing market analysis: house-price movements, planning and local authority records, estate agents' records, builders' own records and migration trends. To these might be added a sixth category: consumer spending and life-style data (see Office for National Statistics, *Social Trends*, annual). These 'indicators of housing demand' are summarised below with the house-builder's needs in mind. A full account, from the perspective of local authority housing strategy, is provided by Nicol (2002).

House price data

Selling prices are a logical starting point for any marketing strategy. Disaggregated at regional, sub-regional and postcode levels, price data give a reliable impression of economic health, competition for the available housing stock and potential for new-build. Data-sets on mortgage transactions prepared by the Halifax Bank and Nationwide Building Society have for some time been accepted as primary sources. These data-sets do not claim to be comprehensive, as they cover only mortgages arranged by those two businesses (together less than 20 per cent of the market); but they are highly regarded for their'scientific' mix-adjusting approach. The most geographically comprehensive data source on house prices today is Her Majesty's Land Registry (HMLR) which 'catches' all market transactions, including cash purchases and sales subject to mortgages. The data-sets run back to 1995, and can be disaggregated to relatively small geographical areas (e.g. postcode sectors). The HMLR data are however not adjusted for sales of different types of dwelling from quarter to quarter. A 5 per cent sample survey by the Office of the Deputy Prime Minister, originated by the Department of the Environment based on completed transactions, is a useful confirmatory source but these data cannot be disaggregated to areas smaller than shire counties and metropolitan districts. Other supporting data can be gleaned from the Inland Revenue's Valuation Office and from local newspapers. To illustrate the complexities of comparing different house-price sources, the banks and building societies compile their data purely on the basis of approved mortgages, whereas the other compilations include all types of transaction.

Local authority housing and planning data

In marketing terms local authority housing policy is relevant because waiting lists are still a part of general demand. House-builders can respond to social need by developing designs and ethical policies appropriate to the supply of affordable housing through partnerships and mix-use developments. Vacancy and occupancy rates are similarly useful in preparing company strategies for conversion work oriented to social housing and buy-to-let. Care must be taken however in the interpretation of low occupancy rates as they may indicate low general demand resulting from economic and environmental distress. Planning data (Coopers & Lybrand Associates, 1987) offer a more immediate impression of demand, though caution is again needed before drawing conclusions. Throughput of planning applications is not itself a perfect indicator of demand as the shift in emphasis from large greenfield sites to small infill sites may generate a lot of separate applications for relatively few completions. Moreover, the plan-led system has discouraged developers from submitting repeated applications speculatively, therefore a downturn may not necessarily signal reduced demand. The number of planning appeals is equally problematic: high numbers could be interpreted as indicating strong consumer demand while low numbers could simply reflect a lot of pre-application advice. Size of site, dwelling type, developer type and time between planning permission and building-start are the real key local authority variables for market monitoring but they can be difficult to obtain for commercially significant sub-areas.

Estate agent data

Buoyancy in the housing market is traditionally gauged by levels of activity in estate agents' offices. Key measures include the ratio of applicants to instructions to sell, and appointments to view per sale. Double counting can result from 'sporting' viewers who tour properties to get decorating tips with no intention of buying. The main problem with estate agent data is its patchiness due to confidentiality. RICS produce bulletins of regional trends but the data are co-ordinated aggregates. There are however encouraging signs (Nicol, 2002) that agents are prepared to co-operate with planning authorities where there is a perceived likelihood of getting marketable land allocated in the local plan (Wiltshire County Council, 1993). Qualitative information based on estate agents' conversations with customers is arguably as important to house-builders as area-based statistics. Estate agents also have unique insights into the privately rented sector and more specifically the build-to-let market.

House-builder data

Starts and completions are recorded by the National House-Building Council (NHBC) as part of their role in assuring standards. These data are close to figures derived from local authority building control records and cover the whole UK (National House-Building Council, annual). Data of a more qualitative and reflective kind are less forthcoming because of the industry's highly competitive, site-based and short-term culture. The Valuation Office and the Land Registry (HMLR) each keep records of transactions. HMLR, for example, can break down their data in terms of new and second-hand property sales. Otherwise, key data-sets compiled by individual house-builders include: (1) sales to reservation ratios, (2) sales times and sales rates, (3) visitors to sites, and (4) proportion of houses sold prior to structural completion. The last of these appears from research to be the most robust (Coopers & Lybrand Associates, 1987). The incidence of 'buying from plan' could also be an indicator of buoyancy.

Migration data

The number and type of people moving into a house-builders' perceived market area is clearly an indicator of potential customers for new-build and converted properties. The Census provides occasional snapshots of residential movements between regions but data are not disaggregated on the basis of income or house-size preference. Coopers & Lybrand Associates (1987) suggest that estate agent records provide potentially the best insights into reasons for moving, although a mechanism for making these, and house-builders' show-house records, available on a synoptic basis has yet to be perfected. The council tax register can provide information on out-migration and the National Health Service Central Register can be used to monitor net household movement between counties. Special sample surveys conducted at local level are however likely to remain the best method for ascertaining migration.

Consumer data

Levels of consumption of motor cars, household appliances and other goods and services provide further confirmation of an area's purchasing power and general economic vitality (Office for National Statistics, *General Household Survey*, annual). Disaggregation to meaningful sub-areas, and cross-referencing between types of household, types of dwelling and different environmental settings, are the principal problems in making any data of this kind usable for marketing purposes. Special sample surveys are again likely to be necessary to gauge specific housing requirements.

Home-buyers' guides

To assist home-buyers in finding the property of their choice, special guides are being commercially produced in increasing numbers. In addition to newspaper supplements, systematically researched profiles of economic regions now provide a factual basis for the strategic marketing of homes. These do not focus exclusively on new-build or conversion; they also take in the much larger second-hand market. The value of such all-embracing studies is that they eliminate the need for house-builders to duplicate basic research, allowing companies to concentrate on matching local environmental and socio-economic characteristics with their product-mix. One such guide is that produced for the Virgin One account in eleven regional volumes (Nelson, 2000). In tone, content and presentation this series resembles a town and country planning document – a quality that reflects the growing convergence of interests and approach between marketing and the environment. The volume for the East Midlands opens by defining the region's problematical southern border and points out that the constituent counties contain some of the cheapest family homes in Britain. Review of historical building styles, land use and climate set the context for a table of council tax bands in each of the 40 districts. Socio-economic profiles for each county and unitary authority are provided, followed by a more detailed appreciation of the major cities and outstanding landscapes. The contributions of four major house-builders (Redrow, Bloor, Wimpey and Barratt) are tabulated, while the price ranges of seven leading estate agents are presented with corresponding postcodes. A house-price map of the region compiled by Experian, the Nottingham-based credit analysts, is included with a commentary explaining the depressing effect of a declining coalfield on the one hand and the positive effect of good rail connections on the other. Following a section (common to all eleven regional guides) on the financial and legal practicalities of home buying, the East Midlands survey reviews all forms of transport infrastructure, pollution and noise, with a particular focus on airports and military air bases. A 'relative peacefulness' map compiled by CPRE is included to attract home-seekers. Proneness to subsidence, radon gas and flooding are also mapped and related to postcodes. Finally, childcare facilities and schools' performance grades are given for each authority. Appended are lists of local authorities, utilities, tourist information centres, estate agents, local newspapers, retail markets and places of historic interest. London is covered by three of these Virgin guides, the one for the north and west sectors of the capital containing a 'mosaic of neighbourhood types' and a 'shopping centre ranking'. This volume could be regarded as a model for any area-based marketing analysis as it is strong on market sementation.

The marketing of new homes

To make new-build homes sufficiently attractive to justify the higher price charged, house-builders must provide additional features, assure quality and promote their product. Key selling points include additional features within the basic price, more efficient heating and insulation, greater choice of finishes and more luxurious fittings. The idea of providing all this 'up-front' is especially attractive to people who do not wish to spend their time and earnings on DIY improvements and repairs. Not having to worry about the basic efficiency of the dwelling allows resources to be spent instead on a chic backdrop, state-of-the-art possessions and an aspirational life-style. An important role of the new-build dwelling therefore is to define a person's wider living space including the image of the neighbourhood. It is noticeable that new housing developments now contain a greater variety of dwelling types, and are landscaped in advance so that schemes look practically finished when residents move in. House-building companies are also attempting to reconcile corporate and local distinctiveness by design. This is crucial if the new-build sector is to capture a greater share of the second-hand market where most people still feel more comfortable. The image problem of new-build housing up to the 1980s was that of 'boxes' of limited variety and character. While clear improvements in style have since taken place, government policies for increasing site density have made it difficult for house-builders to market homes primarily on the grounds of ample space. Given planning constraints, the emphasis now has to be on delivering quality and performance.

A survey by Mulholland Research Associates for the New Homes Marketing Board and Halifax plc (2001) revealed that 36 per cent of people interviewed would consider buying a new property and 24 per cent of those currently intending to move would prefer to buy brand-new. These percentages were the highest for 5 years and indicated a narrowing in the preference gap between new and second-hand properties. Respondents who had recently visited new developments considered that the homes for sale were better designed, constructed and finished, had bigger rooms and more luxurious fittings, were more attractively laid out, had greater character and exclusivity, and were more efficiently heated.

Consumer preferences

There is a general perception that new-build homes are materially superior in much the same way as a new car is superior, but some of the advertised advantages are still debatable. To justify the premium price, new-build must have incontestable advantages in terms of construction, comfort, running costs and social image. Brick-and-block construction is still preferred by most consumers who fear that timber framing is insubstantial, fire-prone and noisy. Yet those who actually own timber-frame homes typically report greater warmth in winter, smoother finishes and prompter completion dates. A distinguishing feature of new-build homes in general is the incorporation of recent government regulations on quality of construction. Customers interviewed in the NHMB/Mulholland study approved of wider doors and ramps for wheelchairs but felt, for example, that lower light switches were a potential hazard for children.

Inevitably, the image of new homes is slightly tarnished by the government's drive to use brownfield sites where lingering contamination could still be a hazard to human health. Other concerns are the difficulty of navigating the 'calmed' road environment of design-guide compliant layouts, the reduction in off-street car parking, and a lack of parking provision for visitors. Town houses were rejected by many of the Mulholland respondents as impractical for families with children if living space is spread over three storeys. Small gardens, or a lack of garden space alto-gether, are seen by many as a backwards move socially. More favourable reactions to current planning ideology are evident in the views that integral garages should be replaced by additional utility space within the dwellings, and that mixed-use developments have the potential to create balanced communities.

In assessing new homes built over the last few years, the Mulholland report was implicitly drawing comparisons with houses built in recent decades and with the existing housing stock in general. It is not surprising then that new properties are seen as glamorous, convenient and aspirational, and likened to a good-quality motor car or exotic holidays. A particular attraction of new-build is that the consumer's own specifications can be added in at the construction stage, e.g. bath-room colours and specially positioned cable sockets. Women interviewed referred to the cleanliness of untouched surfaces and the fresh smell of a new home.

Branding

Compared with other sectors of production, house-building has few strong brands. A brand is a visual identity that sustains high turnover based on widespread customer perception of reliability (Baker, 1996). Lack of effective branding among UK house-builders is primarily because house purchases are made relatively infrequently; many more sales take place in the second-hand market, and housing is not regarded by most people as a mere commodity. Traditionally, homes were marketed principally by reference to location wherein lay a kind of branding based on the external environment rather than refinements of the product. It is arguable furthermore that while homes were generally in short supply, the branding of companies was less necessary than in motor car manufacturing or electronics where there is global over-supply. On this point the reader may test the generalisation by jotting down the names of any house-building companies that have a memorable brand image. Barratt's helicopter and David Wilson's 'dog and slipper' may spring to mind and it would be instructive to ponder the connection between those icons and housing provision.

While advertising in the national and local newspapers is strengthening brand images, most home-buyers interviewed placed word of mouth well ahead in the scale of influences on purchasing decisions. Factors such as the responsiveness of sales staff and quality of after-service also appear to rank highly (cf. buying a new motor car). Respondents to the Mulholland survey expressed interest in the concept of a 'one-stop shop' service whereby the house-builder co-ordinates legal and financial services (including part-exchange) and provides the home decor and a designer garden. For diplomatic reasons the NHMB-published report does not commend the brand image of any particular house-builder, making it difficult in this discussion to relate any of the survey's conclusions to field evidence.

Show-houses

House-buying of any kind is notoriously stressful and involves both careful comparison of sales literature and instant reaction in the field. To take the latter first, 'kerb appeal' is an important factor in determining whether passing customers will stop at all. This can be made more likely if a 'show-house' is clearly indicated. Potential customers who have already engaged in a systematic comparison of sites from press advertisements may form a positive impression of the development if one of the properties is complete and inviting. Show-houses therefore tend to be sited near the entrance to a development and signalled by notice-boards and other indicators of the product on offer. From the buyer's point of view a show-house is a useful way of comparing the internal 'feel' of a new or converted property with the products of other companies. Thus a visit enables the instinctive 'kerb' impression to be corroborated by the internal practicalities of a particular domestic space.

From the developer's angle there are other functions of the show-house. The extent to which corporate branding has attracted customers must be verified together with an assessment of the influence of loyalty and reputation on sales. These factors can be recorded by means of a short questionnaire completed during

Plate 9.1 A marketing suite for new apartments in a listed building, Weekday Cross, Nottingham: R. N. E. Blake.

prospective buyers' visits. The ease with which the site could be found using maps in advertisements, whether ongoing construction work acted as a deterrent and questions about health and safety on site are just three of many customer-care issues that a house-builder should monitor. In the short term a show-house represents capital tied up until the development is complete, and the cost-effectiveness of staffing and physically maintaining it will depend on the number of units in the development. For flats, a mobile show-flat may be appropriate to reduce disturbance to existing residents but on a conventional housing estate this would create an unhomely impression. In high-grade apartments a 'marketing suite' on the ground floor is appropriate (Plate 9.1).

On large estate developments the throughput of customers in a show-house demands regular maintenance, redecorating and cleaning to be carried out. Some developers still use a 'bare-boards' approach to give an impression of space, flexibility and potential for individual interpretation. It is not unknown for petty thieves to graze show-houses as a cheap alternative to shopping and some developers therefore minimise the fittings on display. Since the average conversion rate of visitors to buyers is as low as 5 per cent, the morale of the sales staff can be maintained by their doubling as market analysts, recording the origins, motivations and preferences of customers. Special training and support is therefore provided for show-house teams, including skills in keeping an eye on who enters and leaves.

The external space of the show-house is important in balancing surveillance with privacy. Fencing is one way to guide customers towards a single entry point where negotiating staff can meet and attend to them, but the lengthy process of reservation should take place in a room near the office (known in the business as the 'sales trap'). The need for at least two sales staff at all times is thus apparent. Large signboards and excessive bunting are to be avoided as the external environment should look as close to an occupied home as possible. A single pole with a corporate flag is a fair compromise between attention-seeking and good taste. Balancing the freedom to roam with personal attention is crucial in persuading an undecided customer to make a follow-up visit. A sensitive approach is to supply the visitor(s) with compact literature and allocate a private room where members of the prospective household can confer without feeling under pressure. For this reason specialist firms of show-house furnishers have been set up over the past two decades to supply a full range of comforts and conveniences that give a user-friendly impression. All-day lighting and plenty of mirrors are proven selling devices. Over-furnishing is however to be avoided because it evokes clutter. Training for show-house staff emphasises that sales persons should cultivate a 'non-pushy' style. Female staff are frequently employed in this role, and it is considered advantageous if staff of either gender live in a similar type of house themselves. Building a friendly relationship with a customer increases the likelihood of a reservation, second visit, or even a repeat purchase in the future.

A show-house can have a lifespan of anything from a few months to several years. There are different opinions as to whether it is better to locate the sales office in a distinct space, for example a double garage, or integrate it with the living area to create the image of a busy professional household. The function of the show-house is to give customers an alternative to buying from plan. A problem occurs when the last few houses on a development have not yet been sold and the cost-effectiveness of maintaining the show-house has diminished. In such cases the price of the final properties may be reduced to speed up the sale and quit the site. Because of their convenient siting, show-homes are often reserved by patient buyers well in advance of availability.

The language of advertising homes

Estate agents' euphemisms have long provided material for comedians. Coded language perfectly fits the second-hand housing market because of the huge throughput of transactions and the unique assemblage of information relating to each property; relationships between vendor, purchaser and agent involve a high degree of semi-formal negotiation and the 'personality' of the house as a lived-in environment encourages informality until legal contracts are exchanged (Garber, 2001). Selling new-build and converted homes involves a different kind of language. Some words and phrases such as 'spacious', 'secluded' and 'conveniently located' are common to all advertisements, but in an era of design guidance and urban regeneration the marketing of new developments has become fiercely competitive and many novel linguistic devices are employed in advertisements and brochures.

To illustrate this fascinating and under-researched subject, the new homes supplement of *Nottingham Evening Post* was scanned during the last quarter of 2002 for key expressions that capture the flavour of contemporary advertising practice.

The critical factor for house-builders is the aspirations of its potential customers. Certain regions, environmental settings and social positions recur in advertisements and can be directly related to the psychology and temperament of the buyer. Regional associations are evident in the nomenclature of new house type, e.g. 'The Windermere' (Wimpey Homes), 'The Mendip' (Barratt) and 'The Belgravia' (Persimmon), where romantic locations are substituted for actual locations (in the Midlands). Names of landed estates such as 'The Buckingham' (Rippon Homes) and 'Cavendish Park' (Bovis Homes) are adopted to imply social grace. Generic locations designed to appeal to the buyer are seen in descriptions such as 'semi-rural' (Fairclough Homes), 'town and country' (Miller Homes) and '. . . close to the city centre' (Crosby Homes). Urbanity is conveyed by 'The Square' (George Wimpey) which shows a plan and a compass in the advertisement to suggest precision and professionalism. Allusion to influential women in history is seen in 'Hamilton Court' and 'Alexandra Court' (Westbury Homes) while 'Queen Elizabeth Court' and 'the fabulous Balmoral' (George Wimpey) illustrate the power of royalty.

In the conventional new-build sector, association with rurality is as strong as ever. 'The Hollies' (Fairclough Homes), 'Poplar Gardens' (Rippon Homes) and 'Bramley Orchard' (Persimmon) are just three references to the seclusion provided by trees. 'The Ridgeway' (Barratt) represents a topographical trigger to buying while 'The Grange' (Standen) is suggestive of leadership in the rural community. The 'Walled Garden' (Bovis Homes) evokes enclosure by mature brickwork with connotations of Tudor England. Respect for folklore is implicit in 'Piper's Court, off Vicarage Lane' (Clarke Homes) while English sporting tradition is upheld in 'The Wickets' (Rippon Homes) and poetry in 'Byron Fields' (Lovell Homes).

In the new environment of city living, other forms of language are deployed to evoke a more cosmopolitan and racier life-style. References to the Italian renaissance are seen in the nomenclature of apartment designs such as 'Largo' and 'Andante' (George Wimpey), while classical antiquity is evoked in 'The Arena' (Crosby Homes) and 'The Atrium' (Westbury Homes). A current conversion scheme based on a former convent (Chase Homes) is described in publicity as '. . . betwixt the Park and the City Centre' (delightful use of an antiquated preposition).

In contrast to terms that espouse older values, a more exciting and challenging form of language is being used by residential developers in the urban context (see Plate 9.2, for example). 'Stunning views' (Chase Homes) relates to the commanding position afforded by apartments in the Park Row area of Nottingham's city centre. Developments with names such as 'The Edge', 'The Zone' and 'The Pinnacle' are part of the aspiration to be above everything else. Crosby's Arena is promoted as '. . . a stylish collection in an elevated position' while David Wilson's 'City Heights' is further indication of the imperative to be 'on top'. Aerial position is further suggested in Wilson Bowden's apartments where prospective buyers can '. . . see the week fly by'.

Plate 9.2 Advertising hoarding for new-build apartments under construction on a commanding hill-top: Standard Hill, Nottingham: R. N. E. Blake.

Appeal to the customer's powers of discernment are evident in the invitation to '. . . take the opportunity to individualise your home with finishing touches . . .' (Persimmon) and in the jest that '. . . this weekend my boyfriend said he needed some space, so he bought us a new home' (Sol Homes). Continuing this jocular tone, 'stylish apartments with "wow" factor' suggests a policy of targeting younger fun-seeking buyers, while a thought-provoking claim '. . . it was easier to have a new home than a new kitchen' (Bryant Homes) demonstrates an increasing boldness in the advertising of customised homes.

To conclude this consideration of marketing language, the presentation of material incentives using eye-catching phrases is noteworthy. 'Treat yourself to a perfect Christmas gift' (George Wimpey) and 'Move in for Christmas' (Bovis Homes) exemplify the use of seasonal optimism to promote sales. The idea of home-buying itself being an occasion for social interaction is encapsulated in the following open invitation: 'Please join us for the premier of our stunning city centre apartments and penthouse – One Fletchergate. There'll be champagne and canapés and plenty of famous faces, and of course the opportunity to acquire a brochure' (Wilson-Connolly/FPD Savills).

Design incentives such as 'the Big Loft Company' and 'L-shaped interest' (George Wimpey) may be contrasted with straight cash incentives such as '£6,000 discount' (Bovis), '100 per cent Part Exchange' (David Wilson Homes) and

'£10,000 cash back' (Wilson Bowden). Further inducements include '500 towards legal fees . . . and your five per cent deposit paid' (George Wimpey). The claim '13 properties reserved before a brick has been laid' (Fairclough Homes) is an effective way of advertising the sales momentum of a popular product.

Other influences on the marketing of new homes

Influence of planning on the new-build market

In general the house-building industry has embraced PPG3 and the 'new urbanism' in good faith. Riverside and canal-side developments fit in well with the aspirational life-style of younger professionals, but are most successful when in the form of high-density apartments designed to keep living space above flood level. Conventional low-rise housing is less marketable near water. House-builders are critical of the blanket target of siting 60 per cent of all new development on brownfield sites. This is perceived as creating too much high-density new-build in the North where consumer preference is for thinning towns out after generations of cramped living amid industry. The prospect of having community facilities and convenience shops such as newsagents 'planned in' as part of mixed-use development is generally popular, although the current doctrine of affordability and social inclusiveness has been challenged by some respondents who aspire to new-build as a means of avoiding unruly neighbours. A perceived hazard of houses sited on recycled land is the possibility that landfill materials are still toxic (see Chapter 7). Town houses are widely perceived as inappropriate in suburban locations, as they give the impression that the area has taken a step back towards the working-class terraces of yesteryear. Higher density is only acceptable to purchasers where gardens and balconies have 'designed-in' privacy. Internal loft space is popular (known as 2.5 storey design) as are French windows. Needless to say, detached properties in 'admired' styles with traditionally proportioned windows, visible front doors and tasteful ironwork are almost universally aspired to. With regard to general layout, most prospective purchasers are critical of design guidelines that reduce off-street parking provision, perceiving a conflict between visitors' cars and passing buses or emergency vehicles. Emphatically, home-buyers are resistant to separate garage and parking courts where theft, vandalism and assault are feared. Shared drives are also seen to be a potential source of conflict between neighbours.

Predictably, first-time buyers in the Mulholland research showed the greatest interest in new properties because of their younger age profile. Intriguingly, men seem slightly more in favour than women, possibly because DIY has now lost some of its macho associations. There appears to be only a marginally stronger preference for new-build among the higher socio-economic groupings, but a disproportionate interest in the north of England may reveal the lower esteem of second-hand houses in that region. The last finding has been seized upon by NHMB as evidence of great marketing potential for the new-build sector in the North. The current distribution of preferences based on NHMB evidence is: new-build (24 per cent), 'recent', i.e. post-war second-hand (37 per cent) and 'old', i.e. pre-1945 second-hand (39 per cent). The north–south divide is confirmed by the finding that older properties are still preferred by the older and more affluent socio-economic groups in the South, almost certainly because in the North the equivalent people would be more likely to have grown up in comparatively small and unfit properties. Since the mid-1990s NHMB has monitored moving intentions and revealed that only 6 per cent of people nationally expect to move over the next twelve months. The north–south gap is closing in the North's favour but a levelling in the number of moves in the Midlands may be an early sign of market cooling.

Competitor analysis and pricing

To remain solvent, companies must normally sell houses at prices exceeding all costs of production. Occasionally prices are purposely lowered to meet a turnover target within a particular accounting period or region, or as a strategy to capture market share as seen recently in the airline business. In times of rapid house-price inflation sales rates may be artificially slowed down in order to sell properties later at a higher price. Residential developers generally operate on a comparative basis, observing the price range of local competitors and the second-hand market. Problems can occur on new estates when a developer lowers prices during the build period, causing resentment among those who moved in first. One way around this is to set a standard price for a particular house type but offer modest discounts to the first batch of purchasers. 'Hidden' incentives can then be offered to the later purchasers that may actually be of greater cash value. Psychologically it is a better marketing strategy to raise prices than habitually slash them. Home-owners are highly sensitive to the social standing of the place where they live and are inclined to find the resources to buy a property at the higher end of the range in order to secure the right kind of physical and social environment.

Analysis of competitors is carried out by companies using information gleaned from roving customers, eight-week records of sales rates and specification data in brochures. Consideration has to be taken of unpublished variables such as mortgage facilities, legal assistance and location which can explain subtle differences in pricing. In so far as these items can be quantified at the level of a particular development, a house-builder may be able to discern from rival figures whether its own properties are overpriced or underpriced. However, because new-build housing is characteristically delivered through sub-markets and as a bundle of attributes rather than a 'basket' of separately costed items (Evans, 1995), pricing decisions are likely to remain 'hedonic', i.e. subjective rather than completely objective. Although the new-build market currently represents a tiny proportion of all UK housing transactions, the increasing availability of detailed specifications through customisation may reduce the hedonic element in pricing and engender a more rational approach to marketing.

Conclusions

In drawing links between finance and marketing, this chapter has highlighted the long and complex process whereby housing is procured and made available to prospective householders. A distinction between consumption and production has enabled the demand and supply sides of the housing equation to be re-examined in financial terms and the role of marketing placed in the context of a development 'loop'. From a traditional procurement perspective house-builders may be seen as high risk-taking speculators acting on behalf of clients unknown and therefore vulnerable to oscillations in the general economy. Opportunities for making short-term changes in their product are limited because the industry is still innately conservative, poorly rated on the stock market and hamstrung by land holdings and planning. In the eyes of the construction industry house-building lacks the glamour of big capital projects, while investors remain timid because of bad publicity over recent financial collapses and controversial products. The industry is perceived as living on the 'never-never', achieving high profit margins but lacking sustainability, flexibility and critical mass. Credibility rests heavily on annual published accounts and image created through strategic marketing. Fund managers need evidence of efficient 'upstream' procurement of production and materials while effective branding is emerging as the key to winning greater market share. In a 'cash-rich/time-poor' economy the provision of special features through customisation evokes parallels with the automobile. Finally, from an academic perspective marketing can be seen to operate at different spatial scales, ranging from house-building's image as a distinct profession, through company branding to the promotion of an individual housing development.

Discussion points

1   Compare the financial advantages and disadvantages to a house-building company of entering the 'affordable housing' market. Focus in particular on the balance between risk and reward relative to oscillations in the economy and government philosophy.
2   Obtain the published annual statements of three house-building companies. Compare the format of the results, the language used to present the achievements and aspirations of each company as declared in their respective documents. Conclude with an assessment of the house-building industry's culture and current mood.
3   In the role of a marketing consultant draw up a framework for the strategic analysis of a trading region on behalf of a medium-sized house-builder.
4   Obtain sales brochures from a selection of current developments by leading house-builders in one locality. Compare the quality of the publicity in terms of information about the surrounding area, estate layout, dwelling construction design, pricing, additional features and after-care services. Comment also on the artwork, articulacy and user-friendliness of the respective brochures.

5   Consider the essential differences and similarities between the advertising of new homes and that of motor cars and other fashionable consumer products. What factors explain the comparative absence of advertisements for homes in the broadcast media?

Key reading

There are no standard works on either finance, procurement or marketing from a UK house-building perspective. For a factual overview of consumption finance, Malpass and Aughton, *Housing Finance: A Basic Guide* (1999) is exemplary. For financial accounting the definitive text is Reid and Myddleton, *The Meaning of Company Accounts* (1971). Helpful generic works on marketing include: Baker, *Marketing: An Introductory Text* (1996), Pettinger, *Construction Marketing* (1998) and Randall, *Principles of Marketing* (1992). A recent collection of essays on marketing issues, edited by Bartlett, *Consumer Choice in House Buying* (2002) is stimulating. Specialist periodicals such as *Building Homes, Show House* and *Which House?*, together with company annual statements, provide useful insights into house-building enterprises.

Part Four

Contemporary Practice in Housing Development

Chapter 10
Sustainable housing development and urban capacity solutions

Andrew Golland and Ron Blake

House-building, urban growth and the sustainable development agenda

Historical shifts in planning policy

It will be clear from a reading of the foregoing chapters that house-building, land and planning policies are closely connected. The need to ensure that the land-use planning system provides enough land for housing development is an obvious objective, as is the need to guide investment in housing via development plans and also, to some extent, to capture the financial benefits ('planning gain') which might otherwise accrue to private interests because of the actions of the state.

These planning 'objectives' may be regarded as constants (although great argument has always arisen over 'planning gain'). From time to time, however, as with housing policy, the emphasis of (planning) policy has shifted. We can identify periods in time when planning policy sought strongly to redistribute; for example during the late 1940s via the Uthwatt report and later, during the 1970s, via the Community Land Act (1975). It can be argued that at other times, the planning system has 'followed' the housing market and housing demand; the policy of 'predict and provide' and the 'presumption to development' of the 1980s planning policy is one example; the 'ribbon development' of the inter-war years, when the planning system was less formalised is another.

The planning system has, however, also been highly prescriptive at times in defining new opportunities for housing development. Green belt policy and the establishment of planning policies for new towns are examples of highly defined spatial development policies. Since the late 1980s, a new 'Leitbild' or 'planning vision' has emerged. In broad terms this is one of 'urban containment' with the aim of bringing about an 'urban renaissance' in the towns and cities. Planning policy, via key guidance such as PPG3 (DETR, 2000b), now encourages planning authorities to work to the principles of 'plan, monitor and manage'. This agenda is less about letting the market decide how planning should react, and more about proactive planning to manage the supply of land where possible. Planning policy is now aimed towards the most efficient use of land in such a way that new settlements and communities can function and be accommodated in a sustainable way for the future. Whilst it is recognised that 'sustainable' communities need adequate space and the necessary physical and social infrastructure, planning policy nevertheless aims to achieve these goals by developing housing more densely than has previously been the case.

The need for a new planning vision for housing development

The reasons for the problems of urban decay, the movement of population from towns to the suburbs and the countryside and the need to address the problems can be understood from the report of the Urban Task Force (1999). This explains:

> More recent urban history has been dominated by a severance in the relationship between people and place. In England, we have paid a particularly heavy price for our leading role in the industrial revolution. The industrial age was a period of phenomenal urban growth which made a lasting and indelible mark on the British attitude towards the role and function of the city. It marked a point of departure from the Continental attitude towards urban development and urban living. The industrial city, with its pollution, its slums and its short-term vision, destroyed our confidence in the ability of the city to provide a framework for humane civic life . . . [however] our attempts to escape the city have had mixed results. At their best, the garden cities and new towns have provided a form of suburban living where the relationship between urbanity and country; of public transport and walkability; of work and residence, continues to hold significant implications for sustainable planning today.
>
> Such places represented, however, only a small fraction of the general process of urban decline at the centre, and expansion at the periphery, of our towns and cities, which began at the turn of the century and continues to this day.
>
> (Urban Task Force, 1999: 26)

Thus whilst events such as the industrial revolution in Britain brought about significant benefits in economic growth, it helped to create the problem of a lack of confidence in the city centre and its immediate neighbourhoods. People, in particular families, moved out and have not been convinced by policy to move back in.

The role of housing development in arresting this decline has not been underestimated in the report of the Urban Task Force or in other leading policy making forums. The focus on housing development as a remedy for arresting urban decline can be justified in a number of ways when the link between house-building and land use is analysed. Bibby and Shepherd (1997), in looking at historic and future trends in the rate of urbanisation state:

> A focus on house-building as the driving force behind the overall rate of land conversion can be justified in a number of ways. First, and most importantly, housing typically accounts for about seven-tenths of land in urban use, slightly less in larger settlements and rather more in smaller ones. . . . Residential land requirements also account for a very substantial proportion of the overall area of land transferring from rural to urban use – just over 90 per cent according to the LUCS [Land Use Change Statistics] for the period 1985–89. . . . Secondly, the demand for non-basic services such as shopping, leisure,

education and so forth, and hence for various forms of urban development other than residential. . . . Thirdly, it is generally argued that it is the decentralisation of population rather than the decentralisation of employment which is leading the evolution of the settlement pattern. . . . Finally, the statutory planning framework lays particular emphasis on housing allocations from which flow the assessment and allocation of land for other uses.

(Bibby and Shepherd, 1997: 93)

Thus, convincing people that living once again in the cities and central urban areas is a key factor which could make a significant difference to the amount of green-field land used in the future. If planning policy can guide housing development increasingly towards the urban, rather than the rural, areas, then this can help towards the broader goals of sustainable development directed towards the conservation of natural resources and the environment.

The policy mechanisms

This chapter is focused to a very significant extent on the policies and mechanisms in place to achieve increased housing development in urban areas. It analyses the key sources of data relating to land-use change (for example, the Land Use Change Statistics) and to the sources of information relating to the supply of sites which have been previously developed (for example, the National Land Use Database, NLUD). It identifies and describes the main facets of planning policy directed towards achieving urban regeneration via housing policy (for example, PPG3) and analyses the role of urban capacity studies and the guidance *Tapping the Potential* (DETR, 2000d).

The chapter considers some important questions relating to the regional dimension, and the way in which 'success' and 'failure' can be evaluated when analysing planning and housing policy. Questions about the role of the housing market are considered when thinking about how policy might move forward. A case study of an urban capacity study carried out in the East Midlands brings together the key issues by highlighting the specific urban problems and opportunities being faced by those charged with implementing the urban renaissance policy agenda.

Land for housing and the brownfield site challenge

If we are to understand better the problems and challenges of housing development, and in particular the increased focus on urban and brownfield sites, then some appreciation is required of the scale of the challenge both at a national and a regional level. This section examines some important questions relating to the role of different types of land supply for housing development, to the extent to which land is being recycled for housing and, most importantly, to the factors which help to explain why some areas are more successful than others in pursuing a brownfield site housing development policy. We begin with a most fundamental question about sources of land for housing development:

Where does land for housing come from?

To develop housing, the industry needs land. But whereas most early and immediately post-war development was built on former agricultural land, this is today no longer entirely the case. As the policy agenda has changed, and as sustainable development has become a key policy issue, housing developers have increasingly had to look at alternative sources of land supply.

The key publication identifying the main sources of housing land supply and, indeed, data relating to recycled land is the DTLR's report *Land Use Change in England* (DTLR, 2001). The publication's trends are reliant to an important extent on Ordnance Survey (OS) data, and this comes about where OS maps are revised. The data recorded by OS in any one year 'depend on OS resources and how these are deployed on different types of map revision' (ibid.). The map revision programme is in turn, 'determined by the amount of change taking place on the ground and its relative importance to OS customers'. Most large-scale revisions in recent years have been focused on urban areas and the urban fringe, while less regular revisions (five and ten yearly) have been undertaken in more settled rural, mountain and moorland areas. The data are thus not perfect, and inevitably there are sometimes lags to be taken account of, although by concentrating on the urban and urban fringe locations, where much of the development occurs, an advantage is given. With this proviso, we make some conclusions.

Figure 10.1 shows the previous uses of land used for residential development in 1997, and it highlights a number of important issues. It divides sources of land for housing into six categories: 'rural agricultural', 'other rural', 'urban residential', 'urban vacant previously developed land', 'urban vacant not previously developed

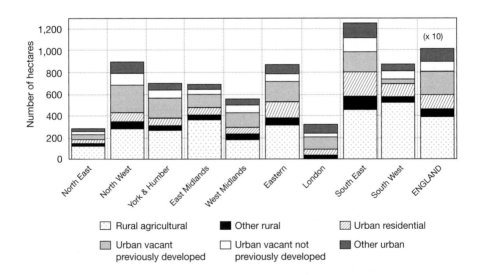

Figure 10.1 Previous uses of land changing to residential use by region in 1997.
Source: DTLR, *Land Use Change in England No. 16*, July 2001

land' and 'other urban'. Of these, agricultural use provides by far the most significant source of supply for house-builders. Figure 10.1 shows that in 1997 40 per cent of all housing development land in England was previously used for agriculture. However, this needs to be seen in context because it also means that 60 per cent of land for housing was not farmland! Indeed a significant proportion (21 per cent nationwide) of housing land came from vacant land which had in some way been previously developed; moreover a further 10 per cent came from other urban uses. The key statistic for England, namely the amount of housing land coming from all types of previously developed land, was 45 per cent (DTLR, 2001).

At the regional dimension, there are significant variations, as Figure 10.1 shows. These are most evident in the volume of land changing from different uses. Whereas for example in the South East, over 1,200 hectares of land changed to housing, less than 300 hectares changed use to housing in the North East. Other areas experiencing significant changes of use that were recorded for 1997 were the North West, the Eastern region and the South West.

Perhaps the most interesting regional variation, however, relates to the particular individual sources of land supply. Many regions are still highly reliant on agricultural land for house-building: for example the South West (60 per cent of all sources recorded in 1997), the East Midlands (52 per cent) and the North East (47 per cent). By contrast, London (0 per cent), the West Midlands (34 per cent) and the North West (32 per cent) have a much greater proportion of land coming from sources other than agriculture. A key source in these regions is previously developed vacant urban land (40 per cent in London; 24 per cent in the West Midlands and 29 per cent in the North West).

The question which arises from these regional variations is 'why?' Perhaps the most important reason for some regions using a high percentage of agricultural land and other regions using more previously developed land is a very simple one: geographical accident. Those regions which are highly urbanised can only build new housing under urban circumstances. This is a double-edged sword. In theory, it makes central government brownfield and land recycling targets easier to meet; in practice, however, the difficulties of developing in these areas have to be carefully considered. By contrast, regions such as the South West, the North East, the East Midlands and Yorkshire and Humberside, which have a much lower proportion of land in urban use, may find it more difficult to meet brownfield development targets, simply because these opportunities are not to be found to such an extent.

Measures of the success of land recycling policy

Because housing development is so reliant on greenfield and agricultural land in many areas of the country, it is important for government and the house-building industry to be able to monitor the volume of development occurring on other sites; namely urban and brownfield development sites. Two ways in which the success of this policy can be measured are: first, to record the proportion of all new dwellings

Table 10.1 Measures of land recycling policy in England, 1989–2000

Year	% new dwellings built on previously developed land (excluding conversions)	% of all land for new housing that was previously developed
1989	52	43
1990	51	43
1991	50	45
1992	53	46
1993	53	47
1994	51	44
1995	54	47
1996	53	45
1997	53	45
1998	54	47
1999	55	47
2000	54	48
Average 1996–2000	54	46

Source: Adapted from DTLR, *Land Use Change in England*, July 2001

built which are constructed on land that has in some way been previously developed; and second, to record the proportion of all land that changes use for housing development which has (in some way) been previously developed. The former data can be broadly viewed as a measure of how much new housing development occurs on previously used land, the latter, as a broad measure of the extent to which previously used land (as opposed to land not previously developed) supplies new housing development.

Interestingly, Table 10.1 shows that there are not significant differences between the two measures on a year-by-year basis. Even taking an average for 1996–2000, the difference between the two measures is only 8 per cent. In many ways government could be satisfied with these measures, although as the table shows there has only been marginal improvement between 1989 and 2000. At a regional level, some regions have actually developed a lower proportion of homes on previously used land as time has passed; the South West (45 per cent in 1989 and 33 per cent in 1997) and the East Midlands (46 per cent in 1989 and 37 per cent in 1997) are good examples. Other regions, for example the West Midlands (46 per cent in 1989 and 57 per cent in 1997) and the North West (50 per cent in 1989 and 58 per cent in 1997) have increased their figures. Whilst this may indicate a more 'successful' brownfield development programme, differences in regional trends should also been seen in the light of wider planning and housing policies. In other words, if planning policy fails to release any new greenfield sites, while at the same time focusing resources on property clearance and regeneration, this will have the effect of increasing the proportion of development on previously used sites.

Why is there a difference between the 'housing' recycling measure and the 'land' recycling measure?

Table 10.1 shows that the proportion of dwellings built on previously developed sites is consistently higher than the proportion of all land for housing that was previously developed. The question is: why this might be the case? The DTLR report concludes that the difference is primarily explained by policy on density:

> The recycling rate is higher in terms of dwellings than land. This is due to the higher density of development (on average, 28 dwellings per hectare) on previously developed land, which is mostly in urban areas and conversely, the lower density of development (22 dwellings per hectare) on land which was not previously developed.
>
> (DTLR, 2001: 14)

The previously developed sites are thus attracting more dwellings pro rata hectare of land than those previously undeveloped with the net effect of an apparent 'gap' between the 'dwellings' and the 'land' recycling figures. From a more critical viewpoint it could be argued that the 'land' measure provides the most accurate reflection of success in 'recycling'. This is because differential density standards are applied according to the specific type of land supply, increasing densities on previously used sites beyond what they might otherwise be. If this did not happen, then the picture of 'recycling' would approximate more to the proportion of all land for housing that was previously developed.

In practice, however, we cannot afford to take such a critical approach. Planning policy in practice recognises that, in many development circumstances, the housing market demands that sites that have been previously developed are developed at higher densities than sites that have not been previously developed. This is to reflect both the economics of development and the desire of planners to respond to the sustainable development and urban renaissance agendas.

Regional land recycling for housing: why do rates of recycling differ?

Rates of 'recycling', whether using the 'dwellings' measure or the 'land' measure, differ considerably at the regional level. There are a number of explanations and relevant factors. We identify at least three.

First, there is a factor which we have already touched on: namely 'geographical accident' and its derivative, industrial history. The fact that some regions are predominantly 'urban', while others are mainly 'rural', is significant in explaining why rates of land recycling for housing differ. Indeed, as the most recent land-use change statistics show (DTLR, 2001: 16), the five most urbanised regions of the country are also the regions with the highest rates of land recycling for housing. However, it is important to note that:

The variation in recycling rates across the regions is not totally explained by the proportion of land in each region that is in urban uses. This implies that there are other factors which affect the rate at which previously-used land is recycled.

Amongst these 'other factors', two appear to be important: first, variation in density (ibid.) and second, variation in regional housing markets.

Density, land recycling and urban regeneration

It is clear from policy set out in PPG3 that government wishes to increase density where possible in order to conserve greenfield land, and promote sustainable development and urban regeneration. It is also clear that a differential policy operates on sites that have been previously developed. On these sites, development is generally denser and this leads to the outcome that there is a difference between the 'land' and the 'dwelling' measures (see previous section).

To understand why there are regional differences in the proportion of land recycled for housing it is important to have further information about regional density policies and development outcomes both for sites on previously developed land and for those on not previously developed land.

In some regions such as London and the West Midlands, densities for housing development on previously used land are significantly higher than elsewhere. In London average density of previously developed land, measured in the average number of dwellings per hectare, was 52 (for the period 1989–2000). The density in London for land which was not previously developed was, for the same period, 36 dwellings per hectare. This means that development on previously used land was 44 per cent more dense than for sites which had not been previously used. For the West Midlands, the differential figure was 30 per cent. In contrast, development densities in regions such as the South East, the Eastern region and the East Midlands hardly differed (only 9 per cent).

These 'differentials' have an exponential effect on the difference in the regional proportion of dwellings built on previously developed land when they are considered alongside regional geographical circumstances. Considered in a very simple comparison, a highly urbanised region which builds relatively densely on previously used sites is likely to achieve a higher (regional) recycling figure than a region which is more rural and does not make density policy distinctions between previously used and not previously used sites.

Increasing density on previously used sites (relative to those which are not previously developed) is one way in which green land can be conserved. However, for sustainable development policies to be successful, it is necessary that the urban development itself is successful. This requires a careful balancing out of market forces, planning policies on density and the physical challenge of sites themselves. Unsuccessful urban regeneration schemes will feed through very quickly into increased pressures on greenfield sites, thereby negating the objectives of the whole policy (Nicol and Blake, 2000).

The impact of market forces on regional land recycling rates

It is important to state that the impact of market forces on rates of land recycling is uncertain. If the market worked in a perfect way, it could be argued that variations in market circumstances make little difference to differential in rates of land recycling. All differences in house prices, building costs and specific site circumstances are reflected in differences in land values. In other words, developers take a 'site neutral' approach and offer land-owners a sum of money simply reflecting the particular set of market and site appraisal data that they have available.

There is evidence to show that these conclusions hold. The proportion of dwellings built on previously developed land in the North West, for example, is similar to that in the South East. This is despite the fact that these are two completely different regional housing markets and that they have similar development density standards. The same conclusions apply when taking a comparison between the Eastern region and Yorkshire and Humberside. Thus the fact that a regional housing market is 'strong' or 'weak' may not have much impact on the amount of land that is recycled or the proportion of dwellings built on previously developed land.

At the margins of the market, however, and particularly at the bottom end, absolute differences in house prices and building costs may matter to a significant extent. On almost every greenfield site development opportunity, positive land values will be generated. Revenue from the sale of housing will exceed development cost and profit margin allowances, meaning that the developer can offer the land-owner 'something'. Because building costs do not vary significantly across the country, in areas where the market is strong developers can pay much more for land, even if a site is 'problematic'. This is particularly the case in Greater London. But this option is not available if house prices are very low and the gap between revenue and development costs small. For regions having a combination of low house prices and a proliferation of difficult brownfield sites, there is likely to be a serious disincentive to bring land forward for development. Although the significance of this 'constraint' is difficult to quantify, it should nevertheless be considered when comparing regional rates of land recycling.

Are we succeeding with our brownfield site housing policy?

As previously stated, the government can be satisfied with the statistics. These show an increase in the proportion of all new dwellings being built on previously used land and in the proportion of all land for new housing that was previously developed. Between 1990 and 1999, there were increases of 2 per cent and 5 per cent respectively in the two 'measures'.

Breheny has questioned the extent to which the policy is actually a success:

> The official figures [Land Use Change data] refer only to percentages. Absolute figures
> . . . are not presented. Thus we do not know how much housing development occurred

on various types of sites: we only know the shares. However . . . the bulletin gives the overall hectarage of land changing to residential use in England each year.

(Breheny, 1998)

This shows that 'the overall amount of new residential development declined significantly over the period [1985–95]; from 8,700 to 5,620 hectares. Thus re-used urban sites were taking an increasing share of a significantly declining total.' This fact, Breheny concludes, 'may be regarded as a modest success, but it gives much less confidence about the future prospects for increased urban compaction than would a genuine recent increase in the absolute amount of new housing on re-used sites'. As Breheny further points out '60 per cent [government's guideline national target] of very little is very little' (ibid.).

It is important to note that the latest version of the Land Use Change statistics shows that between 1990 and 1999 all land changing to residential use declined significantly: from 8,160 hectares (1990) to 4,630 hectares (1999). Thus Breheny's point is as relevant today as it was in 1998.

Policies and mechanisms for delivering more housing in Britain's urban areas

Policies and mechanisms

The very varied situations facing local and regional authorities across the country in delivering the urban housing agenda can be appreciated from the discussion of the previous sections. This section looks at ways and means by which urban housing policy is being delivered, in particular by identifying the key policy statements, the resources and the methods used by planning authorities. We think that three sources of information are crucial: first, PPG3, the government's key policy framework document for housing; second, the National Land Use Database (NLUD); and third, urban capacity studies.

In this section we examine these three sources of information, highlight their objectives, and, where appropriate, explain the tenets of their methodology. We give some considerable attention to the role of urban capacity studies in helping to deliver the urban renaissance. We look at recent government guidance *Tapping the Potential* and at its implications for the way in which local authorities are encouraged to follow a guideline methodology. At the end of the section, a case study of an urban capacity project in the East Midlands Region is presented.

Planning Policy Guidance Note 3: Housing and the 'sequential test'

The role of PPG3 in setting the framework
The framework for the current policy on urban regeneration and the development of housing in urban areas can be understood to a significant extent from Planning Policy Guidance Note 3: *Housing* (DETR, 2000b) ('PPG3'). This policy document

places an important emphasis on a number of key issues including the re-use of land and buildings, policies to promote brownfield site development before greenfield, and the need for local authorities to undertake urban capacity studies.

PPG3 states:

> The government is committed to maximising the re-use of previously developed land and empty properties and the conversion of non-residential buildings for housing, in order both to promote regeneration and minimise the amount of greenfield land being taken for development.
>
> (PPG3, para. 22)

PPG3 suggests further that 'all local planning authorities should undertake urban housing capacity studies' and 'consider the various options in relation to density of development, levels of parking provision, different residential layouts and the mix of housing types'. In doing so, the policy objectives are intended to encourage local authorities, architects, surveyors and builders to develop housing more efficiently and sustainably.

In trying to realise this sustainable agenda, local authorities are further encouraged via PPG3 to draw on all key sources of data and information which can help them to assess potential for additional house-building in their area:

> In compiling the base data for their capacity work, local planning authorities should draw on the National Land Use Database, which will help identify and track available sites and their potential for housing development. The intention is that as the NLUD is developed, it will increasingly provide a common data set which will underpin capacity studies.
>
> (PPG3, para. 27)

Sequential test for development

PPG3 affirms a sustainable principle in setting out a 'sequential test' as a basis for allocating land in plans and for making development control decisions: 'In determining the order in which sites identified in accordance with the criteria set out . . . should be developed, the presumption will be that previously-developed sites (or buildings for re-use or conversion) should be developed before greenfield sites' (PPG3, para. 32).

Thus providing the relevant criteria are met, local authorities should always give preference to sites which have been previously developed rather than those which have not. The relevant 'criteria' outlined in paragraph 31 of PPG3 relate to the availability of previously developed sites, their location and accessibility, the capacity of existing infrastructure to allow for the proposed (brownfield) development, the potential for community building and the physical and environmental constraints. Only where a site performs 'so poorly' against the aforementioned criteria, may the local authority in question depart from the principles engendered in the sequential test.

The operation of a 'sequential' approach could be achieved by a phased release of sites, where previously used sites are phased into the land supply first. PPG3 suggests that 'one possible approach to managing the release of land for housing is to divide the plan into three phases, allocating sites for development' in accordance with the sequential presumption. Local authorities should aim to identify a five-year housing land supply in the development plan as a way of providing a working framework to operate the sequential test. However, PPG3 emphasises that: 'it is essential that the operation of the development process is not prejudiced by unreal expectations of the developability of particular sites nor by planning authorities seeking to prioritise development sites in an arbitrary manner' (PPG3, para. 34).

We now consider in more detail two specific aspects of urban housing policy highlighted in PPG3, namely the National Land Use Database (NLUD) and urban capacity studies.

The National Land Use Database (NLUD)

Background

A key policy initiative to help bring forward more urban development land is the National Land Use Database (NLUD). This initiative does not provide data on land use change (as dealt with in the DTLR Land Use Change statistics), but provides a snapshot of the total amount of 'previously developed land' (PDL) in the country.

The data outputs and analysis are thus focused in a different way from that in the Land Use Change analysis. The key driver to the NLUD is the need to ensure that central and local government have access to information about the amount of land that is available for re-development at a given point in time. NLUD results show, for example, that for England in 1998, there were an estimated 57,710 hectares of previously developed land. The PDL is then broken down in terms of 'vacant land', 'derelict land and buildings' (see Plate 10.1), 'land occupied by vacant buildings', 'land in current use but allocated in the local plan for a change of use with planning permission for housing' and 'land with known development potential but without planning permission' (DETR, 2000b).

The process of monitoring via the NLUD aims to give central government realistic targets for land recycling at a regional level, and for the proportion of homes that are likely to be built on previously used land in any given region. Thus the NLUD serves to not only make information about PDL more widely available but also provide those responsible for housing provision with an opportunity to influence the process by which targets affecting them are set.

The NLUD is managed by a partnership of four organisations: the Department of Transport, Local Government and the Regions (DTLR), English Partnerships, the Improvement and Development Agency (representing the interests of local authorities) and Ordnance Survey. Each of these partners provides a specific input to the NLUD project: DTLR provides the policy driver and the raison d'être for the project, English Partnerships works with local authorities gathering information on specific sites, the Improvement and Development Agency works to

Plate 10.1 Riverside regeneration potential, Norwich: R. N. E. Blake.

ensure that local authority participation in the project is maximised, while Ordnance Survey has 'brought expertise as the mapping agency for Great Britain in collecting, collating, quality assuring, maintaining, developing and marketing geographically related information integrated at a national level' (DETR, 2000b).

What trends are identified via the NLUD?
The results from the NLUD highlight the importance of having several indicators to appraise the urban development challenge. The NLUD results (for May 1999), based on returns from 293 local authorities, show that:

> Much of the vacant and derelict land was located in the large provincial metropolitan areas; the North East, North West and Yorkshire and Humber had particularly high concentrations of both vacant and derelict land whilst London and the South East regions had relatively low amounts. To some extent this regional disparity is offset by the relatively large proportions in the South East of land currently in use with a planning allocation or permission indicating redevelopment, or assessed to have potential for redevelopment even though no planning allocation or permission exists.
>
> (DETR, 2000b)

These specific circumstances are very important when interpreting the trends highlighted in the Land Use Change data. Regions with a high proportion of vacant and derelict land might provide additional housing land, but this must be included as part of the land allocation and planning process if significant levels of land recycling and house-building on brownfield sites are to be achieved. Similarly, those regions with apparently low concentrations of vacant and derelict land may be achieving relatively high levels of land and property recycling if these land and buildings are already included within the land allocation process.

All depends on where we are in the regional development and housing market cycle. If sites do not come forward in regions where there is much spare 'capacity' in the form of vacant land and redundant buildings, then planning permissions for housing will not be identified in the NLUD. The net result of this might be to show significant regional capacity for vacant and derelict land, yet relatively low levels of land recycling (because development is mostly occurring on greenfield sites with planning permission). Similarly in some regions, it may appear from the NLUD that there is little scope for utilising vacant and derelict land simply because all the vacant and derelict land has been included as development opportunities with planning permission.

The different ways in which sources of information on land recycling and brownfield housing development are compiled mean that great care is required when trying to understand the success or failure of urban renaissance policies.

Urban housing capacity studies

What is an 'urban housing capacity study' and why carry one out?

An urban housing capacity study aims to assess the potential extra supply of housing that can be built within a given urban or already developed area. It usually involves an amount of research work covering site visits, commercial viability appraisals of the local housing market and a process of canvassing the views of public and private sector organisations with an interest in the urban regeneration process. It involves making informed judgements about how much of the capacity initially identified (the 'unconstrained capacity') should be 'discounted' to arrive at a 'constrained' or more realistic assessment of (deliverable) capacity.

It has become very important for local authorities to carry out urban capacity studies since the publication of PPG3 (DETR, 2000b). This policy document makes an assumption that housing development will be based on a 'plan, monitor and manage' approach and that housing will be delivered on a 'sequential' basis. Government anticipates that the urban capacity study will be a key mechanism in delivering the PPG3 agenda.

It is important to recognise some of the key issues that are raised by the requirement to carry out such studies. The geographical basis for studies is normally the local authority area, although county-wide studies (Surrey District Planning Authorities, 1999; Urban Initiatives and Chestertons, 1995) and regional studies (Llewelyn Davies, 1997; Baker Associates, 1998; Entec UK and De Montfort University, 1998) assessing capacity are not uncommon. It is clear, however, that many 'urban' capacity studies are studies of areas which are largely not urban, for example, market towns and villages. The extent to which a different approach should be adopted in these cases is left to the discretion of the authority itself, although where capacity opportunities are few in number a 100 per cent survey approach might be expected, rather than the 'sample' approach used frequently elsewhere.

An urban capacity study does not provide an indisputable 'magic figure'. Capacity studies can indicate the additional number of homes that will be forth-coming if certain policies and market conditions are in place. 'Capacity' is, however, ultimately an open-ended concept. It often depends not least on how radical a local authority wishes to be in its forward planning. Whilst physical capacity can be estimated fairly robustly by comparing with, say, the surrounding development, it is much more difficult to assess capacity where a local authority is planning a major re-development or regeneration programme. Under these circumstances it will not just be a case of summing together capacity from vacant sites; it will also be a case of accounting for net additions or reductions to the stock as a result of a demo-lition and re-building process. Always, capacity assessments should be benchmarked against a time period, usually that of the local plan. This process may be more efficiently carried out if the study is done 'in-house', although previous experience shows that very often local authorities lack the resources to do this.

Market factors also play an important role. In this respect, planning bodies run up against much the same problem as when housing needs studies are carried out, namely, in identifying the 'footprint' of the 'local' housing market. Usually this footprint does not shadow precisely the local authority boundary. So any assump-tions about whether sites will be brought forward should be considered in the light of housing demand as it might be affected by competing employment centres, travel distances to work and other critical factors.

Government policy guidance: *Tapping the Potential*

Housing capacity studies aim to produce a realistic deliverable amount of additional housing within the existing urban areas. To this end, government has produced a 'short guide to better practice' in the form of a document called *Tapping the Potential* (DETR, 2000d). This draws on good practice based on the experience of previous capacity studies. However, it is:

> . . . not intended to be the 'final word' on this subject, nor indeed does it attempt to prescribe how urban capacity studies should be carried out. Rather, it is designed to high-light the issues authorities will encounter in undertaking their capacity work and to act as a checklist of the various options available and decisions which have to be made at any point in the capacity assessment process.
>
> (DETR, 2000d)

Thus, it does not define the approach of each and every study, although it does set the context for each assessment.

There are two key considerations highlighted in *Tapping the Potential*: first, the general approach to the sampling of sites; second, the recommended steps that should be taken to arrive at a figure for discounted or net capacity.

Approach to sampling

The approach to the sampling of sites can vary. At the one extreme, all potential sites can be surveyed and assessed for their potential housing 'yield'. This is known as a 'comprehensive' approach. This approach is feasible given substantial human resources and data availability, and is also possible where only a small area is to be assessed, for example, a large village or a market town. At the other end of the scale, a sample approach can be adopted using 'generic' or 'typical' urban areas (Llewelyn Davies, 1998; Entec UK and De Montfort University, 1998; Entec and Nottingham Trent University, 2001). This has the advantage of reducing the number of sites to be assessed, for once similar areas have been identified only one or two need to be physically surveyed. The conclusions based on the findings of one typical area can be extrapolated to give a total number of dwellings that might be expected to be developed from all such areas. This approach has advantages, although it is not without its downsides. *Tapping the Potential* highlights the fact that conclusions are based on an assumption that areas have similar characteristics. This leads to the question of how to identify 'one-off' sites. It is also clear that some areas are more complex than others to assess. A suburban housing estate, for example, is likely to produce only one or two sources of additional supply: say, odd pieces of backland, or over-large corner plots. By comparison, a mixed-use area having housing, commercial office and industrial space is arguably much more complex to assess. Small changes in the market for these commercial uses might yield significant additional housing capacity, so care needs to be taken when arriving at a realistic figure.

Alternatively, urban capacity studies can adopt a 'priority area' approach whereby local authorities identify specific areas where they feel that significant additional capacity may be forthcoming. Very often such an approach works in a 'mixed-use' area. This method can often be usefully combined with a 'design-led' approach. Using fairly detailed drawings and paying close attention to density guidelines, an appraisal of capacity can be carried out. With this approach, however, there is the possible danger that capacity becomes falsely inflated. There can be a tendency with the 'design-led' approach to overlook the existing tone of the neighbourhood, which is an important consideration when arriving at a realistic assessment of capacity.

Steps in the method

There are usually four steps in the approach to the assessment of capacity: identifying the sources of capacity, surveying the capacity, assessing the yield, and discounting.

The first step suggested in *Tapping the Potential* is the identification of sources of capacity. The guidance states that 'appraisals should consider as many sources of capacity as possible' and not omit 'significant' ones. To this end, it is important that 'all previously developed land is brought within the purview of the study'.

Typically, sources of supply for additional housing cover existing properties, vacant sites and sites which could be more densely developed. Existing properties throw up a number of opportunities including empty homes, conversions (of both residential and commercial buildings) and the sub-division of properties to create additional housing occupancies. Vacant sites are sites which have either been previously developed or have lain fallow; further opportunities are often found in under-utilised car parks or garage spacing. The type of site opportunities will vary according to the local authority area, and within the local authority area ('typical urban areas'). There are some areas of the country, for example the North East and the North West, where wide-scale housing estate renewal to create more sustainable communities in line with PPG3 objectives is possible. In many of the major cities of the Midlands, site opportunities are very varied, involving the full range of examples just outlined. In London and the South East, land values are so high that any under-utilised sites create great interest for the market and for developers, who see an opportunity to raise residual land values.

The method of surveying has to a large extent already been covered in the discussion on the approach to 'sampling'. The method of surveying sites will be determined by the approach adopted, which may be 'comprehensive', 'priority area' or 'typical urban area', and the choice will also depend to a great extent on the resources available to the commissioning agent of the urban capacity study.

The assessment of 'yield' is a very important step. Government expect that: 'urban housing capacity studies should be about more than just a mechanical process of identifying more land and buildings for housing. They must also explore the potential to develop these opportunities more efficiently' (DETR, 2000d). To achieve a more 'efficient' use of the opportunities, sound judgements must be made about the appropriate density standards. As the guidance states, it is not sufficient to simply aggregate the number of sites or hectares and use a general multiplier for all site opportunities. This can lead to situation in which some sites become, in relation to their general location, either too densely or too sparsely developed. The density at which sites are developed should take account of the immediate situation and the nature of the existing development and environment. A 'design-led' approach can help in this respect, since schemes can be drawn up in draft form with the relevant densities outlined.

Once the area has been surveyed and an assessment of total housing yield made, the final stage in the study, namely 'discounting', begins. This is perhaps the most important stage of the method, since it is at this stage that capacity that has initially been identified begins to 'disappear'. Capacity can 'disappear' for a number of reasons. The factors to be taken into account are 'developability', 'market viability', 'planning standards' and 'local circumstances'. The assessment of developability is normally benchmarked against physical land constraints, for example, problems of infrastructure provision, problems of flooding, difficult topography or terrain. In addition, the readiness of a land-owner to sell land for development might also be considered at this stage.

The 'market viability' assessment can be done using local market housing data in conjunction with a residual development approach. In other words, an assessment is made of the commercial viability of a site from the viewpoint of a developer or a potential purchaser of that site. On this basis, a judgement can be made about whether the site is likely to realise a land value sufficient for it to be sold for housing development. The process of assessing market viability should be undertaken in close co-operation with local developers who can provide benchmark figures for land values, house prices, and sometimes, profit margin allowances. In addition, the assessment of market viability should take account of the effect of affordable housing quotas on the scheme. This broad approach to the evaluation of commercial viability has been recently used in the Milton Keynes urban capacity study (Entec UK and Nottingham Trent University, 2001).

Planning standards are a further important consideration. The assessment of capacity should take account of the application of parking standards, overlooking distances and ceilings on densities. All these factors can have a significant effect on reducing the yield. Some urban capacity studies (examples: Llewelyn Davies, 1997; Baker Associates, 1998) have adopted a 'policy scenario' approach to deal with different assumptions about planning standards.

Taking the 'local character' of the area into account is often a difficult political issue. The inclusion of sites which are regarded as 'sensitive' by the local community in an estimate of capacity can be a difficult factor to deal with. This is particularly the case with 'open space' which is used for recreation and play areas and for such uses as allotments and paddocks (Nicol and Blake, 2000). Capacity identified within conservation areas is often discounted by 100 per cent. Often only very small percentages of the originally identified capacity in environmentally sensitive areas can be realised. The 'local character' of the area often goes wider than individual sites. In towns and cities which have experienced wide-scale urban sprawl then some 'reigning in' of the trend is desirable. However, it can be argued that in some communities, for example, new towns, which were built with the intent of expanding from a planned base, that extensive in-filling is not in line with the 'local character'. Thus what is discounted depends very much on the acceptability of the proposed development to the local area.

The assessment of discounted capacity depends on the explicit assumptions laid out in the particular study concerned. *Tapping the Potential*, however, has a guideline range of 'discounts' for particular sources of supply. It suggests, for example, that sites with existing housing allocated in plans will achieve between 90 per cent and 100 per cent of the unconstrained capacity, whereas for example, 'Living over the Shop' (LOTS) schemes will only achieve between 25 per cent and 40 per cent of the unconstrained capacity. In other words, with LOTS schemes up to 75 per cent of the capacity originally identified can be lost.

Urban capacity studies: a linear or an iterative process?

The final discounted figure that is arrived at in an urban capacity study is the result of an extensive process of survey and assessment. It is important to emphasise that the robustness of the findings depend very much on the assumptions made. It is also important to recognise that the process of assessing capacity is not necessarily a linear one. Each of the stages outlined in *Tapping the Potential* can itself be subject to review. The process of 'discounting' is itself inherent at all stages: the identification of sites involves some 'discounting' of those sites which are not seen to be viable. Similarly, the assumptions made about density and the yield that can be delivered requires some discounting. Thus the process should be seen not as a 'linear' one, but as an iterative one, where capacity is assessed, reviewed and discounted on an ongoing basis.

Case study: assessing urban housing capacity in the East Midlands

The East Midlands: spatial characteristics and housing markets

In 1998, Entec UK and the Centre for Comparative Housing Research at De Montfort University were commissioned to carry out an urban housing capacity assessment of the East Midlands. The East Midlands is one of the standard English regions and has a wide variety of urban and rural locations. Its main urban locations are Nottingham, Leicester and Derby; in addition, it has other key urban centres such as Northampton and Lincoln. The East Midlands covers a number of very different types of housing market, from the buoyant Northamptonshire and south Leicestershire markets to the more rural markets in Lincolnshire and northeast Nottinghamshire and to the less strong housing markets in the coalfield areas of north-west Nottinghamshire and Leicestershire.

The East Midlands has, however, in the regional context, a very low rate of land recycling. Between 1985 and 1993 the proportion of land which was previously developed for urban uses and which changed to residential use was only 32 per cent. Figure 10.1 shows that in 1997, housing land was still being sourced to a very significant extent from agricultural uses. Arguably, two factors are instrumental in determining these outcomes. First, there is the prevalence of rural areas within the East Midlands region. In other words, compared to other regions (and one might highlight the West Midlands as a good nearby example), the East Midlands has a relative shortage of sites which have been previously developed; it thus follows that it must draw on rural and not previously developed sites.

The second factor is the housing market itself. The research (Entec UK and De Montfort, 1998) examined housing market data and concluded that the East Midlands faced a particularly difficult task in delivering higher proportions of brownfield site housing development and levels of land recycling. This was concluded by examining the price, or the value 'gaps' between house prices and land prices (on the one hand), and (on the other hand) the percentage of land changing to residential use which was previously developed for urban areas. The investigation showed that the price gaps were greatest in regions where the percentage of land changing to residential on previously developed sites was highest. Most notably this occurred in regions such as Merseyside and the North West. By contrast, regions such as the East Midlands and Yorkshire and Humberside had much lower 'margins' between house prices and land prices, and showed a correspondingly low level of land recycling for housing.

The theory underlying this investigation recognised that levels of land recycling would be highly influenced by the balance of urban to rural land. However, it also questioned the way in which the regional housing market operated, and, in particular, the way in which the land market took into account the very real situation on the ground which relates to the supply and demand for more difficult and brownfield sites. There are two ways of elaborating this theory. The first is to suggest that the market does work in a fairly competitive and transparent way, discounting the price of land more (relative to house prices) in regions having a prevalence of brownfield sites. If this happens, it has the effect that areas with many brownfield sites have a way of ensuring they become developed. The second is to suggest that the market does not work so well, and that differences in the price 'gaps' are not so much a function of the balance of brownfield and greenfield sites between regions but of the wider housing markets in general. If it is this second assumption which is more relevant, then land prices in regions with small price gaps may have to fall disproportionately if those regions are to reach higher levels of land recycling.

Methodological approach to assessing housing capacity in the East Midlands region

The variety of urban and rural development offered a corresponding variety in the sources of urban housing capacity. A very significant proportion of additional capacity was thought to exist in areas of industrial decline associated with the major industries of the key urban locations: Leicester (knitwear), Nottingham (lace and textiles) and Northamptonshire (boots and shoes). In particular, structural decline in these industries might be expected to yield a number of sites which included redundant mill buildings or sites where existing industrial units could be demolished to make way for new housing (see Plate 10.2). However, it was also anticipated that there would be sources of supply generic to other regions and areas of the country, for example infill sites, backland, open space, car parks, space over retail units (LOTS schemes) and potential housing space which could be created from obsolescent offices from the 1960s and 1970s.

It was also important to recognise in the regional study the potential sources of housing supply which could be yielded from sites in the key market towns of the region; for example, Boston, Buxton, Chesterfield, Daventry, Gainsborough, Ilkeston, Market Harborough, Spalding, Sutton in Ashfield and Worksop. These were by no means all such market town centres, but rather those which provided a relevant sample of site opportunities.

The approach to the assessment of urban housing capacity can be understood from Table 10.2, which shows the typical urban areas which were surveyed and in

Plate 10.2 Vacant site, High Pavement, Nottingham city centre: R. N. E. Blake.

Table 10.2 Assessing urban capacity across the East Midlands region

Type of urban area	Greater Leicester	Greater Nottingham	Derby	Lincoln	Northampton
Residential					
Pre-1918		✓			
Inter-war			✓		
1950s–1960s	✓				
1970s +					✓
Industrial					
Pre-1945	✓		✓		
Post-1945					✓
Commercial					
City centre		✓		✓	
Town		✓			
District					✓
Mixed-use	✓		✓		

Source: Adapted from Entec UK and De Montfort University (1998)

which housing capacity was assessed. It will be noted that only a sample of area types were undertaken. The main aim was to ensure that an accurate assessment of capacity was achieved for each of the area types. For some area types, for example, pre-1918 housing, it was thought necessary to study only one location (Greater Nottingham). 'Pre-1918' is largely terraced housing, densely built in inner-city locations. This situation does not differ significantly between the major cities. However, for other typical urban areas such as pre-1945 industrial, city-centre commercial and mixed-use, it was thought necessary to examine more than one location and case study.

It was very important in the assessment of capacity to recognise that many different types of urban area can yield additional housing supply. *Tapping the Potential* emphasises the importance of looking at all possible sources. The East Midlands study also took this approach, even though it pre-dated the government guidance. To this end, it was important to assess the potential for existing residential areas to yield more housing. Whilst it was unlikely to be the case that the densely developed terraced housing areas of the pre-1914 period would provide much additional supply, it was seen to be very important to look at the inter-war and 1950s and 1960s housing estates. The inter-war housing was often built to very generous plot standards and could, if access allowed, provide some additional housing land. Housing built after the Second World War also could provide some additional capacity, particularly where open space had been generously allocated in the design of estates (see Figure 2.2).

Industrial land and buildings clearly provide an additional source of supply, particularly where buildings are no longer suitable for industrial production or are badly located for transport links. There was, and still are, significant housing opportunities in redundant textile mill type buildings in the East Midlands. Some of these opportunities have been taken up with success. Most notable is Nottingham city's Lace Market area (see also Chapter 11 case study), where apartments for owner occupation and private rent are being sold by developers. There is also some success in other cities such as Leicester, where former knitwear and hosiery factories have been converted into private flats. 'Industrial' opportunities, however, were identified in many shapes and sizes. Much of the potential which was identified was on smaller industrial units in the inner city. These areas are arguably not so good for access, being positioned neither handily for the city centre employment zones, nor for access to the outer ring-road systems. Neither, often, are the factories themselves architecturally interesting. As such, their potential for housing is less certain, and for this reason, planners are often reluctant to allow for a change of use from industrial to housing.

The study identified very significant potential for housing development in 'town' areas. These are areas usually between the central business district ('city centre') and the inner ring road. Typically, this is where high-rise and medium-rise offices were developed during the 1960s and 1970s. One might identify Maid Marian Way in Nottingham or Vaughan Way and Southgates in Leicester.

Dealing with the regional context

A key aim of the study was to show how typical urban areas would provide specific types of opportunities and constraints to housing development. It was understood that the research would highlight particular issues in relation to specific area types; moreover that this approach would not provide a 'figure' either in terms of an amount of land capable of being developed or a number of dwellings that could be built in the East Midlands region. The regional study should highlight the key constraints and opportunities from which targets and numbers could be worked up by local authorities working in conjunction with the National Land Use Database resource.

On this basis, the regional study sought to identify potential alternative policies for specific types of urban housing development challenge. Various options were identified which are now briefly described.

One option is a 'programme based' approach. This approach is engendered in past initiatives such as City Challenge and more recently the New Deal for Communities. These initiatives are wide ranging in their objectives including physical regeneration as well as social and economic renewal. A partnership approach is usually combined with the use of compulsory purchase powers. Such as approach would be appropriate for larger sites where, for example, contamination existed and where significant environmental benefits could be achieved via a comprehensive approach. A good example identified in the study was Bede Island, south of the River Soar near to Leicester city centre.

A second option is a 'portfolio based' approach. This involves initiatives aimed to tackle specific types of property or land problems. Examples include initiatives to tackle older industrial buildings, vacant floor-space over shops (e.g. LOTS) or policies to tackle vacant sites. Other options identified were more, or less, specific than the previous two. Site-specific approaches, for example, are appropriate. These often involve producing a 'master plan' for a specific site showing precisely how many additional dwellings can be accommodated. Other solutions would require the support of government via mainstream policy changes. For example, removing VAT on building conversions or the imposition of a 'greenfield' or 'environmental' tax which could support house-building on brownfield sites or urban regeneration more broadly.

Main findings of the East Midlands study

As was stated, the study attempted to identify the opportunities and constraints for particular types of urban areas. The study's conclusions addressed this aim by reporting on the potential for additional housing to be accommodated in the area types.

Residential areas generally were not seen to be significant as a source of additional housing supply. Infill developments in the major locations of Nottingham, Leicester and Derby had not made a major contribution to new housing supply over the previous few years. When 'residential areas' were sub-divided into 'age of building' (see Table 10.2) then it could be seen that a contribution to supply was more possible in some locations than in others. Estates built with more generous plots, in particular inter-war housing areas, were clearly more likely to yield additional housing than the pre-1918 housing which is generally more densely developed. Traditional terraced housing was typically found to be built to densities of around 70 dwellings per hectare. In these locations, there is little additional space and any such areas would have to be comprehensively re-developed, probably at a lower density, leading to a net loss of urban housing. In residential areas a significant barrier is amenity space and the political 'premium' placed on it.

Commercial property areas were identified in the study as having a much greater potential for accommodating housing and increasing the number of urban dwellings. The opportunities are significant in the number of office blocks found in the city centres; a prime example identified was the St George's Tower, located near to Leicester's railway station and with a potential for 170,000 ft² of development. Many further good examples were identified around Nottingham's inner ring road. There are, however constraints to developing housing in these buildings. Whilst space abounds, residential use requires particular conversion skills and a confidence in the market for such housing and many questions were raised about the commercial viability of such schemes. Specific issues identified were the cost of sound-proofing, both internally, between residential units, and externally, from the main roads. The viability of such schemes would be highly sensitive to planning policy and, in particular, the requirement to include affordable housing. In addition, housing developed in predominantly commercial areas was seen to be particularly liable to be affected by 'bad neighbour' uses. This was not so much land uses of a noxious nature, but more related to the '24 hour city effect' which means that the living experience is often being conducted in areas where bars, pubs or night clubs remain open until late.

Significant potential for additional housing development was identified in 'mixed-use' urban areas. Mixed-use areas are by their nature rather ill defined and usually have a smattering of many different operations being carried out. It is important to recognise that these areas are ultimately defined somewhat arbitrarily in a capacity study although some local authorities have recognised the varied and often transient nature of land use and have thus designated the area as having potential in a local plan; for example providing a PDA (Potential Development Areas) designation. Housing potential identified in these 'mixed-use' areas would need to be realised via a number of initiatives including new-build, conversions, and in some cases, demolition.

The key barriers identified in mixed-use areas relate mainly to the land market and the planning process. Investment in housing development proceeds only where land or buildings are sold to developers from original land-owners. If land-owners take the view that housing is the best alternative use for a building or a plot, then they will not bother to apply for 'refurbish for commercial use'. However, in a highly volatile property market this is not always the case, and hence housing opportunities are frequently not realised. The local authority can play a crucial role here in increasing the supply of urban housing through the planning process, importantly by being more prescriptive in planning for mixed-use areas. This is a double-edged sword. Developers and investors need to be encouraged by a flexible approach to planning; yet if the approach is seen to be too 'flexible' then the situation can be exploited by land-owners holding back specific plots for speculative reasons.

Sustainable and urban capacity solutions: looking forward

The discussion in this chapter presents several conclusions and 'pointers' towards the future performance of the urban housing policy agenda. Perhaps the most significant way in which the profile of the urban housing development thrust has been promoted is via improved information and, in particular, more extensive data availability. The Land Use Change statistics, for example, have been highly influential in bringing to public attention the need to focus increasingly on the re-use of land where possible. While the basic data are perhaps not widely known beyond those with a specific interest, government targets for house-building and land recycling have been highly profiled in the press and other media. At the same time, initiatives such as NLUD have served to improve information about site opportunities for local planning authorities and the development industry. Urban capacity studies are helping to make known the extent of available land at an individual local authority area level. Government guidance on how these studies should be carried out is helping to firm up estimates of the urban land challenge.

The availability and improved quality of data and information via these means is likely to continue, especially as information technology continues to make an increasing contribution to the way in which we analyse the built environment. So long as local authorities and the development industry have the resources to manage the systems and processes which are now in place, there seems to be considerable scope for delivering the urban housing renaissance.

Nevertheless, it is clear that improved information and data can only assist up to a certain point. It is evident that delivering the urban housing agenda with an increasing proportion of all new homes built on brownfield sites will be more difficult to achieve in some areas than others. Past trends indicate, for example, that whereas in regions such as Greater London, high brownfield site targets will be met in the future, this will not be the case elsewhere. To a large extent, 'high' levels of brownfield site development are achieved where there is a ready supply of 'brownfield' land; more rural regions may not be achieving such high targets. As such, targets can be adjusted so that they are broadly met.

However, there is a significant margin for error in reaching targets associated in particular with the relationship between planning policy and the performance of the housing market. This relationship is likely to hold the key to the successful delivery of the urban housing development programme. There are a number of factors to be considered by local planning authorities and developers: the effects of future downturns in the housing market, the implementation of the sequential test, and, importantly, the delivery of the PPG3 policy relating to density.

The interaction of these factors will be critical in determining the supply and demand balance between greenfield and brownfield sites. This is a very tricky balance to gauge. While, for example, it can be argued that stemming the flow of greenfield sites will encourage the release of brownfield and urban sites, such policy change needs careful implementation if the wider land is to be re-configured. Land-owners and developers, in the absence of prescriptive plans in favour of housing on recycled land, will simply retain land in favour of other uses. Similar arguments can be applied in the case of future downturns in the market where it is assumed that the price paid for land will simply reflect changed circumstances. In many cases this will be the situation. However, in some areas land values are already very low, and a change in market circumstances, conjoined with increased costs of building, may lead to negative land value.

The role of land-use planning policy in delivering increased urban and brown-field housing will be highly critical in the way density standards are applied on brownfield and greenfield sites. Whereas developers can use good local knowledge to gauge fairly accurately the effects of density policy on greenfield sites, there is less certainty about its effect on urban and brownfield sites. This is largely because changes in density do not always have commensurate effects on house prices. A site which is developed twice as densely as another will not necessarily yield double the gross development value. The effects of density on sale prices will usually be much more difficult to assess.

Thus our conclusions about whether the urban housing development policy will succeed are based on the expectation that improved information will raise the awareness to develop housing sustainably; however, successful delivery and imple-mentation of the policy depends largely on the extent to which local planning authorities and developers can co-operate to ride out the fluctuations in the housing market and to respond to the government's new planning agenda.

Discussion points

1   Discuss the role of the Urban Task Force report (1999) in framing the sustain-able housing development debate.
2   Highlight and discuss the measures used for evaluating the success of land recycling policies.
3   Identify and discuss the key mechanisms for delivering more housing in urban areas.
4   Examine the role of policies to alter housing densities in increasing urban housing development.
5   Define the scope of an 'urban capacity study'. What are the strengths and weak-nesses of this tool for increasing housing development in towns and cities?

Key reading

The literature base for this topic is huge. Lord Rogers' Urban Task Force report *Towards an Urban Renaissance* (1999) distils the agenda while the prolific research outputs of the late Michael Breheny, e.g. *Sustainable Development and Urban Form* (1992) chart the topic's emergence and importance. The government bulletin *Land Use Change in England* (for examples, DTLR, 2001) provides a partial basis for statistical monitoring of the housing footprint. For reflections on 'town cramming' see Nicol and Blake, 'Classification and use of open space in the context of increasing urban capacity' (*Planning Practice & Research*, 2000).

Chapter 11
Housing renewal, conversion and city living

Ron Blake and Andrew Golland

Housing and urban renewal

The importance of increasing the volume of housing developed in urban areas and on brownfield sites has been emphasised in the previous chapter. The sustainable development agenda is focused on both the objective of saving greenfield land as well as preserving the existing housing stock. There are advantages in achieving both these goals, particularly from the perspective of reducing public expenditure on new-build housing.

A housing 'renewal policy' has been in evidence in various forms for the greater part of the period since the Second World War. This has been desirable as a way of improving both the quality of housing, as well as increasing its supply. Housing renewal has been desirable in order to increase the number of available homes (where dwellings are 'unfit' for habitation'), to maintain the supply of homes (where dwellings might otherwise fall below the necessary fitness standards) and to create pleasant housing environments where people want to live.

'Housing renewal' can take the form of changes to the built housing form, and it can take the form of changes in the environment in which housing is located. Changes to the built form include physical improvements to the structure of the building, necessary repairs to its fabric, or refurbishment, and an increase in the standard of facilities with which the dwelling is provided. 'Renewal' more broadly can include a change of use between different types of occupier, for example a conversion scheme from an office to housing. It can also include a physical change in the building without a change of use, for example where a large house is converted to smaller units, usually apartments.

Implicit in the term 'housing renewal' is the idea that we move from a situation which is less desirable to one which is more desirable. This is clearly the case where dwellings are brought up to standards of fitness which they were not previously achieving. It should be remembered however that housing renewal does not always achieve its objectives. The best example is perhaps the slum clearance programme which replaced poor-quality terraced housing with better quality high-rise housing. While people moved into higher quality accommodation, their environment was, in many cases, considerable less pleasant following their relocation.

This chapter considers housing renewal in its various forms. More specifically, it focuses on two main forms: the renewal of 'traditional housing environments' and the renewal of 'non-traditional housing environments'. We see 'traditional housing environments' as areas which are predominantly and historically residential in nature. These include inner-city terraced areas, larger suburban mixed dwelling type estates and the various forms of social housing estates, from high to low rise. These areas have, in an urban capacity context, a settled nature where there is limited scope for additional house-building and where there is only a very low chance that different forms of land use will be adopted.

'Non-traditional housing environments' we see as areas which have traditionally not attracted housing development and where other urban land uses predominate: commercial property and industry in particular. In this chapter we focus on the city centre and inner city as a 'non-traditional housing environment'. This is because of the particular interest in, and role played by, city centre housing development schemes at the present time. In these areas, the dynamics of the wider property market are highly significant in determining the volume, type and location of housing development at the urban core. Of course, in seeing these central areas as 'non-traditional housing' environments, we leave ourselves open to the criticism that historically these areas did indeed accommodate most of the housing. However, the trend in the more recent past (since the end of the nineteenth century) has been counter-urbanist, where households have sought to move away from city centres to the suburbs and the countryside. The current urban regeneration policy thrust appears to be making good ground in attracting a certain section of the housing market back to the heart of our cities.

The focus on housing in this chapter shows that 'renewal' is both a remedy for housing problems as well as a consequence of housing development. Government needs to have policies to improve and maintain the housing stock. Yet at the same time, encouragement to housing developers to convert buildings from other uses and to build on brownfield sites is important in helping to renew the wider urban area.

The activities bringing about housing renewal and improvement of urban areas can be grouped into two areas: (1) policies aimed to change the built form (either housing or other property), and (2) policies to change the nature of the wider environment in which housing is located. Policies in practice, however, are inevitably connected where subsidies are made conditional on location.

In this chapter, we examine the main ways in which these two types of activity affect the two types of housing environment: the 'traditional' and the 'non-traditional'. The chapter provides a summary of the key policy initiatives, particularly those employed in the traditional housing areas, as well as recent case study material from cities enjoying a renaissance of housing development in their urban core locations.

Renewal of traditional housing environments

How can traditional housing environments undergo renewal?

In this section, we consider the options for the renewal of traditional housing environments.

Perhaps the most radical solution is a programme of demolition and clearance linked to a development programme of new-build. This method can, and has, proved controversial, as the approach changes not only the form of development but also the entire neighbourhood and environment.

Housing renewal is very often a response to poor housing quality or a need to bring housing up to a given standard of 'fitness'. By far the most common causes of housing 'unfitness' relate to serious disrepair and dampness. For the financial year 1997–98, 57 per cent of unfit dwellings were caused by this problem (DTLR, 1999c). Sanitary unfitness is also prevalent. Unfit food preparation areas and unfit bath, W.C. and hand washing basins accounted for 15 per cent of all unfit dwellings in the same year. The structural stability of dwellings accounted for 7 per cent of unfit homes, while problems with heating, ventilation, lighting, drainage and water supply accounted for a further 21 per cent of all unfit homes.

The traditional solution to poor-quality housing and improvement has usually involved grants paid directly to households to improve the quality of the housing stock. These grants have several bases: grants for repairs, for improvement and conversion and, more latterly, to improve housing for those in particularly difficult financial situations.

Grants have been linked to wider regeneration area policies, where the applicant is entitled to an award higher than would be available were the applicant to be living outside the area. Typical examples have been General Improvement Areas (GIAs), Housing Action Areas (HAAs) and Housing Renewal Areas (HRAs).

We now consider these initatives and policy solutions in more detail.

The role of slum clearance in improving the housing environment

The policy of demolishing homes in order to provide land for new and better-quality housing can be justified on the basis of improving households' standard of living and to obviate the need for long-term repair and maintenance costs.

The decision to demolish, however, is appropriate only under certain circumstances. There are many factors to be counter-balanced, for example whether demolition and new-build will actually achieve the objective of improving households' living standards and quality of life; and the balance of supply and demand. Where housing shortages are very significant, it may be practical to repair and maintain the existing stock rather than clear and build.

'Slum clearance' implies the clearing away of unsatisfactory housing. For many years following the Second War World slum clearance was seen as a key solution to housing problems. In part, this was due to the expectations of people for better housing. In part, it was also a reaction to the need to renew the housing stock. 'Slum clearance' is a particularly British phenomenon. Power (1999: 13) suggests that 'there have been no major slum clearance programmes comparable to Britain elsewhere in Europe'. This in turn is explained by the early advent of the industrial revolution, whereby Britain found itself with a high proportion of relatively old stock.

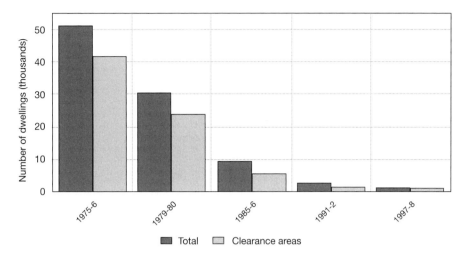

Figure 11.1 Slum clearance: dwellings demolished or closed in England and Wales, 1975–98.
Source: DTLR housing and construction statistics

Slum clearance was thus a key plank of housing policy for the years following 1945. 'Clearance areas' were declared to assist this process and it was intended that many of the beneficiaries should be households in very poor quality private rented homes, who, it was anticipated, would be pleased to move to better quality local authority housing. However, the slum clearance policy became less significant after 1970 and rates of clearance began to fall. Figure 11.1 identifies the dramatic decline in the number of homes demolished from 1975–76, when around 50,000 homes were demolished, to 1997–98, when only around 1,000 homes were demolished.

The roots of the decline can be traced to the mid-1960s, when objections to slum clearance programmes began to emerge. Events began to catch up: older housing was becoming obsolete at a rate faster than the clearance and new-build programme could keep up with. As with many aspects of housing policy, pragmatic solutions won over idealistic arguments. The economic crisis of the late 1960s and the financial arguments in favour of renewal of the stock took over and clearance levels began to fall towards today's levels, which are hardly significant.

The grant framework for housing renewal: an historic overview

Types of grant available
There have been several types of grant available to private owners and housing association tenants. Figure 11.2 shows the main types available since 1970. The grant system has changed considerably since then, most notably during the late 1980s

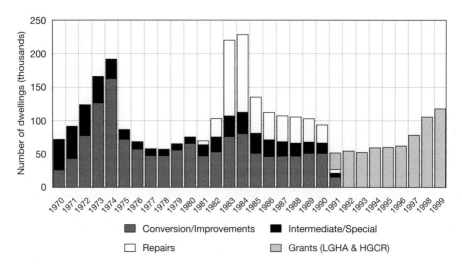

Figure 11.2 Housing grants made to private owners and housing association tenants by type of grant, England, 1970–99.
Source: DoE and DTLR housing and construction statistics

and mid-1990s, under the Local Government and Housing Act (LGHA) 1989 and the Housing Grants, Construction and Regeneration Act (HGCR) 1996.

'Conversion' or 'improvement' grants were first introduced in 1949 and were awarded at the discretion of local authorities 'either for the improvement of existing dwellings or for the provision of new dwellings by conversion' (DoE, 1981). The amount payable related to a proportion of 'eligible' expenses up to a limit; the maximum payable for dwellings outside Greater London during the late 1970s was around £7,000 (ibid.).

'Intermediate grants' were available as of right (i.e. mandatory) for housing where 'standard amenities have been lacking for at least one year' (ibid.). Normally the aim of the grant was to bring the dwelling beyond the basic standard of fitness for habitation. Typically these grants were for basic sanitary (kitchen and bathroom) facilities. Awards were usually much lower than with conversion and improvement grants.

'Special' grants were available on a discretionary basis to owners of houses in multiple occupation in order to provide basic standard amenities and, post-1980, to provide means of escape.

'Repair' grants were introduced in 1974 (England and Wales) and were discretionary for 'substantial and structural repairs to dwellings built before 1919'. Until 1980 these grants were, however, only available in Housing Action Areas and General Improvement Areas (see section below). The maximum payable was £4,000 (£5,500 in Greater London) and the grant was further subject to the condition that the rateable value of the dwelling fell below specified limits.

Collectively, these types of award are known as 'renovation' grants. As from July 1990 a new system of renovation grants was introduced following the Local Government and Housing Act 1989. The main distinction since that time has been in terms of 'mandatory' and 'discretionary' renovation grants. These grants have been made available for all types of housing renewal and renovation: improvement, conversion, repair and sub-division of buildings to flats. The grants are available for private owners, tenants liable for repairs and upkeep under the terms of a lease, and landlords (other than those who are owners of HMOs (houses in multiple occupation) where a separate grant system applies. The system since 1990 has aimed to bring dwellings up to a standard of fitness for human habitation. If the local authority deems renovation to be an appropriate course of action (as opposed to demolition) then the grant is mandatory in these circumstances. The 1990 system has also aimed to provide discretionary grants to repair and/or improve a property. The system provides grants for other facilities such as home insulation, heating, improvement of internal living arrangements and conversions.

Watersheds in the grant system

The grant system has aimed broadly to improve the condition of the housing stock and to improve the living conditions of households. Like many other government policy initiatives, the grant system has not entirely achieved these objectives and there have also been unintended consequences.

There are several points in time which we can regard as 'watersheds' in the recent history of the housing grants system. The post-war grant regime was based to a large extent on the need to ensure a steady supply of housing. To do this, it encouraged housing improvements via appropriate discretionary grants. Local authorities, in many cases, saw improvement as a desirable policy option, particularly in the light of bad experiences with slum clearance and high-rise development.

By the mid-1970s, the take-up of improvement grants had risen significantly. This was a response due in no small part to a rising housing market, where developers and property speculators took advantage of the grant system to convert and improve buildings for their own profitable ends (Balchin, 1996). There was an additional concern over the activities of private landlords, who, fettered by the system of regulated rents, exploited the grant system to buy out secured tenants to realise a considerably enhanced capital value for their property. The Housing Act 1974 was a reaction to this emerging situation. The introduction of the Act was accompanied by a sharp fall in the number of grants taken up (see Figure 11.2). One cause of this is likely to have been a slump in the housing market during the mid-1970s. However, the provisions of the Act tied landlords and owner-occupiers to a 'pay back' clause if they moved or sold within five years of receiving the grant (ibid.).

The Housing Act 1980, introduced by the incoming Conservative Government provided an impetus for a renewed programme of housing repair (see Figure 11.2). It focused the repair programme on older dwellings (pre-1919). It also abolished the 'five years' of anti-speculation rule for owner-occupiers. The main effect was dramatically to increase the amount of repair activity. However, there was concern about who was actually benefiting from the system, and in particular there was a concern that it was better-off owner-occupiers who were taking a major share of the subsidy. The 1985 Inquiry into British Housing and the White Paper of 1987 were important milestones in the change of policy which came in 1989. Balchin (1996: 81) describes the background to the changes:

> The Inquiry into British Housing . . . stressed that although there were three vital areas for government intervention – encouraging voluntary action, dealing with the very worst stock and helping worse off households – its basic philosophy was that the main responsibility for the repair and improvement of private sector housing should be with individual owners. It was therefore considered in government that much greater selectivity in the award of grant was essential.
>
> (ibid.)

The solution was much greater means testing for improvement and repair grants and a greater focus on targeting improvement grants towards the worst housing and to households in greatest need. The 1989 legislation consolidated this policy thrust, where the system of grant allocation was largely based on a 'mandatory' system. Renovation grants, including those for HMOs and for those requiring disabled facilities all became means tested. DTLR Housing and Construction statistics show that the number of mandatory grants since 1990 have far exceeded the number of discretionary grants, indicating the desired effects of the change in policy direction.

Area renewal

In policy making for housing renewal, it has been important to target subsidies towards those areas of housing where quality is lowest. Two initiatives have been significant during the last 35 years: the creation of General Improvement Areas (GIAs) and Housing Action Areas (HAAs).

GIAs were timed to be a response to the ongoing slum clearance programme and were legislatively enabled by the Housing Act 1969. GIAs had the broad aim of providing increased housing supply at a time when housing was being demolished. GIAs provided a twin-track solution in that they aimed to provide a special subsidy framework by which run-down areas could be regenerated. Within a GIA, the occupants of housing in poor condition could attract greater levels of grant subsidy than were available to their counterparts outside the GIA.

The GIA policy experience was not however a happy one. The criticism can be summarised in terms of 'gentrification, speculation and administration'. Gentrification and speculation occurred in the sense that the consequences of GIAs were to improve the profits of developers and wealthier home-owners who had adapted quickly to exploit the grant system. Babbage for example, argued: 'By declaring a general improvement area in an area of housing stress . . . the local authority may just as well have been putting a flag on the developer's office wall map to show where he might operate with the best return on investment' (Babbage,

1973). But it was ultimately a problem of administration of local planning that caused the problem for GIAs. Leather and Mackintosh (1993: 112) state: 'the number of GIAs declared by local authorities was very small and the number of grants awarded in these areas amounted to only five per cent of all grants paid. By 1974, declared GIAs contained only 273,000 dwellings.

A second housing renewal initiative was the introduction of Housing Action Areas (HAAs). Whereas the principle of targeting locations in need of regeneration and housing renewal survived. HAAs further focused housing subsidies towards those on low incomes. Eligible costs were set into a more progressive framework, so that low-income households could recover a higher proportion of total costs.

The extent to which the grant framework was robust enough to significantly improve housing quality was questionable. Leather and Mackintosh (1993: 114) suggest that in some cases, grants up to 90 per cent of eligible costs were not enough. This factor, combined with the slow rate of HAA declarations, made the initiative difficult to evaluate as a 'success'.

Under the Housing Act 1980, GIAs and HAAs were replaced by Housing Renewal Areas (HRAs). These were aimed to go even further in making the link between poor housing quality and low income and to provide grant subsidies to those who most needed it. The system of renewal areas sparked a very significant increase in the number of repair grants awarded (see also Figure 11.2). Towards the middle of the 1980s, however, resources available for grants became subject to the Housing Investment Programme (HIP) and local authorities came under greater pressure to balance repair and improvement subsidies between the private housing stock and their own (council house) stock.

Renewal of non-traditional housing environments via housing development: the market for city centre living

In addition to the up-grading of run-down estates, planning and housing development have a joint role in re-invigorating the commercial and cultural core of cities. This is part of a wider agenda to boost the urban economy and promote cosmopolitan values such as multi-culturalism and greater entertainment choices. By-products of a residential renaissance include the refurbishment of historically interesting buildings and 'townscape repair' via architecturally sensitive infill developments.

City centres, their population and environment

Who lives in city centres?
Todorovic and Wellington (2000) have usefully examined the relationship between household type and geographic location. This is done using data from the Survey of English Housing (DETR, 1999c) and the Office for National Statistics classification of local authority areas (Wallace and Denham, 1996). The analysis of Todorovic and Wellington provides key data for 'urban areas'. These are areas which can be described (ibid.: 14) as 'inner city areas and centres of towns'.

Table 11.1 Tenure by type of area: all households in England, 1998–99

	Urban areas (%)	All area types (%)
House owned outright	13	26
Buying on mortgage	28	42
All owners	42	69
Council tenant	28	16
RSL tenant	11	5
All social rents	39	21
Private renting	19	10

Source: Adapted from Todorovic and Wellington (2000)

Table 11.1 shows the very specific tenure profile of urban areas and the people living there. Urban areas are characterised by a relatively low proportion of owner-occupation and a correspondingly high proportion of social renting. Compared with all areas types for England, the number of homes owned outright in urban areas is half that of all areas for the country; the proportion of registered social landlord (RSL) tenants in urban areas is over twice as much as overall and the proportion of private rentings in urban areas is almost double the proportion elsewhere, on average.

The report, *Living in Urban England* (Todorovic and Wellington, 2000) also examines population density for specific types of local authority area, as defined in the Office for National Statistics classification. Table 11.2 shows that urban areas are much more likely to be densely populated than suburban and rural ones. This

Table 11.2 Population density (persons per hectare) and area type

Area typology		Average population density
DETR classification	ONS classification	
Urban	Inner London	80.14
Urban	Cosmopolitan London	84.56
Urban	Young singles	87.1
Urban	London public housing	90.4
Urban	Scottish inner city	71.35
Suburban	Primary production	18.2
Suburban	Small towns	14.28
Suburban	Better off manufacturing	19.95
Rural	Agricultural heartland	0.26
Rural	Accessible countryside	0.46
Rural	Affluent villages	0.81

Source: Adapted from Todorovic and Wellington (2000)

is not surprising, although the extent to which population density differs is perhaps revealing of the very different environments in which people live.

Table 11.2 highlights the very high densities to which specific groups popu-late different types of urban area. These compare radically with suburban and rural areas, where population density significantly lower. Compared with the urban areas, suburban population is around one-quarter of their density, whilst rural population is as low as one three-hundredth.

The picture of urban population that we might justifiably draw is that of pre-dominantly younger people, often in rented accommodation (both in the private and social sector), who live in relatively densely inhabited urban spaces. Owner-occupier households in urban areas are more likely to be financing house purchase through a mortgage and be less likely than in suburban and rural areas to purchase their home outright (Table 11.1).

The city centre environment

'City centre' is an amorphous geographical concept. Normally city centres are characterised by a retail core, surrounded by office and other commercial property development. The adjacent 'inner-city' is often terraced and less expensive housing developed at relatively high density. The next 'ring' is usually described in terms of 'suburban' and 'estate' type housing with the green belt or open country beyond. However, the precise relations of urban and housing form differ considerably accord-ing to the individual historical development of cities, and in particular, the extent to which local industry has survived changes in economic circumstances during the last half of the twentieth century. The legacy of industrial decline, in the form of redundant warehouses and factories has left some cities better placed than others to regenerate their centres through housing developments. In some cities, particularly those where these buildings lie alongside water, demand for city centre housing can be high; in others, the warehouses and factories are located in much less 'desirable' locations. The city centre environment thus differs considerably from one place to another.

Although it is difficult to delineate the 'city centre', there is little doubt that the wider urban area in which the core areas are found are places where relatively high levels of economic and social deprivation exist. Robson *et al.* (2000) have examined the 'state of English cities'. The city is a place where the highest levels of deprivation, the lowest levels of educational attainment and often the lowest house prices are found. The research found that: there was a high correlation between urban population and multiple deprivation; for inner London, the main metropol-itan areas and the other large cities, the percentage of school children with no or low GCSE results was over 2 per cent higher than the English average; and (with the exception of inner London), the main metropolitan areas contained the highest percentage of houses sold for less than £20,000.

Whether city centres can be revived, and the extent to which this happens, depends not on the macro-urban environment, but on the micro-neighbourhood one. The urban environment can vary radically within very short distances.

Economic indicators such as levels of employment and house prices can vary radically, as can indicators of social and physical well-being: life expectancy, educational achievement and levels of family breakdown.

House-builders, wanting to develop in existing urban areas, have to look not only at the current neighbourhood environment, but also at the drivers and dynamics of change. This is because the economic and social fortunes of neighbourhoods can change in very short spaces of time. Moreover, some areas change significantly, while others remain much more difficult to regenerate:

> The dynamics of neighbourhood change are important . . . snapshots of particular neighbourhoods can show the persistence of high levels of poverty and deprivation over successive time periods. A distinction can, however, be made between more dynamic and more stagnant neighbourhoods. In the more dynamic, there is a higher level of 'churning', a greater tendency for households to move up and out as their individual circumstances improve (and usually for poorer households to take their place, so that the neighbourhood itself shows no improvement). In the more stagnant neighbourhoods, households tend to be trapped over the longer term. These may represent a more intractable problem.
>
> (Robson *et al.*, 2000: 23)

Against this backdrop, developers may be excused for avoiding urban and city centre development. The market could be argued to be too uncertain and too unstable to be worth risking expensive capital on. Many developers still argue along these lines; others, however, have taken the plunge.

Marketing city living

A housing demand or a housing need?

The extent of housing demand for city centre living was always going to be a difficult question for developers to evaluate. Long-term trends show that the demand to live in cities has fallen, since households have been increasingly ready to quit the inner city for the suburbs and the countryside as and where their means allowed. Developers can therefore be forgiven for thinking that city centre development is largely the domain of the housing association, looking to meet the needs of those on low incomes and those who rely on public transport. City centre development would thus largely meet housing needs, rather than housing demand.

To some extent, this assumption is correct because it was the housing association sector that led the way in exploiting the opportunities that arose in urban locations. Housing association development schemes were first completed in the 1980s. Typically these schemes were conversions from secondary office property, located 'outside the core of commercial activity, and dated back to the 1960s' (University of Westminster *et al.*, 1998: 5). By the early 1980s, these buildings could be identified as 'white elephants . . . if the tenant pulled out, the building was left in an isolated location, and as a result was often effectively unlettable' (ibid.).

The marketing challenge

There was thus a precedent of sorts for private sector investment in residential conversion schemes and new-build near to the city centre. The key difference for private developers was lack of subsidy. Whereas the majority of housing association schemes attracted subsidy to cover building costs, this was not the case for private sector developments, which had to be covered by sales, or, in the case of long-term investors, rents.

There have been several obstacles for developers to overcome in marketing schemes in city centres. The first is the general reluctance of the wider house-building industry to embrace brownfield site development. Heath (2001) argues that much of the research carried out for house-builders attempts to deflect policy away from brownfield and conversion work by stressing consumer preference for suburban and greenfield locations:

> Much of the research into the preferences of residential location has been undertaken for organisations with a vested interest in the outcome, and this has often led to biased samples focused on relatively affluent families. In the United Kingdom, research for the House Builders Federation surveyed some 818 households with 76 percent rejecting the idea of living in urban areas. The main reasons were cited as the hostile environment, traffic noise, crime and the poor quality of schools. There were also worries about the density of urban living particularly in relation to the size of houses, gardens, and parking spaces.
>
> (House Builders Federation, 1995; from Heath, 2001: 466)

There is a feeling that developments built in the city centre are 'not for the family'. This 'rule' applies not only to mainstream households but also to those for whom housing is not a financial problem:

> While footballers Fabien Barthez and brothers Gary and Phil Neville are free to invest their hard-won cash from Manchester United FC in luxury penthouses in the city core, their team mate David Beckham is, in effect, barred from living in the centre of town. Not because he lacks the cash . . . but because he has a family. . . . Even if the Beckham family wanted to move there, the shortfall of doctors' surgeries, schools, parking and crèche facilities would still in effect exclude them from the centre of town.
>
> (Allen, 2002: 65)

While developers strive to widen market opportunities, the city remains a place where in-comers have to accommodate a range of activities within their neighbourhood, some of which are decidedly less 'family-orientated':

> Yet here, the brochure's urban fantasy, the council's optimism, Marketing Manchester's sales pitch, meets the city's stubborn realities . . . Mancunians know the streets . . . as a grim red light area, a depressing seedy place . . . where buyers will take their pick of smart new restaurants, bars and cultural entertainments jostling to cater to them, but the way home will be paved with earthier Mancunian experiences.
>
> (Conn, 1999: 7)

Other research, however, provides a more optimistic outlook for new housing developments in the city centre, particularly for specific groups:

> Research for the Joseph Rowntree Foundation supports the view that changing household structures are resulting in different housing choices and claims that 60 percent of single people working in central Leeds in the North of England would welcome the opportunity to rent apartments in the city centre. The research indicated that there was a clear division between the 'urbanised' who appreciated the 'buzz' and social anonymity of city life and the 'country life'/'suburbanised'.
>
> (Heath, 2001: 467)

Research has also shown that a significant proportion of people (around 20 per cent) were prepared to consider living in the city centre. This group have been termed the 'urban pursuadables' (Urban and Economic Development Group *et al.*, 1999) since, whilst they are happy with the benefits brought about by living in the suburbs, they would nevertheless also welcome improved access to city centre amenities and facilities.

Perhaps the most significant factor in encouraging city centre residential development has been a historic precedent of similar development. But because this form of housing development is a relatively new phenomenon, it is difficult to identify 'precedents'. Thus what developers look for is development 'mass'. Once schemes begin to sell profitably, and in particular, to re-sell as second-hand products, a market is established and more supply can be encouraged.

As we shall discuss in the following section looking at supply-side issues, the level of scheme profitability is very difficult to predict in new markets. In some schemes market values, realised even at the very highest level, are not economically viable in terms of covering development costs. However, some schemes which are marginally viable can be turned into developments providing a reasonable return if selling prices can be raised by a small amount. Where it is difficult to raise market values, then some other mechanism is required. The success of many of Manchester's city centre residential conversion schemes, has been attributed to the Central Manchester Development Corporation which has provided funds for building and neighbourhood environmental improvements (Robson *et al.*, 2000: 28).

Case study in city living: Nottingham

Cities such as Nottingham have seen a rapid increase in the number of people buying and renting homes in apartment conversions over the past five years. Figure 11.3 depicts the location and extent of recent residential development in and around the city's central area.

Recent housing schemes, including much conversion work, are located in three main places: (1) in the old Lace Market area, to the immediate east of the old Market Square, (2) near the Castle and Park Terrace area and (3) around Canning Circus and Derby Road on the west side.

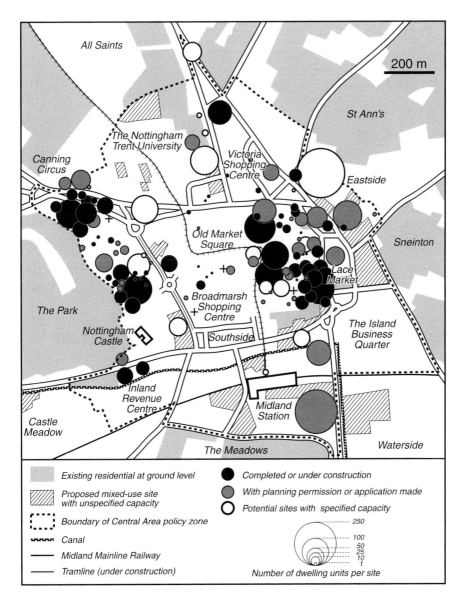

Figure 11.3 New-build and conversions to residential, central Nottingham, 1997–2002.
Source: Mapped by R. N. E. Blake from data supplied by Nottingham City Council

Figure 11.3 shows that in the Lace Market area four schemes of over 100 units have recently (2002) been completed with many more smaller schemes of up to 100 units also being developed. The success of developers in this area of the city is attributable to a combination of factors: timing, the availability of extensive areas of redundant but very attractive mill and warehouse buildings and proximity on foot to the city centre. The other two key areas where development is progressing

Plate 11.1 Building conversion to apartments, Castle Gate, Nottingham: R. N. E. Blake.

apace are also well placed for the city centre. In the case of developments near the Park, the location is topographically demanding in its own right.

Figure 11.3 also shows urban housing potential in the form of sites where planning applications have been made and theoretical open sites with capacity for new housing development. Development in the city centre is being robustly marketed (see Plate 11.1) and the local authority is hoping that an additional 6,000 homes will be created over a ten-year period from 1997.

Renewal of non-traditional housing environments via housing development: developer perspectives

Sources of supply for housing schemes in city centres

In the previous chapter, which examined urban capacity studies, several 'sources of housing supply' were identified. These included vacant sites, sites previously developed and sites where the planning system would encourage a change of use. The focus of the urban capacity policy thrust has, in many places, been on cleared sites, where a new-build scheme is an appropriate solution. However, it is important to recognise that the urban regeneration agenda is also being strongly supported via the re-use of buildings for housing (Plate 11.1).

The re-use of buildings, as we explained in the introduction, can help to meet the objectives of cost saving, sustainability and maintaining heritage. Opportunities for the re-use of many different types of building for housing have arisen during the last few years. Residential use has been a key focus of local authority and government policy because of two main factors. First, an acceptance that the United Kingdom's older industries, in particular textiles and shoe manufacture, were unlikely to recover over the longer term. This has left a wealth of historic mills in and around the city centres in places such as Manchester, Leeds, Nottingham and Leicester. Second, investment in office and commercial buildings, particularly in London, has been of a speculative rather than a planned nature. This has led to situations where there is an extensive over-supply of commercial space, never likely to be in demand again.

Of course, the dynamics of the whole property market are significant in determining how much of the over-supply of commercial and industrial space becomes converted to housing. The property market is dynamic and the owners of land and buildings or their agents will always weigh up very carefully the opportunity cost of making a change of use. If residential use does not provide the highest immediate, medium or long-term returns (depending on the owner's financial 'horizon') then housing will not be developed. The theory behind the timing of re-development and conversion for buildings is set out in some detail in Harvey's book *Urban Land Economics* (1987). This establishes a framework for answering the question of when a building or a site becomes ripe for redevelopment. The many different forms of obsolescence (including 'physical', 'locational' and 'functional') are key to understanding why and when buildings might be re-developed.

The sources of supply coming forward range from low-rise to high-rise office buildings (in particular office development of the 1960s and 1970s which is functionally obsolete), mill buildings across a large size range and which are often architecturally appealing, and smaller industrial units which can sometimes lend themselves to commercial conversion for housing. Further sources of supply include large Victorian villas and terraces which lend themselves to sub-division to smaller homes in the form of apartments. We consider now some of the key development issues affecting these types of opportunity.

Developers and investors for city centre schemes

Developers

As we saw in Chapter 4, the house-building industry is a conservative one, aiming to enhance profits by becoming better at what it has traditionally done, rather than seeking to find new products by which it can take itself forward. Thus the idea that major, let alone minor, house-building firms should become involved in city centre schemes converting building to housing is an ambitious one.

Nevertheless, some house-building firms have become involved in city centre conversion and new-build schemes. The University of Westminster and London

Residential Research (Greater London Authority, 2002) have recently published data on the role and contribution of major house-builders to city centre and inner city housing regeneration. Companies such as the Berkeley Group and Bellway Homes have begun to make important inroads to the Urban Task Force agenda, by developing a significant proportion of their homes within the existing urban areas. St George's (part of the Berkeley Group) developed around 7.8 per cent of all production in central and inner London during the year 2000. Bellway Homes developed 8.4 per cent, while Fairview developed 7 per cent and Barratt 4 per cent (ibid.).

London Residential Research (Greater London Authority, 2002) has also produced a 'typology' of developers in London. It breaks these down in terms of 'Urban Task Force (UTF) Leaders', 'Urban Task Force Followers', 'Suburban House-builders', 'High Value Central London Specialists', 'Local Specialists' and 'Housing Associations'. The 'UTF Leaders' are 'very large scale developers, with the capability of delivering very large schemes over 200 units with at least 25 per cent affordable units, mixed use on brownfield sites. Examples of this type of firm are the Berkeley Group and Laing. 'UTF Followers' are traditional volume house-builders rather than regeneration specialists, but some of whom are cultivating their activities to more urban lifestyle developments. Examples are Bellway, Barratt and Fairview and Wimpey. 'Suburban house-builders' are expected to find it 'difficult to compete' if 'UTF lifestyle schemes do become more prevalent in outer London' (ibid.).

Further research (Jones, 2002) has looked at the role of subsidiary companies in meeting the urban renaissance and sustainable development agenda. This research also considers companies operating outside London. Examples of these subsidiary companies are Redrow's 'In the City', Persimmon's 'City Developments' and David Wilson's 'City Homes' (ibid.). The research shows how the product range of some major companies has changed since the mid-1990s in response to the increased policy on developing brownfield sites. In the case of David Wilson plc, 10 per cent of its production was in the form of apartments in 2000. In 1996, by contrast, the company was developing almost entirely houses.

The motivation for these house-building companies to become involved in new forms of development are several. Clearly, it is desirable that schemes should not lose the company money, i.e. a scheme should show a positive return on capital employed. However, there are cases in our experience (Golland and Spaans, 1996) where developers are prepared to take on specific schemes that the local authority particularly wishes to realise, often as urban regeneration 'flagship' schemes. With some such schemes, the economics of development are often very marginal. House-builders will take them on if they believe that there is sufficient 'goodwill' or 'prestige' which might give them some 'leverage' with the local authority in future negotiations over greenfield sites (earning 'brownie points'), or provide the company with a scheme which can show its ability to take on difficult sites and provide a quality solution. There is also the possibility of greater flexibility with conversion and inner-city high-density developments. With traditional urban fringe (greenfield) or suburban low-rise developments consumers expect a 'finished article', but developers can sometimes sell city centre units as 'shells' which new owners can then personalise (Kelly, 1998a: 13).

Investors

Developers commit money usually only in the short term. Investors look for longer term results. There has been a steady flow of funds into city centre residential conversion schemes in the past few years. 'Investors' range from large-scale (both home and abroad), to small-scale landlords buying units on a 'one-off' basis. A number of factors have combined over the past five years to make investing in city centre new-build and conversion schemes attractive to investors.

Perhaps the most important of these has been stock market performance. This affects both large and small investors, but has particularly affected investors in the Far East, who have seen the UK property market as a potentially valuable place to put their money. The University of Westminster's study (1998) of commercial property conversions found that:

> Many of the recent developments (and to our surprise, some in other cities like Manchester) have been specifically targeted at Far East investors . . . Many schemes are marketed first in the Far East, especially in Singapore (and less often now in Hong Kong) . . . In many cases where investors still have funds to invest, the London property market seems far more attractive than anything in their own volatile home markets.
>
> (University of Westminster *et al.*, 1998: 15)

Overseas investment in city centre residential development has, in our own experience of Nottingham, continued through the late 1990s to 2002. Recent research, looking at the housing market in Nottingham (Golland, 2002) has shown a significant amount of investment flowing into new-build and conversion schemes in the city centre. In particular, there has been a large volume of finance coming from Ireland to support developments in Nottingham city centre.

'Buy-to-let'

Smaller investors have been encouraged into the private rented sector since around 2000 by the so-called 'buy-to-let' schemes. These schemes, targeted at the smaller investors (buying up to around five units) have been promoted by banks and building societies and have helped to expand the private rented sector. Buy-to-let is a mortgage product allowing people to raise money against their own homes and equity in order to purchase another dwelling, which can then be rented out. Borrowing allows investors to take advantage of tax breaks allowing interest payments to be offset against rental income. For investors who balance equity and borrowing judiciously, the scheme can prove fruitful. Since around the end of 2001, however, there has been considerable concern in the press about the exposure of the market to buy-to-let schemes. In London, over-supply of dwellings for rent has been occurring and rental income falling. This situation is being mirrored throughout the provincial city centres, especially in the more prestigious city centre apartment developments (ibid.). The buy-to-let market for city centre conversion developments appears, at the time of writing (late 2002), to have reached its peak. Its long-term success would seem to depend on rental and capital value adjustments, and a second 'generation' of young professional households wanting to rent homes in the city centre.

Student housing

The university sector is a key investor in city centre conversion schemes for student housing. The shortage of institutional (university) accommodation has been an ongoing problem, particularly as universities have had to improve their image to students as the competition to fill places has become much hotter. The need to keep student rents at a reasonably low level has meant that many older industrial buildings have been converted at high densities to considerably increase the supply of accommodation. Two such examples from the Midlands are the Russell Building, a canal-side conversion of an old sock factory in Leicester, and the Maltings in Basford, Nottingham. For the investor, student housing carries the risk of relatively long void periods during the summer recess. To offset this, new conversion schemes often include an element of retail use: a newsagent or an off-licence which can generate additional revenue for the university from the same building.

Viability considerations and conversion schemes

Risk, values and development costs

To convert an existing building for residential use, whether from office or industrial use, involves the developer in some degree of risk. The level of risk will be greater, we argue, for conversion schemes than for new-build. This is the case on two counts: first, there is the risk that predicted sales prices will not be realised; second, there is the risk that development costs will overrun.

Both these forms of risk are encountered in any housing development situation. On a greenfield site, where a low-density traditional estate layout is to be built, there is also the risk that expected prices will not be realised, or that build costs will overrun. With conversions, however, it is usually much more difficult to quantify the level of risk. Converting existing buildings to residential use is a particularly risky exercise where there is no local market precedent for such development. In London, where people have been living in flats and maisonettes for some time, the risk is arguably less. In provincial cities, however, where most households see 'residential development' as low-rise, low-density estates, trying to 'educate' people into a different form of housing could prove an expensive mistake.

On the costs side, conversion schemes are more difficult to predict. The Building Cost Information Service (Royal Institution of Chartered Surveyors) shows that for new-build projects, the range of build costs (per m^2) is very small, compared with the range of costs for conversion schemes. Whilst conversions may demand a much wider range of quality solutions, the question nevertheless remains in the developer's mind: what will be 'found' once the existing building is 'opened up' for conversion.

Location and viability

It might be argued that it is easier to convert buildings in parts of the country where house prices, and hence revenue from schemes, will also be high. In some circumstances, negative land values will be produced for a conversion to residential use because conversion costs exceed gross development value. On this basis, we might imagine that more schemes would come forward in the wealthier southern regions than in the North. Experience shows, however, that many northern and Midlands cities have seen a steady growth in the number of conversions to housing each year.

Ultimately, the viability of conversion schemes depends on the particular site in question. Viability is 'site specific' and can vary significantly depending on the nature of the building to be converted. The density of the conversion scheme is highly important and the developer has to make careful provision in order to maximise revenue from the existing building.

If the building is listed, or in a conservation area, then this can be highly significant for the viability of conversion. It is important that local authorities and heritage bodies understand the implications of their decisions for market viability if buildings are likely to be converted to other uses. Developers will walk away from schemes if planning and conservation regulations make schemes marginally viable. There are currently over 100 listed buildings, many in the north of England, which have been placed on the 'at risk' list, because developers believe the planning restrictions make the schemes too risky.

Mixed communities and residential conversions

Government policy is to try to achieve 'mixed communities'. This is a key tenet of Planning Policy Guidance Note 3, and Circular 6/98 (DETR, 1998b) (see also Chapter 5) sets out that for developments of greater than 25 units (15 in inner London) an element of affordable housing should be included. This policy applies whether the scheme is new-build or a conversion. A mixed development approach is seen to be the key to successful city living: 'The key to the living city is therefore to break down the dogma of zoning and seek an integrated mixed-use. And the key ingredient of that mix is housing' (Royal Institution of Chartered Surveyors, 1992: 7).

Developers typically argue that the inclusion of affordable or social housing within converted multi-occupant buildings is undesirable from a marketing point of view. They argue that accommodating people on low incomes (and in particular people on housing benefit) will have a detrimental effect on their ability to sell homes to private owners. This issue is of particular concern with conversions. On greenfield, low-density, traditionally built estates, developers can begin to generate revenue from private buyers as they complete the building process on an incremental basis. Sometimes developers can 'hide' the fact that affordable housing is to be built on-site until all private homes are sold (although local authorities have tried to restrain them in this practice). But with conversions this is much more difficult to achieve. Because of safety requirements on site, the onus is on the developer to complete all units at virtually the same time. This means that private as well as affordable units come 'on stream' simultaneously at the point at which it is critical for the developer to begin generating revenue. In areas of very high demand, for example in some parts of London, it is possible for the developer to ask for up-front payments so that cash flow can be helped. Some of the more ambitious schemes have included a significant amount of affordable housing. A scheme at Imperial Wharf, in the London borough of Hammersmith and Fulham, for example, includes six forms of affordable housing, ranging from social rent through to key worker housing. Demand is believed to be strong for this particular development location.

The term 'mixed community' is, however, one which is potentially more wide-ranging than the occupancy of a single building. In the mid-1990s, the London Borough of Newham was planning 3,500 new homes on the banks of the Thames in Docklands and 700 near the proposed Eurotunnel station at Stratford. However, it 'wanted to avoid any social housing whatsoever' (Simpkins, 1999: 66). The local authority in Newham explained: 'What we have is a concentration of benefit-dependent people in the area. Social housing attracts people that are economically challenged who can't support local shops and services' (ibid.). The borough adopted a more wide-ranging interpretation of the 'mixed community'. Instead of providing social housing, the developers had to make a payment to Newham. The money was then to be used to buy out housing rented to people on housing benefit in the borough. The houses were then to be sold on to middle-class owner-occupiers.

There is significant potential for the use of commuted sums with conversions, where residual schemes values are not too marginal. In areas where house prices are highest, Greater London being the obvious example, the onus is on the developer to show why affordable housing should not be included in the scheme. In other areas, where development values are lower, the onus is on the local authority to show why it should be included. Where city-centre conversion schemes are first emerging, there is a temptation for wider regeneration objectives (to get the building renovated) to take precedence. Local planning authorities are thereby pressured into moratoriums on affordable housing in multi-occupied buildings. They then find out later that the apartments have sold well and the developer could have provided some affordable housing. Commuted sums, linked to the development's success, could provide a solution.

Reflections on housing renewal and city living

In the early nineteenth century, the centre of Manchester was such a mess that even visitors from Rotherham were shocked. 'The town is abominably filthy', complained one in 1808, 'the steam engine is pestiferous, the dyehouses noisome and offensive, and the water of the river as black as ink or the Stygian Lake.

Now Manchester has just notched up the sale of its first £1 Million apartment
... the development in question, lies right beside the 'Stygian Lake' itself, the River
Irwell, which cuts a deep channel between Manchester and Salford.

(Clark, 2000)

Housing renewal policies are a reflection of contemporary problems and challenges.
In this chapter we have examined the objectives and mechanisms relating to housing renewal and the role of sustainable development policies in increasing housing
supply in the city centres. At the same time, it is important to recognise that
housing development, in the form of conversions and rehabilitation, plays a vital
role in regenerating housing markets in urban areas and city centres.

The focus on housing renewal is largely a focus on traditional housing areas,
typically Victorian terraced housing, particularly where private landlords have left
housing in poor repair for many years. Slum clearance, the post-war grant regime and
area improvement policies have all helped to significantly improve the quality of the
housing stock. These initiatives have, however, not been without their problems.
Slum areas cleared for new housing failed to provide a higher quality of life for many;
failure by local authorities to bring together housing and planning strategies meant
that central government provided a subsidy framework that was not properly
exploited; and grants aimed to assist the most needy in poor-quality older housing
were fully exploited only by speculators and more wealthy housing occupants.

But without government intervention at times when the housing market was
at its most stressed, the housing stock would probably have fallen into a worse
condition. Renewal policies were in many ways the most effective and efficient way
of achieving regeneration objectives.

At the same time, the housing, and more accurately, the property market, has
played a strong role in helping city centres and urban areas towards an urban renaissance. Our focus on city centre development from both the supply and demand side
highlights the complexities involved in developing conversion schemes in city
centres. The property market is dynamic, providing only windows in time when
residential development is feasible; this is because commercial land values usually
exceed residential values. In understanding this dynamic, investors' confidence in
local planning is of paramount importance. The development of housing in these
non-traditional housing areas relies to a great extent on planners providing a clear
framework. This is particularly important in areas where the economics of development are marginal.

The all-important relationship between residential and commercial land value
varies between cities because alternative uses for a building (normally 'commercial')
vary significantly. The form of the building is highly significant and architecturally
interesting buildings (e.g. river-side mills) can provide a high residual land value.
The main source of supply in London has proven to be secondary offices; in cities
such as Manchester, however, converted cotton warehouses have provided the key
supply source for residential development. In Nottingham and Leicester, both types
of building are being brought forward for development.

In looking forward, it is possible to be very optimistic for a greater numbers of homes being built in urban areas. If this is to happen, however, it is vitally important that government directs funds in a very efficient way so as to bring forward buildings and sites which might otherwise remain undeveloped.

Discussion points

1 Describe and evaluate the role of government in housing renewal.
2 Distinguish, using examples, 'traditional' and 'non-traditional' housing environ-ments.
3 Highlight and describe the key housing market issues facing city centre devel-opment.
4 Identify the key players involved in city centre development schemes. What are the main challenges facing them?
5 Set out your expectations for the city centre conversion market. Provide reasons for your expectations.

Key reading

Like Chapter 10, this topic has a rich and rapidly expanding literature base. The theo-retical background is well expressed in Balchin, *Housing Policy: An Introduction* (1996) and Harvey, *Urban Land Economics* (2000). For new ideas on planning and design the following reports are recommended: Royal Institution of Chartered Surveyors, *Living Cities* (1992); University of Westminster *et al.*, *Back to the Centre* (1998); and DTLR and CABE, *By Design: Better Places to Live* (2001). An exemplary research article is Heath, 'Revitalising cities' (*Journal of Planning Education and Research*, 2001).

Chapter 12

Housing development in Europe

Andrew Golland and Michael Oxley

European housing development: an overview

Housing development from an historical perspective

Housing development and the production of housing to meet targets has been a key feature of policy for many years. Chapter 3, which focuses primarily on the UK, explains why housing development has been needed and, in particular, why it has commanded such a high profile in policy debate. It is perhaps no surprise therefore to find that housing development has also featured highly as a political issue in other European countries.

The focus of housing policy in European countries has been significantly influenced by the need to ensure that enough housing is available to the population at a given point in time. To some extent this process can be managed via knowledge about demographic change. Other impacts have been less easy to deal with. Boelhouwer and van der Heijden (1992: 237) have shown how many European countries focused policies on meeting quantitative housing need in the wake of, in particular, the Second World War. In some ways, the 1950s and 1960s can be regarded as a golden age of housing production where many countries sought, and succeeded, in meeting very demanding production targets. The need to replace war-damaged housing stock, combined with sharper increases in the population defines today, in a marked way, the age profile of the housing stock.

Figure 12.1 shows that in many European countries (here the European Union 15), the largest proportion of all dwellings were built during the period 1945–70. This group includes Belgium, Germany (the housing of the former West Germany), France, Italy, Luxembourg, Sweden and the UK. While this period of housing development is highly significant, it is also important to point out that the temporal emphasis on development has varied greatly between countries.

It is clear from Figure 12.1 that some countries have developed relatively fewer homes since the end of the First World War. The UK, where 28 per cent of the housing stock was developed before 1918, is a good example; France at 29 per cent and Belgium at 27 per cent are the other two cases. Indeed, nearly 50 per cent of the UK's housing stock is pre-Second World War. By contrast, many European countries have developed a large proportion of their housing stock since 1945: Greece, Spain, the Netherlands and Finland are countries with relatively new housing stocks, although all European countries, with the exception of Belgium

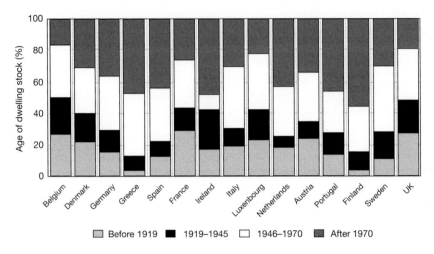

Figure 12.1 Housing development in EU countries: by age of the stock (1990s).
Source: European Commission, *Housing Statistics in the European Union* (1998)

(50 per cent of the housing stock developed before 1945), have developed more housing since 1945 than the UK (53 per cent of the stock developed since 1945). In the future therefore the UK will need to develop new housing at a faster rate than its European partners if it is to achieve a similar age profile in the housing stock.

From quantity to choice

In the immediate post-1945 period the housing policy emphasis was on quantity. Although quantitative shortages have re-appeared, for example in the unified Germany, housing policy in European countries has been increasingly directed towards improving housing choice, in particular, by trying to meet the aspirations of households wanting to own their own homes. Figure 12.2 shows housing development in ten European countries according to 'investor' (i.e. whether the demand for a house is driven by a public or a private sector agency).

For the greater part, housing developed by 'private' investors is housing built for owner-occupiers, although this is by no means completely correct for all country cases (United Nations, 2000). It is clear from Figure 12.2, however, that private sector investors are far more significant in creating development demand for housing. This is the case in all countries despite the variation in the annual number of dwellings developed. Moreover, it is clear to see that between 1985 and 1995 the number of dwellings developed by the public sector has, in most countries, declined. This is particularly the case in the UK and France (Figure 12.2) where housing policy has favoured increasing private sector involvement. It is however also the case in countries such as the Netherlands and Sweden, which are countries with a very strong public sector ethos.

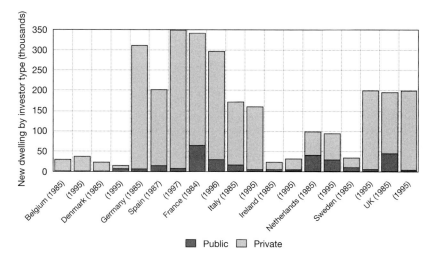

Figure 12.2 New dwellings by type of investor in a selection of European countries, 1985 and 1995.
Note: Not all countries provided data for both 1985 and 1995, but at appropriate times when data became available.
Source: United Nations: Annual Bulletin Housing and Construction Statistics

More should be asked about the nature of 'private' and 'public' investment in new development. The United Nations bulletin states that 'public sector investment' includes 'both central government and governmental bodies on all lower levels' as well as 'other public bodies' which should have functions with 'public aspects'. In many countries today, including the UK, 'public' sector development is principally undertaken by housing associations, with central and local government playing a very small role; other countries falling into this category are Belgium, Denmark, France, the Netherlands and Austria (European Commission, 1998: 48). Whilst the objective of social housing development by these organisations is mainly 'non-profit', many European housing association models are run as private entities.

'Private sector' housing development also needs further clarification. The official statistics (United Nations, 2000) sub-divide the 'private sector' into 'private persons', 'co-operatives' and 'other private bodies'. In the UK, 'private sector' development is largely development built on a speculative basis for home-owners (Golland and Boelhouwer, 2002). It is a very distinct model. In other countries, notably, Germany, France and, to a lesser extent, the Netherlands, 'private sector development' is housing built for home-owners, but built on a contract basis, where home-owners have a much greater role in the development process themselves (B.M.Bau, 1993a). In Sweden and Finland, 'private sector' development is built on a 'co-operative' basis, whereas elsewhere in Europe private investment for new housing development comes from private landlords and intermediaries such as estate agents.

Housing development in Europe: what and for whom?

When studying housing development in Europe, one of the most interesting aspects is the variety of housing form. In particular, it is important to highlight the major differences that exist in the balance of housing stock between apartments and houses. This varies significantly as can be seen from Table 12.1. Countries such as Italy, Spain, Germany and Greece have developed mainly apartments with the result that less than 50 per cent of all homes are houses. By contrast, the UK, Ireland and Belgium have developed mainly houses, and all three countries have less than 25 per cent of the stock as apartments. In between, a significant number of countries (France, Denmark, Luxembourg, the Netherlands and Portugual) have a housing stock in which around 60 per cent or more are houses. The supply of housing from the stock is thus very different across Europe and households in countries such as Italy, Spain and Germany will find it much more difficult to access a house than will be the case in, for example, the UK or Ireland.

It is also important to consider the tenure of housing that has been developed and its relationship with housing form. This is important because it helps us to refine our understanding of housing choice in each country. Table 12.1 shows that some countries have a very high overall or 'absolute' level of home ownership. We can say these have 'absolute tenure bias'. The best examples are Italy, Spain and Greece. Some countries have absolute or overall tenure bias towards renting; these are, for example, the Netherlands and Germany. To obtain a better understanding of housing choice, we have to look however at how tenures are relatively distributed

Table 12.1 Housing tenure and dwelling type in a selection of European countries

Country	Apartments			Houses		
	% of total	Owner occupation (%)	Rented (%)	% of total	Owner occupation (%)	Rented (%)
Italy	66	42	24	34	28	6
Spain	64	49	15	36	31	5
Germany	61	10	51	39	31	8
Greece	52	34	18	48	44	4
France	42	10	32	58	45	13
Denmark	41	7	34	59	46	13
Luxembourg	34	10	24	66	56	10
Netherlands	32	5	27	68	43	25
Portugal	30	15	15	70	47	23
Belgium	21	6	15	79	62	17
United Kingdom	18	5	13	82	61	21
Ireland	5	0.5	4.5	95	81	14

Source: Adapted from European Community Household Panel (ECHP, 1994); Eurostat (2000)

within the housing stock. We can clarify these points by grouping countries together as follows:

Group One: 'Absolute tenure-bias (towards owner-occupation) with relative dwelling type bias' (towards owner-occupation within flats): comprising Italy and Spain;

Group Two: 'Absolute tenure-bias (towards owner-occupation) with relative dwelling type bias' (towards owner-occupation within *houses*): comprising Luxembourg, Portugal, Belgium and the UK;

Group Three: 'Absolute tenure-bias (towards *rented housing*) with relative dwelling type bias' (towards owner-occupation within *houses*): comprising Germany and the Netherlands;

Group Four: Absolute *tenure-neutrality* with relative dwelling type bias' (towards owner-occupation within *houses*): comprising Denmark and France;

Group Five: 'Others'; examples, Greece (tenure bias towards ownership but across flats and houses) and Ireland which has virtually its entire owner-occupied stock in the form of houses.

It can thus be seen that housing choice varies significantly depending on the country in which particular tenures are sought. In Germany and the Netherlands, for example (Group Three) home ownership is very strongly associated with the house, rather than the flat while in those two countries, rented housing predominates. Italy and Spain are also interesting cases, since there, home ownership is the dominant tenure, although mostly available in the form of flats. In the UK, home ownership dominates, with supply mainly being in the form of houses

Understanding differences: the role of comparative analysis

Understanding differences: why bother?

The overview in the previous section has highlighted key differences between countries in the level of output, the tenure of housing built and its form and design. The question which now arises is 'Does this actually matter?' and, moreover, 'How can a comparative study assist in understanding housing development in our own country?' There are several ways in which comparative analysis can assist.

Oxley (1991) has set out a number of key purposes for doing comparative housing research. Not all the aims of investigation are specifically analytical; for example, research into other countries can be carried out on the basis of 'generally extending knowledge' (ibid.: 73), or to 'get ideas for new policies'. Simply finding out that, for example, a country has an effective planning policy, might be a good enough reason to ask the question whether that policy might be effective in one's home country. Similarly, studying another country, or set of countries, can help to develop hypotheses about the relationship between housing markets, the economy and the house-building industry. If, for example, the government of another country regulates its land market to a much greater extent and thereby reduces volatility in the market, could the same happen in our own country? Equally important would seem to be the need to 'obtain material that can be used to reject arguments based on narrow perceptions' (ibid.); the need to challenge and re-visit 'home grown truths' should always be an objective of countries wishing to improve housing provision. Comparative analysis can be used to show examples of where commonly held 'truths' actually do not prove correct in all cases. However, as Oxley also points out, there is a need to 'beware of those who substitute stories to support a set of pre-held value judgements which they hold. Those who hold strongly [these] beliefs, will have no difficulty in finding material to support their convictions by careful choice of time and country' (ibid.).

Needham (1999) adds further weight to the case for doing comparative or 'cross-national' research. He states that cross-national research can be grouped in terms of:

> Descriptions of a certain practice in one country, using a framework which is used for descriptions of the same practice in other countries;
> Drawing general conclusions from a study of the same practice in several countries;
> Putting forward a general law, which is then tested in more than one country;
> Policy transfer, or institutional transplantation.
>
> (Needham, 1999: 2–3)

In some senses these comparative objectives are similar to those identified by Oxley (1991) in that they broadly relate to identifying the implications for policy transferability and to the potential for hypothesis testing. Indeed the debate about comparative studies and their implications is a rich one. It is a debate which is unlikely to go away. Pickvance (1999) discusses varieties of comparative analysis in which a key distinction is made between 'universalising comparison' and 'individualising comparison'. The aims of these approaches are quite different. The first seeks to 'establish that every instance of a phenomenon follows essentially the same rule', whereas the latter contrasts a number of cases 'in order to grasp the peculiarities of each case'. Comparative housing research has been focused around these two broad approaches for some time. We shall identify some important examples of each.

Explaining differences: previous research efforts

An important investigation using an approach which can be described as broadly 'universalist' was undertaken by Schmidt (1989). Taking what is known as 'convergence theory' an attempt was made to explain the development of housing policy and housing markets in advanced industrialised countries from the early 1970s to the mid-1980s. The hypothesis tested was one set by earlier researchers (Donnision and Ungerson, 1982) which stated that: 'housing policies and the housing markets of industrial society are converging – irrespective of party-political, ideological or institutional circumstances'.

An implicit expectation of the research was that industrial society, being exemplified in the countries chosen, would increase the likelihood of there being similar 'housing' outcomes in the form of housing policy and housing market behaviour. While it was found that a pattern existed between the extent of government welfare spending and levels of owner-occupation (ibid.: 96), the main conclusion was that convergence theory, driven by the 'logic of industrialism' did not adequately explain housing outcomes across the board:

> The results show that contrary to convergence theory, and its associated thesis of a partic-
> ular 'logic of industrialism', institutional and ideological factors loom large. Analysing the
> structure of the market, ideological factors are found to be of the greatest importance.
> At the same time, housing market processes and the character of housing policy are
> primarily determined by institutional factors, that is, the way in which market actors have
> been organised into or out of the housing policy system.
>
> (Schmidt, 1989: 83)

Previous attempts using a universalist approach have also failed to identify an all-encompassing variable capable of explaining particular housing outcomes across a number of countries. Marcuse's analysis (1983) for example, looked at West German and US housing policy with an aim of showing that housing policy in capitalist societies took a particular form, namely that of supporting the 'private housing industry'. Marcuse concluded that, when he examined the legislation that made up housing policy, his thesis was proven in the case of the US. However, in the case of Germany, although for much of the post-war period, housing policy had favoured the private sector, this was not the case for sustained shorter periods of policy making. Thus the thesis could not be supported.

Universalist approaches have a key contribution to make in that they provide a 'big thesis', or an 'all-encompassing' theory from which individual country circumstances can be evaluated. Their weakness is that, very often there are too many exceptions to the 'rule'. Some researchers have focused in a different direction, namely on the individuality of housing systems, housing markets and housing policy. Ball and Harloe (1992) developed what is known, as the 'Structure of Housing Provision' thesis. A key emphasis of the 'thesis' is to promote understanding of housing outcomes by focusing on the particular element in systems of housing supply and demand; for example, modes of production, consumption and finance. The social, economic and institutional relations between the agencies of production, consumption and finance are a key factor in explaining how housing is produced, consumed and financed. A potential danger of this type of approach for comparative analysis is that there becomes too much emphasis on describing the particularistic structures in each country; so much so, that no generally applicable lessons emerge.

Between the general and the particularistic approach

Comparative research into housing development has recognised that both general and particularistic approaches have weaknesses. Specific research work, notably that by Barlow and Duncan (1994) has sought to take a middle road. In a comparison of systems of housing provision in Britain, France and Sweden, housing outcomes are benchmarked against the political and welfare system in which they take place. Drawing on the work of Esping-Andersen (1990), systems of housing provision are set within the context of the welfare state to which they are associated. Britain, France and Sweden represent countries in which, respectively, a 'liberal', 'corporatist' and 'social democratic' welfare state policy is pursued. Thus, it should be no surprise to find in Britain that many housing solutions are driven by a free market private sector philosophy, whereas in France corporate solutions to development and other housing issues are adopted. Similarly, although there are no 'pure' examples of welfare state regimes (Barlow and Duncan, 1994), we might expect housing policy in Sweden to place a greater emphasis on democratic and inclusive solutions to housing challenges.

This approach is helpful in that draws attention to the multi-dimensional nature of comparative analysis. That is to say, to answer questions about why things are different now, we need to understand how, in each country, over time, the particular systems of housing provision have grown up. The benefits of comparative analysis come not only from a description or snap-shot which is compared, but also from tracing why, and under what conditions, housing policies and processes change over time.

The problem of equivalence in comparative analysis

When we compare whole housing systems, or just part of those systems, for example a development process, it is important to be able to state that we know what we are comparing. We must be able to say that we have established, in a formal way, equivalence of concept; so that we know, when we are comparing 'the development process' in two countries, where the broad conceptual boundaries actually lie. We may not identify similar stages or procedures in the process, but we should seek to identify how the concept of the 'development process' is formulated in the countries we are comparing so that an accurate picture can be drawn up. Failure to establish a broad equivalence is serious. If a comparison were to be made between, for example, 'home-ownership' in Bangladesh, one of the poorest countries in the world, and 'home-ownership' in Switzerland, one of the richest, we would find that home-ownership in Bangladesh is over twice as high a level. However, to say anything useful about, say, the implications of increasing Swiss home-ownership levels, we would undoubtedly have to come to terms with very different forms of home-ownership and housing quality in the two countries.

Another however, more complex form of equivalence has to be dealt with in comparative analysis. This is known as 'dynamic equivalence' (Hatim and Mason, 1990: 240). Dynamic equivalence becomes an issue where particular facets of a policy or a process have different significance in different countries. Good examples of this problem are given in the extensive research carried out into urban land and property markets (B.M.Bau, 1993b) by the German Government during the late

1980s and early 1990s. It is clear from the study that, for example, development plans have a different level of importance in different countries; development plans take on a much greater level of significance in countries like the Netherlands, France and Germany, where they are legally binding once made, than in the UK, where they do not provide an automatic right to develop according to the land use stated. It therefore follows that other aspects of the development process, in particular planning 'gain' have greater significance than in other countries where development plans, or municipal land-ownership largely determine the outcome of the development process. We expand on this theme using a four-country case study example below.

Problems of equivalence: case study of planning in the UK, France, Germany and the Netherlands

The role of land use planning is potentially very broad in so far as comparative studies are concerned. At the local level, however, where planning is implemented, and land is brought forward for development, we are concerned principally with two aspects: the physical development plan and, the process for granting planning permission. Both these stages of local planning influence the overall volume of land supplied to the market and behaviour of individual land-owners.

There is significant variation between countries in the importance of both local plans and the process of giving planning permission. Leading research (DoE, 1989; B.M.Bau, 1993b) has shown that the actual process by which planning permission is granted is far more significant in the UK for development outcomes than it is in mainland European countries. This is particularly the case when the UK is compared with the Netherlands and Germany, where development plans are more prescriptive and there is less scope for negotiation in the development control process. The process of development control in the UK has a much greater potential impact on the land market and on land values than in countries where prescriptive development plans 'bind' land-owners and developers to specific land uses (B.M.Bau, 1993b: 109). Although in the UK the land-use plan steers, and is indicative of, end land use, there is nevertheless still scope for developers to influence land values (and hence land supply) via negotiation over standards of infrastructure provision, affordable housing quotas and other social infrastructure.

In the three mainland European countries considered here, 'local development plans' are not comparable in content with those in the UK. Research that has previously compared planning systems in European countries (B.M.Bau, 1993b) has shown that local development plans in the UK are much less detailed than elsewhere. In all the countries compared, namely the Netherlands, Germany and France, there are development plans which are far more 'local', i.e. prepared for a smaller area, than is the case in the UK, where development plans normally relate to a district or borough.

The Dutch Bestemmingsplan is prepared in 'outline form', but is then worked through at a more detailed site level as a basis for planned development.

In Germany, the Bebauungsplan prescribes development at a site level. Both these documents are, in effect, not only 'land use' plans, but also 'infrastructure' plans setting out the necessary street and green space layouts. The French local plan (the Plan d'Occupation du Sol, POS) can be broadly equated at a level of detail with the UK local plan; however, the POS is detailed further either in a plan for 'lotissement' (see also below) where plot and road layouts are prescribed, or via a 'Plan d'Aménagement de Zone, PAZ), where a detailed infrastructure plan is produced for urban renewal areas.

Thus comparing 'local plans' in the European context is somewhat difficult and, arguably, spurious. What matters is their significance in their own national and local context. Previous research stresses the importance of understanding the impact of local plans for land supply. In this respect, the key question is whether very prescriptive, detailed plans assist land supply and land assembly, or whether they act as a deterrent. This is a complex question and to a large extent one which can only be dealt with by considering how plans link into, and affect, the housing development process.

European models of housing development

What do we know about how housing is developed elsewhere in Europe?

Research into, and knowledge about, how housing is developed in other European states outside the UK, is rather thin. Compared with, for example, research into housing policies in Europe (Donnison and Ungerson, 1982; Lundquist, 1991; Barlow and Duncan, 1994; McCrone and Stevens, 1995), or research into investment and European housing markets (Oxley and Smith, 1995; Ball *et al.*, 1996; Royal Institution of Chartered Surveyors, 2000), the housing development process has attracted rather less research interest.

What has been done is mainly of a 'fact-finding' nature and usually has not been synthesised into a comparative format. The Department of the Environment, for example, commissioned research to look at planning and the development control process in selected European countries (DoE, 1989). Its successor, the Department of the Environment, Transport and Regions included a European dimension to inform its policy on urban regeneration. From time to time, the housebuilding industry has shown an interest in finding out more about the development process abroad (National House-Building Council and Coopers & Lybrand, 1990). At the other end of the analytical scale there has been some theoretical progress on the development process. Notably, Healey (1991) has modelled the process in a number of ways where development can be seen as a process arrived at in various ways, for example, through a process of 'equilibrium', where the forces of market and capital investment monitor outcomes, or via an 'event-sequence' where the process is carefully planned and outcomes are the consequence of that process. Attempts to dovetail the theory into comparative analysis, however, have not been many in number. Golland (1998) has attempted to use Healey's theoretical framework in a comparative study, although difficulties were encountered with the abstractions of certain approaches.

Perhaps the most useful and robust study of the housing development process in Europe is that commissioned by the German Government during the early 1990s (B.M.Bau, 1993b). The study is an investigation of 'urban land and property markets in Europe'. The findings are presented in two ways. First, they are presented in a series of books, published in English, relating to the selected countries studied: the UK (Williams and Wood, 1994); the Netherlands (Needham *et al.*, 1993); Germany (Dieterich *et al.*, 1993); France (Acosta and Renard, 1993); Italy (Ave, 1994). These books are produced with a standard format approach so that the reader can identify the salient facts and understand, through detailed descriptions, how particular stages of the urban land and property (housing and commercial) markets function. Second, in a separate publication, the findings are presented in a thematic way by drawing on specific aspects of the development process in each country and then synthesising these findings (B.M.Bau, 1993b). This is arguably a more useful way of providing understanding of how the process works, although the success of this approach depends largely on how well the author is able to keep sight of the associated events in the development process of each country. In practice, this is done successfully and the text is arguably the best current example of a comparative study of models of European housing development. As far as we are aware, however, the text has not been translated from the German, and for some readers this will undoubtedly prove a barrier. A summary in English nevertheless is provided with the report.

This overview shows, if nothing else, how challenging the assimilation of knowledge in this field can be. We now turn to the key factors influencing differences in the housing development process and its outcomes.

Housing development processes in Europe: key influences

In understanding why new housing development differs across Europe, we need to identify the key factors which influence the development process. These factors are several, although previous research has been focused to a significant extent on the role of the state in the regulation of land in housing supply. We consider these now in relation to the Netherlands, Germany and France, countries which we believe provide a robust spectrum of development processes.

Role of the state in land regulation and housing supply

Typical complaints of the UK house-building industry are that development is too 'heavily regulated' or that the planning system is a 'burden' on the economy. It is indeed a fact that the planning system in the UK is a mature and potentially powerful mechanism for controlling development. Planning has it roots in the immediate post-war reforming legislation and it has been used to regulate land use in urban and rural areas. Planning regulates the volume of development and its location and therefore the house-building industry ignores it at its peril.

However, it has also been consistently argued elsewhere that 'planning' is too narrowly defined and that it therefore lacks 'bite' and does not have the power to bring about satisfactory development solutions. The planning system in the UK cannot, for example, make land available, it can only allocate land and this is a potential 'circle' that has not been squared (Chiddick and Dobson, 1986). The planning system, via development plans and development control, could not for the greater part of the last 60 years ensure that affordable housing was included as an integral part of new housing developments. This has only happened in the latter part of the 1990s (see for example, Circular 6/98: DETR, 1998b). Thus a potentially important function of planning, namely to facilitate beneficial externalities, has not been fully exploited. Furthermore, the planning system is arguably ill equipped to deal with the need for urban renaissance as highlighted in the recent report of the Urban Task Force (Urban Task Force, 1999). The planning system in the UK does not by itself provide the means to assemble land; the assembly of land, very important for development sites in multiple ownership on brownfield sites, occurs not simply because land is allocated for development but because market forces determine that the sites are commercially viable and hence should be developed.

Thus although the planning system might from a UK perspective appear to be overbearing and onerous, there are many more things which it could achieve, were government to take a more radical approach to land supply. Indeed, the lessons of some other European countries are that a more interventionist stance in land and planning policy can deliver more rounded development outcomes and in some cases, help to smooth out volatility in the housing development cycle (Barlow and Duncan, 1993). We now examine three approaches to housing development in mainland European countries.

Three European approaches to housing development

The three approaches are important models for developing housing in the Netherlands, Germany and France respectively. The description of each provides an example of a different way of approaching housing development from that described in earlier sections of the book, which have focused primarily on the UK model. We begin with the traditional approach to housing development in the Netherlands. This is a fully comprehensive and interventionist model of housing development.

The comprehensive development model in the Netherlands

The focus on strategic planning at all levels in the Netherlands has been accompanied by a comprehensive approach to development: the physical preparation of the land, estate layout and building construction. This situation is the result of a combination of factors where a planning 'mind-set' and a political will has been necessary to deal with very significant land and water management challenges. The model works on the basic principle of municipal intervention in the land market;

in short local authorities purchase land from farmers and other original land-owners, rather than this being done by developers, as happens in the UK. There are several detailed descriptions of how this (Dutch) process works, widely explored by Needham (1992 and 1997), and Needham *et al.* (1993). A summary of the key points in the process are given here. The 'customary practice' of Dutch land assembly is described thus:

> The development process can be divided into two phases. In the first, land in its existing use is converted into building plots for its new use (the land development process); in the second, the plots are built upon (the building development process). In most countries, both phases are carried out by the same actor. In the Netherlands however, the land development is usually carried out by the municipality where the land is located; then the municipality disposes of the serviced building plots to building developers (which can be private, public, or semi-public, such as housing associations). That division of labour is called 'an active municipal land policy'.
>
> (Needham, 1997: 291)

The key distinction is made clear here: that in the traditional, or 'customary' Dutch approach to land assembly (what is termed 'land development' in the description), it is the local authority, or municipality, that has the key role in land assembly. In acquiring the land, the municipality takes responsibility for site preparation (importantly drainage), infrastructure provision and estate and street layout.

Dutch local authorities in this model assemble land on a 'cost-benefit' basis (see also Wigmans, 1992). The costs and benefits are assessed across the full range of services and types of development which will eventually be provided on the site. This can include housing, commercial, education and recreational uses. The task of the municipality is to assess the extent to which the costs will be offset by the benefits. The municipality will be concerned to maximise the revenues accruing from 'market' land uses (e.g. private housing and commercial property) so that it can maximise the amount of 'social' provision in the form of affordable housing, schools, green space and or/other recreational facilities. It focuses on land value and aims to sell plots to the market users at high enough prices so that the costs of social uses and infrastructure do not mean the whole scheme shows a negative residual land value. The process is described in the following extract:

> The municipality bought the land, usually from farmers and for a price only a little above agricultural value. It drained this land and put in all the on-site infrastructure (roads, play surfaces, local parks, cycle tracks, etc). To these costs it added the costs of any off-site infrastructure: widening feeder roads, expanding the capacity of the sewage works, etc. The costs of borrowing the necessary money came on top of that. Then it added an arbitrary percentage (up to 19 per cent) to those costs in order to pay for making the plan and supervising the implementation. From the total costs it subtracted the income from the sale of the land for public and commercial services such as local schools, doctors' surgeries, local shops. The remaining costs had to be recouped from the sale of land for

private housing and for social housing. In so far as those sales prices were more than necessary to cover the costs, if a profit was made on the land development process, then this went to the municipality. And the public facilities, both on-site and off-site, were paid by the users (the purchasers of the private housing, the local shops, etc) via the land prices. Sometimes it was not possible to cover the costs by disposing of the land, and the 'land development' was subsidised by central and/or local government.

(Verhage, 2000)

The viability of the land assembly process has traditionally been assessed via a 'land exploitation document' (the 'exploitatierekening'). The preparation of this document allows the municipality to assess whether they need to request top-up funding from the province or from central government. Historically, central government has funded 'exploitation deficits' more generously than is the case today. This has meant that more recently, municipalities following the traditional approach to land assembly have had to either decrease the level of social infrastructure (it is difficult to cut corners with physical infrastructure in the Netherlands) or increase the costs of developed and building-ready land to private housing and commercial property developers.

Clearly this model of land assembly (set out in diagrammatic form in Figure 12.3) allows for control to be vested fully in a single agency, the municipality. The local authority has not only land use planning powers, but also powers for land

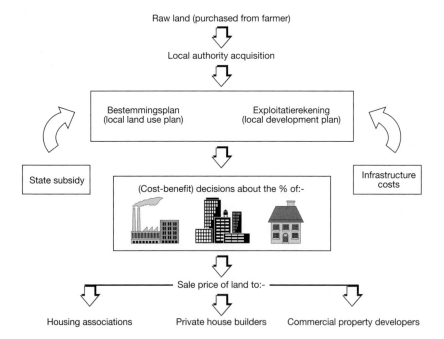

Figure 12.3 The traditional approach to land assembly in the Netherlands.
Source: A. J. Golland, adapted from leading sources on the Dutch development process

supply. Thus it can control the release of sites in a 'sequential' or 'plan, monitor and manage' fashion, and therefore has great potential for planning and managing the urban development process in most circumstances.

The model also provides the possibility to create mixed uses and mixed communities. Municipalities, once land is assembled, are in control of serviced and 'ready' building land, and in a strong position to negotiate with private developers and housing associations.

The ability to implement these policies via this method of land assembly relies on sites of a reasonable size. Historically, many of the urban 'expansion areas' have been realised via the 'customary' practice. As large site opportunities reduce in number, and regeneration of existing smaller sites becomes a policy focus, the older model may not be so important in the future.

Land pooling ('Umlegung') and housing development in Germany

As discussed earlier, 'land allocation' and 'land availability' are two different things. The process of allocating land is fully within the control of planning, although making land available is not. A key obstacle to housing development is land availability. This in turn depends on land-ownership and the objectives of land-owners in holding land. Where house-builders have to deal with one land-owner, perhaps on a large greenfield site, the problems are not usually so complex. However, it is increasingly becoming the case within the focus on brownfield and urban development that sites have to be assembled from many small land plots. The process of 'Umlegung' in Germany (literally, the 'turning over' (of land)), offers a tried and tested solution to this problem scenario.

The process of Umlegung has arisen to a large extent out of the system of passing down land between generations. This process, created by the inheritance laws is known as 'Realteilung' and leads eventually to a situation where: 'in the case of inheritance by several heirs, one piece of land is divided into individual plots, which leads to sites that are too small for development' (Dieterich *et al.*, 1993).

Under these circumstances, a development solution had to be found. The Umlegung process provided such a solution. Depending on the particular circumstances involved, Umlegung can be carried out on a 'Freiwillige' ('voluntary') basis, or can be carried out according to the statutory procedures for Umlegung set out in the Building Law book ('Baugesetzbuch').

It is often the case that Umlegung is carried out on a voluntary basis. 'Freiwillige Umlegung' is a process of land 'turnover' driven largely by original and intermediate (those who own land immediately prior to, or during, the construction process) land-owners ('Owner-Owner'). However, 'Umlegung' is also carried out under statutory provisions ('Owner-LA') and is highly significant in making development land available.

The process of Umlegung works on the basis of land 'pooling'. In general terms, several land-owners agree to 'securitise' their 'bundle of rights and obligations' (land value) in such a way that a larger more developable site can be realised. Umlegung has two main aims: 'to provide owners with usable or developable building plots; and to enable the municipality to take ownership of areas necessary for public development, such as streets or other public spaces' (Dieterich *et al.*, 1993: 66.) In theory, the benefit for land-owners of adopting the process lies in realising 'marriage value' that will be created by planning, infrastructure provision and the pooling of land resources. The initial assumption is that the sum of the value of the individual plots will be less than the value of the whole (once 'pooled') provided that the 'whole' provides a developable site. In practice, the process is based on the reasonable assumption that planning and building consent will provide a significant increase in land value and hence benefit most, if not all, land-owners.

At the same time, the process must be understood in the context of the German planning system at the local level. Highly important is the legally binding local plan (Bebauungsplan) and the Umlegungsplan, which together set out the areas to be set aside for infrastructure, roads and green space. The municipality can acquire the public space needed for infrastructure without having to compensate the land-owners. Thus the land is free and value is lost to the land-owners. Provided, however, that the increase in land value created by the grant of planning permission offsets the land 'contribution', land-owners will usually agree to an Umlegung.

The process of umlegung

Umlegung works according to the following steps. First, all individual land rights and interests are identified and valued. This provides what is known as the 'Umlegungsmasse' (the 'pooled total value'). Second, a deduction is made from each land-ownership which relates to infrastructure and public land use. Third, is the use of the 'Verteilungmaßstab'. This is, literally, the 'sharing out mechanism', and in practice is a process for re-allocating land interests back to individual owners.

The mechanism operates mainly in two ways, either on the basis of land redistribution or on the basis of value redistribution. This is to say, land-owners can, following the Umlegung process, be given either the same amount of land (hectares) they had prior to it (less land for public use), or they can receive land to an equivalent 'value' to that which they possessed prior to the use of the Verteilungmaßstab. The purpose of the exercise is to provide plots which the original land-owners can build on, or which they can sell to a developer. There is flexibility in the outcome of the Umlegung in that where it is not possible to provide a perfect solution in terms of land redistribution, financial compensation is payable between land-owners.

Umlegung can be implemented on a statutory basis, using all the mechanisms described, or it can be based on an approach using professional advisers working for individual land-owners. A number of factors influence which method is used. One factor is the complexity of the 'value' based approach. Using this method, it is arguably sounder for all land-owners to opt for a statutory Umlegung, where the valuation procedure is taken on principally by the municipality. Another factor is the infrastructure burden imposed by the municipality. If this is significantly high,

Planning and development process   **Pooling and valuation process**

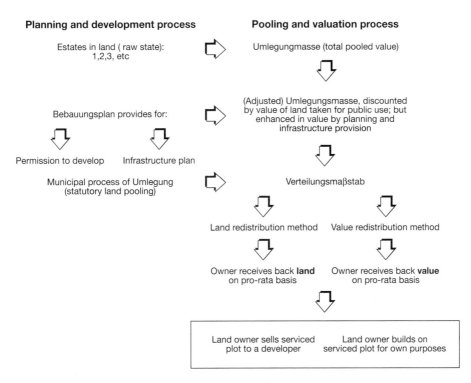

Figure 12.4 Umlegung via the statutory process in Germany.
Source: A. J. Golland, adapted from leading sources on the German Umlegung process

a flexible, privately negotiated solution is less likely to be successful. This is because some land-owners will be less likely to accept the high burden than others. Where, however, the municipality makes it transparent that there are significant benefits to land-owners in working together, a flexible negotiated solution will result. Figure 12.4 sets out these processes in diagrammatic form.

The role of the Umlegung process has been significant, particularly on green-field sites, although the approach is also used on brownfield areas, not least because the proportion of land which can be appropriated by the municipality for public use is 10 per cent maximum (Dieterich *et al.*, 1993: 67). In greenfield areas, the figure is 30 per cent (ibid.).

The process is also particularly effective in meeting the demands of housing provision in Germany, where a very large proportion (*c.*50 per cent) of all new homes for owner-occupation are 'self-build' (Golland, 1998). This method of housing provision conventionally involves a household finding a building plot and commissioning an architect, who then in turn contacts a building company to construct the house. This process is in contrast to the usual mode of private housing development in the UK, for example, where large tracts of land are purchased by speculative developers and then sold 'off-the-shelf' to purchasers.

Plate 12.1 Speculative new-build housing in rural France: R. N. E. Blake.

The French allotment ('lotissement') model

The need to find a way of providing serviced building plots for purchase by private households, and the lack of a fully fledged speculative house-building industry, has led to the growth of the process of 'lotissement' in France. The history, and the reasons for the growth of this model in France, are well explained in Booth (1991). Particularly important has been the fact that 'French house-builders had no experience to compare with that gained by their British counterparts in the vast public and private estates of the 1920s and 1930s' (ibid.: 243). Much of the pre-war and inter-war French housing for owner-occupation was in multi-family blocks and flats. The desire for home-owners to have low-rise and detached housing since the 1950s has led to a growing role for the lotisseur company.

Lotisseurs are promoted and regulated as a specific profession by the Syndicat National des Aménageurs-Lotisseurs (SNAL). It is estimated that companies associated with SNAL are responsible for preparing more than a quarter of all the plots required for development in France each year (SNAL, 1999: 18). Currently, around 60,000 to 80,000 dwellings per annum are provided through the process of lotissement (Renard, 2001a).

Most firms are small, and lotissement for housing can be organised with a very limited number of people covering sales, buying and administration. Larger firms who extend the function of lotissement to a land management role are sometimes known as 'aménageurs-lotisseurs'. They have a full technical team including architects, geologists, engineers and ecologists, and can deal with more complex development situations (ibid.). Many lotisseur companies are set up from scratch to meet the demand for lotissement; however, some of the most important lotisseur firms are breakaway groups from the larger construction and development companies. Foncier-Conseil, amongst the largest (lotisseur) firms in France, was originally the land-buying department of a major house-building company. Some of the smaller lotisseur companies are franchised to the larger 'promoteurs' (developers).

The lotissement model is most significant for housing at the urban fringe and has been used to expand many of France's major cities. Thus far, the use of the model has not been directed towards the regeneration of urban sites and vacant land in cities. The more appropriate solution has been seen to be the 'ZAC' (Zone d'Aménagement Concerte). This is a more interventionist approach involving a stronger local policy steer, but one which can provide a more comprehensive and socially sustainable solution. The application of the conventional lotissement model to brownfield and urban sites is currently being debated by SNAL.

The process of lotissement

The process of 'allotment' or 'lotissement' is inherent in all development processes. It is always necessary at some point in time. The process involves the sub-division and servicing (with infrastructure) of land into plots that can be sold for housing. The key difference in France, however, is that this process is carried out by a specialised actor (the 'lotisseur') operating within a highly defined stage of the planning process. Booth explains how the French system differs from the system in Britain:

> In Britain planning approval for residential estates is seen as being essentially an act of control in which the proposal's relationship to the development plan in force is at issue, whereas, in France, permission to subdivide land or lay it out for development is considered as part of the forward planning process, which itself will give rise to the need for further permissions.
>
> (Booth, 1991: 240)

Thus lotissement is seen as a logical, yet separate step in the development process. This 'step' is marked by changes in land-ownership: from original land-owner, to lotisseur to the final user. The 'final user' will usually be a private household, although sometimes it will be a 'promoteur' (a private housing developer). In the case of a housing development built by a large speculative firm in the UK this change in land-ownership will not usually occur, since the firm will own the land from the point at which it purchases it from the original land-owner to the time at which the dwelling is sold to a private buyer. Lotisseurs are short-term operators who do not 'bank' land.

There are several practical issues raised by the process, despite the fact that most lotissement schemes involve the creation of plots for only around 10–15 dwellings (Renard, 2001). One of the potential problems relates to how common areas will be managed subsequent to the lotisseur having sold all the plots. Some areas will fall to the households themselves to manage; others will fall to the local authority. The local authority can levy a one-off tax payment from the lotisseurs relating to infrastructure provision; this will be a percentage of the cost of provision. Ongoing costs will need then to be agreed between authority, households and lotisseur.

Further control is exercised by the lotisseur through what is known as a 'cahier des charges' (a specification document). This document sets out the conditions under which the land is sold to the end-user. Typically, these relate to changing the design of dwellings, maintaining access and ensuring that quiet is enjoyed by the neighbourhood.

The operation of lotissement has been supported by the tax system, in particular, VAT. Lotisseurs, when they sell land, pay VAT at only 13 per cent, when standard rate is 18 per cent. This allows them to reflect these reduced costs in the sale of land to buyers and developers.

Housing development in the UK in a European perspective

Towards the urban renaissance: the role of comparative models?

The value of looking at different ways of developing housing is to highlight the possibilities for transferring those 'lessons' to our own country. The three case studies outlined in the previous section provide different solutions to particular land and housing development problems abroad. Indeed, the models, if they are not directly transferable, provide ideas for ways of solving the urban housing development challenge in the UK today.

First and foremost, this challenge is about ensuring a supply of land under often difficult urban site conditions. The government's vision for regeneration, set out in *Towards an Urban Renaissance* (Urban Task Force, 1999) can be met only by tackling head on the problems of land development and of site assembly. The role of comparative research has, it is argued, not been fully exploited. The comparative focus of *Towards an Urban Renaissance* is largely one which emphases the design solutions adopted in other countries, but does not really explore the potential lessons to be gained through a greater understanding of the way in which the urban development process operates in different countries. Further exploration of the applicability of models such as those discussed in the previous section could well yield benefits for the development of more difficult urban sites. Happily, there is an emerging body of research now looking at the possibilities of comprehensive cost-benefit and land-pooling approaches (for example: Urban Villages Forum, 1995 and Verhage, 2000).

However, as a student of comparative housing development, it is important to be aware that the success of a particular approach needs to be seen in the context in which it is operating. The Dutch 'comprehensive' development approach can be seen as a response to difficult ground conditions that do not exist to such an extent in the UK. In some senses the need for such a solution has not been so great although that does not mean it should not be tried. Indeed, one could argue that such an approach, with a single land acquisition body, has been successfully in use for developing new towns and for planning large-scale urban development schemes in the UK.

Development models often arise out of country-specific circumstances, however; the German Umlegung process is a good example, and it has some similarities with the Japanese process of 'land adjustment'. Similarly, the French 'lotissement' process is found within other European development models, albeit those where the process is undertaken by the same agency that originally acquires land and builds the houses. It is important when trying to implement models from abroad to look at how they are working in their own country's context.

The pressure for convergence

A key theme of comparative housing studies is convergence: the extent to which housing development, in both its processes and outcomes, is likely to become more similar in the future. As ever in comparative analysis it is important to recognise the forces driving things together as well as those forcing them apart.

Demographic pressures

One convergent pressure is demographic, in particular, the trend towards smaller and single-person households. Eurostat statistics show that, 'according to 1990/1 censuses, EU-12 had 131 million private households compared with 111 million in the 1981/2 censuses. This 18 per cent rise was far higher than the 2.6 per cent increase in total population'. Thus, as the rate of growth of the overall population increases, so it is overtaken by the rate of increase in the number of households. In terms of what is happening in individual countries:

> Only in Greece did household size stay stable from 1981–91. And only in Spain, Portugal, Greece and Ireland was the average household size still above three in 1991. The fall elsewhere was due to fewer babies, more divorce and people living longer and on their own, especially widows. One-person households now account for over 30 per cent of the total in Denmark, Germany and the Netherlands. Of the EU-15's 140 million households, the country with the smallest average size is Sweden (2.1 people). And in Sweden 40 per cent of households consist of one person and half of all households have no children. In EU-12 there are nearly nine million single-parent households, 85 per cent of them headed by the mother.
>
> (Eurostat, 2000)

The trend towards smaller, and predominantly single-person, households in many European countries has profound implications for planners and housing developers. It not only affects the overall numbers and need for housing but also, importantly, raises questions about the form, space standards and design of new dwellings. It is

Plate 12.2 Conversion of an agricultural building to homes, Brittany, France: R. N. E. Blake.

frequently argued by the house-building industry that dwellings for single people should not necessarily be 'small' but that they should allow for a full range of activities that a family or a larger household would undertake. This in turn has implications for the use of space and land-take.

The challenge for housing developers across Europe is to meet the demographic changes against a backdrop of very different land policy and planning policy frameworks. Some planning systems will undoubtedly fare better than others. What is uncertain is where the smaller households will want to be located. Undoubtedly many will lack purchasing power and be excluded from the market, while others will have greater choice and perhaps move out of the inner cities to the suburbs or the countryside. In France, particularly, the rehabilitation of abandoned cottages and farm buildings is an increasing trend (Plate 12.2). Some will want to move to fashionable city-centre apartments where services and employment are at hand. The development of new homes for this demographic group is arguably a much greater challenge than, say, providing homes was for the large number of family households seeking a suburban home in the immediate post-war period.

Monetary union

Another convergent influence will be monetary union. By 2002, many European countries, with the notable exception of the UK, had adopted the euro currency. Inevitably there will be some effects on the behaviour of housing markets and on the demand for new dwellings. The main effect will be bought about by the ability of housing consumers, and indeed housing developers, to acquire credit at similar levels of interest in different countries.

The effects on the supply of, and demand for, new housing will be varied. Taking the case first of a relatively 'low' interest rate, this may have particularly beneficial effects in countries such as the UK where developers are often highly geared by land banking policies. In other countries, for example, the Netherlands and Sweden, where house-building firms have traditionally operated as housing construction companies, the benefits may be less tangible. The opposite conclusions would of course be drawn were interest rates to be set at a higher level. In practical terms, the level at which interest rates are set will be important for the size of the new-build market. The relationship between the number of sales in the second-hand and new housing markets differs considerably between countries. Whereas in the UK, the number of sales in the new-build housing market are relatively low compared to turnover in the second-hand market, this is not the case in many other European countries. If a single interest rate is to bring about convergence in the demand for new-build (relative to second-hand housing), then a considerable shift will be needed from the current situation in European housing markets.

Inevitably any conclusions about the effects of the single European currency on housing development in different countries will be speculative at this early stage. In so far as the demand for new owner-occupied or private homes is concerned, there is much evidence to show that housing developers across Europe are increasingly building for this sector at the expense of social and private rented housing (see also Figure 12.2). The extent to which there will be a future demand for new-build home-ownership relative to other tenures will depend to a large extent on the level of interest rates in the euro zone. However, interest rate effects are uncertain. Whilst it can be argued that a relatively low interest rate will increase the demand for home-ownership because repayments will be low for house buyers, it can equally well be argued that the cost of providing affordable housing will also be lowered for housing associations, government and other social housing providers.

As in other areas of comparative interest, the effect of monetary union needs to be seen in wider context. Whether a single European currency, and its likely consequence of similar interest rates, will bring about similar housing development outcomes depends not just on interest rates but on the whole financial context. Tax and subsidy policies, and the extent to which these are harmonised, will be a key factor. For private developers in the UK there have historically been very few direct subsidies for house-building. In other European countries, and the case study countries considered above (France, Germany and the Netherlands), direct subsidies and tax reliefs are available for the developers of housing for home-ownership. Very often these are subsidies of a 'conditional object' nature (Oxley, 1987), where a subsidy is made available subject to a housing developer agreeing to provide a dwelling in line with specific conditions. One of the more interesting examples of this is where a developer obtains a subsidy to build a dwelling for low-cost home-ownership but where the price is fixed to the end consumer. This 'continental' model now appears to be emerging as a derivative of 'affordable housing' in the UK today.

At the same time, private developers in the UK, although they have traditionally received few direct subsidies, have had the scope to make significant gains from the process of development itself. Inflated land values, from which private developers have often gained, can be regarded as a form of 'subsidy' in comparison with other countries where these sorts of development 'gains' are taxed. On the basis of this comparative conclusion alone, it is difficult to gauge the effects of converging interest rates; if monetary (interest rate) policy and fiscal (tax and subsidy) policy do not also converge, the effects on the volume of new housing produced, its tenure and its location within countries will be very difficult to predict.

Political change, housing development and convergence

Perhaps one of the most significant factors in trying to evaluate the extent of convergence in housing development trends is the political dimension. In respect of the overall demand for housing this is unlikely to be affected by the political 'colour' of European governments. Governments in this relatively highly industrialised and developed continent are unlikely to under-provide new homes to any great extent because politically this would be unacceptable. The key debates therefore concern, the tenure, form and location of new housing development.

Historically, the UK can be singled out as a country in which housing development has been a highly political issue. Typically, Conservative governments have favoured the private sector as a way of meeting housing demand and need, whereas Labour governments have favoured social and council housing development. This trend is most marked when studying the period 1970–90. By contrast, other European political parties have adopted a much more 'tenure-neutral' approach to housing development. What this has meant is that new housing development has reflected the prevailing economic conditions rather than some inflexible ideology. New private development in countries such as the Netherlands and Germany, for example, has responded to these economic conditions, irrespective of the fact that there have been changes in political power over the years; for a full analysis of this debate see Golland (1998). Countries such as Sweden have also adopted a tenure-neutral approach.

Whether housing development, or housing 'production' as it has often been seen by politicians, can be manipulated in the UK to such an extent in the future, is debatable. It seems clear that 'New Labour' are as convinced by the arguments for private-sector provision and a scaling back of the welfare state as were their predecessor Conservative government. This raises an important question about the extent to which new housing development is appropriate to the changing economic circumstances. Arguably, the preference for private-sector provision will not matter if the definition of 'affordable housing' remains wide; if, for example, some 'affordable housing' is, in practice, low-cost home-ownership, then it can be argued that the private sector is developing a 'social housing good'. It can also be argued that policies on the tenure of new housing development, if not the outcomes themselves, are converging, at least in so far as some of the northern European countries are concerned. In southern European countries such as Greece, Italy and Portugal, private housing development cannot be so easily compared with the northern systems of housing supply which are arguably more institutionalised.

There are, then, questions about the extent to which environmental policies will bring about convergence in housing development trends. Undoubtedly, there are political pressures on European governments to conserve and recycle land where possible. The extent to which this is happening is uncertain because data on the topic are rather scarce. It is interesting to note, however, that the United Nations has recently (2000) begun to provide data on urban land building. What is certain is that the pressure to recycle and build on 'brownfield' sites is significantly greater in some countries than in others. The situation is very different in densely developed countries such as the UK, Belgium and the Netherlands from that in more rural countries such as France, Spain, Ireland and the Scandinavian countries. Countries such as Germany, which has a strong environmental policy and is represented by a 'Green-Social Democrat' alliance, has, to some extent, defined an individual framework for housing development. Much depends on planning; where planning systems are arguably less 'developed' and where often 'informal' housing development emerges, these situations are unlikely to be mirrored in other countries where planning is more rigidly enforced.

Because countries place different emphases on the environment and on planning policy, and because different levels of urbanisation exist, it is very difficult to foresee common or converging housing development outcomes. Clearly, the way to conserve land is to build more densely. This is certainly a lesson for the UK in that it has a very low proportion of multi-family and apartment housing by European standards. New (PPG3) policy is now reflecting the environmental agenda to some extent. It is also clear that countries where development is also relatively dense, for example the Low Countries (Netherlands and Belgium), are also placing increased emphasis on brownfield site development. However, if convergence on levels of urbanisation are to be sought, then very different housing development solutions will be necessary. Less urbanised countries could afford to develop less densely, probably in the form of free-standing housing on greenfield sites, while highly urbanised countries would have to develop very densely, using apartments and multi-family housing as a norm.

Discussion points

1   Compare, contrast and evaluate the merits and demerits of three European housing development processes.
2   Examine some of the problems involved in comparative housing research.
3   Analyse the role for 'state' and 'market' in housing development, based on European examples.
4   Rehearse the case for convergence in European housing development processes and outcomes.

5   Discuss the proposition that the UK can learn much from mainland Europe when looking for solutions to the land assembly problem.

Key reading

A number of books taking a pan-European overview of housing are available, notably: Barlow and Duncan, *Success and Failure in Housing Provision* (1994); Boelhouwer and van der Heijden, *Housing Systems in Europe* (1992); RICS *European Housing Markets* (2000); and Verhage, *Local Policy for Housing Development; European Experiences* (2002). Useful research articles include: Needham, 'A theory of land prices' (*Urban Studies*, 1992); Oxley, 'The aims and methods of corporative housing research' (*Scandinavian Housing and Planning Research*, 1991); and Schmidt, 'Convergence theory, labour movement and corporatism' (*Scandinavian Housing and Planning Research*, 1989).

Chapter 13

Innovation and emerging trends in housing development

Chris Nicol and Andrew Golland

The innovation challenge in housing development

Innovation has an important role to play in all industry activities relating to development or production, including housing. However 'innovation' can mean several different things. A dictionary definition (Fowler and Fowler, 1998: 702) suggests that to 'innovate' is to 'bring in new methods or ideas', or to 'make changes'. 'Textbook' approaches to innovation, particularly those being written for students of economics and business, tend to focus on the subject from the perspective of changes either in a manufacturing process, or in a manufactured product.

Often 'innovation' is associated with invention or discovery: the 'big find', or the 'earth-shattering solution'. In practice, however, innovation is often a more modest event, taking place over a period of time, happening incrementally or being adopted in different ways by different organisations. Innovation in many cases takes the form of manual tasks being replaced by mechanised or computerised operations. This does not always happen overnight and occurs sometimes by way of a 'trial and error' approach towards making things happen.

Although there have been significant improvements over time in the quality of new housing development, for example, the use of improved materials and improved environmental and thermal performance, the house-building industry has in many ways failed to come up with really innovative ways of developing housing or indeed for creating different types of housing 'product'. 'New housing development', particularly that built for private interests, conforms to a particular image: traditional build, which is normally a two-storey structure with brick-and-block frame combined with a pitched tiled or slate roof with some attention in minor features to conform with a local vernacular style. This 'new housing development' is likely to be built by a large speculative housing development company, probably on a greenfield fringe or large infill urban site. Housing tends to be built to relatively low density, in many cases at around 20 to 35 dwellings per hectare, which is not significantly different from housing developed under Tudor Walters' inter-war standards. This process (and product) has been with us for some considerable time, and although housing development solutions have become more imaginative as the urban renaissance policy has had an impact, housing development nevertheless remains a fairly conservative process. It is thus fair to ask: Why does this situation exist and what might be done about it?

The literature examining the reasons for the lack of innovation in the UK's house-building industry and its development process is fairly extensive. The 'barriers' to innovative housing product and innovative development techniques and processes are well catalogued. In the early stages of this chapter we highlight a few of the key arguments, before moving on to look at some actual innovations in housing production.

Innovation and house building: an historical perspective

A brief history of (a lack of) innovation

> At the top end of the market you will sit down with the company's designers and design your own house. The computer simulations will be 'totally real', just like visiting a show house. You will be able to decide exactly where every internal wall is and it will be defined on the computer model to within a millimetre. Once you have finalised your design it will be transmitted to the factory's production line and construction workers – helped by robots – will build the various modules of the house, and stack them onto a lorry for later assembly on site. This technology could happen in five years . . . All the elements are there and all the technology is proven.
>
> (Miles, J. from *Housebuilder* (Lamont, 1999)).

The picture built up by the above quotation offers an exciting view of choice and flexibility in housing development based on a responsive method of housing supply. Unfortunately, it is very unlikely that this image of the perfectly planned development process is one which is familiar to new housing purchasers. But why might this be the case and why has there traditionally been a low level of innovation in new housing development?

One relatively simple paradigm which we can use to try to answer the question is that of 'supply and demand'. On the supply side, house-building firms are concerned to balance out the requirement to meet housing demand as precisely as possible at given points in the economic and housing market cycle with the need to ensure that there is sufficient supply of labour and materials. This complex interaction is examined in more detail by Ball:

> [British builders producing houses for owner occupation have] functional activities . . . spread across a number of markets. On the one side is the housing market in which their products are sold in competition with each other and the existing stock of dwellings and, on the other side, the inputs for land, labour, materials, plant and equipment. On occasions, the labour, plant and materials components are subcontracted as a package, so that there is only one market relation rather than three. Yet . . . the managerial abilities of housebuilding firms are not simply concerned with productive activities . . . Instead they have to deal with five specific types of market as well as conceive developments and oversee their building'
>
> (Ball, 1999: 11)

Although the house-building industry is not alone in serving several markets, it is the 'special characteristics of each market' (ibid.: 12) that discourages innovation and change. The volatile nature of the housing market in post-war Britain can be argued to have contributed to a lack of innovation.

However, innovation and its relationship with the performance of the housing market is a two-way process. It is understandable that house-building companies are unlikely to take a longer term view of house-building and invest greater resources trying to innovate products and processes, if future revenue streams and profits can be easily predicted. The unpredictable and sometimes cumbersome process of planning can also be argued to militate against house-builders trying out new processes and products. However, it can equally well be argued that were house-builders to become more innovative in their approach, particularly in increasing productivity, they could respond better to changes in the housing market, thus overcoming some of the short-term inelasticity in housing supply and in its price effects.

Volatility of housing market performance has been accompanied by a restructuring of the house-building industry both in terms of output (see also Chapter 3) and in terms of product. The effects of these changes have been studied by Nicol and Hooper (1999). They show that firms have consolidated and merged to concentrate house-building output in a smaller number of (larger) firms. The impact at the individual firm level has been, however, to increase the number of standard new housing products offered by the firms. Thus more variety of 'standard' products is allowed for. There has also been some scope for purchasers to customise and personalise their homes, particularly if they can negotiate changes from the standard product early enough in the building process. However, the scope to make changes to the planned dwelling is normally limited to internal, rather than external, alterations and to features that do little to affect the structural integrity of the building (ibid.: 74).

Standardisation of product is, in part, a response to the need to deal with the question of the skills available in the house-building industry. It can be argued that a highly skilled workforce will be able to respond more effectively to changes in product demand than one which is less skilled. Research by Clarke and Wall (1996) has shown that, in contrast with other European countries, Britain is relatively disadvantaged in being slow to respond to new demands:

> . . . the construction process [in Britain] has the economic disadvantage of being considerably less productive and slower than in either Germany or the Netherlands [which the study mainly compares]. There is also little room to improve this without radical change, given the low level of technology involved in the process and the relatively narrow and low level of skills assumed. In both Germany and the Netherlands, in contrast, the high level of training – imparting flexible and transferable skills – allows for much greater adaptability of the workforce to new technologies, materials and processes
>
> (Clarke and Wall, 1996: 84)

From the demand side, housing consumers for new-build products have been shown to be extremely cautious in their tastes (Bramley *et al.*, 1995; Ball, 1999). As Ball states (Ball, 1999: 12) 'car designs come and go, but the two-storey, pitched roofed, semi – but preferably – detached house, in a limited range of styles, is the mainstay of the housing market'. The detailed reasons for this conservatism in housing choice is a source of continual concern to those with an interest in new building. A recent research survey commissioned jointly by the New Homes Marketing Board of the House Builders Federation (HBF) and the Halifax plc (2001), found that: 'for many, innovation in construction was a closed book' (ibid.: 35).

The HBF and Halifax survey showed that there was a reasonable awareness of alternative construction techniques such as timber and steel frame and more innovative methods of heating homes, such as solar panels and new-style radiators. However, it was also clear that households' concepts of 'innovation' were more realistically interpreted in terms of what might be considered 'cosmetic changes or differences'. Thus (particularly for women) a visually interesting exterior or an improvement to internal fittings was a significant 'innovation'. Similarly features such as energy saving bulbs, fitted smoke alarms and air conditioning were considered to be an 'innovation' more generally. Perhaps most concerning was the expectation that homes built in an 'innovative' way would take less time to construct and therefore not be of such a high quality. One buyer suggested 'what worries me is how quickly they build houses nowadays . . . are they putting enough into them? Sometimes you wonder if they can be safe if they're built so quick' (ibid.: 36). This consumer attitude, or perceived consumer attitude, has meant that innovations in construction technique, such as timber-frame construction, have proved difficult to introduce to a public who since the 1970s have thought that timber frame represents poorer quality. Or at least this is what the house-builders think they think (Hooper and Nicol, 2000: 307). Forms of 'modular' construction, where units of the dwelling or parts are brought onto site and assembled there in 'kit' form, were thought either to be 'wacky' or associated with the kind of construction approach used 'for McDonald's restaurants'.

The constraints on innovation in the house-building industry are thus considerable; from both the supply side, in terms of the way in which the market for land works, as well as from the point of view of skills and labour shortages. Perhaps, however, the greatest deterrent, particularly with respect to the new-build product, is the consumer him/herself.

Although these points had to be made, there are, in fact, important new and emerging trends in the way in which housing development is carried out, which we now consider in order to deal with the topic more fully.

Innovation and emerging trends

Despite perceptions that the house-building industry is reactionary and slow to change, changes have nevertheless occurred. Over the last 30 years, some house-builders have tried to introduce innovation to the construction process. For instance in the 1980s Laing introduced their 'superhome' concept. This project would deliver all the materials required to build a home in a pre-packed, weather protected and highly secure container. The materials were to be assembled off-site, packed and stored ready for 'order', whereupon they would be delivered to the location, 'unpacked' and assembled. The innovation here was focused squarely on the material, construction and management side of house-building. The finished home would look exactly the same as one built in a more traditional way. The project floundered, however, due to the lack of suitable computer systems and technology to manage the store keeping, ordering and delivery.

Innovations may not be as fundamental and large-scale as Laing's superhomes, nor may they be visible to the house purchaser, but innovations are occurring if only incrementally in areas such as procurement, energy efficiency, and general construction (Gann, 1996; Hooper and Nicol, 1999; Nicol and Hooper, 1999; Hooper and Nicol, 2000). It may be fair to say that many of these changes are driven by factors such as building regulations and more importantly the need to retain profitability in times of rising land prices, rather than a grand plan on the part of the individual companies to develop innovative houses. These may not be as 'sexy' as some of the innovations that have taken place in the design, in the purchase or procurement of the house or even in simple things such as water use, issues which we will return to later in this chapter. However, as the large house-builders dominate new-housing production in the UK the small incremental innovations that they introduce are likely to have a greater effect on the housing supply than the large innovations being undertaken through the bespoke procurement mechanisms that will be discussed next.

The next sections of this chapter will focus on different aspects of innovation in housing development: the innovative development process; the innovative product placement; and environmentally sustainable innovation. Innovation in the development process will focus on self-build, while the product placement innovation will focus on one project, INTEGER, which sought to introduce radical house features to the public and construction industry, through a pilot construction which ran as a TV series during the late 1990s. The final example will focus on the 'green' environmental innovations that are being introduced into a small number of example homes.

Although all three can be seen as being the antithesis of the operation of the private speculative house-building industry, with its standard house types, material procurement and profit driven agenda, innovative processes and products nevertheless do influence the industry; rather as concept cars and developments in the world of motor sports eventually reach the family saloon, features that are seen as enhancing the values of the house-builders product and allowing it to sell more easily are introduced, first, as options and then, slowly into mainstream housing design. Although not everyone will be in a position to build their own green-roofed house, with 'smart' kitchen equipment, we can find house-builders willing to adapt. For instance some house-builders are already installing more environmentally friendly features, which reduce energy and water use. Others build homes that are designed to accommodate the internet and ones where customers can request additional space, either in the loft or instead of an integral garage.

Innovation in the development process: the self-build market

What is self-build and how important is it?

The term 'self-build' is one which needs introduction and explanation. Most publications concerned with housing development and housing production focus largely on the 'private' and the 'social' sector. It is often overlooked that there are subsections of these (larger) sectors which have a development process that is quite distinct. In the mainland European context, self-build is highly significant; in Germany it is the conventional approach to new-build for home-owners (Golland, 1998), and it also has an important role to play in countries such as France and the Netherlands (ibid.). In those countries, households wanting to acquire a new home look to take a much more pro-active role in the process than is the case in the UK, where it is normal for people to buy new homes on a 'ready to occupy' basis on a speculatively developed estate. Abroad, it is more usual for households to buy a plot of land, commission an architect to draw up plans, acquire full planning permission and set up a building contract. The difference in approach owes much to the way in which the respective house-building industries have been established in each of the countries. This aspect is examined in some depth by Booth (1991).

Self-build, as a mode of housing development is a difficult term to define. Whereas the speculative private housing development process is characterised by almost total responsibility falling on the private firm, self-build is a moving 'target'; some self-build schemes can be argued to deserve the accolade 'self-build' more than others. Some people say they have undertaken a 'self-build' when in actual fact they have only perhaps commissioned an architect who has, on their behalf, acquired the land, drawn the plans and made a contract with a builder. Other people have actually been involved in the building process themselves. The term 'self-build' should be regarded rather like the term 'mountain climbing': there is often no way of distinguishing between the 'ramblers, the scramblers and the danglers'! Some arrive by the 'hard' route, others by the easy one. There is also often no way of finding out how much help the self-builder has been given along the way, from friends, relatives or the community at large. A broad definition of 'self-build' is thus appropriate. Recent research carried out for the Joseph Rowntree Foundation (Barlow *et al.*, 2001) provides the following definition:

> We use the term 'self-build' to cover all instances where home buyers are involved in the production of their new home rather than purchasing from a speculative developer or renting from a landlord. The extent of personal involvement will vary. In some instances, it can entail self-builders physically building all or part of a dwelling themselves. At the other end of the spectrum, the self-builder might make only a few key decisions relating

to land, design and construction and hand over responsibility for construction to other parties. Self-build may also be undertaken collectively, often with groups of people pooling their expertise and resources to produce what is commonly referred to as a 'group' or 'community' self-build.

(Barlow et al., 2001: 1)

Thus the 'self-build' route to new development has many different options. Although it is normally associated with building for home-ownership, it is also promoted by housing associations through, for example, shared ownership. Using this model, households can acquire the land using a conventional mortgage, and then the build costs can be funded on a part-mortgage, part-rental basis. The key parameters to consider when trying to understand the nature of the 'self-build' scheme are the mode of housing promotion (in self-build, always the household), the method of housing construction (either the household itself or contracted out to a builder) and the way in which the financial benefits of the project are apportioned. This latter aspect needs further clarification: if the household has purchased the building plot, then there may be some financial benefit to be gained if the land has been purchased at below 'market' value. Where a development company buys the land, clearly that potential benefit will lie with the firm. If the household has carried out much of the actual building work itself, then any potential cost-savings are in its hands. It follows therefore that these potential savings are in the hands of the building contractor if the project is managed in that way.

Households who are prepared to make significant physical inputs and who take a strong role in organising the scheme have the greatest potential for cost-savings and for financial return on their investment. Being committed to do a lot of the work oneself has potential advantages with respect to finance; lenders, under some circumstances, will accept the 'sweat equity' argument (where a household can show how costs are reduced by its own labour) and provide greater levels of funding so that a high-standard dwelling can be built. On the other side of the coin, self-build is generally recognised as being a challenging way of acquiring new housing.

The scale and emergence of the self-build market

The self-build sector makes a key contribution to housing output on an annual basis. The actual number of dwellings completed is not certain. Any analysis of the exact number of 'self-build' housing projects is made difficult by the official (ODPM) housing and construction statistics which classify out only according to 'private enterprise', where it is likely that most self-build schemes are 'found'. There are a number of market research and specialist self-build and DIY journals that from time to time publish data on the size of the sector. Figures such as 20,000 completions per year are not unusual. Bespoke research looking at the question of how much self-build is carried out casts doubt on these figures. The current scale of the self-build market is likely in practice to be nearer 15,000 units per annum, according to the recent Joseph Rowntree Foundation report (Barlow *et al.*, 2001: 8). This estimate is based on data relating to the number of VAT claims made for self-build housing. The report estimates that the number of completions has grown from around 2,000 in 1978 to 15,000 in 1999 (ibid.: 11). In very round terms, self-build accounted for about 5 per cent of all private sector completion during the 1980s and about 8 per cent during the 1990s. Although this trend is rising, the report's authors have suggested that output will stabilise at current levels throughout this decade to 2010 (ibid.: 35).

What is the role of self-build in housing supply?

Self-build as a mode of housing development meets several objectives. First, it provides a way for people to express their own individuality in a housing project. Rather than relying on a large house-building company to provide them with a newly built dwelling, they take things into their own hands. It is perhaps instructive to note that self-build emerged as a significant force in housing production during the 1980s (DTLR housing and construction statistics), a time when contemporary politics promoted individuality as a solution to the country's problems. Edge and Duncan have suggested:

> Self-build housing is far more consistent with the cult of the individual than many conventional models of . . . housing provision. In a political climate in which the individual and the family have been stressed at the expense of a 'society' which some politicians have been known to claim does not exist, self-build has much to commend it. It involves the small-scale organisation of individuals 'getting on their bikes' and helping themselves. The homes which are produced are likely to be individual and tailored to particular needs. Self-build ostensibly offers an express route from the underclass to the middle class.
>
> (Edge and Duncan, 1998)

Thus, one function of self-build is to empower households to take charge of their own housing destinies. In a broader way, self-build increases household choice, via the opportunity to decide the plot on which the household wants to live, to decide the design of the dwelling and other associated features. It could be argued that self-build, as a description, covers a number of different types of housing consumers, ranging from the eco-warrior environmentalist school of thought, through self-build as a cost-effective way of entering owner-occupation or developing skills, through to affluent households who feel that they want something different from what is on offer. Self-build is possibly the most diverse housing solution, with each different group gaining and adding something different to the process.

In a very different way, however, self-build provides people with an opportunity to build communities for themselves. This is particularly important in social models of self-build, as Hutson and Jones explain:

> What better way to address the problem of youth homelessness and localised demand
> than to use a community development approach which enables better use to be made of
> social networks and builds on resources currently untapped. Self-build, as a distinctive
> aspect of self-help or community development, recognises the complex nature of social
> exclusion facing some young people, acknowledges the inter-relationship between home-
> lessness and unemployment as well as making possible lower rents for some young people.
>
> (Hutson and Jones, 1998)

The role of self-build, under these circumstances, is to procure housing for those
who might not otherwise have it, to build communities and, as a by-product of
the scheme, provide employment opportunities. Self-build is encouraged by local
authorities for a number of additional reasons. First, it cements their role as
local enablers in the process of housing provision and demonstrates a readiness
to take a flexible approach to development; second, it can help to meet housing
needs at the local level. Finally, self-build can be one solution to local authority
estate management challenges; some authorities, for example, are prepared to
demolish existing poor housing and sell or lease the land plots for self-build if they
believe that this policy provides a better long-term solution than selling land-directly
to private or social housing organisations.

Self-build provides a potential advantage, relative to the speculative house-
building process, to improve the quality of housing and to produce more innovative
design solutions. Whereas with speculative housing production the operator, namely
the private development firm, normally builds in a profit margin to reflect the
element of risk, this is not normally required for the self-builder. Whereas the profit-
motivated firm is concerned to ensure that there is 'return' in the short run, the
self-builder can spread the costs (particularly of finance) over the longer period of
owner-occupation. The result is potential cost-savings via the self-build route and
hence an opportunity to improve the design specification or to include sustainable
features not usually included via more traditional development routes. Empirical
research suggests that the financial viability equation is fundamentally different for
self-builders:

> Self-build essentially decouples the land development process from the construction
> process . . . the distribution of the gain in land value is different under self-build – where
> the household is also the developer – from speculative development. Most of the cost-
> reducing opportunities are unique to the self-build sector – self-builders have greater
> control over the production process and, because they own the site and the dwelling, are
> able to retain the savings.
>
> (Barlow *et al.*, 2001)

The precise cost benefits of self-build versus speculative housing development are
difficult to evaluate and the case for self-build should not be overstated. It is probable that on a plot-by-plot basis, large house-building firms can acquire land more
cheaply, because of economies of scale and purchasing power. Thus, it might be

argued that it is the large firms, not the small self-builders, who are more likely to produce innovative, cost-effective development solutions.

In practice, however, it is always important to keep in mind that housing provides two 'returns': first, 'investment' and second, 'consumption'. Whereas development firms are only concerned with the former, most self-builders are concerned with both issues. As a result, it is the self-builders who are more likely in practice to take a broader, long-term view, and include innovative solutions which the private firm might consider to be not worth the additional attention.

Who are the self-builders and what advantages do they see in self-build?

There are clear advantages for self-builders who are themselves employed full-time in building, or have close connections with the industry. These households understand the building process, have access to contacts for labour and raw materials, and probably have one or two key skills which can help the process on its way. Research consistently shows (Davidson, 1998; Barlow *et al.*, 2001) that those employed in the building trade are more likely to be involved in both self-build as well as DIY more generally. A study of the role of DIY in the renovation of owner-occupied homes found

> a disproportionately high amount of DIY work [was] done by households where the head or partner works or has worked in one of the building trades. These households account for less than 10 per cent of owner-occupied households, but they do around a quarter of the total volume (value) of DIY work.
>
> (Davidson, 1998)

Builders may thus be expected to have a head-start when it comes to self-build projects. However, evidence suggests (Ellis, 1998; Barlow *et al.*, 2001) that those employed in non-manual careers are also significantly involved in self-build projects. This is particularly the case for households on higher incomes with younger children, where the household is looking to expand its space and sees self-build as an efficient way of doing so. Another key group of self-builders are those just approaching retirement, or those just having reached it. These households often do not have significantly high outgoings and can often take advantage of a lump sum or pension annuity which can be used to fund a land plot.

There is yet another 'group' of people who favour self-build: those who are very keen to use the self-build process to develop environmentally and ecologically friendly housing. This group often see self-build not only as a way of providing a roof over their head and finding a pleasant place to live but also as a way of meeting some environmental or sustainable objective. Typically, this is in the form of using sustainable or local materials, but self-build is also often seen as a way of experimenting with innovative technology over and above that which would be likely to be found in speculatively built housing. Self-build is seen as being a flexible approach which can meet sustainable objectives:

The 'amateur' self-provision of housing can be argued, irrespective of the exact form and materials used, to fit particularly well into [the] fashionable ecological model. In addition, it can often be the case that the relative flexibility and possible ad hoc nature of many self-build schemes, particularly for individual houses, favours both rehabilitation and the incorporation of recycled materials into construction.

(Edge and Duncan, 1998).

Similar arguments relating to flexibility apply to the financing of self-build projects. There are now bespoke mortgage products for self-build, so called 'accelerator mortgages' to allow for stages payments to a building contractor as the project progresses (Ellis, 1998). Thus the self-build can progress at a rate which is suitable for the household itself.

A key advantage claimed for self-build is that it can reduce costs and provide better 'value for money'. It is important to substantiate this claim for a number of reasons. First, anecdotal evidence (based on household experiences in typical self-build TV programmes) usually suggests that costs significantly overrun budget. It would, however, be incorrect to suggest that this is wholly attributable to the process, since in most cases households improve the specification of the dwelling in some way as the build progresses. One key way in which costs are claimed to be reduced is by using a timber frame. This occurs more frequently in the self-build sector than in the speculative sector, which has steered clear of timber frame since the 1980s due to adverse publicity. Timber frame clearly provides an opportunity to speed up the building process, although its precise benefits, relative to traditional building methods, are difficult to quantify.

There is much debate about the benefits of self-build in reducing building costs. In support of the argument that self-build can reduce costs is the obvious advantage of the household's own 'inputs' in ordering materials and doing some work on the dwelling itself. Ultimately, much depends on how the additional quality of the house is balanced against the fact that 'one-off' housing is, according to key data sources, more expensive than that built in large estates (Royal Institution of Chartered Surveyors, 2001). Against the claimed advantages for self-build must be balanced the possibility that land is acquired relatively expensively compared to that acquired by large speculative housing development companies.

Technical innovation and intelligent housing

The need for technical innovation

While more innovative processes of housing development are beginning to emerge as we have seen with self-build, it is also important to highlight technical innovations in housing design and function. These 'technical' innovations are a response in no small measure to the need to improve the functional performance of new housing as well as to ensure that new homes are built as sustainably as possible. In this section, we look at case studies demonstrating the ways in which these needs are being met. We look at the INTEGER project, and its Millennium House.

The INTEGER project and the Millennium House

The INTEGER project is a 'holistic approach to innovation in housing' (INTEGER, 2002). The project, which started in 1996, 'addresses issues about living, working and playing in the twenty-first century and beyond' and was the brainchild of architects Cole Thompson and information technologist Alan Kell. The idea that developers should be looking harder at the connections between places of work, places to live and the performance of buildings is implicit in the project's promotion.

Although the parameters of the project are broad, it has been given particular focus via the construction of the 'Millennium House' which featured in the BBC television series 'DreamHouse'. The Millennium House is innovative in the construction techniques used, the use of intelligent technologies and the use of environmental techniques, and it was developed (from design stage to completion) in around three months.

Features of the Millennium House

The INTEGER Millennium House differs from traditionally constructed dwellings in several ways, in particular the extent to which dwelling components were manufactured off-site. Timber and glass panelling was used extensively and the bathrooms were installed as complete modules. In this way, work on-site was minimised, and, as an added benefit, so was the need to dispose of waste materials as the construction process proceeded.

A key concept of the home is 'intelligent technology', where the aim is to better manage the residential environment for the benefit of the occupiers and the sustainability of the house itself. The house includes several systems which can be termed 'intelligent' in the sense that they anticipate the needs of the user or can be operated independently by the user where required. The underlying concept for the interaction of the house's systems is the 'central nervous system' of the human body. The systems in the house are set up along the principles of 'sight, sound and communication'. Blinds, for example, respond to the level of sunlight; the amount of daylight and time of day is used to control the electrical lighting system so that a suitable room appearance can be achieved at all times; the security system is controlled in such a way that once it is set, external doors are locked and the heating system is set to an appropriate lower level. When the house is returned to, and the householder de-activates the alarm, the house 'wakes up' in the appropriate manner. The house is kitted out with an extensive provision of IT and multi-media connections. Additional features include a low-energy vacuum fridge and a low water use washing machine.

The house promotes low energy use, water conservation and generally sustainable materials. It is orientated to maximise the amount of sunlight, and the solar collector ensures that the house uses only around half as much energy as a conventional house. Hot water is also solar powered, while heating, when required, is generated from hot water circulated around the house to floor-mounted natural convectors. The cold water system is 'grey' in that it recycles used water for toilet flushing and rainwater is collected from the roof, reducing water usage by 30 per cent as against a conventional dwelling. The roof surface is turfed to 'contribute to a cleaner atmosphere and . . . an attractive, low maintenance and natural alternative to conventional roof materials' (ibid.).

To test the performance of the Millennium House, a family was asked to live in it for a week; the feedback they gave was 'overwhelmingly good' (Building Research Establishment, 1998). The house was subject to further scrutiny as a result of a survey asking people for their reactions once they had visited the house. The survey showed a number of features that were to be particularly welcomed, including those which saved energy, the design of the house and the control systems. Some other aspects were of concern to the visitors. These included specific features of design such as the (grass) roof and automatic doors (ibid.). Whilst it is clear that intelligent homes provide the potential for households to have a greater level of control over their lives, it is equally clear that 'control' can also be seen as a problem. Households may see 'intelligent houses' in terms of homes that are full of gadgets that are out of control, or indeed put them in a situation where the house itself 'takes control of their lives'.

People's past experiences of domestic technologies and appliances are highly significant when considering the scope for more advanced technologies. People not only often find new technologies difficult to incorporate into the home environment but they are often also concerned that the pattern and balance of their lives will be detrimentally affected. Under these circumstances it will be difficult to widen the scope for more advanced technology in the home.

Sustainable and green housing

Earth sheltered dwellings: origins and typology

Earth sheltered dwellings are nothing new, having been used for millennia, particularly in Asia but more recently in Europe and America. Over recent years these dwellings have increased in popularity as they are seen as sustainable housing forms. As at 1998 there were 27 earth sheltered dwellings in the UK, either complete or with construction ongoing. The oldest, Westonbirt in Gloucestershire, had been occupied since the early 1980s (Littlewood *et al.*, 1998).

There are three basic types of earth-sheltered dwellings. The first is known as the 'exposed south wall' type. This, as the name suggests, is very much focused on solar gain and achieves this through exposing all windows and doors to the south and enveloping the rest of the building in earth. This is by far the most common type of earth-sheltered home in Britain with 17 of the 27 sites falling within the category. The popularity of this type is possibly due to the fact that from the southern aspect it can look very conventional, can provide the occupants with views and, more importantly for some, have much (if not all) of their heating needs achieved through solar gain.

The second type of earth-sheltered dwellings is less able to collect solar heat and may be less popular in terms of sustainability. This alternative has been classed as the 'rooflight' type, where all light penetrates through shafts. As of 1998 there was only one such rooflight type in the UK, 'Undermill' in Hertfordshire, built in 1992. The third type is a variation of the rooflight home, classed by Littlewood *et al.* as the 'sunken courtyard type'. It is probably fair to say that the courtyard type is a hybrid of the rooflight type. The most significant difference is that instead of light entering individual rooms directly through domes in the roof, light enters through conventional vertical windows which face onto open courtyards and provide the necessary light. In the study conducted by Littlewood *et al.* they found that there was only one such dwelling in the UK, near Bradford upon Avon.

One of the sustainable aspects of earth-sheltered dwellings is in terms of land use, since the earth-sheltered roofs are often used as gardens ('No Man's Land' in Wadebridge, Cornwall, and Caer Llan in Monmouth). An additional advantage is that they can be less intrusive into the landscape, which was a factor in allowing the Hockerton development to proceed on (or under) green belt land in Nottinghamshire. However, the most sustainable aspect of earth-sheltered dwellings is probably the fact that they reduce space-heating requirements, although an additional factor could be that they reduce the materials needed in construction.

The Hockerton Project

Background to the project

As the Hockerton development (see Plate 13.1) is the largest earth-sheltered residential project in the UK it is appropriate to look at this interesting project in more detail. Not only is it the largest, it also has the most residential units and is the first to aim for self-sufficiency in all aspects. The original aim at Hockerton was the development of five ecologically sensitive homes in a rural setting, built on a 10-hectare site. The extensive size of the site was necessary to enable the occupants to be self-sufficient in food, water and energy, with land being set aside for agriculture.

The homes were designed by Brenda and Robert Vale, architects who had designed and built similar energy-efficient and autonomous single dwellings elsewhere in the East Midlands. The occupiers of the dwellings then treated much of the work as a self-build project, and although there were five families involved in the project, the varying degrees of construction skills and experience meant that minor contracting out was required. The level of outside skill that was required was reduced by the fact that the design was relatively simple. Work began on-site in August 1996 with the first of the five homes being occupied in March 1998 and the last being occupied in September of the same year.

Construction

The five-unit terrace is principally concrete. The floor slabs and roof are 300 mm reinforced concrete, the back wall is 450 mm concrete and the whole development is

Plate 13.1 Earth-sheltered housing at Hockerton, Nottinghamshire. Note solar roofing, earth bank and intensive horticulture: Gavin Tunstall.

encased in approximately 500 mm of earth to provide additional insulation. It should be pointed out that the depth of earth on the Hockerton units are less than elsewhere and a third of the depth that Littlewood *et al.* suggest as an optimum thickness for the UK climate. For example, Underhill has only 300 mm of earth covering and requires a central heating system, and Carpenter (1994) estimated that this meant that heating costs of £500 per annum were to be expected. It should be pointed out that this dwelling is near Huddersfield in Yorkshire and 400 m above sea level so the climate would be considered harsher than the lower-level site in Nottinghamshire.

Hockerton overcomes the reduced soil covering by ensuring that all the external concrete walls are insulated by a 300 mm expanded polystyrene surround. The net result is a very high level of thermal insulation with the roof, walls and ground floor having a U-value of $0.11 \, \text{W/m}^2\text{K}$. Placing the insulation on the external side of the concrete walls ensures that the house does not 'overheat' when occupied. The heat within internally insulated rooms are prone to react suddenly to occupation and heat generated from electrical items. Littlewood *et al.* cite a visit to Caer Llan where a study bedroom experienced a temperature rise of 5 degrees after being occupied for only 10 minutes by 12 University of Glamorgan students. This is an unfortunate side effect of over-insulating the interior walls where any passive heat gain is not stored in the mass of the building, but kept in the air temperature by the insulation. Placing the insulation on the outside of the mass results in air temperature changing slowly as the heat is stored in the massive structure, which then finds it difficult to dissipate into the surrounding soil and is slowly charged back into the dwelling.

Space heating

Although very well insulated, the five homes need to gain heat from somewhere, and this is achieved through a conservatory, which is built the length of the terrace and collects solar gain from its south-facing aspect. The windows separating the main habitable parts of the dwellings from the conservatory are triple-glazed with low-emissivity coatings. Due to its site, even in mid-winter solar energy is collected by the glazed conservatory and passed through the unit. In addition to the solar gain, the homes are so well insulated that occupancy itself provides a heat source, and the concrete mass of the building fabric acts as a heat store, retaining heat when the air temperature drops below that of the concrete. Using the fabric of the building as a 'storage heater' does mean that the walls should remain free of wallpaper and the floors free of carpet (clay tiles are used), both of which can inhibit heat conductivity.

Water use

Potable water is collected from the rainwater falling on the large area that is the conservatory roof and is then filtered and collected for drinking. Water for washing and laundry is collected and stored in a reservoir at the north end of the site. All waste water and sewage flows through a reed bed system that cleans the water before it enters a recreational lake situated to the front of the dwellings. Sludge does build up and has to be removed at certain intervals. Only certain types of detergent can be used in the showers, sinks and laundries, as the reed bed is fragile when confronted with harsher modern detergents. All water-using facilities, such as toilets and showers, incorporate water-saving features.

Electricity

Electricity is still required, even though much effort is made to reduce energy use, both through the use of easily accessible technology such as low-energy lightbulbs, and development-wide design features (e.g. the cold stores at each end of the terrace and buried beneath the same soil that insulates the dwelling; these are large concrete pipes, in which fresh food can be stored at around refrigeration temperatures without any need for electricity use). A wind turbine was seen as providing the electricity required on site; however, initial problems with obtaining planning permission meant that for the first couple of years the site had to rely on mains electricity. Once the wind turbine became operational, reliance on the grid reduced substantially, but not entirely. Electricity has to be used for water heating: one-fifth of hot water comes from an immersion heater; the remainder is heated through an air-to-water pump located in the conservatory.

As part of the government's drive for energy efficiency, the Hockerton site was monitored in terms of energy consumption. They found that each house used around 11 kWh per day over a twelve-month monitoring period. Unsurprisingly, due to reduced use of lighting and more time spent outdoors, summer energy use was around 25 per cent lower than in the winter. It is estimated that the energy use at Hockerton is around one-third of a conventional home of a similar size. In addition, the temperature in the homes remains relatively stable fluctuating between 17°C in the winter and over 24°C in the summer. The occupants did admit to using supplementary heating at times over the winter, and some occupants found that the homes were sometimes too hot and that there was no scope for opening windows.

As the dwelling is designed to build up reservoirs of heat slowly and then to store the heat within the building, ventilation is clearly an issue. Too much ventilation and the heat 'capital' is lost; too little and the dwelling becomes over stuffy. The Vales designed a mechanical ventilation system to overcome this and the intention was to run this continuously over the winter, drawing the incoming air through ducting at ceiling level in the solar corridor and permitting heat exchange. The residents did not use this as designed over the winter of the monitoring period, and this created problems with condensation and mildew.

BRESCU concluded that many of the elements of the housing at Hockerton could be replicated in more mainstream developments. These included: the level of insulation; the use of thermal mass as a heat store; the greater use of renewable energy for developments; the use of heat pumps to harness the heat in a conservatory to produce domestic hot water. They found the five units were built to a comparable cost to conventional housing, although they pointed out that the self-build element of the work distorts a simple comparison.

Evaluation: the scope for further innovation in housing development

The scope for innovation

The foregoing discussion and case study examples of this chapter provide a fair benchmark against which we may consider the future scope and potential for innovation in housing development. Much of the previous research focus has been directed towards a deeper understanding of the reasons underlying the lack of progress in making change and in introducing innovative solutions to housing development problems. There is much evidence to suggest that despite the fact that new technologies are available, they are not being adopted by the house-building industry to a satisfactory extent.

Rather than re-iterating the problems, it is perhaps useful at this stage of the book to consider what needs to be done. This can be tackled by setting out a framework criterion or set of conditions which need to be fulfilled if the house-building industry and its products are to become more innovative in nature.

Conditions for increased innovation in house-building

The self-build process provides an opportunity to expand the role for innovative solutions. Those who undertake self-build are, by virtue of the route to housing provision, not tied to a 'standard' house type or housing form. The reality of those who undertake self-build suggests that such households are inherently more adventurous and more likely to want to put their own 'stamp' on their dwelling. Herein lies an opportunity for more experimental housing, and an expansion of the self-build route to new housing can only enhance the opportunities for more innovative solutions.

If we are to see more innovative solutions in the housing development and housing construction process, then the house-building industry needs to find ways in which risk in the market can be minimised. Research consistently shows that the volatility of the housing market militates against more daring solutions and house-builders look for more 'conservative' solutions. The current planning policy, which has shifted house-builders increasingly towards brownfield sites and conversions, may assist the process of innovative thinking, but in the absence of subsidy or some other form of 'cushion', house-builders will continue to do things as they have always done: by building to the public's perception of 'speculative housing'.

Where building standards are more closely regulated, or where there is a quality 'norm', there may be scope for improving the amount of sustainable and energy-efficient housing. The social housing sector is an area where higher quality standards can be enforced and there are a number of schemes around the country now adopting more innovative technical solutions to improve building performance and energy consumption. That said, the balance between affordable housing regulated by building standards and methods of procurement (for example, those set out in the 1998 Egan report) and the subsidy system is a delicate one. It is sometimes the case that the Housing Corporation will pay subsidy at a greater rate than 100 per cent of build costs in order to achieve a certain standard, or to realise a 'flagship' scheme. However, in many cases, social housing is built to a tight timetable and budget which allows very little scope for experimentation in housing design or function.

Innovation is also unlikely to flourish in the absence of greater transparency of information about the benefits of sustainable features. People are aware that money can be saved if they purchase a home that is 'energy-efficient'. But the savings made on costs in use need to be balanced against potential additional costs of, for example, servicing and maintenance of devices that are not commonly installed.

Perhaps more significantly, households are often unsure about the 'costs versus value added' question which relates to more innovative housing solutions. That is to say, whilst costs can be saved by having a house that is more 'energy-efficient' or one which has a wealth of 'sustainable features', there is no guarantee that this type of house will appreciate in value as quickly as a more conventionally built one. It is no use to the UK owner-occupier to find that an intelligent and sustainable house saves him 50 per cent of energy costs if the dwelling only appreciates in value half as quickly as a conventional house. What matters in terms of the financial equation over the period of the life of the dwelling is not the costs saved, but the value accrued!

Better understanding and appreciation of the nature of the emerging housing demand is a prerequisite to expanding the number of homes built in an 'innovative' way. The greater part of current household demand is estimated to be in the form of single-person households. Yet this group is by no means homogenous; it is made up of young people leaving home earlier, people separating and elderly lone people. Younger people are generally believed to be more amenable to new and high-tech solutions and here there is an opportunity for the house-building industry to meet a specific demand. But the level to which housing should be made 'intelligent' is not easy to gauge. Busy people usually want easy and accessible solutions, particularly those facing challenging family situations, for example lone parents. If innovative and intelligent solutions are to be widely adopted, it is very important that the features incorporated in new homes should make plain the benefits and not just the 'wizardry' of the technology.

Discussion points

1   Discuss the way in which the term 'innovation' can be applied in the context of the house-building industry and its development processes.
2   Identify the main barriers to innovation in house-building and analyse how more innovative practices might be introduced.
3   Analyse the merits and problems of the 'self-build' route to housing development.
4   With the use of case study examples, show how 'intelligent' and 'green' development solutions can meet the contemporary housing needs of twenty-first century Britain.
5   Evaluate the hypothesis in relation to house-building innovation that what is needed is not 'intelligent housing' but 'intelligent people'!

Key reading

A good basic text on innovation in the dwelling house is Vale and Vale, *Design for a Sustainable Future* (1993). The self-build market is covered in the report by Barlow *et al.*, *Homes to DIY for* (2001) and the article by Nicol and Hooper, 'Contemporary change and the house-building industry' (*Housing Studies*, 1999). Websites on the BRE's INTEGER house and the 'Bedzed' development (Beddington Zero Energy Development, London Borough of Sutton) are highly recommended.

Part Five

Conclusions

Chapter 14

Summary, conclusions and reflections

Andrew Golland and Ron Blake

Retrospect and prospect

> Britain is the quintessential example of a society obsessed with housing values ... The
> obsession with housing has diverted resources away from more productive activities. It is
> sometimes alleged, for instance, that Britain has invested too much in bricks and mortar.
> Clearly though, to have any economic significance, this needs to be true of the amount
> of resources spent on new house-building, and not just the amount of money spent on
> recycling second-hand houses. In fact, new house-building activity in Britain has been
> low by international standards.
>
> (Bootle, 1996: 83)

There is a paradox at the centre of the debate on housing development today. In
some senses, housing development has assumed a high profile role in the public's
mind and media focus, as new exciting development in our city centres makes a
contribution to the urban renaissance policy agenda. Environmental concerns inad-
vertently push housing development up the political agenda, as central and local
government attempt to steer ever more development onto brownfield sites. The
buoyancy of the housing market and the British pre-occupation with home-
ownership have bought the issue of house-building more closely into focus as people
ask whether new development can bring about more affordable homes.

At the same time it can equally strongly be argued that housing development
is declining in importance both as a policy issue and in the minds of the general
public. While land recycling and the brownfield site development have become key
features of the housing debate, the public in general are more interested in 'house
recycling' and the exchange of second-hand homes. Without much ado, house-
building rates have fallen to their lowest point for several decades, begging a
question about which agency – government or the private sector – will be responsible for raising completions to a level that can accommodate growing household
numbers. Housing development has effectively become de-politicised. The political
dogma of the 1970s and 1980s which overhung the development debate has evap-
orated. The re-formed political parties see speculative development as playing the
key role in new provision, with housing associations providing a fall-back position
for those outside the housing market.

Speculative developers, for their part, are not committed to any specified
production targets and will build housing provided there is a return. Developers are

increasing their marketing activities to meet the demand for new housing products, especially focusing on brownfield sites, high-density and mixed-use development solutions. In doing so, they are making strong objections to the planning process where they see insufficient land supply.

The institutional content in which housing development takes place is also a present concern. There is no what might be termed house-building 'profession', leading to problems of recruitment at all levels. The need for closer co-operation between the industry, social housing providers and policy makers has never been greater, particularly as housing markets across Europe look to converge.

This chapter identifies several of these key themes, expanding them in a forward looking way.

The de-politicisation of housing production

> Housing politics used to be about accommodating the poorest. Now it concerns the perils of prosperity.
>
> (Walker, 2002: 12)

Housing production, which can be broadly regarded as the 'sum' of housing development activity, was, in the past, a highly politicised issue. Once, the concern was with which political party in government could achieve the highest number of completions in a single year. Against a backdrop of significant housing shortage, this was an entirely understandable, if not commendable, objective. Failure to deliver enough new homes could lead to failure at the electoral ballot box.

The solution to housing shortages was politicised, however, in another important way. From the 1960s onwards, it became evident that the Conservative Party was to be the party of the private sector and importantly, owner-occupied provision, whereas the Labour Party was more keen to promote council and social housing. These associations are most readily identified via studies of housing output during the 1970s and 1980s. Housing development tended to be seen by each of the political parties as a product of their own ideologies; the Conservative Party wishing to promote home-ownership, personal responsibility and an increased role for the private house-building industry, with the Labour Party promoting social housing to a greater extent and (during the 1970s in particular) combining this with a strongly interventionist and redistributive agenda aimed at the land market.

These policies largely reflect what is now known as 'Old Labour' and the 'New Right' (old conservatism transformed to Thatcherite laissez-faire policies). The early 1990s marked a change in thinking in both major parties; in their place came 'New Labour' and a Conservative Party adopting policies that might best be described as a 'watered down' version of Thatcherism. This shift in the political spectrum has resulted in a framework for housing development in which policies are broadly convergent.

New Labour has embraced the market and private-sector provision with the result that there has been no significant shift since 1997 in the balance of output between private and social sector providers; the private house-building industry has continued having a very significant role. The Conservative Party, for its part, has not produced any evidence to suggest it would try to erode of the social housing sector; indeed, much was achieved during the early 1990s to ensure that planners had increased powers to deliver affordable housing in new developments.

Housing development is now placed firmly within a market environment. While governments will intervene to provide affordable housing where markets are failing (most evidently in London and the South East), it looks unlikely that they will attempt to solve the problem by intervening in the land market or by introducing prohibitively high development taxation; whilst measures such as development tariffs are being considered, they will be very closely evaluated before being introduced. The current government knows that it will be difficult to deliver the required number of homes without the co-operation of the private house-building industry, which is currently facing the new challenges of brownfield sites and denser development solutions under PPG3. Indeed it will be fully aware that new housing output fell to a record low for the year 2001 and will be concerned to ensure that development levels are increased, particularly to combat the problem of the strength of the housing market.

All major political parties can now be expected to promote housing development policies which attune to the market environment. Owner-occupation will be promoted where economic conditions allow; where the market fails to provide, governments will resort to some form of affordable provision within the constraints of the budget allocated for housing.

Increasing choice and diversity in housing development

> The government believes that it is important to help create mixed and inclusive communities which offer a choice of housing and lifestyle. It does not accept that different types of housing and tenures make bad neighbours. Local planning authorities should encourage the development of mixed and balanced communities: they should ensure that new housing developments help to secure a better social mix by avoiding the creation of large areas of housing of similar characteristics.
>
> (DETR, 2000b)

An important symptom of the de-politicisation of housing development is increased choice and diversity. While this is significant in terms of the form of housing being developed, it is particularly important in respect to the tenure of new-build.

Diversification in new-build product has become a feature of the de-politicisation of housing development, where recent governments have encouraged social housing development away from local authorities and towards housing associations, which are now providing a wide range of affordable housing. At the same time, further liberalisation of the system of housing finance has broadened the scope for smaller investors to acquire private rented housing to let. A particularly significant recent issue has been 'buy-to-let'.

Housing associations, via Circular 6/98, now have the scope to develop new homes across a range of tenures. This is a flexible approach allowing affordable housing to be provided to suit market conditions at a local level. In areas where there look to be long-term difficulties of affordable housing, local authorities, via housing associations, can develop social-rented homes. These can be retained as affordable housing in perpetuity. In areas where there are already a significant number of owner-occupied homes at low prices, there is little point in building social-rented housing; under these circumstances it is usually better that public subsidy, if available, be directed towards making new (owner-occupied) homes even more affordable.

Whether it is right for the state to subsidise new social-rented housing development, even in areas where house prices are very high, is debatable. Whilst there have always been a significant number of households who cannot gain access to the housing market (because of lack of employment), there are nevertheless a further large number of households in work who aspire to home-ownership, but cannot raise the necessary levels of finance because of low wages. The development of low-cost home-ownership and shared-equity properties meets this demand to some extent. However, we must ask whether subsidies for social-rented housing, so often the key recommendation of housing needs studies, should be re-directed towards mainstream private-sector lending (i.e. to banks and building societies) to reduce the cost of home-ownership for households who might otherwise 'waver' between the two tenures.

Housing markets and the declining role of housing development

> The suggestion that supply does not matter will seem bizarre to most people. It means that building several hundred thousand additional homes in the South East would not help relieve today's supply shortages, nor would it have any impact on house prices.
>
> (Stewart, 2002: 8)

The relationship between housing markets and new housing development is a complex one which has come under particular scrutiny in recent years as development has fallen to historically low levels. Statistics invariably show that where house prices are high, the price of land is also high. Thus, the argument runs, house prices determine land prices: where house prices are valuable, so land becomes valuable; where house prices are low, land is cheap. There is merit in the direction of this argument, although it may not fully explain the relationship. Where developers find a particularly attractive or 'desirable' location, they can, under some circumstances, create their own 'market'. Similarly, where they build on already used sites (and hence the location cannot be said to be in any way 'different'), developers can create a new 'market' by developing new housing 'products'. Under these circumstances, developers take a 'view' on land prices and calculate house prices from what they have paid for the land and what it has cost to build.

Developers are inclined to blame the planning system for the high cost of land (and hence the high price of housing). If more land were to be released, so the argument runs, then its price would fall and in turn, so would the price of housing. There is substance in this argument, since if supply could be increased to such a level that there was a surplus of housing relative to households, then its price would eventually fall. Researchers also argue that highly priced housing results from supply inelasticity, an inefficient planning and development process; and new building not keeping pace with demand: arguments that developers readily seize upon.

The price of new housing is, however, not only a function of supply inefficiencies, we would argue, but also of the buoyancy of the national (regional and local) economy. If an economy is very strong, and, importantly, there is availability of credit, then even significant releases of land might make little impact in lowering the price of housing; the planning system might be considerably relaxed without much effect on house prices; it is not a necessary consequence of increased housing supply that housing is made more affordable. If sufficient credit is available, additional housing supply may simply act as a sponge for more money. Investors provide more expensive housing for rent, and home-owners pay more to consume housing. Housing 'need' in its broadest sense (household-dwelling units equation) is met, but affordability is not dealt with. It is the 'money versus bricks and mortar' equation that matters as much as the 'household versus dwelling units' equation; we argue that the current level of house prices in the UK today reflects not only problems with the planning system but also the success of the economy and the availability of mortgage finance.

Perhaps the greatest challenge for the development industry lies in matching supply with significant variations in regional demand. While the South East and Greater London have significant housing shortages, particularly in affordable housing, large run-down estates exist in other parts of the country, where no-one wants to live. Some house-builders will not have to be concerned with these variations as they do not operate across regional markets. The larger companies, however, have constantly to be aware of the way in which the national housing market is shifting. There are at least three key drivers governing the relationship between regional housing markets. The first is economics, the second population profile and the third social trends. Economics is a key factor, and households priced out of the market in one region can be expected to look for work in another (the problem of 'key workers' in Greater London and the South East). Highly paid work draws in households until the price of housing reaches such a level that it becomes unaffordable. The price then falls back in that region to an affordable level. In the past, there has been much attention in research to the 'ripple effect', whereby house prices in one region begin to rise, following a fall in other regions. Clever developers can time their land acquisitions and production sales to maximise profit in line with (regional) housing market cycles. Sub-themes emerge in housing markets: an important driver since the early 1980s has been the growing gap between those on very high and those on very low incomes. A significant number of households in the South East, for example, have sufficient wealth or income to have purchased a second home elsewhere in the country. Others have sufficient income to retire early and build a home for themselves away from the larger urban areas. In recent years, this has been an important driver for new development in locations such as Norfolk and Lincolnshire.

The population profile is changing, creating new demand for house-builders. Households are getting smaller with most leading-edge reports suggesting that 80 per cent of all future housing demand will come from single-person households. Social trends and, in particular, increases in the divorce rate are creating a demand for new housing, especially as it is a product which is easy to maintain. As may be expected, much of this demand is centred on the larger urban areas. This creates a new focus for house-builders who are now looking to develop smaller units, particularly flats in the cities, while at the same time continuing to develop their traditional low-rise estates at the urban fringe and in the countryside. Regional focus is a key determinant of the relative success of urban schemes, particularly conversions. Whereas the larger cities such as London, Manchester and Birmingham have seen considerable success in city centre developments, the provincial cities such as Nottingham, Leicester and Leeds have taken a while to catch up. As with the mainstream housing market, timing is critical to involvement in regional housing markets.

The outlook seems bright for housing developers at the beginning of the twenty-first century. A key driver of housing market demand is affordability. Traditionally banks and building societies have measured 'affordability' in a fairly simple way: by the house price/income ratio. More recently, however, commentators from the financial institutions have made much of the prevailing rate of interest, which, at the time of writing in autumn 2002, is at a historically low rate. Although the house price:income ratio is low in many places, so the argument goes, affordability remains good. Increasing disposable income, combined with ever more targeted mortgage and loan packages, is likely to fuel the demand for new-build housing for some time yet.

The growing importance of brownfield site development

> City living has not, traditionally, been a very British thing, at least for anyone with choice. The middle-class ideal was a semi or detached house with a big garden in a quiet suburb or, even better, a place in the country near a convenient train line to town. When manufacturing industries gradually collapsed and great swathes of streets were replaced in the 1960s with dual carriageways, subways and office blocks, the death of our city centres seemed assured.
>
> (McConnell, 1999)

Government has set out clear aims and targets for the proportion of homes to be developed on brownfield sites. As we have shown in this book, the target varies considerably depending on where one happens to be in the country. Regions such as Greater London and the North West naturally have higher 'brownfield' targets as a greater proportion of the land area is already brownfield. Regions such as the East Midlands and Yorkshire and Humberside have lower targets for land recycling.

The housing development industry has generally risen well to the challenge of brownfield site development, although there are some very clear 'Urban Task Force Leaders' and some (of the largest house-builders) who are not yet involved. Many developers have been caught out by the policy change and, having no land bank, are forced into brownfield site developments. At the local level, there are specialist companies who have followed the example of firms such as Urban Splash and renovate and rehabilitate old factories, warehouses and space over shops.

'Brownfield site development' however covers many different scenarios. It is often the case that a 'brownfield site' is, for example, an old hospital standing in extensive grounds. The 'brownfield site challenge' is in practice, under these circumstances, a case of renovating the hospital buildings (usually for flats) and then building new homes in the grounds (a similar exercise to conventional 'greenfield site' development. A very different proposition is an old mill building with very little space around it, located in a city centre. The latter is a much more challenging site requiring the developer to think outside the conventional mode of house-building.

The success of the brownfield site development policy has depended (and indeed will do in the future) on confidence in the housing product. While brownfield sites also produce traditional low-rise 'estate-type' development, more often than not they produce high-density dwellings, usually flats and terraces. The marketing of such development has had to be expertly done, as historically people in this country have shied away from flats. In London this is not so much the case, but in cities in the Midlands and the North such as Nottingham and Manchester, city-centre living in flats was something of the very distant past. Indeed, a key factor in the success of the new conversion market has been location. Where there is an established market in the housing 'product' then the new forms of development are easily subsumed in the evolving housing market.

In many cities, however, it has taken a substantial amount of new development to create the 'market' in order that the 'new' housing product can be traded, providing confidence in property values. Once the market is up and running then more development follows. The city-centre conversions market in cities such as Birmingham, Nottingham and Leeds has been energised in this way.

Developing housing in unconventional forms is of course risky. It is no coincidence that the first significant tranche of residential conversions took place in London, the city where values and house prices were highest. Developers realised that if the experiment did not work there, then there would be little point in trying it elsewhere, as development costs can be higher than for new-build. The trend spread most readily to cities with watersides.

The burning question affecting the development of buildings converted to residential is: 'can it last?'. Initially it should be pointed out that a very significant number of city centre homes have already been created during the last three to four years. In this respect the policy has been highly successful and the local authorities behind the schemes can take a good deal of the credit for promoting them. The potential for more conversions and brownfield site developments more generally is limited by supply and demand factors. Clearly, the opportunities for conversions are becoming more limited as sources of supply run out. On the demand side, it is frequently pointed out that the market for city centre living is one limited to younger and single households, who place a high preference on the convenience and proximity of shops and leisure facilities. Families, who usually require some play space or garden, and in time, schooling, are much more limited in their choice; moving families back into the city centres still seems to be a long way off, particularly as the best schools are often to be found in suburban and rural locations.

The market for city centre apartments has undoubtedly been fuelled by private landlords and investors. A significant injection of finance into this sector via such initiatives as 'buy-to-let' has increased the level of activity. There is currently (September 2002) an over-supply of apartments to rent and rents are falling in response. The national press frequently report that returns are insufficient or dangerously close to break-even level. Without an expansion of this form of demand, it may be difficult to increase the level of development for this form of housing.

The consumer and housing development

> Understanding customers' needs is fundamental in any market. In the new-build market it is clear that customers are prepared to pay for a premium product but only if the quality in design, construction and aftercare is delivered.
>
> (New Homes Marketing Board: Halifax plc, 2001: 3)

The consumer is being given an increasingly higher profile in the minds of developers. Developers know that if they are to compete effectively in the wider housing market, then their products must be distinct, well targeted and affordable. This is a difficult task against a background of rising land prices which make it difficult to keep sales competitive and ensure that sites are fully exploited via design.

New homes are, in the eyes of a large segment of the public, in direct competition with the second-hand market. Would-be purchasers of new homes normally have regard to the opportunity cost of buying a new dwelling. Second-hand housing, particularly that built before 1945 often has more generous accommodation (for example compare modern town houses with pre-war terraces) and, in many cases, is built to higher standards. Semi-detached inter-war housing can compete well in the family market with its modern 'equivalent' since the latter usually has far less space and garden.

As a result, housing developers expend considerable energies marketing the benefits of new homes. A key trend helping the sales of new homes is changing lifestyles. New homes are marketed as being 'convenient', 'easy to maintain' and 'cheap to run'. Developers have seen the growth in working hours for many households as an opportunity to market new homes. Despite the fact that the UK's DIY industry has never been so popular, for many households, housing maintenance and improvement is still a real challenge. For smaller and single-person households, which will form the main growth focus over the coming years, maintenance-free and easy-to-run new homes will provide an attractive solution.

A key marketing thrust at the current time is being directed towards the sale of new apartments in city centres. These homes are being promoted to appeal in particular to young, busy, professional people who want to be near work, shops and leisure facilities. The marketing has to be good, when it is considered that in many towns and cities this form of accommodation is very inferior in terms of space and recreational area; that is to say, only a very low proportion of apartments have garden space, while some are sold without parking provision. The price is often high, and in some areas of the country the opportunity cost of a city-centre apartment would be a two or three bed country cottage with a reasonable sized garden. Apartments are however being sold in such a way as to appeal to buyers who are not looking to the conventional market, but want a completely different (life-style) housing product. But the jury is still very much 'out' on the robustness of this market over the next few years.

House-builders can market new homes on the basis of additional features provided over and above those in second-hand ones. These 'features' can be a range of things; from a simple double-glazing unit through to a fully integrated grey-water system. Information technology requirements and expectations are growing and new homes are now generally equipped with cabling to suit all forms of IT.

The challenge for house-builders, however, is to decide the appropriate level of provision. A new home can be expected to be different from a second-hand one in providing higher quality in some shape or form. However, new homes which are over-specified with complex, challenging features can cause problems for sales. This is not only for buyers using the features, but also in the sales process where bank and building society valuers may not accept the price premium added by the developer (and agreed with the buyer) for additional features. Lenders may see additional features in some circumstances as being a potential problem, leading to the conclusion that they actually devalue the home, not add to it. Innovation in the new-build product needs to be carefully introduced so as to ensure that the additional costs of inclusion do not outweigh the value added to the home.

The particular requirements of the consumer need to be considered in each and every local circumstance. The supply of new homes to the local market needs to be considered against the supply of second-hand homes. This relationship has important consequences for the pricing of new housing. A developer building in two locations near to each other may price homes very differently if one site competes better with the second-hand market than another. The price, affordability and saleability of new homes depends on a complex mix of factors including location, house-type mix, strength of the second-hand market and the quality of new build. Although the housing market is not entirely transparent, most house-buyers know a good 'deal' when they see one, and developers have a challenging task meeting local housing demand in the light of increased consumer expectations.

Above all, new homes have to be safe. This goes without saying, recent years have hazards hitting the housing market, such as telecommunication masts. Flooding has become a high-profile issue over the past five years with large areas of Yorkshire and Sussex, for example, being exposed. With an increased proportion of brownfield sites being developed, the risk of contamination also increases, bringing with it the need for developers to overcome any consumer fears about purchasing housing there. In an increasingly litigious and insurance-aware society, house-builders will have in the future to be able to ensure both minimum as well as maximum standards of building provision.

Towards a European approach to housing development?

> Most Britons are home-owners, with 68 per cent of households in the tenure. The majority of dwellings are also single-family houses – in England in 2000, 82 per cent of households live in houses, 16 per cent in self-contained accommodation. The housing stock, furthermore, is relatively old in comparison to many other European countries – with 41 per cent built before 1945; another 45 per cent between 1945 and 1984; and only 13 per cent since the mid-1980s. Housing stock growth slowed from the 1970s, although it experienced a minor revival during the boom years of the 1980s. Since the early 1990s house-building has been at historically low levels, despite the sharp upswing in house prices since the mid-1990s.
>
> (Ball, 2002: 119)

As the quotation above suggests the UK housing system is a very particular one; in comparison with key trading partners such as the Netherlands, Germany and France, the UK is an owner-occupied system, with relatively old housing stock. This reflects relatively low levels of house-building and a very specific (speculative) mode of housing supply. Housing development challenges for other European countries have been greater in terms of meeting housing shortages and in many cases, social housing has been the preferred mode of provision. The system of housing finance in the UK remains relatively liberal compared with other European countries, and mortgage packages are very much more flexible. This in turn has helped the owner-occupied sector to flourish relative to other countries. There are further key differences. In mainland Europe planning systems are in the main more prescriptive, and in some cases (the Netherlands and Sweden being perhaps the best examples) underpinned by norms of municipal intervention in the land market. These approaches to making housing land available remain a far cry from the approach in the UK, which still operates largely on the basis of developer confidence in the housing market.

Despite the rather polarised nature of systems of housing supply, however, there is some evidence to suggest a degree of convergence in the way new housing is being developed. One emerging trend is the move in the UK towards developing city centres. A key thrust of the Urban Task Force agenda was to consider housing as a tool of regeneration. It based this notion to some extent on examples from abroad where many European cities have been developed with different building uses in close proximity and mixed use within single buildings being an acceptable mode of development. Importantly, cities outside London are now embracing the idea of developing flats in and around city centres, as is the norm in many urban areas outside the European capital cities. There is some way to go before developers in the UK swing completely away from suburban estates, but there is a significant change towards a more European way of life through re-vitalisation of former derelict urban areas.

The thrust towards city centre developments is bringing with it another trend more akin to mainland Europe, namely that of private renting. Apartments lent themselves to this sector particularly well because they are relatively cheap for investors to acquire and relatively cheap for tenants to rent. In the UK, this sector has grown in strength since 2000 on the back of a housing market boom, combined with financial packages such as 'buy-to-let'. London Residential Research (2002) calculates that up to 70 per cent of new residential units developed in London in the year 2001 were sold to investors. Were this trend to be repeated in other major UK towns and cities, we could see a significant expansion of the private-rented sector towards the levels of some other major European countries. Whether this can be achieved depends very much, we suggest, on whether rented housing can provide robust returns relative to other investments, and in particular equities.

Some of the most successful European housing development results from policy frameworks very different from those in the UK. Several North European and Scandinavian countries have managed housing output very efficiently to fit the housing market cycle. Furthermore they have targeted production of particular tenures to meet the economic conditions and in many developments owner-occupied and social housing sit side by side in an integrated way. These 'successful' developments are often enabled via a prescriptive land-use planning system combined with innovative techniques of land assembly.

The UK is still some considerable way from having the full range of policy mechanisms available to local authorities and other policy makers in other European countries. Solutions to problems of land assembly in this country fall either to the market or to compulsory purchase procedures; in other European countries, local authorities can employ additional mechanisms such as rights of pre-emption, statutory land pooling and the building rights model. Developers in those countries are well aware of the broad scope of public sector powers and this to some extent allows the public-sector to drive a hard bargain with respect to planning gain. Physical infrastructure provision, affordable housing and education or recreation contributions are all issues over which the local authority has a strong hand, particularly in a rising housing market. In the UK, the emphasis has always been very much with the local authority to see how much planning benefit can be 'extracted' from the developer.

Over the past decade, however, policy has moved in favour of the public sector to some extent, moving the UK more in the direction of mainland Europe. The planning system as a whole has tightened, giving development plans greater significance, and land supply has been more highly regulated as authorities are directed to focus on brownfield sites. There have been significant strides made to link together economic planning (in particular for affordable housing) and land-use planning to allow local authorities to capture some of the additional value that accrues with the grant of planning permission. Government is looking at mechanisms such as tariffs which could be used to better achieve both physical regeneration and mixed communities. These initiatives suggest that the policy framework is moving to attune more closely with that abroad.

The housing development process itself in the UK is becoming more varied. While the speculative process is likely to be maintained as the main mode of development, new forms of provision are emerging. The increasing significance of self-build as a way of accessing new owner-occupied housing is becoming apparent. In common with countries such as France and Germany, UK households are now increasingly realising the benefits of this route, both as a way of attaining a bespoke dwelling and a sound investment.

While there are aspects of housing development which appear to be moving closer together, there are others aspects which remain apart. The price of housing varies considerably across Europe. This is not at all surprising when the significant price differences within the UK itself are considered. Some argue that entry to the euro may help housing markets to converge, since prices will become more 'transparent'. This argument is, however, weak in the light of the 'north–south' divide in house prices within the UK. House prices tend to reflect local economic conditions and altering only the means of exchange is unlikely to change the intrinsic value of housing. Convergence in the level of mortgage rate lending, as has occurred in mainland Europe, also seems unlikely to bring about house-price convergence. Rather its impact may distort price levels and make them even more unequal. Taking again the case of the UK's north–south housing market divide, the solution to bringing house prices more in line across the country would seem to be to have differential interest rates, one high (for the South) and one low (for the North). Of course this situation cannot occur without one fundamental change to the UK's economy: the introduction of a second currency allowing different interest rates to be available at the same time. To bring house prices in line across Europe may thus require more currencies and not fewer.

The outstanding challenges for housing development today

> Our country, the United Kingdom, is 60 million acres in size. Some 59 million of us live on those 60 million acres. The area taken up by the homes of these 59 million people takes up less than 10 per cent of the land, a maximum of six million acres, but more probably just 4.4 million acres. It is impossible to settle on a more accurate figure as the statistics for most of the UK are estimates, drawn from samples, while the government of Northern Ireland has no figure at all for its residential acreage.
>
> (Cahill, 2001: 6)

There are perhaps two key outstanding challenges for housing development today: first, the need for improved information and an associated enhanced research programme, and second, the need for a more co-ordinated approach to solving the day-to-day problems of housing development.

The need for improved information and enhanced research is of paramount importance in informing the housing development agenda. The key conflict between development and environmental conservation is one which is played out largely in a vacuum. The size, for example, of the national housing 'footprint' is not known since it is not officially recorded. Whilst we know how many hectares change use from year to year, we do not know the base from which this takes place. Thus, the significance of the impact of the housing development 'problem' is difficult to gauge. Robust research into housing markets is in short supply; this is particularly the case for new development. Whereas the newspapers are full of articles on the housing 'market' (typically, how much 'prices have risen since last year') they rarely deal with new development, other than to provide examples of schemes. We are thus still largely ignorant as to whether, for example, developers charge too much (or too little?) for their products, whether new housing provides benefits for communities as a whole, or whether increased land supply will lead to an increase in affordable housing?

Public policy-making relies heavily on sound information and data in forming development decisions at the local level. Housing market research, housing needs studies and urban capacity assessments stand or fall on the basis of well sourced primary and secondary data. In certain areas, there have been significant improvements in data availability; one might mention house prices (HM Land Registry) or local income data (CACI). However, there are still many other areas where data are far from complete. Data on the housing development process are sparse. Land prices are notoriously difficult to come by, as are development costs. While speculative house-building firms are sometimes willing to provide information on a confidential basis, they do not share this information in the wider sphere. As a result, negotiations over land deals, affordable housing quotas and other forms of planning gain are often protracted. This all feeds into increased housing costs.

An additional problem is a lack of human resources. While skilled (on-site) labour shortages are of concern to the house-building industry, it is equally concerning to identify skills shortages amongst policy-making organisations and in particular, local authorities. Just at a time when central government appears to be putting into place a fairly focused regeneration programme, local councils find themselves short of planners, housing development officers and estate surveyors. To those in the university sector, this is perhaps of little surprise, considering the demise of many planning and estate development courses. The need for skilled personnel in the public sector has never been more acute: to bring about land assembly, to negotiate affordable housing quotas and to assess the viability of potential development areas.

If new housing is to be developed successfully, that is, to a high standard, and to affordable prices, then the key development institutions need to come together to generate solutions. This will be a great challenge. Currently 'housing problems' are seen as the domain of organisations such as the Housing Corporation, the

National Housing Federation and the Chartered Institute of Housing; organisations which look primarily to 'social' housing solutions. 'Development problems' fall within the domain of the industry and in particular the House Builders Federation. Problems relating to the financing of housing fall within the ambit of the Council of Mortgage Lenders, and, to a lesser extent the Royal Institution of Chartered Surveyors. Housing and planning problems are seen as a policy issue for organisations such as the Royal Town Planning Institute and the Town and Country Planning Association. Central government, whilst it is moving towards a regional housing solution to the problem of 'housing numbers', does not currently have the necessary structures to deliver successful housing development solutions on the ground.

What is needed is a single 'all-in-one-place' institutional body that can respond to the diverse challenges of modern housing development. This 'body' could act to promote housing development, to raise awareness of supply side obstacles, to provide innovative land assembly solutions and to encourage innovative housing construction techniques.

Appendix A
Chronology of housing related events

1801	Census of population first taken in Britain
1817	Owen's 'New Lanark' model village established near Glasgow
1841	Household data first collected as part of the Census
1842	Chadwick's report on the sanitary conditions of the labouring population
1845	Halifax Building Society founded
1848	Public Health Act, requiring sewers, ventilation and daylight in new housing
1853	Titus Salt's model village 'Saltaire' founded near Bradford
1858	Ordnance Survey resolves to map urban areas at 1:2,500 and 1:10,000 scales
1868	Artisans' and Labourers' Dwellings Act (Torrens Act) introducing the idea of slum clearance
1871	Local Government Board established to administer housing, and later planning, matters at national level
1872	Public Health Act requiring sanitary inspection by Local Authorities throughout the country
1875	Public Health Act requiring minimum street width and rear access in new housing: the end of back-to-back construction
1879	Cadbury's 'Bournville' model village established near Birmingham
1888	Lever's 'Port Sunlight' model village established near Liverpool
1890	Housing of the Working Classes Act giving local authorities discretionary power to build houses for need
1891	Overcrowding first investigated as part of the Census
1898	Ebenezer Howard's *Tomorrow: A Peaceful Path to Reform* published
1902	Ebenezer Howard's *Garden Cities of Tomorrow* published
1903	Letchworth Garden City established
1907	Hampstead Garden Suburb established
1909	Housing and Town Planning Act permitting planning schemes

1912	Unwin's pamphlet 'Nothing Gained by Overcrowding' published
1918	Tudor Walters report *Provision of Dwelling for the Working Classes* published
1919	Housing and Town Planning Act providing subsidies to build council houses and requiring planning schemes in certain areas
1920	Welwyn Garden City established
1923	Housing Act emphasising that local authorities should build high-quality homes for rent
	Le Corbusier's *Towards a New Architecture* published
1932	Town and Country Planning Act introducing the idea of development control including 'country' areas for the first time
1935	Restriction of Ribbon Development Act
1936	National House-Builders Registration Council (NHBRC) founded
1938	Green Belt (London and Home Counties) Act
1942	Scott report *Land Utilisation in Rural Areas* published, advocating control of urban sprawl to protect natural resources
	Uthwatt report *Compensation and Betterment* published
1944	Dudley report *The Design of Dwellings* published
	Abercrombie's *Greater London Plan* published
	White paper *The Control of Land Use* published
1945	Labour Party won the general election
1946	Thomas Sharp's *The Anatomy of the Village* published
	New Towns Act
1947	Town and Country Planning Act requiring development plans and development control everywhere
1951	Conservative Party returned to power at general election
1952	Town Development Act
	Government's *The Density of Residential Areas* published
1953	Historic Buildings and Ancient Monuments Act
1954	Development charge abolished
1955	Circular 42/55 *Green Belts* issued
	Ian Nairn's *Outrage* published
1956	Clean Air Act
	Housing Subsidies Act encouraging high-rise public sector housing
1957	Housing Act accelerating mass slum clearance
	Rent Act deregulating private-sector rents

1959	Conservative Party won the general election
1961	Parker Morris report *Homes for Today and Tomorrow* published
1962	Ministry of Housing and Local Government opens Northern Office in Manchester
	Ministry of Housing and Local Government's *Residential Areas: Higher Densities* published
1963	Greater London Council created
1964	Labour Party won the general election
	Housing Corporation established to encourage housing associations
1965	Planning Advisory Group (PAG) report *The Future of Development Plans* published
	Milner Holland report *Housing in Greater London* published, advocating fair rents
1966	The charity *Shelter* formed
	Government's 'Deeplish Study' (Rochdale), demonstrating feasibility of general housing improvement
1967	Ronan Point disaster in which a residential tower block partially collapsed following gas explosion
	Civic Amenities Act introducing urban conservation areas
	Land Commission Act giving central government wide powers of compulsory purchase
1968	Countryside Act including provision for country parks near centres of population
	White paper *Older Houses into New Homes* published
1969	Housing Act, advocating General Improvement Areas (GIA)
1970	Conservative Party won the general election
	Department of the Environment (DoE) formed from other ministries
	Circular 10/70 asking local authorities to ensure housing land supply
1971	Land Commission abolished
1972	Local Government Act heralding a major shake-up of local government
1973	NHBRC re-branded as the National House-Building Council (NHBC)
	Oscar Newman's *Defensible Space* published
	DoE's *Better Homes: The Next Priorities* published
1974	Labour Party won the general election
	Major shake-up of local government and planning responsibilities
	Essex County Council's *A Design for Residential Areas* published
	Housing Act providing for Housing Action Areas (HAAs)

1975   Community Land Act giving additional powers of land assembly to local authorities

1978   Inner Areas Act advocating partnerships to regenerate the older areas of cities

1979   Conservative Party won the general election

1980   Housing Act introducing option for council tenants to purchase homes below market value

1981   Brundtland Commission's *Our Common Future* published, articulating the principles of sustainable development

          Countryside and Wildlife Act requiring environmentally sensitive areas to be protected

1983   Consortium Developments formed to build housing-led 'new settlements' in the South East

          MIRAS introduced to assist owner-occupation

          Controversial programmes on Granada TV's *World in Action* leading to a downturn in timber-frame housing construction

1984   Building Act consolidating various building regulations

1985   Housing Association Act increasing the 'right to buy' discount

          White Paper *Lifting the Burden* published

          NHBC Building Control Services Ltd established

          Alice Coleman's *Utopia on Trial* published

1986   Housing and Planning Act introducing urban regeneration grant

          Greater London Council and six metropolitan county councils abolished

1987   Planning Use Classes Order revised to streamline development control

1988   Planning Policy Guidance (PPG) introduced

          Housing Act introducing 'tenants' choice' and near-market rents for social housing

1989   Regional Planning Guidance first published

1990   Town and Country Planning Act accompanied by 'daughter' acts on listed buildings and hazardous substances

          White Paper *This Common Inheritance: Britain's Environmental Strategy* published

          Environmental Protection Act introducing the idea of contaminated land registers on the 'polluter-pays' principle

1991   Planning and Compensation Act reinforcing the plan-led system

          City Challenge five-year regeneration initiative announced

	Property Misdescriptions Act making it an offence to promote false attributes of housing
1992	Audit Commission's *Building in Quality: A Study of Development Control* published
1993	Single Regeneration Budget set up to fund land assembly and reclamation
1994	English Partnership created
1995	Environment Act setting up the Environment Agency to co-ordinate monitoring of flooding, contaminated land and air pollution
1996	White Paper *Household Growth: Where Shall We live?* published
1997	Labour won the general election; DoE replaced by the Department of the Environment, Transport and the Regions (DETR)
1998	Countryside Agency formed to widen the rural agenda to include socio-economic issues
	New Deal for Communities announced, including funds for housing
	Egan Report *Rethinking Construction* published, advocating new approaches to procurement through partnering between constructors and suppliers
	DETR circular 6/98 on affordable housing in all tenures
	Private Finance Initiative pilot project for refurbishment of council estates
2000	Urban White Paper *Delivering an Urban Renaissance* published
	Rural White Paper *Our Countryside: The Future* published
	DETR/CABE report *By Design* published
	DETR *Tapping the Potential* (for urban housing capacity) published
2001	Labour won a second term at the general election
	DETR redefined as the Department of Transport, Local Government and the Regions (DTLR)
2002	DTLR abolished and planning and housing functions transferred to the Office of the Deputy Prime Minister (ODPM)
2003	Planning and Compulsory Purchase Bill before parliament

Note

Suggested further reading: Eleanor Smith Morris, *British Town Planning and Urban Design: Principles and Policies*, Harlow: Addison Wesley Longman, 1997.

Housing related organisations and websites

Age Concern
    Contact: www.silver-surfers.org/ageconcern
Alfred McAlpine Homes
    Contact: www.alfredmcalpine.com
The Association of British Insurers
    Contact: www.abi.org.uk
Audit Commission
    Contact: www.audit-commission.gov.uk
Barratt Homes
    Contact: www.barratthomes.co.uk
Beazer Homes
    Contact: www.beazer.co.uk
Beddington Zero Energy Development
    Contact: www.bedzed.org.uk
Bellway Homes
    Contact: www.bellway.co.uk
Berkeley Homes
    Contact: www.berkeleyhomes.co.uk
Brick Development Association
    Contact: www.brick.org.uk
The British Brick Society
    Contact: www.britishbricksoc.free-online.co.uk
British Geological Survey
    Contact: www.bgs.ac.uk
British Urban Regeneration Agency
    Contact: www.bura.org.uk, or www.sourceuk.net/articles/a01025.html
Bryant Homes
    Contact: www.bryant.co.uk/pattern
Building Research Establishment
    Contact: www.bre.co.uk
Cambridge Econometrics
    Contact: www.camecon.com

Central Statistical Office
Contact: www.statistics.gov.uk

Centre for Alternative Technology
Contact: www.cat.org.uk

Centre for Education in the Built Environment
. Contact: http://ctiweb.cf.ac.uk

Centre for Housing Policy
Contact: www.york.ac.uk/inst/chp

Centre for Research in Ethnic Relations
Contact: www.warwick.ac.uk/fac/soc/CREC_RC

Centre for Residential Development, Nottingham Trent University
Contact: www.construction.ntu.ac.uk

Chartered Institute of Building
Contact: www.ciob.org.uk

Chartered Institute of Building Services Engineers
Contact: www.cibse.org

Chartered Institute of Environmental Health
Contact: www.cieh.org

Chartered Institute of Housing
Contact: www.cih.org

Chartered Institute of Public Finance and Accountancy
Contact: www.cipfa.org.uk

Commission for Architecture and the Built Environment
Contact: www.cabe.org.uk

Commission for New Towns
Contact: www.archive.official-documents.co.uk/document/caboff/pubbod97/cnt.htm

Construction Industry Environmental Forum
Contact: www.ciria.org.uk/cief.htm

Construction Industry Research and Information Association
Contact: www.ciria.org.uk

Construction Industry Training Board
Contact: www.archive.official-documents.co.uk/document/caboff/pubbod97/citb.htm

Council for the Protection of Rural England
Contact: www.cpre.org.uk

Countryside Agency
Contact: www.countryside.gov.uk/index.htm

Crédit Lyonnais
Contact: www.creditlyonais.com

David Wilson Homes
Contact: www.dwh.co.uk

Demos
Contact: www.demos.co.uk

Department of Land Economy, University of Cambridge
Contact: www.landecon.cam.ac.uk

The Economist
Contact: www.economist.co.uk

Empty Homes Agency
Contact: www.emptyhomes.com

English Heritage
Contact: www.english-heritage.org.uk

English Partnerships
Contact: www.englishpartnerships.com

Estates Gazette
Contact: www.egi.co.uk

European Network for Housing Research
Contact: www.enhr.ibf.uu.se

Fabian Society
Contact: www.fabian-society.org.uk

Financial Times
Contact: http://news.ft.com/home/uk

Forum for the Future
Contact: www.forumforthefuture.org.uk

General Household Survey
Contact: www.doh.gov.uk/public/househol.htm

Government Actuary's Department
Contact: www.gad.gov.uk

Greater London Authority
Contact: www.london.gov.uk

Halifax Bank
Contact: www.halifax.co.uk/home/index.shtml

Health and Safety Executive
Contact: www.hse.gov.uk

Help the Aged
Contact: www.helptheaged.org.uk

Henley Centre
Contact: www.henleycentre.com

House Builders Federation
Contact: www.hbf.co.uk

Housing Corporation
Contact: www.housingcorp.gov.uk

The Housing Forum
Contact: www.thehousingforum.org.uk

Housing Research Foundation
Contact: www.housingresearch.org

Housing Research Group (at Anglia Polytechnic University)
Contact: www.be.anglia.ac.uk/phrg/phrg1.html

Institute for Fiscal Studies
Contact: www.ifs.org.uk

Institute of Materials
Contact: www.iom3.org

Institution of Civil Engineers
Contact: www.ice.org.uk

Institution of Structural Engineers
Contact: www.istructe.org.uk

International Federation For Housing and Planning
Contact: www.ifhp.org

Joseph Rowntree Foundation
Contact: www.jrf.org.uk

Land Registry HM
Contact: www.landreg.gov.uk

Landmark Information Group
Contact: www.landmark-information.com

Landscape Institute
Contact: www.l-i.org.uk

Local Government Association
Contact: www.lga.gov.uk

Local Government Management Board
Contact: www.lgmb.gov.uk

London Residential Research
Contact: www.egi.co.uk

MORI
Contact: www.mori.com

National Assembly for Wales
Contact: www.wales.gov.uk

National Audit Office
Contact: www.nao.gov.uk

National Building Agency
Contact: www.nationalbuildingagency.ie

National Dwelling and Household Survey
    Contact: www.statistics.gov.uk/STATBASE/xsdataset.asp?vlnk=115

National Family Formation Survey
    Contact: www.statistics.gov.uk/STATBASE/xsdataset.asp?vlnk=111

National Federation of Builders
    Contact: www.builders.org.uk

National Federation of Housing Associations
    Contact: www.housing.org.uk

National House-Building Council
    Contact: www.nhbc.co.uk

National Housing Condition Survey
    Contact: www.odpm.gov.uk

National Housing Federation
    Contact: www.housing.org.uk

National Land Use Database
    Contact: www.nlud.org.uk

National Radiological Protection Board
    Contact: www.nrpb.org

Nationwide Building Society
    Contact: www.nationwide.co.uk/hpi

Office for National Statistics
    Contact: www.statistics.gov.uk

Office of the Deputy Prime Minister
    Contact: www.odpm.gov.uk

Ordnance Survey
    Contact: www.ordsvy.gov.uk

Peabody Trust
    Contact: www.peabody.org.uk

Persimmon Homes
    Contact: www.persimmonhomes.com

Planning and Environmental Training
    Contact: http://bts.gov/DOCS/423.html

Planning Officers Society
    Contact: www.planningofficers.org.uk

Policy Studies Institute (PSI)
    Contact: www.psi.org.uk

Popular Housing Group
    Contact: www.popularhousing.org.uk

Promap
    Contact: www.prodat.co.uk

Quality of Life Capital
> Contact: www.qualityoflifecapital.org.uk

Redrow Homes
> Contact: www.redrow.co.uk

Roof
> Contact: www.roofmag.org.uk

Room
> Contact: www.room.org.uk

Royal Institute of British Architects
> Contact: www.architecture.com

Royal Institution of Chartered Surveyors
> Contact: www.rics.org.uk

Royal Town Planning Institute
> Contact: www.rtpi.org.uk

Secured by Design
> Contact: www.securedbydesign.com

Shelter
> Contact: www.shelter.org.uk

Society for the Protection of Ancient Buildings
> Contact: www.spab.org.uk

The Stone Federation
> Contact: www.stone-federationgb.org.uk

Town and Country Planning Association
> Contact: www.tcpa.org.uk

Urban and Economic Development Group
> Contact: www.urbed.co.uk

Urban Splash
> Contact: www.urbansplash.co.uk/us.php

Urban Villages Forum
> Contact: www.urban-villages-forum.org.uk

Valuation Office
> Contact: www.voa.gov.uk

Westbury Homes
> Contact: www.westbury-homes.co.uk

Wilcon Homes
> Contact: www.wilcon.co.uk

Wimpey Homes
> Contact: www.wimpeyhomes.co.uk

Glossary

Affordable housing Dwellings built specifically for those on incomes that deny them the opportunity to purchase or rent on the open market.

Aggressive ground conditions Conditions in the soil or sub-soil where chemical or physical action affects the durability of building structures.

Allocation Land identified in a local plan as appropriate for a specific land use in advance of any planning permission for that use.

Amenity A facility or environmental attribute that increases a place's residential desirability.

Ancillary use A use which is secondary to, but associated with, the main use, e.g. a car park for flats.

Aquifer A geological structure that acts as a reservoir, or conduit, for water.

Archaeological constraints area Shown in the local plan to indicate where development would be detrimental to archaeological remains.

Area of outstanding natural beauty An area of attractive countryside where there is a very strong presumption against development, e.g. the Chilterns.

Article 4 direction Removal by the local planning authority of permitted development rights to safeguard an amenity or the built heritage.

Backland Yards and rear gardens where space is frequently under-utilised.

Bad neighbour use A use not appropriate within a specific area, e.g. a haulage depot in a residential neighbourhood.

Biodiversity A term denoting a richness of plant and animal species, ecosystem complexity or genetic variation.

Blight A fall in property and amenity values caused by neglect, anti-social activity or vague planning proposals on adjacent land.

BRE Environmental Assessment Method (BREEAM) A system for the certification of housing based on modelling energy efficiency and environmental impact.

Brief A document drawn up by a client, developer, designer, consultant or planning authority setting out the parameters of a proposed scheme.

Brownfield site Land which is, or has been, developed with buildings or otherwise disturbed but is currently abandoned or under-utilised.

Building Regulations A set of national standards ensuring that buildings are constructed safely, durably and efficiently.

Built environment Those parts of the environment comprising buildings and the ancillary spaces between them.

Capacity assessment A method of analysing sites in terms of development opportunities and constraints and the anticipated impact on environmental stock.

Carrying capacity The level of population or physical development that can be supported by an area without degrading the visual environment, overloading the transport infrastructure or destroying natural habitats.

Catchment area The area surrounding a facility, e.g. a hospital or school, from which the great majority of users travel.

Cellular living A trend whereby the individual members of a household pursue their own interests in different spaces within their home.

Census of population A complete survey of the inhabitants of the United Kingdom every ten years, with sampling, estimates and updates in between.

Circular A government publication that gives advice to local authorities and other agencies on how to interpret national policy on specific issues

Commitment Land with an unexpired planning permission but not yet developed.

Community severance Separation of residents from community facilities or from each other caused by a new road or 'improvement' in traffic flow.

Commuted payments Contribution made by a developer towards the cost of providing or maintaining an off-site facility, e.g. affordable housing, or a play area.

Conservation The wise use and management of resources in the natural and built environments. Allows for sympathetic change and not to be confused with rigid preservation.

Conservation area Designation in the local plan relating to a part of the built environment judged to be of special architectural or historic interest that contributes to the area's character.

Consultation draft The first draft of a local plan, made publicly available for any organisation or individual to comment upon.

Contaminated land Land that contains concentrations of substances, e.g. asbestos, cadmium or arsenic, and likely to be harmful to humans or the natural environment.

Core and periphery A concept recognising that in any geographical space there is a relatively accessible and well developed centre and a less accessible and under-developed outer edge.

Curtilage The area containing a dwelling, its out-buildings and garden space normally co-extensive with ownership and regarded as a planning control unit.

Cut and fill A process in the construction of buildings on slopes whereby soil is cut away at high level and used to fill voids or create a platform at low level.

Defensible space Ground within a dwelling curtilage or group of dwellings that is visibly defined by walls, vegetation or a change of surface so as to deter interlopers and create territorial identity.

Demographic transition Changes in the size, density or distribution of the population on a scale that significantly alters the character of a place.

Density The degree of development within a given area, variously measured as persons per square kilometre, or number of dwellings per hectare.

Deposit draft The stage in the local plan review where initial public comments have been incorporated and made available for public inspection.

Derelict land Land so damaged by industrial and other uses that it requires special treatment before re-use. Not necessarily contaminated but visibly disturbed.

Design guide A non-statutory published explanation of design principles intended to assist developers in meeting environmental standards through their schemes.

Design statement A type of brief accompanying a planning application that amplifies the proposal with design-based reasoning.

Desire lines An imaginary straight line linking trip origins and destinations based on the largest number of people wanting to make a journey, e.g. from a cul-de-sac to the local primary school.

Detention basins (or ponds) Features designed to withhold stormwater to help reduce peak surface flow, assist absorption and improve water quality through sedimentation.

Development In planning terms any building operation or change of use between classes defined in the General Development Order. More generally, an increase in building construction or land occupancy for social or economic benefit.

Development corporation Generic term embracing government appointed bodies responsible for new towns and inner-urban regeneration in specified locations.

Development potential A measure of the accessibility and environmental capacity of an area's assets relative to a given demand for development.

Earth-sheltered houses Houses constructed with a significant proportion of the building in contact with the earth so as to maximise insulation, reduce unwanted sound and permit plant growth above.

Eco-system A biological community of interacting organisms in their physical environment.

Ecology The study of the relationships of organisms with each other and with their total environment, including humans beings.

Embodied energy The amount of energy consumed in the extraction, manufacture, transport and assembly of building materials, on-site and off-site.

Environmental assessment Collection of information on the likely environmental effects of a proposed development. Mandatory for certain specified types of project and any other project likely to have a significant impact by virtue of its size, location or operating process.

Environmental capacity The ability of a particular environment to sustain its current functions and absorb additional development.

Environmental Impact Statements Prepared by developers whose proposals constitute a major change to the environment. An American idea adopted in the EU.

Environmentally friendly A development, process or material that does minimal damage to the environment.

Escutcheon A protective plate, sometimes decorated, surrounding the keyhole of a door, a light switch etc.

Fenestration Spacing of windows in a building's facade.

Filter strips Grassed earthworks constructed to improve the natural recharge of underground water supplies through infiltration.

Gearing The ratio of a company's debt to its equity. High gearing indicates risk to shareholders' investments.

Gentrification The transformation of a residential area by people on high incomes to the exclusion of people on low incomes.

Granny flat A self-contained unit within a dwelling to accommodate a single elderly person enabling that person to live independently, but close to their family.

Green belt An area of land defined by local authorities around a conurbation or large free-standing town with the intention of preventing the spread of development into open countryside.

Green roof A roof, usually flat or low-pitched, where a thin soil and vegetation cover is used to detain stormwater, absorb CO_2 and replicate garden conditions. Designs vary from intensive and high-maintenance to extensive and low-maintenance.

Green wedge An area of open land representing an important break between settlements or tentacles of an urban agglomeration.

Greenfield site An area of land that has never been built upon or shows no evidence of previous building activity in modern times.

Greenhouse effect Mechanism by which the Earth absorbs solar energy and is kept warmer that it would otherwise be.

Greenhouse gases Water vapour, CO_2, methane, chlorofluorocarbons (CFCs) and other gases that absorb radiation at infrared wavelengths.

Grey water Waste water from the bath or washing machine that can be recycled for toilet flushing or garden irrigation. Includes 'harvested' rainwater.

Gross density The overall density of a neighbourhood including open spaces, commercial uses, roads and other local infrastructure.

Hectare An area measuring 10,000 square metres (2.471 acres), roughly equivalent to two and a half football pitches.

Home zone A residential area where the streets are 'calmed' and given over primarily to pedestrians and cyclists by restricting motor vehicles to 20 m.p.h.

Housing association An independent, non-profit making organisation funded primarily by government to build, improve and manage affordable housing for sale or rent.

Infrastructure Facilities necessary to open up an area for development, especially roads, water supply and sewerage. Social infrastructure includes schools and health service centres.

Jamb A vertical member at either side of a doorway or window frame.

Kerb appeal The value ascribed to a dwelling by a prospective buyer based on its immediate visual impact and general ambience.

Land bank An accumulation of parcels of land acquired by private developers on the expectation that market conditions and planning permission will allow development in due course.

Land supply The amount of land readily available or likely to become available within a specified planning period, usually five years.

Legibility Building design or estate layout that allows the user to locate functions easily from the logical arrangement of elements.

Life-cycle analysis Assessment of energy costs over the long term from construction to the continuing use of the built form. Includes the extraction, processing, maintenance and disposal of the materials involved.

Life-cycle costing Buildings designed to be durable and flexible, with a planned operational life of 100 years or more.

Listed buildings A building of special architectural or historic interest included on a list prepared under Section 1 of the Planning (Listed Buildings and Conservation Areas) Act, 1990.

Local plan Generic term covering three main types of detailed land use plan: district-wide plan, action area plan and subject plan.

Local plan inquiry Held before an inspector appointed by central government to consider formal objections to the local plan.

Local planning authority Generic term covering county councils, district councils and unitary councils depending on the structure of local government in a particular area (see Cullingworth and Nadin, 2002, and Duxbury, 2002).

Marginal land (1) Land with low agricultural productivity, e.g. moorland edge or heathland grazing. (2) Industrially degraded, flood-prone or inaccessible sites where development would be of marginal economic benefit without additional infrastructure.

Material consideration A legal term describing a matter or principle relevant for a local authority to take into account when exercising its powers under planning law, sometimes overriding allocations on the physical plan.

Mixed-use development A planned mixture of housing, offices, light industry, community facilities, leisure and shopping deemed desirable on a particular site. The opposite of rigid zoning.

Mortgage A loan secured against the value of a property.

Multiple occupation Occupation of non self-contained accommodation in a house or flat by persons who do not form a single household.

National nature reserve An area designated as being of national importance for the preservation of flora, fauna or geological features including opportunities for research and education.

Negative equity Occurs where house prices fall and the debt on an individual home exceeds its capital value. Most severe for those with a very high per cent mortgage.

Net density An occupancy measure based on number of dwellings per area exclusive of all ancillary land uses. Frequently confused by the inclusion of frontage roads and minor landscaping in area measurement.

New town Strictly refers to state-financed urban developments following the New Towns Act 1946, overwhelmingly on greenfield land. A term sometimes used generically for other large urban extensions.

Nodes Points at which main roads and public transport routes meet or intersect, usually attracting development or creating an opportunity for it.

Obstruction angles Angles above the horizontal plane used to assess the obstruction of natural light by one building in relation to neighbouring property.

Outline planning permission Confirms the principle that a piece of land or a building may be developed for a given use, normally valid for a period of three years.

Overshadowing The obstruction of sunlight by buildings, trees and landforms. Important factor in passive solar design and daylighting standards.

Overtrading Conducting business on a scale that cannot be sustained by the firm's capital or short-term cash-flow.

Passive solar gain Use of energy from the Sun to heat buildings by the design of windows, choice of fabric materials and orientation of the building itself. Aims to maintain comfort by displacing normal energy use, partially or completely.

Patio houses Mostly single storey dwellings, typically terraced, incorporating a patio. An alternative to the conventional land-hungry bungalow plus garden.

Pedestrianisation Complete removal of vehicular traffic from an area to give total priority to people on foot.

Perimeter development Buildings that are located around the edge of a site so as to focus community activity inside the development.

Permeability (1) Ground conditions whereby water passes through the structure rather than eroding the surface by run-off. (2) The attribute whereby an area or place has convenient, safe and agreeable routes through it.

Photovoltaic devices Energy converters using semiconductors which directly convert sunlight into usable electrical current.

Planning appeal A provision in planning law whereby an applicant who is refused permission to develop land or property may appeal to the Secretary of State for a reconsideration of the local authority's verdict and possibly a reversal in the applicant's favour.

Planning brief Prepared by the local authority to guide the development of a particular site. Includes opportunities, constraints and relevant policy implications.

Planning conditions Requirements attached to a grant of planning permission to ensure the effective and proper implementation of the proposed development.

Planning gain A benefit conferred on an area where the local council imposes an obligation on a developer to provide works or a payment towards facilities in return for planning permission.

Planning Policy Guidance (PPG) Concise and practical guidance on a range of planning matters issued by government (originally DoE and currently ODPM). Routinely embodied in development plans and cited as 'material considerations' in development control.

Proposals map A map of a planning area illustrating the location and extent of all land development allocations and policy designations articulated in the written document.

Public local inquiry To be distinguished from an EIP (for structure plans) in that the final decision on the findings is made by the local planning authority.

Ransom strip A parcel of land impeding access to a potential development site where the site's owner can command a price above normal market value.

Rat-run Motorists' use of back streets or residential estate roads as short cuts, avoiding traffic congestion on designated highways.

Reclamation Traditionally, the restoration of land to its former use, e.g. return to farming of abandoned mineral workings and airfields. Also refers to the purification of foul water.

Recycling Generic term covering re-use of building materials, buildings, land, water and consumer goods to help reduce levels of extraction of raw materials from the unspoilt environment.

Reed bed technology Alternative to conventional sewage treatment using ponds and reed beds to treat waste water.

Refuges Retention of semi-natural ecological sites within developments. In highway design the term also refers to designated places where pedestrians can wait in comparative safety until vehicles have passed.

Regional Planning Guidance (RPG) Government guidance on housing construction targets to be met via local development plans in each region.

Rehabilitation Re-use of degraded land where disturbance precludes complete restoration to the former use, but where an alternative, adaptive use is possible.

Remediation Treatment of contaminated land by physical containment, removal elsewhere or *in situ* biological processes to meet standards acceptable for redevelopment. Proposed end-use, e.g. housing, open space or industry, will determine the technology employed and the thoroughness of the treatment.

Renewable resources A somewhat imprecise term covering 'continuous' resources, e.g. solar energy, wood and rainwater that are relatively free of human control. To be contrasted with minerals, fossil fuels and dwindling plant and animal species.

Residential institutions Domestic accommodation where care is given (e.g. old people's, or convalescent homes) or institutional lodgings (e.g. a college or a detention centre).

Restoration Land reclamation involving replacement of the original topography and vegetation, usually to the former use. Most commonly practised in relation to open-cast coal extraction sites returned to agriculture.

Risk assessment An attempt to make rational decisions about the likelihood of a site becoming hazardous to human health or compromising economic investment.

Rurban fringe Landscape and land-use mix where development is fragmented and neither truly urban nor truly rural in character.

Section 106 agreement A voluntary legal agreement under s.106 of the Town and Country Planning Act 1990 between a local authority and a developer intended to enhance development beyond the scope of normal planning conditions.

Secured by Design The corporate title for a family of national projects involving the design of new homes, refurbished homes, commercial premises, car parks and other crime prevention projects. Managed by the Association of Chief Police Officers (ACPO) with Home Office and ODPM (formerly DoE, DETR and DTLR) backing.

Seller's pack A suggested device where any seller of residential property will be legally obliged to provide a prospective purchaser with full documentation concerning the site's history and condition.

Sequential test Methodology under PPG3 whereby previously used or infill sites within the built-up area are brought forward for development before any detached greenfield sites are released.

Social costs Those externalities that must be paid for by the community rather than the individual, e.g. noise, blight, inaccessibility.

Substructure Ground conditions and foundations of a dwelling up to and including ground floor level.

Supplementary Planning Guidance (SPG) Non-statutory policy guidelines, e.g. estate design, individual site briefs and affordable housing provision, invoked by the local authority to enhance development control.

Sustainable construction Choice of materials, assembly methods and site practices designed to make the minimum impact on the natural environment, directly and indirectly.

Sustainable development/sustainability Defined by the World Commission on Environment and Development (1987) as 'development that meets the needs of the present without compromising the ability of future generations to meet their own needs'.

Sustainable urban drainage systems (SUDS) Drainage channels and vegetated surfaces designed into a development to absorb rainwater gradually by slowing the rate of run-off.

Technocentrism A belief that environmental problems can be overcome by the application of technology without restraining economic growth. Its opposite is ecocentrism.

Town cramming Over-development of built-up areas resulting in environmental damage and threatening the character of established residential properties.

Townscape (1) A landscape visibly consisting primarily of built forms. (2) A land-use mix consisting predominantly of purposefully developed land.

Traffic calming Reduction of the intrusive effects of motor vehicles, especially speed, by a co-ordinated series of measures including road humps, chicanes, speed limits and one-way systems. The objective of such measures is to improve safety and amenity, particularly in relation to pedestrians and cyclists.

Trigger values Used to determine at what point ground contamination becomes a hazard and what level of remediation is then required.

Trombe wall A blackened concrete wall fronted by glass whereby the intervening airspace collects solar heat for transmission later into the dwelling via controlled vents.

Urban capacity study Assessment of the number of extra dwellings an area could accommodate assuming environmentally acceptable densities.

Urban sprawl The unrestrained expansion of an urban area.

Use Classes Order (UCO) Section 55 of the Town and Country Planning Act 1990 provides that a change of use does not require planning permission if the existing use and the proposed use are both within the same class. The UCO specifies the official class to which any use belongs.

Useful energy The energy available as heat and light within the home, after combustion within a boiler or appliance, or as a result of internal heat gains and solar collection.

U-value A measure of the heat transmission performance of different building materials.

Vernacular Use of readily available local materials and construction methods. Strongly advocated in most design guides.

Voids (1) Space underground resulting from either natural geomorphic processes or non-engineered fill, giving rise to possible failure of buildings sited above. (2) Vacant buildings and space within buildings that may be counted as commercial or social development potential as part of an urban capacity study.

Washlands Flat areas adjacent to rivers which are set aside to accommodate flood-waters, and accordingly shown as a constraint on development.

Water catchment areas The areas defined by the watersheds between surrounding river systems.

Wet trades Construction involving concrete, mortar and plaster on site (as opposed to 'dry' component assembly).

Wildlife corridors Linear features such as motorway verges and redundant railway lines that provide a habitat for animals, insects and plant seeds. Valuable in maintaining a sense of visual continuity in suburban developments.

Wind rose diagrams A method of assessing prevailing and topographic winds at a particular location. Wind direction is mapped using arrows that are aligned in length and width in proportion to frequency, force and temperature.

Windfall sites Areas of land capable of accommodating more than about ten dwellings and for which planning permission is likely to be granted for that purpose despite not having been previously identified as such in the local plan.

Wirescape An environment dominated by telephone and other overhead wires suspended across streets and gardens.

Written statement That part of a local plan which explains and justifies the planning authority's land use policies. Forms the basis for development control decisions and in the event of a contradiction the written word prevails over the map.

Yuppies Young, upwardly mobile professionals.

References

Abercrombie, P. (1945) *Greater London Plan 1944*, London: HMSO.

Acosta, R. and Renard, V. (1993) *France: Urban Land and Property Markets*, London: UCL Press.

Adair, A., Berry, J. and McGreal, W. (1991) 'Land availability, housing demand and the property market', *Journal of Property Research*, 8: 59–69.

Adair, A., Berry, J. and McGreal, W. (1993) 'The interaction between macroeconomic and housing policy in the UK', *Journal of Property Research*, 10: 121–34.

Adams, D. (1992) 'The role of land-owners in the preparation of statutory local plans', *Town Planning Review*, 63: 297–323.

Adams, D. (1994) *Urban Planning and the Development Process*, London: UCL Press.

Allen, E. (1995) *How Buildings Work* (2nd edition), Oxford: Oxford University Press.

Allen, L. (2002) 'Family unfriendly', *Estates Gazette*, 30 March: 64–5.

Allmendinger, P. and Chapman, M. (eds) (1999) *Planning beyond 2000*, Chichester: Wiley.

Alonso, W. (1964) *Location and Land Use*, Cambridge (Mass): Harvard University Press.

Ambrose, P. (1974) *The Quiet Revolution: Social Change in a Sussex Village 1871–1971*, London: Chatto & Windus.

Ambrose, P. (1986) *Whatever Happened to Planning?*, London: Methuen.

Ambrose, P. and Barlow, J. (1987) 'Housing provision and house-building in Western Europe: increasing expenditure, declining output?' in van Vliet, W. (ed.) *Housing Markets and Policies under Fiscal Austerity*, London: Greenwood Press.

Ave, G. (1994) *Italy: Urban Land and Property Markets*, London: UCL Press.

Babbage, A. (1973) 'House improvement in stress areas', *Environmental Health*, 81 pages.

Bailey, N., Barker, A. and MacDonald, K. (1995) *Partnership Agencies in British Urban Policy*, London: UCL Press.

Bailey, N., Findlay, J. and Gibb, K. (1998) *Deregulation and the Structure of the Urban Rental Housing Market*, RICS Cutting Edge Conference, September.

Baker Associates (1998) *Study of Settlement Capacity and Regional Development Options in Yorkshire and Humberside*, London: Baker Associates.

Baker, M. J. (1996) *Marketing: An Introductory Text* (6th edition), Basingstoke: Macmillan.

Balchin, P. (1996) *Housing Policy: An Introduction*, London: Routledge.

Balchin, P. and Kieve, J. (1977) *Urban Land Economics*, London: Macmillan.

Ball, M. (1983) *Housing Policy and Economic Power*, London: Methuen.

Ball, M. (1986) *Home Ownership: A Suitable Case for Reform*, London: Shelter.

Ball, M. (1988) *Rebuilding Construction: Economic Change and the British Construction Industry*, London: Routledge.

Ball, M. (1996) *Housing and Construction: A Troubled Relationship?*, Bristol: The Policy Press.

Ball, M. (1999) 'Chasing a snail: innovation and housebuilding firms' strategies', *Housing Studies*, 14: 9–22.

Ball, M (2002) *RICS European Housing Review*, London: Royal Institution of Chartered Surveyors.

Ball, M. and Grilli, M. (1997) *Housing Markets and Economic Convergence in the European Union*, London: Royal Institution of Chartered Surveyors; South Bank University.

Ball, M. and Harloe, M. (1992) 'Rhetorical barriers to understanding housing provision: what the "provision thesis" is and is not', *Housing Studies*, 7.

Ball, M., Wood, A. and Morrison, T. (1996) 'Structures investment and economic growth: a long-term international comparison', *Urban Studies*, 33: 1687–706.

Barke, M., Henderson, P. and Morphet, C. (1993) 'Mapping the census', *Geographical Magazine*, 65: 36–9.

Barley, M. (1961) *The English Farmhouse and Cottage*, London: Routledge & Kegan Paul.

Barley, M. (1986) *Houses and History*, London: Butler & Tanner.

Barlow, J. (1990) *Who Plans Berkshire? Land Supply, House Price Inflation and Housing Developers*, Working Paper No. 72, University of Sussex.

Barlow, J. and Duncan, S. (1993) 'Controlling the housing land market: some examples from Europe', *Urban Studies*, 30: 129–49.

Barlow, J. and Duncan, S. (1994) *Success and Failure in Housing Provision: European Systems Compared*, Oxford: Elsevier Press.

Barlow, J. and King, A. (1992) 'The state, the market and competitive strategy: the house-building industry in the UK, France and Sweden', *Environment & Planning A*, 24: 381–400.

Barlow, J., Jackson, R. and Meikle, J. (2001) *Homes to DIY For: The UK's Self-build Housing Market in the Twenty-first Century*, York: Joseph Rowntree Foundation.

Barrett, S. and Healey, P. (1985) *Land Policy: Problems and Alternatives*, Farnborough: Gower.

Bartlett, K. (ed.) *Consumer Choice in House Buying: The Beginnings of a House Buyer Revolt*, York: Joseph Rowntree Foundation.

Bartlett School of Planning and Llewelyn Davies (1998) *The Use of Density in Urban Planning*, London: Department of the Environment, Transport and the Regions.

Barton, H., Davis, G. and Guise, R. (1995) *Sustainable Settlements: A Guide for Planners, Designers and Developers*, Luton: Local Government Management Board.

Bather, N. (1976) *The Speculative Residential Developer and Urban Growth*, Geographical Paper No. 47, University of Reading.

Baum, A. and Mackmin, D. (1989) *The Income Approach to Property Valuation* (3rd edition), London: Routledge.

Beckett, J. (ed.) (1997) *A Centenary History of Nottingham*, Manchester: Manchester University Press.

Begg, D., Fischer, S. and Dornbusch, R. (1989) *Economics*, London: McGraw Hill.

Bell, F. (1993) *Engineering Geology*, London: Blackwell.

Best, R. H. (1964) *Land for New Towns: A Study of Land Use, Densities and Agricultural Displacement*, London: Town & Country Planning Association.

Best, R. H. (1981) *Land Use and Living Space*, London: Methuen.

Best, R. H. and Rogers, A. (1973) *The Urban Countryside: The Land Use Structure of Small Towns and Villages in England and Wales*, London: Faber & Faber.

Best, R. H. and Ward, J. (1956) *The Garden Controversy*, London: Wye College.

Bibby, P. and Shepherd, J. (1997) 'Projecting rates of urbanisation in England, 1991–2016: method, policy, application and results', *Town Planning Review*, 68: 93–124.

Binnen, M. (1998) *Town Houses: Evolution and Innovation in 800 Years of Urban Domestic Architecture*, London: Mitchell Beazley.

Blake, R. (1981) 'Land use surveys for town and country planning', *Cartographic Journal*, 18: 50–5.

Blake, R. (1994) 'Measuring greenness in the built environment by synoptic cartography', *Buildings and the Environment*, CIB Taskgroup 8 Conference proceedings 16–20 May, Watford: Building Research Establishment.

Blake, R. (2001) 'Geoenvironmental factors in the regeneration of military airfields in Great Britain' in Ehlen, J. and Harmon, R. (eds) *The Environmental Legacy of Military Operations: Reviews in Engineering Geology*, 14: 203–19.

B.M.Bau (Bundesministerium für Raumordnung, Bauwesen und Städtebau) (1993a) *Die Eigentumsbildung im Wohnungsbau*, Bonn: Bad-Godesburg: B.M.Bau.

B.M.Bau (Bundesministerium für Raumordnung, Bauwesen und Städtebau (1993b) *Funktionsweise städtischer Bodenmärkte in Mitgliedstaaten der Europäischen Gemeinschaft: ein Systemvergleich*, Bonn: Bad-Godesburg: B.M.Bau.

B.M.Bau (Bundesministerium für Raumordnung, Bauwesen und Städtebau) (1998) *Haus und Wohnung: in Spiegel der Statistik*, Bonn: Bad-Godesburg: B.M.Bau.

Boelhouwer, P. and van der Heijden, H. (1992) *Housing Systems in Europe: Part 1*, Delft: Delft University Press.

Booth, P. (1991) 'Preparing land for development in France: the role of the aménageur-lotisseur', *Journal of Property Research*, 8: 239–51.

Bootle, R. (1996) *The Death of Inflation: Surviving and Thriving in the Zero Era*, London: Nicholas Brealey Publishing.

Bramley, G. (1989) *Land Supply, Planning and Private House-building: A Review*, SAUS Working Paper No. 81, University of Bristol.

Bramley, G. (1993) 'The enabling role for local authorities: a preliminary evaluation' in Malpass, P. and Means, R. (eds) *Implementing Housing Policy*, Buckingham: Open University Press.

Bramley, G., Bartlett, W. and Lambert, C. (1995) *Planning, the Market and Private House-building*, London: UCL Press.

Bramley, G., Pawson, H. and Third, H. (2000) *Low Demand Housing and Unpopular Neighbourhoods*, London: DETR.

Breheny, M. (1992) *Sustainable Development and Urban Form*, London: Pion.

Breheny, M. (1997) 'Local authorities and residential densities – an attitude problem?', *Town & Country Planning*, 66: 84–6, March.

Breheny, M. (1998) 'Success in re-using urban land', *Town & Country Planning*, 67: 24–5, January/February.

Brett, L. (1965) *Landscape in Distress*, London: Architecural Press.

Brett, P. (1997) *An Illustrated Dictionary of Building*, Oxford: Butterworth Heinemann.

Briggs, A. (1963) *Victorian Cities*, London: Odhams.

British Standards Institution (1981) *Code of Practice for Site Investigation* (BS5930), London: BSI.

Britton, W., Davies, K. and Johnson, T. (1989) *Modern Methods of Valuation* (8th edition), London: Estates Gazette.

Broome, J. and Richardson, B. (1991) *The Self-Build Book*, Devon: Green Books.

Brotherton, D. (1992) 'On the control of development by planning authorities', *Environment & Planning B*, 19: 465–78.

Brown, N., Gerard, F. and Fuller, R. (2002) 'Mapping of land use classes within the CORINE land cover map of Great Britain', *Cartographic Journal*, 39: 5–14.

Brunskill, R. (2000) *Vernacular Architecture*, London: Faber & Faber.

Burgess, E. W. (1925) 'The growth of a city: an introduction to a research project' in Park, R. E., Burgess, E. W. and Mackenzie, R. D. (eds) *The City*, Chicago: University of Chicago Press, pp. 47–62.

Building Research Establishment (1991) *Sulphate and Acid Resistance of Concrete in the Ground*, BRE Digest No. 363, Watford: BRE.

Building Research Establishment (1998) *Constructing the Future: INTEGER*, Watford: BRE, Autumn 1998, Issue 1.

Burke, G. (1976) *Towns in the Making*, London: Edward Arnold.

Burnett, J. (1978) *A Social History of Housing 1815–1970*, Newton Abbot: David & Charles.

Burns, L. and Grebler, L. (1967) *The Housing of Nations*, London: Macmillan.

Burton, T. (1992) 'The protection of rural England', *Planning Practice & Research*, 7: 37–40.

Cahill, S. (2001) *Who Owns Britain: The Hidden Facts Behind Land-Ownership in the UK and Ireland*, Edinburgh: Canongate.

Carpenter, P. (1994) *Sod It: An Introduction to Earth Sheltered Development in England and Wales*, Coventry University.

Carter, N., Brown, T. and Hill, M. (1986) *The Private Housing Development Process*, Department of Land Management, Leicester Polytechnic.

Cassettari, S. (2003) 'A new generation of land use mapping in the UK', *Cartographic Journal*, 40: 121–30.

Champion, A. and Townsend, A. (1994) *Contemporary Britain: A Geographical Perspective*, London: Edward Arnold.

Cherry, G. (1972) *Urban Change and Planning: A History of Urban Development in Britain Since 1750*, Henley: GT Foulis.

Chiddick, D. and Dobson, M. (1986) 'Land for housing – circular arguments', *The Planner*, 72: 10–13, March.

Ching, F. (1996) *Architecture: Form, Space and Order* (2nd edition), Cambridge: J Wiley & Sons.

Civic Trust and Ove Arup (1999) *Sustainable Renewal of Suburban Areas*, York: Joseph Rowntree Trust.

Clapham, D. (1996) 'Housing and the economy: broadening comparative housing research', *Urban Studies*, 33: 631–47.

Clapham, D. and English, J. (1987) *Public Housing: Current Trends and Future Developments*, London: Croom Helm.

Clark, C. (2000) 'Manchester disunited – the new and the old', *Property: Daily Telegraph*, 22 January.

Clarke, L. and Wall, C. (1996) *Skills and the Construction Process: A Comparative Study of Vocational Training and Quality in Social House-building*, Bristol: The Policy Press.

Clayton, C., Matthew, M. and Simons, N. (1995) *Site Investigation: A Handbook for Engineers*, Oxford: Blackwell Science.

Clifton-Taylor, A. (1972) *The Pattern of English Building*, London: Faber & Faber.

Cloke, P. and Shaw, D. (1983) 'Rural settlement policies in structure planning', *Town Planning Review*, 54: 338–54.

Coleman, A. (1969) 'A geographical model for land-use analysis', *Geography*, 54: 43–55.

Coleman, A. (1976) 'Is planning really necessary?', *Geographical Journal*, 142: 411–37.

Coleman, A. (1977) 'Land use planning: success or failure?', *Architect's Journal*, 165: 94–134.

Coleman, A. (1985) *Utopia on Trial: Vision and Reality in Planned Housing*, London: Hilary Shipman Ltd.

Coleman, A. and Shaw, J. (1980) *Field Mapping Manual*, London: Second Land Use Survey, King's College.

Coles, A. (1993) 'Housing finance: some international comparisons', *Housing Finance*, 20: 15–19, November, London: Council of Mortgage Lenders.

Coley, C. (1998) 'Aiming high with Tim and Tamsin', *Property: Weekend Telegraph*, 12 September.

Conn, D. (1999) 'Oasis of urban sophistication: New Homes', *The Daily Telegraph*, 27 March.

Construction Industry Research and Information Association (1999) *Sustainable Urban Development Systems*, (Design Manual) London: CIRIA.

Cook, O. (1984) *The English House through Seven Centuries*, London: Penguin Books.

Cook, P. (2000) 'Managing customers', *House Builder*, 59 (2): 20–3, March.

Coopers & Lybrand Associates (1987) *Land Use Planning and Indicators of Housing Demand*, London: Coopers & Lybrand.

Cornford, T. (1998) 'The control of planning gain', *Journal of Planning & Environment Law*, 1998: 731–49.

Council for the Protection of Rural England (1988) *Welcome Homes: Housing Supply from Unallocated Land*, London: CPRE.

Council for the Protection of Rural England (1994) *The Housing Numbers Game*, London: CPRE.

Countryside Agency (1996) *Making Local Character Count in New Development*, London: Countryside Agency.

Crédit Lyonnais (1995) *Private House-building*, Building Research UK, London: Crédit Lyonnais.

Cullen, A. (1980) *The Production of the Built Environment*, Proceedings of the Bartlett Summer School 1979, BSAP.

Cullingworth, J. B. and Nadin, V. (2002) *Town and Country Planning in the United Kingdom* (13th edition), London: Routledge.

Cunliffe, B. (1995) *Iron Age Britain*, London: Batsford (for English Heritage).

Darke, R. (1999) 'Public speaking rights in local authority planning committees', *Planning Practice & Research*, 14: 171–83.

Davidson, M. (1998) 'DIY and unpaid help in renovating owner-occupied homes', *European Network for Housing Research Conference*, Cardiff University, 7–11 September.

Davies, H. (1998) 'Continuity and change in the British planning system', *Town Planning Review*, 69: 135–52.

Davy, B. *et al.* (1998) *Aktion: Mehr Bauland + 5*, Fakultät Raumplanung an der Universität, Dortmund: Deutsche Bank Bauspar AG.

De Montfort University and Entec (1998) *Urban Housing Capacity in the East Midlands*, Leamington Spa: Entec UK Ltd.

Derek Lovejoy Partnership (ed.) (1997) *Spon's Landscape Book* (4th edition), London: E. & F. N. Spon.

DETR (Department of the Environment, Transport and the Regions) (1997) *The Demand for Owner Occupied Housing*, London: DETR and Cambridge University.

DETR (Department of the Environment, Transport and the Regions) (1998a) *Housing and Construction Statistics*, London: HMSO.

DETR (Department of the Environment, Transport and the Regions) (1998b) *Planning and Affordable Housing*, Circular 06/98, London: DETR.

DETR (Department of the Environment, Transport and the Regions) (1999a) *Projections of Households in England to 2021*, London: HMSO.

DETR (Department of the Environment, Transport and the Regions) (1999b) *Housing and Construction Statistics*, London: HMSO.

DETR (Department of the Environment, Transport and the Regions) (1999c) *Survey of English Housing 1998/9*, DETR.

DETR (Department of the Environment, Transport and the Regions) (2000a) *Quality and Choice: A Decent Home for All*, London: DETR.

DETR (Department of the Environment, Transport and the Regions) (2000b) *Housing*, Planning Policy Guidance Note 3, London: The Stationery Office.

DETR (Department of the Environment, Transport and the Regions) (2000c) *National Land Use Database*, www.nlud.org.uk

DETR (Department of the Environment, Transport and the Regions) (2000d) *Tapping the Potential – Assessing Urban Housing Capacity: Towards Better Practice*, London: DETR.

DETR (Department of the Environment, Transport and the Regions) (2001) *Housing and Construction Statistics*, London: HMSO.

DETR (Department of the Environment, Transport and the Regions) (2002) *Housing and Construction Statistics*, London: HMSO.

DETR (Department of the Environment, Transport and the Regions)/Planning Officers Society/House Builders Federation (1998) *Housing Layouts: Lifting the Quality*, London: HBF.

Dieterich, H., Dransfeld, E. and Voss, W. (1993) *Germany: Urban Land and Property Markets*, London: UCL Press.

DoE (Department of the Environment) (1976) *Housing and Construction Statistics*, London: HMSO.

DoE (Department of the Environment) (1977) *Housing Policy: A Consultative Document*, Cmnd 6851, London: HMSO.

DoE (Department of the Environment) (1980a) *Housing and Construction Statistics*, London: HMSO.

DoE (Department of the Environment) (1980b) *Circular 9/80 Affordable Housing*, London: HMSO.

DoE (Department of the Environment) (1980c) *Circular 22/80 Development Control – Policy and Practice*, London: HMSO.

DoE (Department of the Environment) (1981) *Housing and Construction Statistics*, London: HMSO.

DoE (Department of the Environment) (1984) *Circular 22/84 Memorandum on Structure and Local Plans*, London: HMSO.

DoE (Department of the Environment) (1985) *Circular 14/85 Development and Employment*, London: HMSO.

DoE (Department of the Environment) (1987) *Housing: The Government's Proposals*, Cmnd 214, London: HMSO.

DoE (Department of the Environment) (1989) *Planning Control in Western Europe*, London: HMSO.

DoE (Department of the Environment) (1990) *Planning Policy Guidance 14: Development on Unstable Land*, London: HMSO.

DoE (Department of the Environment) (1992a) *Residential Roads and Footpaths: Layout Considerations*, Design Bulletin 32, London: HMSO.

DoE (Department of the Environment) (1992b) *Housing and Construction Statistics 1982–1992*, London: HMSO.

DoE (Department of the Environment) (1995) *Our Future Homes*, London: DoE.

DoE (Department of the Environment) (annual) *Local Authority Housing Statistics*, London: DoE.

DoE (Department of the Environment) and House Builders Federation (1978) *Land Availability: Study of Land with Residential Planning Permission*, London: DoE.

Donnison, D., and Ungerson, C. (1982) *Housing Policy*, Middlesex: Harmondsworth Penguin.

Doyle, P. (1989) *The Strategic Importance of Brands*, London: Economist Intelligence Unit.

DTLR (Department for Transport, Local Government and the Regions) (2001) *Land Use Change in England No. 16*, London: Government Statistical Service.

DTLR (Department for Transport, Local Government and the Regions) (2002a) *Development on Land Affected by Contamination: Consultation Paper on Draft Planning Advice*, London: DTLR.

DTLR (Department of Transport, Local Government and the Regions) (2002b) *Planning Obligations Green Paper*, London: DTLR.

DTLR (Department for Transport, Local Government and the Regions) and CABE (Commission for Architecture and the Built Environment) (2001) *By Design: Better Places to Live*, London: Thomas Telford.

Dunleavy, P. (1981) *The Politics of Mass Housing in Britain 1945–1975: A Study of Corporate Power and Professional Influence in the Welfare State*, Oxford: Clarendon Press.

Dunn, R. and Harrison, A. R. (1994) *Feasibility Study for Deriving Information about Land Use Stock* (Department of the Environment, Planning and Research Programme Contract PECD 7/1/411), London: HMSO.

Duxbury, R. (2002) *Telling and Duxbury's Planning Law and Procedure*, London: Butterworth.

Edge, M. and Duncan, P. (1998) *Motivations in the Self-Provision of Social Housing: The Political Economy of Self-Build*, Cardiff, European Network for Housing Research, September.

Egan Report (1998) *Rethinking Construction* (Report to the DETR by the Construction Task Force), London: HMSO.

Ellis, S. (1998) 'Don't miss a brick with wall-by-wall mortgage', *Daily Telegraph*, 12 September 1998: B11.

Elson, M., Walker, S. and Macdonald, R. (1993) *The Effectiveness of Green Belts*, (Report for the DoE), London: HMSO.

Emms, P. (1990) *Social Housing: A European dilemma?*, Bristol: School for Advanced Urban Studies.

Energy Efficiency Best Practice Programme Documents (2000) *The Hockerton Housing Project*, New Practice Profile No. 119, BRESCU.

Ennis, F. (1994) 'Planning obligations in development plans', *Land Use Policy*, 11: 195–207.

Ennis, F. (1997) 'Infrastructure provision, the negotiating process and the planner's role', *Urban Studies*, 34: 1935–54.

Entec UK and De Montfort University (1998) *Assessing Urban Capacity in the East Midlands Region*, Leamington Spa: The East Midlands Regional Planning Forum.

Entec UK and Nottingham Trent University (2001) *Urban Capacity Assessment in Milton Keynes Borough*, English Partnerships and Milton Keynes Borough Council.

Environment Agency and Scottish Environment Protection Agency (1999) *Sustainable Urban Drainage Systems*, Stirling: SEPA.

Esping-Andersen, G. (1990) *The Three Worlds of Welfare Capitalism*, Cambridge: Polity Press.

Essex County Council (1974) *Design Guide for Residential Areas*, Chelmsford: Essex County Council.

European Commission (1994) *European Community Household Panel*, Brussels: EC.

European Commission (1998) *Housing Statistics in the European Union*, Brussels: European Commission.

Eurostat (2000) *Europe in Figures* (5th edition), Eurostat: London: The Stationery Office.

Evans, A. (1985) *Urban Economics: An Introduction*, Oxford: Blackwell.

Evans, A. (1995) 'The property market: ninety per cent efficient?', *Urban Studies*, 32: 5–29.

Everett, A. (1994) *Part I: Mitchell's Materials* (5th edition), Harlow: Longman.

Field, B. and McGregor, B. (1987) *Forecasting Techniques for Urban and Regional Planning*, London: Hutchinson.

Fielding, N. (1982) 'The volume house-builders', *Roof*, 7 (6): 16–18, Nov./Dec.

Fleming, G. (ed.) (1991) *Recycling Derelict Land*, London: Thomas Telford.

Fleming, S. (1984) *House-builders in an Area of Growth: Negotiating the Built Environment of Central Berkshire*, Geographical Paper No. 84, University of Reading.

Ford, J. and Pawson, H. (2001) *Low Demand for Housing Association Housing*, London: The Housing Corporation.

Fordham, R., Findlay, S., Gardner, J., Macmillan, A., Muldoon, O., Taylor, G. and Welch, G. (1998) *Housing Need and the Need for Housing*, Aldershot: Ashgate.

Fowler, H. and Fowler, F. (1998) *The Concise Oxford English Dictionary* (9th edition), Oxford University Press.

Fuller, R. Sheail, J. and Barr, C. (1994) 'The land of Britain, 1930–90: a comparative study of field mapping and remote sensing techniques', *Geographical Journal,* 160: 173–84.

Gallent, N. (2000) 'Planning and affordable housing: from old values to New Labour', *Town Planning Review,* 71: 123–47.

Gallent, N. and Bell, P. (2000) 'Planning exceptions in rural England: past, present and future', *Planning Practice & Research,* 15: 375–84.

Gallent, N., Mace, A. and Tewdwr-Jones, M. (2002) *Second Homes in Rural Areas of England,* Cheltenham: The Countryside Agency.

Gann, D. (1996) 'Construction as a manufacturing process? Similarities and differences between industrialised housing and car production in Japan', *Construction Management & Economics,* 14: 437–50.

Garber, M. (2001) *Sex and Real Estate: Why We Love Houses,* New York: Anchor Books.

Gibb, K. and Munro, M. (1999) *Housing Finance in the UK: An Introduction,* Basingstoke: Macmillan.

Gibb, K., Munro, M. and McGregor, A. (1995) *The Scottish House-building Industry: Opportunity or Constraint,* Scottish Homes Research Report No. 44, Edinburgh: Scottish Homes.

Gibberd, F. (1945) *The Architecture of England: From Norman Times to the Present Day,* London: Architectural Press.

Gillen, M. (1995) *Sectoral Restructuring in the Private House-building Industry,* Working Paper No. 10, Centre for Residential Development, The Nottingham Trent University.

Gillen, M. (1998) 'The application of structure and agency to the residential development process: the interrelationship between volume housebuilding companies and the land-use planning system', PhD Thesis, Nottingham: Nottingham Trent University.

Glasson, B. and Booth, P. (1992) 'Negotiation and delay in the development control process', *Town Planning Review,* 63: 63–78.

Golland, A. (1992) *Returns from Owner Occupied Housing,* Department of Land Management, Leicester Polytechnic.

Golland, A. (1998) *Systems of Housing Supply and Housing Production in Europe: A Comparison of the UK, the Netherlands and Germany,* Aldershot: Ashgate Publishing.

Golland, A. (2002) *Nottingham Housing Market Study and Needs Assessment 2002,* Nottingham: Nottingham City Council and B. Line Housing Information.

Golland, A. and Boelhouwer, P. (2002) 'Speculative housing supply, land and housing market', *Journal of Property Research,* 19: 231–351, Abingdon: Spon Press.

Golland, A. and Spaans, M. (1996) *Local Housing Development: A Comparison of Leicester and Rotterdam,* Working paper, Leicester: De Montfort University.

Greater London Authority (GLA) (2002) *Future Housing Provision: Speeding Up Delivery,* report commissioned by the GLA and the House Builders Federation: SDS Technical Report No. 2, London: GLA.

Greed, C. (1996) *Introducing Town Planning,* London: Addison Wesley Longman.

Hall, D. (1989) 'The case for new settlements', *Town and Country Planning,* 58: 11–14.

Hall, P. (1992) *Urban and Regional Planning* (3rd edition), London: Routledge.

Hall, P. and Ward, C. (1998) *Sociable Cities: The Legacy of Ebenezer Howard,* Chichester: John Wiley.

Hampshire County Council (1990) *Market Demand for Housing in Hampshire,* Winchester: Hampshire County Council.

Harriott, S. and Matthews, L. (1998) *Social Housing: An Introduction,* Harlow: Longman.

Harvey, J. (1987) *Urban Land Economics: The Economics of Real Property,* Basingstoke: Macmillan.

Harvey, J. (2000) *Urban Land Economics* (5th edition), Basingstoke: Macmillan.

Hatim, B. and Mason, I. (1990) *Discourse and the Translator*, Harlow: Longman.

Healey, P. (1991) 'Models of the development process: a review', *Journal of Property Research*, 8: 219–38.

Healey, P. (1992) 'An institutional model of the development process', *Journal of Property Research*, 9: 33–44.

Healey, P. (1998) 'Regulating property development and the capacity of the development industry', *Journal of Property Research*, 15: 211–28.

Healey, P. and Barrett, S. (1990) 'Structure and agency in the land and property development processes: some ideas for research', *Urban Studies*, 27: 89–104.

Healey, P., Purdue P. and Ennis, F. (1993) *Gains from Planning: Dealing with the Impacts of Development*, York: Joseph Rowntree Foundation.

Heath, T. (2001) 'Revitalising cities: attitudes toward city-centre living in the United Kingdom', *Journal of Planning Education and Research*, 20: 464–75.

Henley Centre (1994) *UK Economic Forecasts*, London: Henley Centre.

Hennessy, P. (1992) *Never Again: Britain 1945–1951*, London: Jonathan Cape.

Herington, J. (1984) *The Outer City*, London: Harper & Row.

Hillebrandt, P., Cannon, J. and Lansley, P. (1995) *The Construction Company In and Out of Recession*, London: Macmillan.

Holmans, A. (1995) *Housing Need and Demand*, Findings No. 157, York: Joseph Rowntree Foundation.

Home, H. (1985) 'Forecasting housing land requirements', *Land Development Studies*, 2 (1): 19–34.

Hooper, A. (1979) 'Land availability', *Journal of Planning & Environmental Law*, November: 752–6.

Hooper, A. (1980) 'Land for private house-building', *Journal of Planning & Environmental Law*, December: 795–806.

Hooper, A. (2001) *The Restructuring of the House-building Industry and Future Trends*, London: House Builders Federation.

Hooper, A. and Nicol, C. (1999) 'Design practice and volume production in speculative house-building', *Construction Management & Economics*, 18: 295–310.

Hooper, A. and Nicol, C. (2000) 'The design and planning of residential development: standard house-types in the speculative house-building industry', *Environment & Planning B*, 26: 793–805.

Hoskins, W. G. (1955) *The Making of the English Landscape*, London: Hodder & Stoughton.

House Builders Federation (1995) *Towns or Leafier Environments? A Survey of Family Home-buying Choices*, London: HBF.

House Builders Federation (1997) *New Homes: Because Britain Deserves Better*, London: HBF.

House Builders Federation (1998a) *Urban Life: Breaking down the Barriers to Brownfield Development*, London: HBF.

House Builders Federation (1998b) *Housing Layouts – Lifting the Quality*, London: HBF/DETR/Planning Officers Society.

House of Commons Environment Committee (1996) *Inquiry into Housing Need* (February), London: HoC.

Housing Corporation (2001) *A Toolkit of Sustainability Indicators*, London: Housing Corporation.

Housing Corporation (2002) *The Housing Corporation*, www.housingcorp.org.uk

Housing Monitoring Team, (1981) *The House-building Industry and Changes in the Market for House-building Work: A Review of the British Experience*, CURS Research Memorandum No. 87, University of Birmingham.

Howe, J. and White, I. (2001) 'Sustainable urban drainage: a neglected area of planning', *Town & Country Planning*, 70: 242–4.

Howe, J. and White, I. (2002) 'The geography of Autumn 2000 floods in England and Wales: causes and solutions', *Geography*, 87(2): 116–24.

Hutson, S. and Jones, S. (1998) 'Self-build as a solution to youth homelessness?', European Network for Housing Research Conference, Cardiff University, 7–11 September.

INTEGER (2002) *INTEGER Project website*, INTEGER, www.interproject.co.uk

Jaffe, A. (1989) 'Concepts of property, theories of housing and the choice of housing policy', *Netherlands Journal of Housing & Environmental Research*, 4, Delft: Delft University Press.

Johnson, P. (1979) *What Makes Me Tick, Writings*, Oxford: Oxford University Press.

Jones, O. (2002) 'The impact of land use planning policy on the structure of the UK house-building industry', Master of Science Dissertation in Residential Development, Nottingham Trent University.

Joseph Rowntree Foundation (1994) *Inquiry into Planning for Housing*, York: JRF.

Kelly, R. (1998a) 'Loft dwellings march North', *The Times Weekend: Property*, 26 September.

Kelly, R. (1998b) 'Designer housing scares off customers', *The Times*, Saturday, 3 October.

King, P. (1998) 'Needs and choice in housing: an individualist approach', *Scandinavian Housing & Planning Research*, 15: 5–17.

King, P. (2001) *Understanding Housing Finance*, London: Routledge.

Knox, P. and Pinch, S. (2000) *Urban Social Geography: An Introduction* (4th edition), Harlow: Prentice Hall.

Kotler, P. (1999) *Kotler on Marketing*, London: The Free Press.

Labour Party (1991) *A Welcome Home*, Housing Policy Document, London: The Labour Party.

Lambert, C. (1990) *New House-building and the Development Industry in the Bristol Area*, SAUS Working Paper No. 86, University of Bristol.

Lambert, S. (1993) *Form Follows Function? Design in the 20th Century*, London: V & A Museum.

Lamont, Z. (1999) 'Innovative angle', *Housebuilder*, 58 (4): 39, May.

Latham Report (1994) *Constructing the Team: Joint Review of Procurement and Contractual Agreements in the UK Construction Industry*, London: HMSO.

Lawless, P. and Brown, F. (1986) *Urban Growth and Change in Britain*, London: Harper & Row.

Lawson, B. (1997) *How Designers Think* (3rd edition), London: The Architectural Press.

Leather, P. (1999) 'Housing renewal policy in the UK' in Skifter Andersen, H. and Leather, P. (eds) *Housing Renewal in Europe*, Bristol: The Policy Press.

Leather, P. and Mackintosh, S. (1993) in Malpass, P. and Means, R. *Implementing Housing Policy*, Buckingham: Open University Press.

Leather, P. and Morrison, T. (1997) *The State of UK Housing: A Factfile on Dwelling Conditions*, York: Joseph Rowntree Foundation.

Le Corbusier (1923) *Towards a New Architecture*, London: Architectural Press.

Levy, M. and Salvadori, M. (1994) *Why Buildings Fall Down*, London: W. W. Norton & Co.

Lincolnshire County Council (1994) *Design Guide for Residential Areas*, Lincoln: Lincolnshire County Council.

Lipsey, R. (1975) *An Introduction to Positive Economics*, London: Weidenfeld & Nicholson.

Littlefair, J. (2000) *Environmental Site Layout Planning*, Watford: Building Research Establishment.

Littlewood, J., Penn, R. and Wild, S. (1998) *Earth Sheltered Housing: A Sustainable Form of Housing for the UK*, University of Glamorgan (mimeo).

Llewelyn Davies (1997) *Exploring Potential for Housing in the North West*, London: North West Regional Association.

Llewelyn Davies (1998) *Sustainable Residential Quality: New Approaches to Urban Living*, London Planning Advisory Committee.

Llewelyn Davies (2000) *Urban Design Compendium*, English Partnerships and The Housing Corporation.

London Residential Research (2002) *Residential Development in London 2002*, London: Reed Publishing.

Lundquist, L. (1991) 'Rolling stones for the resurrection of policy as the focus of comparative housing research', *Scandinavian Housing and Planning Research*, 8(2): 79–90, Oslo: Scandinavian University Press.

Lyons, A. (1997) *Materials for Architects and Builders*, London: Edward Arnold.

Maclennan, D. (1982) *Housing Economics*, Harlow: Longman.

Maclennan, D. (1994) *A Competitive UK Economy: The Challenges for Housing Policy*, York: Joseph Rowntree Foundation.

Maclennan, D., Gibb, K. and More, A. (1994) 'Housing systems, regions and the national economy', *Economic Modelling*, 11: 228–37.

McConnell, S. (1999) 'A new buzz in the heart of our cities', *Daily Telegraph*, 3 April.

McCrone, G. and Stephens, M. (1995) *Housing Policy in Britain and Europe*, London: UCL Press.

Madden, L. (1982) 'The volume house-builders', *Building*, 16 April.

Malpass, P. (1986) *The Housing Crisis*, London: Croom Helm.

Malpass, P. and Aughton, H. (1999) *Housing Finance: A Basic Guide*, London: Shelter.

Malpass, P. and Murie, A. (1990) *Housing Policy and Practice* (3rd edition), London: Macmillan Press.

Marcuse, P. (1983) 'Determinants of housing policy in West Germany and the US' in Fainstein, N. and S. (eds), *Urban Policy Under Capitalism*, Newbury Park: Sage.

Marshall, D. and Worthing, D. (2000) *The Construction of Houses*, London: Estates Gazette.

Meen, G. (1994) *Ten Propositions in UK Housing Macro-Economics: An Overview of the Eighties and Early Nineties*, University of Reading Discussion Paper in Urban and Regional Economics, No.94.

Merrett, S. (1979) *State Housing in Britain*, London: Routledge & Kegan Paul.

Merrett, S. (1982) *Owner Occupation in Britain*, London: Routledge & Kegan Paul.

Middleton, M. (1991) *Cities in Transition: The Regeneration of Britain's Inner Cities*, London: Michael Joseph.

Millington, A. (1988) *An Introduction to Property Valuation* (3rd edition), London: Estates Gazette.

Millward, A. and Wheway, R. (1997) *Child's Play: Facilitating Play on Housing Estates*, London: Chartered Institute of Housing.

Ministry of Housing and Local Government (1963) *New Life for Dead Lands*, London: HMSO.

Ministry of Housing and Local Government (1955) *Circular 42/55 Green Belts*, London: HMSO.

Ministry of Housing and Local Government (1965) *The Future of Development Plans*, (PAG report) London: HMSO.

Ministry of Housing and Local Government (1966) *Housing Statistics*, London: HMSO.

Ministry of Housing and Local Government (1970) *Circular 10/70 Land Availability*, London: HMSO.

Monk, S. (1991) *The Speculative House-builder: A Review of Empirical Research*, Property Research Unit, Land Economy Discussion Paper No. 31, University of Cambridge, Granta Editions Ltd.

Morecombe, K. (1984) *The House-building Process*, Aldershot: Gower.

Morgan, N. (1987) *A History of the NHBC and Private Homebuilding*, Carnforth: Parthenon Publishing.

Morledge, R. and Sharif, A. (1996) *The Procurement Guide: A Guide to the Development of an Appropriate Building Procurement Strategy*, London: The Royal Institution of Chartered Surveyors.

Morris, E. S. (1997) *British Town Planning and Urban Design: Principles and Politics*, Harlow: Addison Wesley Longman.

Murie, A. and Forrest, R. (1994) 'Home ownership in recession', *Housing Studies*, 9.

Nairn, I. (1955) 'Outrage', *Architectural Review*, 117: 363–454.

Nathanail, J., Bardos, P. and Nathanail, C. (2002) *Contaminated Land Management: Ready Reference*, Richmond: EEP Publications and Land Quality Press.

National House-Building Council (1993) *New House-Building Statistics*, Amersham: NHBC.

National House-Building Council (1994) *NHBC Standards, Vols I and II*, Amersham: NHBC.

National House-Building Council (2000) *New House-Building Statistics*, Amersham: NHBC.

National House-Building Council (annual) *New House-Building Statistics*, Amersham: NHBC.

National House-Building Council and Coopers & Lybrand (1990) *The NHBC Euro-guide: A Review of European Housing Development*, Amersham: NHBC.

Nationwide Building Society (2000) *Quarterly Housing Review*, Swindon: Nationwide.

Needham, B. (1992) 'A theory of land prices when land is supplied publicly: the case of the Netherlands', *Urban Studies*, 29: 669–86.

Needham, B. (1997) 'Land policy in the Netherlands', *Tijdschrift voor Economische en Sociale Geografie*, 88: 291–6.

Needham, B. (1999) 'Approaching the cross-national comparison of urban, housing and planning phenomena; cross national research: the epistemology and the practice, or, what kind of statements do we want to make?', Paper for the Netherlands Graduate School of Housing and Urban Research International Workshop on Cross-National Comparison, Amsterdam, 16–17 December.

Needham, B., Kruijt, B. and Koenders, P. (1993) *The Netherlands: Urban Land and Property Markets*, London: UCL Press.

Nelson, J. (ed.) (2000) *The Essential Home-buyer's Guide* (in eleven regional volumes), Bury St Edmunds: IP Publishing (for Virgin One).

Nevitt, A. (1966) *Housing, Taxation and Subsidies: A Study of Housing in the United Kingdom*, London and Edinburgh: Thomas Nelson.

New Homes Marketing Board and Halifax plc (2001) *New Homes Today: Consumer Attitudes to New Homes*, a report prepared by Mulholland Research Associates, London: New Homes Marketing Board and Halifax plc.

Newman, O. (1973) *Defensible Space: People and Design in the Violent City*, London: Architectural Press.

Nicholls, D., Turner, D., Kirby-Smith, R., and Cullen, J. (1981) 'The risk business; developers' perceptions and prospects for house-building in the inner city', *Urban Studies*, 19: 331–41.

Nicol, C. (1994) *House Price Series: Interpretation, Compatibility and Applications*, Working Chapter No. 4, Centre for Residential Development, Nottingham Trent University.

Nicol, C. (2002) *Formulation of Local Housing Strategies: A Critical Evaluation*, Aldershot: Ashgate.

Nicol, C. and Blake, R. (2000) 'Classification and use of open space in the context of increasing urban capacity', *Planning Property & Research*, 15: 193–210.

Nicol, C. and Hooper, A. (1999) 'Contemporary change and the house-building industry: concentration and standardisation in production', *Housing Studies*, 14: 57–76.

Northcott, J. (1991) *Britain 2010*, London: Policy Studies Institute.

Nottingham City Council (2001) *Nottingham Plan Review: First Deposit Draft*, Nottingham: Nottingham City Council.

Nuttgens, P. (1989) *The Home Front*, London: BBC.

Nuttgens, P. (1998) *The Story of Architecture*, London: Phaidon Press.

Office for National Statistics (annual) *Regional Trends*, London: ONS.

Office for National Statistics (annual) *General Household Survey*, London: The Stationery Office.

Office for National Statistics (annual) *Social Trends*, London: HMSO.

Oliver, R. (1993) *Ordnance Survey Maps: A Concise Guide for Historians*, London: The Charles Close Society.

Oxley, M. (1987) 'The aims and effects of housing allowances in Western Europe' in van Vliet, W. (ed.) *Housing Markets and Policies under Fiscal Austerity*, London: Greenwood Press.

Oxley, M. (1991) 'The aims and methods of comparative housing research', *Scandinavian Housing and Planning Research*, 8: 67–77, Oslo: Scandinavian University Press.

Oxley, M. (2001) *Viability and Affordable Housing in London*, London: Greater London Authority.

Oxley, M. (2004) *Economics, Housing and Planning*, London: Palgrave.

Oxley, M. and Smith, J. (1995) 'Housing investment, macroeconomics and demographics in Europe', *Netherlands Journal of Housing and the Built Environment*, 10: 187–207, Delft: Delft University Press.

Oxley, M., Golland, A., Dunmore, K. and Cousins, C. (2001) *Affordable Housing in London*, London: Greater London Authority (April).

Perkins, C. and Parry, P. (1996) *Mapping the UK: Maps and Spatial Data for the Twenty-first Century*, London: Bowker-Saur.

Pettinger, R. (1998) *Construction Marketing: Strategies for Success*, Basingstoke: Macmillan.

Pickvance, C. (1999) 'Four varieties of comparative analysis', Paper for the Netherlands Graduate School of Housing and Urban Research International Workshop on Cross-National Comparison, Amsterdam, 16–17 December.

Popular Housing Forum (1998) *Kerb Appeal: The External Appearance and Site Layout of New Houses*, York: Popular Housing Forum.

Powell-Smith, V. (1999) *The Building Regulations Explained and Illustrated*, Oxford: Blackwell Science.

Power, A. (1993) *Hovels to High Rise: State Housing in Europe since 1850*, London: Routledge.

Power, A. (1999) *Estates on the Edge: The Social Consequences of Mass Housing in Northern Europe*, Basingstoke: Macmillan.

Prest, A. (1981) *The Taxation of Urban Land*, Manchester: Manchester University Press.

Prizeman, J. (1975) *Your House: The Outside View*, London: Hutchinson.

Quiney, A. (1990) *The Traditional Buildings of England*, London: Thames & Hudson.

Radley, S. (1996) *Sustainable Home Ownership: A New Concept*, York: Joseph Rowntree Trust and the Henley Centre.

Randall, G. (1992) *Principles of Marketing*, London: Routledge.

Ratcliffe, J. (1976) *Land Policy: An Exploration of the Nature of Land in Society*, London: Hutchinson.

Reeves, P. (1996) *An Introduction to Social Housing*, London: Arnold.

Reid, W. and Myddleton, D. (1971) *The Meaning of Company Accounts*, Farnborough: Gower Press.

Renard, V. (2001) Interview, Ecole Polytechnique, Paris.

Rhind, D. (1983) *A Census User's Handbook*, London: Methuen.

Ricardo, D. (1817) *The Political Economy and Taxation* (reprinted London: Penguin, 1971).

Rideout, B. and Smith, D. (1986) 'Historic maps in the investigation of land use and the identification of possible contamination' in Craig, C. (ed.) *Advances in Site Investigation Practice*, London: Thomas Telford.

Riley, M. and Howard, C. (2002) *House Construction*, London: Palgrave.

Roberts, B. (1987) *The Making of the English Village: A Study in Historical Geography*, Harlow: Longman.

Robinson, R. (1979) *Housing, Economics and Public Policy*, London: Macmillan Press.

Robson, B., Parkinson, M., Boddy, M. and Maclennan, D. (2000) *The State of English Cities*, London: DETR.

Roger Tym & Partners (1987) *Land Use for Residential Development in the South East*, London: HMSO

Rogers, R. A. (1996) *Residential Estate Layout* (Distance Learning Text) Nottingham: Nottingham Trent University, School of Property & Construction.

Rogerson, R. (1997) *Quality of Life in Britain*, Glasgow: University of Strathclyde.

Royal Institution of Chartered Surveyors (1992) *Living Cities*, London: RICS.

Royal Institution of Chartered Surveyors (2000) *European Housing Markets*, London: RICS and Southbank University.

Royal Institution of Chartered Surveyors (2001) *Building Cost Information Service*, London: RICS.

Rudlin, D. (1998) *Tomorrow: A Peaceful Path to Urban Reform*, London: Friends of the Earth.

Rudlin, D. and Falk, N. (1999) *Building the 21st Century Home: The Sustainable Urban Neighbourhood*, London: Architectural Press.

Rydin, Y. (1983) *House-builders as an Interest Group: The Issue of Residential Land Use Availability*, Geography Discussion Papers (New Series) No. 6, London: London School of Economics.

Rydin, Y. (1985) *House-building and the Planning System*, Oxford: Pergamon.

Rydin, Y. (1998) *The British Planning System: An Introduction*, London: Macmillan.

Salvadori, M. (1990) *Why Buildings Stand Up*, London: W. W. Norton & Co.

Saunders, P. (1990) *A Nation of Home Owners*, London: Unwin Hyman.

Schmidt, S. (1989) 'Convergence theory, labour movements and corporatism: the case of housing', *Scandinavian Housing and Planning Research*, 6: 83–101, Oslo: Scandinavian University Press.

Shankland-Cox Partnership (1972) *Land Availability for Residential Development*, London: Housing Research Foundation.

Shore, P. (1977) in Department of the Environment, *Housing Policy: a Consultative Document*, Cmnd 6851, London: HMSO.

Short, J., Fleming, S. and Witt, S. (1986) *House-building, Planning and Community Action*, London: Routledge & Kegan Paul.

Shucksmith, M. (ed.) (1990) *House-building in Britain's Countryside*, London: Routledge.

Simpkins, E. (1999) 'Shelter for the middle class', *Estates Gazette*, 13 March.

Smithies, K. (1981) *Principles of Design in Architecture*, London: Van Nostrand Reinhold.

Smyth, H. (1982) *Land Banking, Land Availability and Planning for Private House-building*, SAUS Working Paper No. 23, Bristol: University of Bristol.

Smyth, H. (1984) *Land Supply, House-builders and Government Policies*, SAUS Working Paper No. 43, Bristol: University of Bristol.

SNAL (Syndicat National des Aménageurs-Lotisseurs) (1993) *La Zone d'Aménagement Concerté: Rencontre d'une volonté politique et du savoir-faire d'un professionnel*, Working Paper, Paris: SNAL.

SNAL (Syndicat National des Aménageurs-Lotisseurs) (1999) *Annuaire du Snal*, Paris: SNAL.

Stamp, L. D. (1962) *The Land of Britain: Its Use and Misuse*, London: Longman.

Stewart, J. (2002) 'New Labour, Old Labour', *Housebuilder*, 61 (3): 8–9, April, London: House-builder Publications Ltd.

Stratton, I. (1983) *Building Land and Estates: Their Acquisition and Development*, London: Oyez.

Stroud Foster, J. (2000) *Mitchell's Structure and Fabric* (5th edition), London: Pearson Educational.

Suffolk Local Planning and Highways Authorities (1993) *Suffolk Design Guide for Residential Areas*, Ipswich: Suffolk.

Surrey District Planning Authorities (1999) *Surrey County Capacity Study*, Kingston-upon-Thames: Surrey County Council.

Surrey Local Government Association (2001) *Surrey Design: A Strategic Guide for Quality Built Environments*, Kingston-upon-Thames: Surrey County Council.

Syms, P. and Knight, P. (2000) *Building Homes on Used Land*, Coventry: RICS Books (for the Joseph Rowntree Foundation).

Thomas, R. (1996) 'The economics of new towns revisited', *Town & Country Planning*, 65: 305–8.

Thompson, G. (2002) 'Don't you want me?', *Building*, 19 April: 24–7.

Thompson, J. (1970) 'The growth phenomenon' in Taylor, L. R. (ed.) *The Optimum Population for Britain*, London: Academic Press (for the Institute of Biology).

Thorburn, A. (1971) *Planning Villages*, London: Estates Gazette.

Thornley, A. (1993) *Urban Planning under Thatcherism: The Challenge of the Market*, London: Routledge.

Todorovic, J. and Wellington, S. (2000) *Living in Urban England: Attitudes and Aspirations*, London: DETR.

Tunstall, G. (2000) *Managing the Building Design Process*, Oxford: Butterworth Heinemann.

Turner, A. (1990) *Building Procurement*, London: Macmillan.

United Nations (2000) *Annual Bulletin of Housing and Building Statistics*, New York and Geneva: United Nations.

University of Westminster, Grimley and London Residential Research (1998) *Back to the Centre*, London: RICS Research.

Urban and Economic Development Group (URBED) (1998) *Tomorrow: A Peaceful Path to Urban Reform*, Manchester: URBED.

Urban and Economic Development Group (URBED) (1999) MORI Social Research and the University of Bristol *But Would You Live There? Shaping Attitudes to Urban Living*, Urban Task Force, London: HMSO.

Urban Initiatives and Chestertons (1995) *Hertfordshire: Dwelling Provision through Planned Regeneration*, Ware: Hertfordshire County Council.

Urban Task Force (1999) *Towards an Urban Renaissance: Final Report* (chaired by Lord Rogers of Riverside), London: E & F Spon.

Urban Villages Forum (1995) *The Economics of Urban Villages*, York: Urban Villages Forum.

Uthwatt Report: Final Report of the Expert Committee on Compensation and Betterment, Cmd 6386, HMSO, 1941.

Vale, B. and Vale, R. (1993) *Design for a Sustainable Future*, London: Thames & Hudson.

Verhage, R. (2000) 'Financing public facilities in housing projects: method for understanding negotiating processes', The European Network for Housing Research Conference, Gävle, Sweden.

Verhage, R. (2002) *Local Policy for Housing Development: European Experiences*, Aldershot: Ashgate Publishing.

Von Thünen, H. (1826) *Der Isolierte Staat* (English translation by Wartenburg in Hall, P. (1966) *The Isolated State*, London: Pergamon).

Walford, R. (ed.) (1997) *Land Use – UK: A Survey for the Twenty-first Century*, Sheffield: The Geographical Association.

Walker, D. (2002) 'Falling behind', *Search*, 37, Summer 2002, York: Joseph Rowntree Foundation.

Walker, R. (1986) 'Planning and the house-building industry', *The Planner*, 72 (2): 76–8, February.

Wallace, M. and Denham, C. (1996) *The ONS Classification of Local and Health Authorities of Great Britain*, London: HMSO.

Ward, C. (2002) *Cotters and Squatters: Housing's Hidden History*, Nottingham: Five Leaves.

Wellings, F. (1993) 'After the recession: strategy, rationalisation and finance', *House-builder*, 52 (9): 27–8, September.

Wellings, F. (1994) *Construction Equities: Evaluation and Trading*, Cambridge: Woodhead Publishing Ltd.

Wellings, F. (2000) *Private House-building Annual 2000*, Crédit Lyonnais Securities.

White, P. (1986) 'Land availability, land-banking and the price of land for housing: a review of recent debates', *Land Development Studies*, 3: 101–11, May.

Whitehand, I. and Carr, C. (1999) 'England's inter-war suburban landscapes: myth and reality', *Journal of Historical Geography*, 25: 483–500.

Whitehand, I. and Carr, C. (2001) 'The creators of England's inter-war suburbs', *Urban History*, 28: 218–34.

Wigmans, G. (1992) *Uiteenzetting Grondexploitatiebegroting*, Faculteit Bouwkunde, T. U. Delft, Netherlands.

Williams, D. and Wood, B. (1994) *The United Kingdom: Urban Land and Property Markets*, London: UCL Press.

Wiltshire County Council (1993) *Housing Market Survey*, Trowbridge: Wiltshire County Council.

Woodforde, J. (1976) *Bricks to Build a House*, London: Routledge & Kegan Paul.

World Commission on Environment and Development (1987) *Our Common Future* (The Brundtland Report), Oxford: Oxford University Press.

Yamaichi (1993) *UK Housing*, Sector Comment, London: Yamaichi International (Europe) Ltd.

Index